Professional Examinatio[n]

PART 3

Paper 3.6

Advanced Corporate Reporting

REVISION SERIES

Official Publisher

FOULKS*lynch*

5299/J01

British Library Cataloguing-in-Publication Data

A catalogue record for this book is available from the British Library.

Published by Foulks Lynch Ltd
Number 4
The Griffin Centre
Staines Road
Feltham
Middlesex
TW14 0HS

ISBN 0 7483 4529 9

Printed and bound in Great Britain by Ashford Colour Press, Gosport, Hants.

Acknowledgements

The past ACCA examination questions are the copyright of the Association of Chartered Certified Accountants. The answers to the questions from June 1994 onwards are the answers produced by the examiners themselves and are the copyright of the Association of Chartered Certified Accountants.

We are grateful to the Chartered Institute of Management Accountants for permission to reproduce past examination questions. The answers have been prepared by Foulks Lynch Ltd.

Contents

Examiner plus – the examiner's official answers

At the end of this book we include the new syllabus Pilot Paper with the examiner's official answers. At the end of each topic in the contents page below we indicate which questions from this examination are relevant to that topic.

Preparing the financial statements of complex business entities

Examiner plus – the examiner's official answers

Preface – How to use this book

The 2001 edition of the ACCA Revision Series, published for the December 2001 and June 2002 examinations, contains a wealth of features designed to make your prospects of passing the exams even brighter.

We have taken the opportunity with the introduction of the new syllabus to reorganise this book. All the practice questions are organised by key syllabus topic categories. This will help you see at a glance a range of questions relevant to each syllabus area to date, topic by topic. The Pilot Paper and the last two years' exams (where relevant) have been cross-referenced to the syllabus category in the contents pages.

Key features

1 Examiner plus

This book includes a wide selection of questions from recent ACCA exams including the 2001 Pilot Paper. In addition, there are full, up-to-date answers, many of which have been prepared by examiners. Where relevant under the new syllabus, the last two years' exams have also been included.

The inclusion of these questions and answers gives you clear picture of the way the new syllabus examinations are set, and the Pilot Paper shows you examples of the examiner's actual approach.

2 Key answer tips

An important new feature in this Revision Series is the inclusion of a Key answer tips for all practice questions.

For each question we have highlighted the most important part of the answer and displayed it as the Key answer tip. This will ensure that you focus on the essential part of the question and will help you give the best possible answer.

3 Examination technique

It is very important that you are prepared before sitting the examination. Section 3 provides practical advice on sitting the examination and valuable guidance on examination technique, such as how to approach a question and write an answer plan.

4 The revision series also contains the following features:

- The syllabus and format of the examination
- An analysis of recent exams from June 1996 to December 2000 (where relevant), and the new syllabus examination Pilot Paper
- Specific revision guidance for each paper
- Examination technique and general revision guidance - an essential guide to ensure that you approach and prepare for the examinations correctly
- Key revision topics
- Essential update notes (where appropriate) to bring you up to date for new examinable documents and inform you of any changes to important legislation
- Practice questions and answers grouped by syllabus topic – a substantial bank of questions and answers in this book
- The Pilot Paper and relevant questions from the last two years' exams
- Formulae and tables where appropriate.

Section 1

EXAMINATION FORMAT AND SYLLABUS

Format of the examination

A three-hour examination will be set, with the following structure:

Section A	One compulsory question		25 marks
Section B	Choice of 3 questions from 4	(25 marks each)	75 marks
			100 marks

Aim

To ensure that candidates can exercise judgement and technique in corporate reporting matters encountered by accountants and can react to current developments or new practice.

Objectives

On completion of this paper candidates should be able to:

- explain and evaluate the implications of an accounting standard or proposed accounting standard for the content of published financial information
- explain and evaluate the impact on the financial statements of business decisions
- explain the legitimacy and acceptability of an accounting practice proposed by a company
- prepare financial statements for complex business situations
- analyse financial statements and prepare a report suitable for presentation to a variety of users
- evaluate current practice in the context of the needs of users and the objectives of financial reporting
- evaluate current developments in corporate reporting in the context of their practical application, implications for corporate reporting, and the underlying conceptual issues and
- demonstrate the skills expected in Part 3.

Syllabus content

1 The UK regulatory framework

(a) Financial Reporting Standards, Financial Reporting Exposure Drafts, Discussion Papers, Urgent Issues Task Force pronouncements including accounting for equity and liabilities, assets, provisions and contingencies, segments, related parties, financial instruments, taxes, leases, retirement benefits.

(b) The content of the UK regulatory framework in a given range of practical situations.

(c) The problems with the current and proposed changes to the UK regulatory framework including measurement and recognition issues.

(d) The impact of current and proposed regulations on the financial statements of the entity.

(e) The effect of business decisions and proposed changes in accounting practice by the entity on the financial statements.

(f) The legitimacy of current accounting practice and its relevance to users of corporate financial statements.

2 Preparation of the financial statements of complex business entities

(a) The financial statements of complex groups including vertical and mixed groups.

(b) Group cash flow statements.

(c) Accounting for group reorganisations and restructuring including demergers, take-overs and group schemes.

(d) Accounting for foreign currency transactions and entities.

3 Preparation of reports for external and internal users

(a) Appraisal of financial and related information, the purchase of a business entity, the valuation of shares and the reorganisation of an entity.

(b) Appraisal of the impact of changes in accounting policies and the regulatory framework on shareholder value.

(c) Appraisal of the business performance of the entity including quantitative and qualitative measures of performance and the potential for corporate failure.

(d) The assessment of the impact of price level changes and available methods of valuation on business decisions and performance.

(e) The effectiveness of corporate governance within an entity.

4 Current issues and developments

(a) The accounting impact of environmental, cultural and social factors on the entity.

(b) The impact of the content of financial statements on users including changes in design and content of interim and year-end financial statements and alternate ways of communicating results to users.

(c) Proposed changes in the structure of national and international regulation and the impact on global harmonisation and standardisation.

(d) The applicability of the regulatory framework to small and medium sized entities.

(e) Current developments in corporate reporting.

5 Ethical considerations

(a) Ethics and business conduct.

Section 2

ANALYSIS OF PAST PAPERS

Topics	*J96*		*D96*		*J97*		*D97*		*J98*		*D98*		*J99*		*D99*		*PP01*	
Foreign currency translation	1	□					2	○	1	□								
Consolidated financial statements	1	□	1 5	□ ○	1 3 4	□ ● ●	3	○	1	□	1	□	1 3	□ ○	1	□		
Reconstructions and reorganisations	4	○	4	○							3	○					3	○
Inflation accounting											2	○						
Interpretation of financial statements	2	□	2	□	2	■			2	○								
Application of accounting standards and accounting principles	5	○	3	○	2 4	□ ○			3 4	○ ●	4	○			4	○		
FRS 5									3	○								
Tangible fixed assets											4	●						
SSAP 9																		
SSAP 15	3	○					4	○										
SSAP 24					4	○												
The cash flow statement							1	□									1	□
Financial instruments															3	○		
International issues					2	■												
Distributable profits																		
Ethical issues							5	○	5	○	6	○			6	○	5	○
Intangible assets					3	○							1	■			2	○
Related party disclosures					5	○									2	○	4	○
Segmental reporting													2	○				
Earnings per share													4	○				
Liability of auditors							6	○										
Share valuation									4	○								
Current issues in auditing									6	○	5	○	5 6	○ ○	5	○		

Key

The number refers to the number of the question where this topic was examined in the exam.

□ This topic formed the whole or a substantial part of a compulsory question.

■ This topic formed a non-substantial part of a compulsory question.

○ This topic formed the whole or a substantial part of an optional question.

● This topic formed a non-substantial part of an optional question.

Section 3

GENERAL REVISION GUIDANCE

PLANNING YOUR REVISION

What is revision?

Revision is the process by which you remind yourself of the material you have studied during your course, clarify any problem areas and bring your knowledge to a state where you can retrieve it and present it in a way that will satisfy the examiners.

Revision is not a substitute for hard work earlier in the course. The syllabus for this paper is too large to be hastily 'crammed' a week or so before the examination. You should think of your revision as the final stage in your study of any topic. It can only be effective if you have already completed earlier stages.

Ideally, you should begin your revision shortly after you begin an examination course. At the end of every week and at the end of every month, you should review the topics you have covered. If you constantly consolidate your work and integrate revision into your normal pattern of study, you should find that the final period of revision - and the examination itself - is much less daunting.

If you are reading this revision text while you are still working through your course, we strongly suggest that you begin now to review the earlier work you did for this paper. Remember, the more times you return to a topic, the more confident you will become with it.

The main purpose of this book, however, is to help you to make the best use of the last few weeks before the examination. In this section, we offer some suggestions for effective planning of your final revision and discuss some revision techniques that you may find helpful.

Planning your time

Most candidates find themselves in the position where they have less time than they would like to revise, particularly if they are taking several papers at one diet. The majority of people must balance their study with conflicting demands from work, family or other commitments.

It is impossible to give hard and fast rules about the amount of revision you should do. You should aim to start your final revision at least four weeks before your examination. If you finish your course work earlier than this, you would be well advised to take full advantage of the extra time available to you. The number of hours you spend revising each week will depend on many factors, including the number of papers you are sitting. You should probably aim to do a minimum of about six to eight hours a week for each paper.

In order to make best use of the revision time that you have, it is worth spending a little of it at the planning stage. We suggest that you begin by asking yourself two questions:

- How much time do I have available for revision?
- What do I need to cover during my revision?

Once you have answered these questions, you should be able to draw up a detailed timetable. We will now consider these questions in more detail.

How much time do I have available for revision?

Many people find it helpful to work out a regular weekly pattern for their revision. We suggest you use the time planning chart provided to do this. Your aim should be to construct a timetable that is sustainable over a period of several weeks.

Time planning chart

	Monday	Tuesday	Wednesday	Thursday	Friday	Saturday	Sunday
00.00							
01.00							
02.00							
03.00							
04.00							
05.00							
06.00							
07.00							
08.00							
09.00							
10.00							
11.00							
12.00							
13.00							
14.00							
15.00							
16.00							
17.00							
18.00							
19.00							
20.00							
21.00							
22.00							
23.00							

1 First, block out all the time that is **definitely unavailable** for revision. This will include the hours when you normally sleep, the time you are at work and any other regular and clear commitments.

2 Think about **other people's claims on your time**. If you have a family, or friends whom you see regularly, you may want to discuss your plans with them. People are likely to be flexible in the demands they make on you in the run-up to your examinations, especially if they are aware that you have considered their needs as well as your own. If you consult the individuals who are affected by your plans, you may find that they are surprisingly supportive; instead of being resentful of the extra time you are spending studying.

3 Next, give some thought to the times of day when you **work most effectively**. This differs very much from individual to individual. Some people can concentrate first thing in the morning. Others work best in the early evening, or last thing at night. Some people find their day-to-day work so demanding that they are unable to do anything extra during the week, but must concentrate their study time at weekends. Mark the times when you feel you could do your best work on the timetable. It is extremely important to acknowledge your personal preferences here. If you ignore them, you may devise a timetable that is completely unrealistic and which you will not be able to adhere to.

4 Consider your **other commitments**. Everybody has certain tasks, from doing the washing to walking the dog, which must be performed on a regular basis. These tasks may not have to be done at a particular time, but you should consider them when planning your schedule. You may be able to find more convenient times to get these jobs done, or be able to persuade other people to help you with them.

5 Now mark some time for **relaxation**. If your timetable is to be sustainable, it must include some time for you to build up your reserves. If your normal week does not include any regular physical activity, make sure that you include some in your revision timetable. A couple of hours spent in a sports centre or swimming pool each week will probably enhance your ability to concentrate.

6 Your timetable should now be taking shape. You can probably see obvious study sessions emerging. It is not advisable to work for too long at any one session. Most people find that they can only really concentrate for one or two hours at a time. If your study sessions are longer than this, you should split them up.

What do I need to cover during my revision?

Most candidates are more confident about some parts of the syllabus than others. Before you begin your revision, it is important to have an overview of where your strengths and weaknesses lie.

One way to do this is to take a sheet of paper and divide it into three columns. Mark the columns:

OK Marginal Not OK

or use similar headings to indicate how confident you are with a topic. Then go through the syllabus (reprinted in Section 1) and list the topics under the appropriate headings. Alternatively, you could use the list of key topics in Section 5 of this book to compile your overview. You might also find it useful to skim through the introductions or summaries to the textbook or workbooks you have used in your course. These should remind you of parts of the course that you found particularly easy or difficult at the time. You could also use some of the exercises and questions in the workbooks or textbooks, or some of the questions in this book, as a diagnostic aid to discover the areas where you need to work hardest.

It is also important to be aware which areas of the syllabus are so central to the subject that they are likely to be examined in every diet, and which are more obscure, and not likely to come up so frequently. Your textbooks, workbooks and lecture notes will help you here, and section 2 of this book contains an analysis of past papers. Remember, the examiner will be looking for broad coverage of the syllabus. There is no point in knowing one or two topics in exhaustive detail if you do so at the expense of the rest of the course.

Writing your revision timetable

You now have the information you need to write your timetable. You know how many weeks you have available, and the approximate amount of time that is available in each week.

You should stop all serious revision 48 hours before your examination. After this point, you may want to look back at your notes to refresh your memory, but you should not attempt to revise any new topics. A clear and rested brain is worth more than any extra facts you could memorise in this period.

Make one copy of this chart for each week you have available for revision.

Using your time planning chart, write in the times of your various study sessions during the week.

In the lower part of the chart, write in the topics that you will cover in each of these sessions.

Example of a revision timetable

Revision timetable Week beginning:							
	Monday	Tuesday	Wednesday	Thursday	Friday	Saturday	Sunday
Study sessions							
Topics							

SOME REVISION TECHNIQUES

There should be two elements in your revision. You must **look back** to the work you have covered in the course and **look forward** to the examination. The techniques you use should reflect these two aspects of revision.

Revision should not be boring. It is useful to try a variety of techniques. You probably already have some revision techniques of your own and you may also like to try some of the techniques suggested here, if they are new to you. However, do not waste time with methods of revision that are not effective for you.

- Go through your lecture notes, textbook or workbooks and use a highlighter pen to mark important points.
- Produce a new set of summarised notes. This can be a useful way of re-absorbing information, but you must be careful to keep your notes concise, or you may find that you are simply reproducing work you have done before. It is helpful to use a different format for your notes.
- Make a collection of key words that remind you of the essential concepts of a topic.
- Reduce your notes to a set of key facts and definitions that you must memorise. Write them on cards that you can keep with you all the time.
- When you come across areas which you were unsure about first time around, rework relevant questions in your course materials, then study the answers in great detail.
- If there are isolated topics that you feel are completely beyond you, identify exactly what it is that you cannot understand and find someone (such as a lecturer or recent graduate) who can explain these points to you.
- Practise as many exam standard questions as you can. The best way to do this is to work to time, under exam conditions. You should always resist looking at the answer until you have finished.
- If you have come to rely on a computer in your day-to-day work, you may have got out of the habit of writing at speed. It is well worth reviving this skill before you sit down in the examination hall: it is something you will need.
- If you have a plentiful supply of relevant questions, you could use them to practise planning answers, and then compare your notes with the answers provided. This is not a substitute for writing full answers, but can be helpful additional practice.
- Go back to questions you have already worked on during the course. This time, complete them under exam conditions, paying special attention to the layout and organisation of your answers. Then compare

them in detail with the suggested answers and think about the ways in which your answer differs. This is a useful way of 'fine tuning' your technique.

- During your revision period, do make a conscious effort to identify situations that illustrate concepts and ideas that may arise in the examination. These situations could come from your own work, or from reading the business pages of the quality press. This technique will give you a new perspective on your studies and could also provide material that you can use in the examination.
- Read good newspapers and professional journals, especially the ACCA students' newsletter, the Student Accountant. The articles will keep you up-to-date and the examiners' reports on previous sittings will give you an advantage in the exam.

Additional revision aids

To help with your revision, and in addition to the Revision Series, Foulks Lynch has prepared two other resource series:

- Lynchpins - these pocket-sized books complement the Textbooks by providing a distillation of the core information necessary to pass the paper and include illustrations, examples, focal points and space for your own notes
- Tracks audio tapes - designed to be used throughout your course as well as during revision, these user-friendly audio tapes are fully integrated with other ACCA publications and include chapter and topic summaries and highlight key points of the syllabus.

Section 4

EXAMINATION TECHNIQUES

THE EXAMINATION

This section is divided into two parts. The first part considers the practicalities of sitting the examination. If you have taken other ACCA examinations recently, you may find that everything here is familiar to you. The second part discusses some examination techniques that you may find useful.

On the day of your exam

What to take with you

You should make sure that you have:

- your ACCA registration card
- your ACCA registration docket.

You may also take to your desk:

- pens and pencils
- a ruler and slide rule
- a calculator
- charting template and geometrical instruments
- eraser and correction fluid.

You are not allowed to take rough paper into the examination.

If you take any last-minute notes with you to the examination hall, make sure these are not on your person. You should keep notes or books in your bag or briefcase, which you will be asked to leave at the side of the examination hall.

Although most examination halls will have a clock, it is advisable to wear a watch, just in case your view is obscured.

If your calculator is solar-powered, make sure it works in artificial light. Some examination halls are not particularly well lit. If you use a battery-powered calculator, take some spare batteries with you. For obvious reasons, you may not use a calculator that has a graphic/word display memory. Calculators with printout facilities are not allowed because they could disturb other candidates.

Getting there

You should arrange to arrive at the examination hall at least half an hour before the examination is due to start. If the hall is a large one, the invigilator will start filling the hall half an hour before the starting time.

Make absolutely sure that you know how to get to the examination hall and how long it will take you. Check on parking or public transport. Leave yourself enough time so that you will not be anxious if the journey takes a little longer than you anticipated. Many people like to make a practice trip the day before their first examination.

At the examination hall

Examination halls differ greatly in size. Some only hold about ten candidates. Others can sit many hundreds of people. You may find that more than one examination is being taken at the hall at the same time, so don't panic if you hear people discussing a completely different subject from the one you have revised.

While you are waiting to go in, do not be put off by other people talking about how well, or badly, they have prepared for the examination.

You will be told when to come into the examination hall. The desks are numbered. (Your number will be on your examination docket.) You will be asked to leave any bags at the side of the hall.

Inside the hall, the atmosphere will be extremely formal. The invigilator has certain things that he or she must tell candidates, often using a particular form of words. Listen carefully, in case there are any unexpected changes to the arrangements.

On your desk you will see a question paper and an answer booklet in which to write your answers. You will be told when to turn over the paper.

During the examination

You will have to leave your examination paper and answer booklet in the hall at the end of the examination. It is quite acceptable to write on your examination paper if it helps you to think about the questions. However, all workings should be in your answers. You may write any plans and notes in your answer booklet, as long as you cross them out afterwards.

If you require a new answer booklet, put your hand up and a supervisor will come and bring you one.

At various times during the examination, you will be told how much time you have left.

You should not need to leave the examination hall until the examination is finished. Put up your hand if you need to go to the toilet, and a supervisor will accompany you. If you feel unwell, put up your hand, and someone will come to your assistance. If you simply get up and walk out of the hall, you will not be allowed to reenter.

Before you finish, you must fill in the required information on the front of your answer booklet.

Examination techniques

Your general strategy

You should spend the first few minutes of the examination reading the paper. Where you have a choice of question, decide which questions you will do. You must divide the time you spend on questions in proportion to the marks on offer. Do not be tempted to spend more time on a question you know a lot about, or one that you find particularly difficult. If a question has more than one part, you must complete each part.

On every question, the first marks are the easiest to gain. Even if things go wrong with your timing and you do not have time to complete a question properly, you will probably gain some marks by making a start.

Spend the last five minutes reading through your answers and making any additions or corrections.

You may answer written questions in any order you like. Some people start with their best question, to help them relax. Another strategy is to begin with your second best question, so that you are working even more effectively when you reach the question you are most confident about.

Once you have embarked on a question, you should try to stay with it, and not let your mind stray to other questions on the paper. You can only concentrate on one thing at once. However, if you get completely stuck with a question, leave space in your answer book and return to it later.

Answering the question

All examiners say that the most frequent reason for failure in examinations, apart from basic lack of knowledge, is candidates' unwillingness to answer the question that the examiner has asked. A great many people include every scrap of knowledge they have on a topic, just in case it is relevant. **Stick to the question and tailor your answer to what you are asked. Pay particular attention to the verbs in the question.**

You should be particularly suspicious if you come across a question that appears to be almost identical to one that you have practised during your revision. It probably isn't! Wishful thinking makes many people see the question they would like to see on the paper, not the one that is actually there.

Read a question at least twice before you begin your answer to ensure you focus on precisely what is required. Underline key words on the question paper, if it helps focus your mind on what is required. Look closely at the mark allocation and how many components there are to each question. You must ensure that you answer all components relative to their mark allocation. For essay questions, take a little time to plan your answer before starting to write. This will help you identify and concentrate on the main points that need to be covered in your answer.

If you do not understand what a question is asking, state your assumptions. Even if you do not answer in precisely the way the examiner hoped, you may be given some credit, if your assumptions are reasonable. Include clear definitions of important terms and concepts, and where necessary, include examples and cases to illustrate your answer.

Presentation

You should do everything you can to make things easy for the marker. Although you will not be marked on your handwriting, the marker will find it easier to identify the points you have made if your answers are legible. The same applies to spelling and grammar. Use blue or black ink. The marker will be using red or green.

Use the margin to identify clearly which question, or part of a question, you are answering.

Start each answer on a new page. The order in which you answer the questions does not matter, but if a question has several parts, these parts should appear in the correct order in your answer book.

If there is the slightest doubt when an answer continues on another page, indicate to the marker that he or she must turn over. It is irritating for a marker to think he or she has reached the end of an answer, only to turn the page and find that the answer continues.

Use columnar layouts for computations. This will help you to avoid mistakes, and is easier to follow.

Use headings and numbered sentences if they help to show the structure of your answer. However, do not write your answers in one-word note form.

It is a good idea to make a rough plan of an answer before you begin to write. Do this in your answer booklet, but make sure you cross it out neatly afterwards. The marker needs to be clear whether he or she is looking at your rough notes, or the answer itself.

Multiple-choice questions

Don't treat these as an easy option – students often gain low marks on this section because they rush them.

Read the questions carefully and work through any calculations required. If you don't know the answer, first eliminate those options you know are incorrect and see if the answer is then obvious. If you are still unsure, make a note and come back to the question later. When returning to the question, if you are still unsure, guess – at least you will have some chance of getting the mark; if you leave a blank, you won't have any chance.

Computations

Before you begin a computation, you may find it helpful to jot down the stages you will go through. Cross out these notes afterwards.

It is essential to include all your workings and to indicate where they fit in to your answer. It is important that the marker can see where you got the figures in your answer from. Even if you make mistakes in your computations, you will be given credit for using a principle correctly, if it is clear from your workings and the structure of your answer.

If you spot an arithmetical error that has implications for figures later in your answer, it may not be worth spending a lot of time reworking your computation.

If you are asked to comment or make recommendations on a computation, you must do so. There are important marks to be gained here. Even if your computation contains mistakes, you may still gain marks if your reasoning is correct.

Many computational questions require the use of a standard format: company profit and loss account, balance sheet and cash flow statement for example. Be sure you know these formats fluently before the examination and use the layouts that you see in the answers given in this book and in model answers. A clear layout will help you avoid errors and will impress the marker. Show workings, but don't overdo things by presenting ledger accounts for every item in a balance sheet question, as some candidates still do.

Essay questions

You must plan an essay before you start writing. One technique is to quickly jot down any ideas that you think are relevant. Re-read the question and cross out any points in your notes that are not relevant. Then number your points. Remember to cross out your plan afterwards.

Your essay should have a clear structure. It should contain a brief introduction, a main section and a conclusion. Do not waste time by restating the question at the start of your essay.

Break your essay up into paragraphs. Use sub-headings and numbered sentences if they help show the structure of your answer.

Be concise. It is better to write a little about a lot of different points than a great deal about one or two points.

The examiner will be looking for evidence that you have understood the syllabus and can apply your knowledge in new situations. You will also be expected to give opinions and make judgements. These should be based on reasoned and logical arguments. You must also explain any concepts used – imagine the examiner as an intelligent layperson.

Case-studies

To write a good case-study, first identify the area in which there is a problem, outline the main principles/theories you are going to use to answer the question, and then apply the principles/theories to the case.

When applying the principles, first outline the facts of the case problem in relation to principles/theories you are using. Be careful only to include relevant points and then reach a conclusion, and – if asked for – recommendation(s). If you can, compare the facts to real-life examples – this may gain you additional marks in the exam.

Reports, memos and other documents

Some questions ask you to present your answer in the form of a report or a memo or other document. It is important that you use the correct format - there are easy marks to be gained here. Adopt the format used in sample questions, or use the format you are familiar with in your day-to-day work, as long as it contains all the essential elements.

You should also consider the audience for any document you are writing. How much do they know about the subject? What kind of information and recommendations are required? The examiner will be looking for evidence that you can present your ideas in an appropriate form.

Section 5

KEY REVISION TOPICS

The aim of this section is to provide you with a checklist of key information relating to this Paper. You should use it as a reminder of topics to be revised rather than as a summary of all you need to know. Aim to revise as many topics as possible because many of the questions in the exam draw on material from more than one section of the syllabus. You will get more out of this section if you read through Section *3, General Revision Guidance* first.

1 Overview of UK GAAP

You should be able to do the following:

- Understand and discuss the nature of UK GAAP
- Outline the reporting exemptions available to small companies, including the Financial Reporting Standard for Small Entities (FRSSE)
- Discuss the solutions to differential financial reporting.

2 Corporate governance

You should be able to do the following:

- Understand the role and need for the reform of corporate governance
- Describe the nature of reporting under the Combined Code
- Understand the need for corporate governance in small companies
- Describe the nature and content of the Operating and Financial Review.

3 Group financial statements 1

You should be able to do the following:

- Explain the principles of measurement relating to the fair value of the consideration and the net assets acquired
- Prepare consolidated financial statements where control is established by a step-by-step acquisition.

4 Group financial statements 2

You should be able to do the following:

- Account for complex group structures.
- Understand the basic principles relating to the disposal of group companies.
- Understand the treatment of goodwill on disposal
- Account for full, partial and deemed disposals.

5 Mergers

You should be able to do the following:

- Understand the basic principles and philosophy of merger accounting
- Account for equity eliminations, expenses and dividends of the subsidiary
- Prepare consolidated financial statements using merger accounting techniques
- Determine whether merger accounting could be used in specific circumstances
- Understand the relative merits of different methods of accounting for business combinations.

6 Group re-organisations and restructuring

You should be able to do the following:

- Discuss the creation of a new holding company
- Explain changes in the ownership of companies within a group
- Understand the nature of demergers and divisionalisation
- Prepare group financial statements after re-organisation and restructuring
- Appraise the benefits of a reorganisation and restructuring.

7 Associates, joint ventures and joint arrangements that are not entities

You should be able to do the following:

- Account for associates, joint ventures and joint arrangements that are not entities (JANE's).
- Apply the equity and gross equity methods of accounting
- Prepare group financial statements including accounting for associates, joint ventures and JANE's.

8 Foreign currency

You should be able to do the following:

- Understand the recording of transactions and retranslation of monetary/non-monetary items at the balance sheet date for individual companies
- Account for the treatment of exchange differences re the above
- Understand the nature of the closing rate/net investment method and the temporal method
- Account for foreign equity investments financed by borrowings
- Prepare group financial statements incorporating a foreign subsidiary
- Discuss the problem areas in foreign currency transactions.

9 Group cash flow statements

You should be able to do the following:

- Discuss the usefulness of cash flow information
- Prepare a group cash flow statement classifying cash flows by standard headings and including acquisition and disposal of subsidiaries
- Deal with associates, joint ventures, joint arrangements and foreign currencies.

10 Fixed assets 1

You should be able to do the following:

- Understand the nature of impairment and the impairment review
- Apply the impairment review and deal with losses on assets
- Account for the amortisation of goodwill and intangible assets including impairment
- Explain and apply the provisions of FRS 11.

11 Fixed assets 2

You should be able to do the following:

- Account for revaluation gains and losses and the depreciation of revalued assets
- Account for the disposal of revalued assets
- Discuss the effect of revaluations on distributable profits
- Understand the problem areas in accounting for fixed assets.

12 Financial instruments

You should be able to do the following:

- Account for debt instruments, share capital and the allocation of finance costs
- Account for fixed interest rate and convertible bonds
- Understand the measurement issues relating to complex instruments
- Understand the definition and classification of a financial instrument
- Explain the current measurement proposals for financial instruments
- Describe the nature of the disclosure requirements relating to financial instruments
- Discuss the key areas where consensus is required on the accounting treatment of financial instruments.

13 'Off balance sheet' transactions

You should be able to do the following:

- Explain the nature of the 'off balance sheet' problem and the principle of substance over form
- Understand common forms of 'off balance sheet' finance and apply current regulatory requirements
- Discuss the perceived problems of current regulatory requirements.

14 Leases

You should be able to do the following:

- Discuss the problem areas in lease accounting
- Account for sale and leaseback transactions and recognition of income by lessors
- Discuss and account for proposed changes in lease accounting.

15 Segmental reporting

You should be able to do the following:

- Discuss the problem areas in segmental reporting
- Understand the different approaches used to disclose segmental information
- Discuss the importance of segmental information to users of financial statements.

16 Accounting for retirement benefits

You should be able to do the following:

- Understand the nature of defined contribution, multi-employers and defined benefits schemes
- Explain the recognition of defined benefit schemes under current requirements
- Understand the measurement of defined benefit schemes under current requirements
- Account for defined benefit schemes
- Discuss perceived problems with current requirements on accounting for retirement benefits.

17 Taxation

You should be able to do the following:

- Understand the different approaches to accounting for deferred taxation
- Understand current proposals for the recognition of deferred taxation in the balance sheet and performance statements
- Explain the nature of the measurement of deferred taxation under current proposals
- Understand the differences between the recognition requirements of the International Accounting Standard and proposed UK regulation
- Calculate deferred tax amounts in financial statements under current proposals.

18 Reporting financial performance and earnings per share

You should be able to do the following:

- Understand the proposed changes to reporting financial performance
- Explain the rationale behind the proposed changes in reporting financial performance
- Calculate basic and diluted earnings per share.

19 Post balance sheet events, provisions and contingencies

You should be able to do the following:

- Understand the problems of accounting for post balance sheet events
- Understand the issues relating to recognition and measurement of provisions
- Explain the use of restructuring provision and other practical uses of provisioning
- Understand the problems with current standards on provisions and contingencies.

20 Related parties and share based payment

You should be able to do the following:

- Understand the related party issue
- Identify related parties and disclose related party transactions
- Discuss the effectiveness of current regulations on disclosure of related party transactions
- Describe the current proposals for the recognition and measurement of share based payment
- Show the impact of the proposals on the performance statements of an entity.

21 Preparation of reports 1

You should be able to do the following:

- Calculate and appraise a range of acceptable values for shares in an unquoted company
- Advise a client on the purchase of a business entity
- Analyse the impact of accounting policy changes on the value and performance of an entity.

22 Preparation of reports 2

You should be able to do the following:

- Discuss the financial and non-financial measures of performance
- Describe the procedures in designing an accounting based performance measurement system
- Appraise the different performance measures
- Compare target levels of performance with actual performance.

23 Preparation of reports 3

You should be able to do the following:

- Understand the alternative definitions of capital employed and measurement bases for assets
- Discuss the impact of price level changes on business performance
- Appraise the alternative methods of accounting for price level changes
- Evaluate the potential for corporate failure.

24 The impact of environmental, social and cultural factors on corporate reporting

You should be able to do the following:

- Appraise the impact of environmental, social and ethical factors on performance measurement
- Describe current reporting requirements and guidelines for environmental reporting
- Prepare an environmental report in accordance with current practice
- Understand the effect of culture on accounting
- Understand why entities might include socially oriented disclosures in performance statements
- Understand the concept of a social contract and organisational legitimacy
- Evaluate ethical conduct in the context of corporate reporting.

25 International issues

You should be able to do the following:

- Evaluate the developments in global harmonisation and standardisation
- Assess proposed changes to national and international regulation
- Identify the reasons for major changes in accounting practices
- Restate overseas financial statements in line with UK accounting policies.

26 Current issues and developments

You should be able to do the following:

- Identify ways of improving communication of corporate performance
- Understand current proposals relating to year-end financial reports and business reporting on the internet
- Discuss the problem areas in interim reporting
- Discuss current issues in corporate reporting including disclosure of accounting policies and discounting.

Section 6
UPDATES

Examinable documents

Every six months (on 1 June and 1 December) the ACCA publish a list of 'examinable documents' which form the basis of the legislation and accounting regulations that will be examinable at the following diet.

The ACCA Official Textbooks published in February 2001 were fully up-to-date for these examinable documents published by the Association on 1 December 2000 and this section gives details of additional examinable documents listed by the ACCA.

Students are reminded that they should also read the ACCA Students' Newsletter. This is particularly important for students sitting Paper 3.6, because FREDs and Discussion Papers will be examined on the basis of articles published in the Newsletter.

The following technical developments are discussed in this section:

1 FRS 18: Accounting policies
2 FRS 19: Deferred tax
3 FRED 22: Revision of FRS 3 'Reporting financial performance'
4 Consultation Paper: Financial instruments and similar items
5 Discussion Paper: Review of the Financial Reporting Standard for Smaller Entities (FRSSE)

FRS 18: Accounting policies

Background

FRS 18 was issued in December 2000 and replaces SSAP 2 *Disclosure of accounting policies.* SSAP 2 was originally issued at a time when there were few accounting standards and was intended to assist in developing accounting policies. However, this approach is now out of date. The emphasis in FRS 18 is on selecting accounting policies from those allowed by legislation and accounting standards.

UITF Abstract 7 *True and fair view override disclosures* and UITF Abstract 14 *Disclosure of changes in accounting policy* are also superseded.

FRS 18:

- updates the discussion of the four fundamental accounting concepts (going concern, accruals, consistency and prudence) so that they are consistent with the *Statement of Principles for Financial Reporting*
- clarifies the distinction between accounting policies and estimation techniques
- makes explicit many of SSAP 2's implicit requirements.

Selecting accounting policies

The main requirements of the FRS are as follows:

(a) An entity should adopt accounting policies that enable its financial statements to give a true and fair view. Those accounting policies should be consistent with the requirements of accounting standards, Urgent Issues Task Force (UITF) Abstracts and companies legislation.

(b) If in exceptional circumstances compliance with the requirements of an accounting standard or UITF Abstract is inconsistent with the requirement to give a true and fair view, the requirements of the accounting standard or UITF Abstract should be departed from to the extent necessary to give a true and fair view.

(c) Where it is necessary to choose between accounting policies, an entity should select whichever of those accounting policies is judged by the entity to be most appropriate to its particular circumstances for the purpose of giving a true and fair view.

(d) An entity should prepare its financial statements on a going concern basis, unless

(i) the entity is being liquidated or has ceased trading, or
(ii) the directors have no realistic alternative but to liquidate the entity or to cease trading.

Directors should assess whether there are significant doubts about an entity's ability to continue as a going concern.

(e) An entity should prepare its financial statements, except for cash flow information, on the accrual basis of accounting.

(f) An entity should judge the appropriateness of accounting policies to its particular circumstances against the objectives of:

- relevance
- reliability
- comparability
- understandability.

The objectives are the qualitative characteristics of useful financial information discussed in Chapter 3 of the *Statement of Principles*.

(g) An entity should take into account the following constraints:

- the need to balance the different objectives above; and
- the need to balance the cost of providing information with the likely benefit of such information to users of the entity's financial statements.

(h) An entity's accounting policies should be reviewed regularly to ensure that they remain the most appropriate to its particular circumstances. In judging whether a new policy is more appropriate than the existing policy, an entity will give due weight to the impact on comparability.

Unlike SSAP 2, FRS 18 does not emphasise the fundamental concepts of going concern, accruals, consistency and prudence. Entities are required to observe the concepts of going concern and accruals, but consistency and prudence are now viewed as desirable qualities of financial information, rather than accounting concepts.

However, note that the Companies Acts and EC Directives **still require** entities to observe the four fundamental concepts, unless there are special reasons for departing from them.

Estimation techniques

Estimation techniques are defined as the methods and estimates adopted by an entity to arrive at estimated monetary amounts, corresponding to the measurement bases selected, for assets, liabilities, gains, losses and changes to shareholders' funds.

Examples of estimation techniques:

- methods of depreciation
- methods used to estimate doubtful debts.

SSAP 2 did not cover the selection of estimation techniques (as opposed to accounting policies). The requirements of FRS 18 are as follows:

(a) Where estimation techniques are required to enable the accounting policies adopted to be applied, an entity should select estimation techniques that enable its financial statements to give a true and fair view and are consistent with the requirements of accounting standards, UITF Abstracts and companies legislation.

(b) Where it is necessary to choose between estimation techniques, an entity should select whichever of those estimation techniques is judged by the entity to be most appropriate to its particular circumstances for the purpose of giving a true and fair view.

(c) A change to an estimation technique should not be accounted for as a prior period adjustment, unless

(i) it represents the correction of a fundamental error, or
(ii) another accounting standard, a UITF Abstract or companies legislation requires the change to be accounted for as a prior period adjustment.

In other words, a change in estimation technique is not normally the same as a change in accounting policy.

An Appendix to FRS 18 provides guidance as to how to distinguish between changes to accounting policy and changes to estimation technique. It contains several practical examples. These illustrate the principle that a change of accounting policy involves a change to:

- recognition; or
- measurement; or
- presentation.

If none of these has changed, there is a change of estimation technique, rather than a change of accounting policy.

Disclosures

FRS 18 requires the following disclosures, which are more extensive than those required by SSAP 2:

(a) a description of each of the accounting policies followed for material items

(b) a description of estimation techniques used that are significant

(c) details of any changes to accounting policies that were followed in preparing financial statements for the preceding period (the disclosures are similar to those required by UITF Abstract 14 *Disclosure of changes in accounting policy*)

(d) where the effect of a change to an estimation technique is material, the effect and a description of the change

(e) in relation to the going concern assessment required by the FRS:

(i) any material uncertainties that may cast significant doubt upon the entity's ability to continue as a going concern

(ii) where the foreseeable future considered by the directors has been limited to a period of less than one year from the date of approval of the financial statements, that fact

(iii) when the financial statements are not prepared on a going concern basis, that fact, together with the basis on which the financial statements are prepared and the reason why the entity is not regarded as a going concern.

In addition, FRS 18 incorporates disclosure requirements similar to those set out in UITF Abstract 7: *True and fair view override disclosures*.

FRS 19: Deferred tax

Background

FRS 19 was issued in December 2000 and replaces SSAP 15 *Accounting for deferred tax*.

SSAP 15 has been coming under increasing criticism, mainly because of problems arising from the fact that it requires deferred tax to be accounted for using the partial provision method:

- SSAP 15 was originally issued at a time when generous capital allowances and high inflation meant that many entities had a 'core' of timing differences that would never reverse. Therefore partial provision reflected economic reality. Since then, conditions have changed, and there is now a far greater likelihood that timing differences will reverse.
- Partial provision is subjective and dependent on management intentions. It is potentially complicated to apply because it involves predicting future events, such as changes in the taxation system, capital expenditure and the useful economic lives of assets.
- It takes into account future transactions. This is inconsistent with the ASB's *Statement of Principles* (a liability can only exist as a result of a past transaction).

There were other problems:

- There were inconsistencies within the SSAP. Full provision was required for timing differences in respect of post-retirement benefits, but partial provision was required for all other timing differences.
- There were inconsistencies in the application of partial provision (eg, some entities provided deferred tax on fair value adjustments on acquisition while some did not). There is evidence that some entities make full provision on grounds of simplicity and this reduces the comparability of financial statements.

However, arguably the most important reason for changing the basis on which deferred tax is provided is that partial provision is now inconsistent with international practice. Almost all other major standard setters (including the FASB and the IASC) now require full provision.

Full provision

FRS 19 requires that **full provision** should be made for all deferred tax assets and liabilities arising from timing differences.

(a) Deferred tax assets or liabilities only arise if the transactions or events that increase or decrease future tax charges have occurred by the balance sheet date. This means that deferred tax should be recognised on timing differences arising from:

  - accelerated capital allowances
  - elimination of unrealised intra group profits on consolidation
  - unrelieved tax losses
  - other sources of short term timing differences.

(b) Deferred tax should not be recognised on timing differences arising when:

  - a fixed asset is revalued without there being any commitment to sell the asset; or
  - the gain on sale of an asset is rolled over into replacement assets;

  The principle behind this is that deferred tax is only provided where it represents an asset or a liability in its own right (this is called the incremental liability approach). The *Statement of Principles* defines a liability as an obligation to transfer economic benefit as the result of a past transaction or event.

  For example, if an entity has capital allowances in excess of depreciation it has an **obligation** to pay more tax in future. It cannot avoid this obligation. Therefore it has a liability. In contrast, if an entity revalues a fixed asset, it will not have an obligation to pay more tax unless it enters into a binding agreement to sell the asset. Therefore it does not have a liability.

Further requirements of FRS 19

These include the following:

(a) Deferred tax attributable to gains or losses recognised in the statement of total recognised gains and losses (STRGL) should also be recognised in the STRGL. (This is consistent with the requirements of FRS 16.)

(b) Deferred tax should be measured at the average tax rates that are expected to apply in the periods in which the timing differences are expected to reverse, based on tax rates and laws that have been enacted or substantively enacted by the balance sheet date. (This is also consistent with the requirements of FRS 16.)

In practice this means that there is no change from the liability method required by SSAP 15. However, SSAP 15 did not stipulate that enacted rates must be used.

(c) Reporting entities are permitted but not required to discount deferred tax assets and liabilities to reflect the time value of money.

The change from partial provision to full provision will result in increased liabilities and reduced earnings for many entities. Such entities might wish to discount deferred tax provisions for this reason. In addition, the *Statement of Principles* states that discounting should be used where carrying amounts are based on future cash flows. However, the ASB has recognised that for many entities the practical problems of discounting outweigh the benefits and has made discounting optional.

Presentation and disclosure

The main requirements are as follows:

(a) Deferred tax liabilities should be classified as provisions for liabilities and charges.

(b) Deferred tax assets should be classified as debtors.

(c) Deferred tax assets and liabilities should be separately disclosed on the face of the balance sheet if the amounts are so material in the context of the total net current assets or net assets that readers might misinterpret the accounts otherwise.

(d) All deferred tax recognised in the profit and loss account should be included within the heading 'tax on profit or loss on ordinary activities'.

Many of the disclosures required are similar to those of SSAP 15. FRS 19 contains one significant additional requirement:

- Information should be disclosed about factors affecting current and future tax charges. This should include a reconciliation of the current tax charge for the period to the profit before tax on ordinary activities multiplied by the standard rate of corporation tax.

Further points

The ASB has admitted that it is not wholly convinced by the arguments for the full provision basis. Nevertheless, it does not believe that this is one of the areas where a good case can be made for going against international opinion. It believes that continuing with the partial provision basis would damage the credibility of UK financial reporting.

Although the ASB has accepted the need for full provision, it has not adopted the same approach as the IASC. Unlike FRS 19, IAS 12 *Income Taxes* requires deferred tax to be provided on revaluation gains and retained profits of associates and joint ventures.

FRED 22: Revision of FRS 3 'Reporting Financial Performance'

Background

FRED 22 was issued in December 2000 and its proposals have been developed from the 'G4+1' group's Discussion Paper: Reporting Financial Performance.

The ASB believes that a review of FRS 3 is necessary for the following reasons:

- Its recent and current projects on derivatives, impairment and pensions have highlighted the need to reconsider the purpose of the statement of total recognised gains and losses (STRGL). When fixed assets, financial instruments or pension scheme assets and liabilities change in value some gains and losses arise that could in theory be reported in either the profit and loss account or in the STRGL.

- There is also some evidence that users and preparers of accounts are confused by the existence of two performance statements. Therefore they concentrate on the profit and loss account and largely ignore the STRGL.

The main proposal

FRED 22 proposes that the profit and loss account and STRGL should be replaced by a single performance statement. This would be divided into three sections:

- operating
- financing and treasury
- other gains and losses.

The main principle behind the statement of financial performance is that items with similar characteristics are grouped together.

In addition, entities would still be required to analyse their operating results between continuing operations, acquisitions and discontinuing activities.

The 'operating' section of the statement would be the 'default' section. Only items specified by accounting standards or UITF Abstracts would be reported in the other sections. FRED 22 lists the items that would be reported in the other sections under the requirements of current accounting standards.

(a) Financing and treasury:

- interest payable and receivable
- the unwinding of the discount on long-term items, eg, pensions
- income from investments held as part of treasury activities.

(b) Other gains and losses:

- revaluation gains and losses on fixed assets (including investment properties)
- gains and losses on disposal of properties in continuing operations
- actuarial gains and losses arising on defined benefit schemes
- profits and losses on disposal of discontinuing operations
- exchange translation differences on foreign currency net investments.

Some of these items are currently reported in the STRGL while others are currently reported as exceptional items on the face of the profit and loss account (as required by FRS 3 para 20).

An Appendix to FRED 22 contains illustrations of a statement of financial performance.

Appendix 1 Example formats and notes

Statement of financial performance (Example 1)

		2001	2000 Restated
Operating	*£m*	*£m*	*£m*
Turnover			
Continuting operations	600		525
Acquisitions	50		
	650		
Discontinued operations	175		190
		825	715
Cost of Sales		(650)	(570)
Gross profit		175	145
Net operating expenses		(124)	(93)
Operating profit			
Continuing operations	60		40
Acqusitions	6		
	66		
Discontinued operations	(15)		12
Operating income/profit		**51**	**52**
Financing and Treasury			
Interest on debt		(26)	(15)
Financing relating to pension provision		20	11
Financing and Treasury income/profit		**(6)**	**(4)**
Operating and financing income before taxation		**45**	**48**
Taxation on operating and financing income		(5)	(10)
Operating and financing income after taxation		40	38
Minority interests		(5)	(4)
Income from operating and financing activities for the period*		**35**	**34**
Other gains and losses			
Revaluation gain on disposal of properties in continuing operations		6	4
Revaluation of fixed assets		4	3
Actuarial gain on defined benefit pension scheme		276	91
Profit on disposal of discontinued operations		3	–
Exchange translation differences on foreign currency net investments		(2)	5
Other gains and losses before taxation		**287**	**103**
Taxation on other gains and losses		(87)	(33)
Other gains and losses after taxation		200	70
Minority interests		(30)	(10)
Other gains and losses for the period		**170**	**60**
Total gains and losses for the period		**205**	**94**

MEMORANDUM ITEMS

Earnings per share	39p	41p
Adjustments (to be itemised and described)	Xp	Xp
Adjusted earnings per share	Yp	Yp
Diluted earnings per share	Zp	Zp
Dividend per share: equity	3.0p	1.8p
preference	0.6p	0.6p
Total dividend for the period: equity	£6.7m	£0.7m
preference	£1.3m	£1.3m
Prior period adjustment recognised during the period		(£10m)

* Any extraordinary items would be shown after this line, with a subsequent subtotal for the statutory 'profit for the financial year' after extraordinary activities.

Exceptional items

FRED 22 makes the following proposals:

- Exceptional items should be included in the appropriate section of the performance statement under the format headings to which they relate and analysed under continuing or discontinuing operations as appropriate. The amount of each exceptional item should be disclosed separately in the notes to the financial statements or on the face of the performance statement if this is necessary in order to give a true and fair view. An adequate description of each exceptional item should be given to enable its nature to be understood.

  (At present, FRS 3 requires three types of exceptional item to be separately disclosed on the face of the profit and loss account below operating profit:

  - profits and losses on sale or termination of an operation
  - profits and losses on disposal of fixed assets
  - costs of a fundamental reorganisation or restructuring.)

- A history of exceptional items should be shown in the notes to the statement. This should give a breakdown of the exceptional items reported during each of the last five years with a description of each item.

  This new disclosure is intended to enable users to see the nature and pattern of exceptional items reported and to assist them in forecasting future results and cash flows.

Discontinuing operations

FRED 22 proposes that:

- the definition of discontinued operations is changed, so that they become discontinu*ing* operations; and that

- discontinuing operations should be separately disclosed from the accounting period in which either a binding sale agreement or the approval and announcement of a detailed formal plan takes place.

The effect of this is that the results of an operation that is discontinued gradually over a long period are separately analysed under discontinuing operations on the face of the performance statement. This contrasts with FRS 3, which states that an operation can only be classified as discontinued if the sale or termination is completed within a short time after the period end. An operation that is discontinuing is reported under continuing operations. This can be misleading to users of the financial statements.

This change also means that UK practice in this area will become consistent with the requirements of IAS 35 *Discontinuing operations.*

Other changes

- The reconciliation of movements in shareholders' funds (reconciliation of ownership interests) would become a primary statement (FRS 3 allows it to be presented as either a primary statement or a note).
- The note of historical cost profits and losses would become optional.
- Entities would be required to disclose total dividends and dividends per share as memorandum items at the foot of the performance statement.
- Dividends would no longer be shown in the performance statement but instead would be reported as a movement in ownership interest for the period. The ASB believes that dividends are not part of financial performance but appropriations of profit and has requested an amendment to the Companies Act 1985 so that dividends paid and proposed no longer have to be disclosed on the face of the profit and loss account.

Most of the other requirements of FRS 3 would remain unchanged.

Comments

The ASB believes that the new performance statement will be clearer than the existing profit and loss account and STRGL and will enable users to appreciate the performance of the entity as a whole.

However, FRED 22 has had a mixed reception. Critics of the ASB argue that its concept of performance (which reflects the 'balance sheet' based approach taken by the *Statement of Principles*) is fundamentally flawed. This means that the performance statement will include items (such as currency translation differences) that are not strictly part of an entity's performance at all.

Consultation paper: financial instruments and similar items

Background

The Consultation Paper was developed by the Financial Instruments Joint Working Group of standard setters (JWG) and issued by the ASB in December 2000.

The JWG consists of representatives of standard setting bodies and professional organisations in Australia, Canada, France, Germany, Japan, New Zealand, the Nordic countries, the UK, the USA and the IASC. It was set up to develop a proposed comprehensive standard on accounting for financial instruments. Each standard setter participating in the JWG will publish the Paper and invite comments from interested parties.

In 1996 the ASB issued a Discussion Paper on derivatives and other financial instruments. Some of its proposals were developed into FRS 13 *Derivatives and other financial instruments: Disclosures*. The ASB has been awaiting the JWG Consultation Paper so that it can take these proposals into account in developing a standard on recognition and measurement of financial instruments.

Although the Consultation Paper is in the form of an Exposure Draft, in the UK it has a similar status to a Discussion Paper. The ASB will set out proposals in a FRED before issuing a UK standard on financial instruments.

Main proposals

These are as follows:

- Financial instruments other than certain unquoted equity investments should be measured at fair value when recognised initially. They should be re-measured at fair value at each subsequent balance sheet date.

FV Measurement.

The ASB's Discussion Paper proposed that financial instruments should be measured at current value, rather than fair value.

- Changes in the fair value of financial instruments should be recognised in the profit and loss account. There would be one exception: exchange gains and losses on translation of investments in foreign operations using the closing rate method would continue to be recognised in the STRGL.

- Hedging should be prohibited. This means that SSAP 20 would need to be amended (at present it permits hedging where foreign currency borrowings are used to finance an entity's foreign equity investments.) Exchange gains and losses on foreign currency borrowings used as a 'hedge' would be recognised immediately in the profit and loss account.

The ASB's Discussion Paper proposed that hedging should be prohibited or restricted.

- There should be extensive disclosure about financial instruments, financial risk positions and their effects on the profit and loss account.

Classification of capital instruments

Under FRS 4 *Capital instruments*, capital instruments are reported either as shareholders' funds or as liabilities. Non-equity shares are reported within shareholders' funds. Convertible debt is reported within liabilities.

The JWG draws a different distinction: between equity shares issued by the reporting entity (which are outside the scope of the proposals) and liabilities. This means that non-equity shares would be treated as liabilities. Convertible debt would be required to be split between equity and debt elements which would be accounted for separately. Only the debt elements would fall within the scope of the proposals.

Recognition and derecognition

The Paper sets out proposed criteria for determining whether financial assets and financial liabilities should be recognised and derecognised. The JWG believes that financial assets and financial liabilities are made up of bundles of contractual rights and obligations that are financial assets and financial liabilities in their own right. These are called 'components'. Some components of a financial instrument might expire before others, or be transferred while others are retained. The derecognition principles recognise this by focusing on contractual rights and contractual obligations.

This contrasts with the recognition and derecognition criteria in FRS 5 *Reporting the substance of transactions*, which are based on changes in assets and liabilities. Note that any changes to recognition criteria would only affect financial instruments; the principles in FRS 5 would continue to apply to other transactions.

Discussion paper: review of the Financial Reporting Standard for Smaller Entities (FRSSE)

When the FRSSE was first issued in November 1997, the ASB stated that it would review how it was working in practice after two full years of effective operation. The ASB has commissioned research into the operation of the FRSSE and in February 2001 it issued a Discussion Paper. The Paper makes no firm proposals, but seeks the views of interested parties on the following issues:

- Should there continue to be a FRSSE?
- Can a single FRSSE cater for the range of smaller entities?
- How and when should the FRSSE be updated?
- Which aspects of smaller entities' reporting should the FRSSE cover?
- How should the requirements of the FRSSE be determined?
- How should the FRSSE be drafted and presented?

The ASB believes that the FRSSE (or something like it) should continue to exist, but that this is an appropriate time to consider what changes, if any, might be made to the existing regime.

Section 7
PRACTICE QUESTIONS

1 FSR group

The FSR Group consists of the holding company FSR plc and two subsidiary companies, GBH plc and Short plc. FSR plc had acquired 75% of the ordinary shares in GBH plc and 80% of the ordinary shares in Short plc on 1 December 20X2. The ordinary shares in Short plc are held exclusively with a view to subsequent resale; the ordinary shares in GBH plc are held on a long-term basis. FSR plc prepares its accounts to 30 November each year.

A trainee accountant working on the consolidation for the year ended 30 November 20X3 has proposed the following adjustments.

(i) Treatment of profit arising from intra-group sales

During October 20X3 GBH plc sold goods costing it £200,000 to FSR plc for £220,000. All of the goods were in stock as at 30 November 20X3.

Proposed to reduce the stock and consolidated profit and loss account by £15,000.

During September 20X3 FSR plc sold goods costing £60,000 to GBH plc for £72,000. All of the goods were in stock as at 30 November 20X3.

Proposed to reduce the stock and consolidated profit and loss account by £12,000.

(ii) Treatment of goodwill arising on acquisition of GBH plc

The 75% shareholding in GBH plc was acquired on 1 December 20X2 for £3,000,000 when the fair value of the total net assets in GBH plc was estimated to be £3,000,000.

Proposed to apply the entity concept and credit the minority interest with £250,000 and record the goodwill at 1 December 20X2 at £1,000,000. In accordance with group policy, this goodwill was to be written off over five years. The charge in the 20X3 accounts was to be £200,000.

(iii) Treatment of profit arising from sale by Short plc

Short plc sold goods costing £100,000 to FSR plc for £110,000 on 31 August 20X3. All of the goods were in stock as at 30 November 20X3.

Proposed to reduce the stock and the consolidated profit and loss account by £8,000.

Required:

(a) Describe the accounting treatment required in the consolidated accounts of the FSR Group as at 30 November 20X3 of the investment in Short plc.

  (i) to comply with the Companies Act 1985
  (ii) to comply with Financial Reporting Standards with a brief explanation as to why this differs from the provisions of the Companies Act 1985. **(5 marks)**

(b) Inform the trainee accountant whether the proposed consolidation adjustments in (i) to (iii) above comply with accounting standards. State any additional information which could affect the accounting treatment. **(9 marks)**

(c) Explain briefly the reasons for the accounting treatment recommended for (i) to (iii) above. **(6 marks)**

(Total: 20 marks)
(ACCA Dec 93)

2 Complex plc

You are the Chief Accountant of Complex plc, a listed company with a number of subsidiaries located throughout the United Kingdom. Your assistant has prepared the first draft of the financial statements of the group for the year ended 31 August 20X9. The draft statements show a group profit before taxation of £40 million. She has written you a memorandum concerning two complex transactions which have arisen during the year. The memorandum outlines the key elements of each transaction and suggests the appropriate treatment.

Transaction 1

On 1 March 20X9, Complex plc purchased 75% of the equity share capital of Easy Ltd for a total cash price of £60 million. The Directors of Easy Ltd prepared a balance sheet of the company at 1 March 20X9. The total of net assets as shown in this balance sheet was £66 million. However, the net assets of Easy Ltd were reckoned to have a fair value to the Complex group of £72 million in total. The Directors of Complex plc considered that a group reorganisation would be necessary because of the acquisition of Easy Ltd and that the cost would be £4 million. This reorganisation was completed by 31 August 20X9. Your assistant has computed the goodwill on consolidation of Easy Ltd as follows:

	£ million	£ million
Fair value of investment		60
Fair value of net assets	72	
Less: reorganisation provision	(4)	
	68	
Group share		(51)
Goodwill relating to a 75% investment		9
Goodwill relating to a 25% investment $\left(\frac{25}{75}\right)$		3

Your assistant has recognised total goodwill of £12 million (£9 million + £3 million). The goodwill attributable to the minority shareholders (£3 million) has been credited to the minority interest account. The reorganisation costs of £4 million have been written off against the provision which was created as part of the fair value exercise.

Transaction 2

On 15 May 20X9, Complex plc disposed of one of its subsidiaries – Redundant Ltd. Complex plc had owned 100% of the shares in Redundant Ltd prior to disposal. The goodwill arising on the original consolidation of Redundant Ltd had been written off to reserves in line with the Accounting Standard in force at that time. This goodwill amounted to £5 million.

The subsidiary acted as a retail outlet for one of the product lines of the group. Following the disposal, the group reorganised the retail distribution of its products and the overall output of the group was not significantly affected.

The loss on disposal of the subsidiary amounted to £10 million before taxation. Your assistant proposes to show this loss as an exceptional item under discontinued operations on the grounds that the subsidiary has been disposed of and its results are clearly identifiable. The loss on disposal has been computed as follows:

	£ million
Sales proceeds	15
Share of net assets at the date of disposal	(25)
Loss on disposal	(10)

Your assistant has noted that unless the goodwill had previously been written off, the loss on disposal would have been even greater.

Required:

Draft a reply to your assistant which evaluates the suggested treatment and recommends changes where relevant. In each case, your reply should refer to the provisions of relevant Accounting Standards and explain the rationale behind such provisions.

The allocation of marks is as follows:

Transaction 1	**(10 marks)**
Transaction 2	**(8 marks)**
	(Total: 18 marks)

3 Exotic Group

The Exotic Group carries on business as a distributor of warehouse equipment and importer of fruit into the United Kingdom. Exotic plc was incorporated in 1975 to distribute warehouse equipment. It diversified its activities during the 1980s to include the import and distribution of fruit, and expanded its operations by the acquisition of shares in Madeira plc in 1979, in Melon plc in 1989 and in Kiwi plc in 1991.

Accounts for all companies are made up to 31 December.

The draft profit and loss accounts for Exotic plc, Melon plc and Kiwi plc for the year ended 31 December 1994 are as follows:

	Exotic plc	*Melon plc*	*Kiwi plc*
	£'000	£'000	£'000
Turnover	45,600	24,700	22,800
Cost of sales	(18,050)	(5,463)	(5,320)
Gross profit	27,550	19,237	17,480
Distribution costs	(3,325)	(2,137)	(1,900)
Administrative expenses	(3,475)	(950)	(1,900)
Operating profit	20,750	16,150	13,680
Interest paid	(325)		
Profit before tax	20,425	16,150	13,680
Tax on profit on ordinary activities	(8,300)	(5,390)	(4,241)
Profit on ordinary activities after tax	12,125	10,760	9,439
Dividends – proposed	(9,500)		
Retained profit for year	2,625	10,760	9,439
Retained profit brought forward	20,013	13,315	10,459
Retained profit carried forward	22,638	24,075	19,898

The draft balance sheets as at 31 December 1994 are as follows:

	Exotic plc	*Melon plc*	*Kiwi plc*
	£'000	£'000	£'000
Fixed assets (NBV)	35,483	24,273	13,063
Investments			
Shares in Melon plc	6,650		
Shares in Kiwi plc		3,800	
Current assets	1,568	9,025	8,883
Current liabilities	(13,063)	(10,023)	(48)
	30,638	27,075	21,898
Share capital and reserves			
Ordinary £1 shares	8,000	3,000	2,000
Profit and loss account	22,638	24,075	19,898
	30,638	27,075	21,898

The following information is available relating to Exotic plc, Melon plc and Kiwi plc:

(1) On 1 January 1989 Exotic plc acquired 2,700,000 £1 ordinary shares in Melon plc for £6,650,000 at which date there was a credit balance on the profit and loss account of Melon plc of £1,425,000. No shares have been issued by Melon plc since Exotic plc acquired its interest.

(2) On 1 January 1991 Melon plc acquired 1,600,000 £1 ordinary shares in Kiwi plc for £3,800,000 at which date there was a credit balance on the profit and loss account of Kiwi plc of £950,000. No shares have been issued by Kiwi plc since Melon plc acquired its interest.

(3) During 1994, Kiwi plc had made inter-company sales to Melon plc of £480,000 making a profit of 25% on cost and £75,000 of these goods were in stock at 31 December 1994.

(4) During 1994, Melon plc had made inter-company sales to Exotic plc of £260,000 making a profit of $33\frac{1}{3}\%$ on cost and £60,000 of these goods were in stock at 31 December 1994.

(5) On 1 November 1994 Exotic plc sold warehouse equipment to Melon plc for £240,000 from stock. Melon plc has included this equipment in its fixed assets. The equipment had been purchased on credit by Exotic plc for £200,000 in October 1994 and this amount is included in its current liabilities as at 31 December 1994.

(6) Melon plc charges depreciation on its warehouse equipment at 20% on cost. It is company policy to charge a full year's depreciation in the year of acquisition to be included in the cost of sales.

(7) It is group policy to capitalise and amortise all goodwill through the profit and loss account over three years from the date of acquisition.

The following information is available relating to Madeira plc:

(1) In 1979 Madeira plc was incorporated as a wholly owned subsidiary of Exotic plc to carry on business importing bananas from Madeira to the United Kingdom. Increased competition from growers in other world markets has resulted in recurring trade losses.

(2) In 1991 the directors of the parent company arranged for all warehousing and distribution for Madeira plc to be physically handled by Melon plc. Madeira plc retained its office accommodation.

(3) In the financial year ended 31 December 1992 Exotic plc wrote off its investment in Madeira plc in its accounts.

(4) In 1993 Exotic plc decided to discontinue the trade carried on in Madeira plc's name as early as possible in 1994. However, due to protracted negotiations with employees, the termination was not completed until November 1994.

(5) The following data relates to Madeira plc in 1994:

	£'000
Turnover	2,000
Cost of sales	(2,682)
Distribution costs	(18)
Administrative expenses	(100)
Redundancy costs	(427)
Profit on sale of fixed assets	115
Loss on sale of net current assets	(36)

Required:

(a) Excluding Madeira plc:

(i) prepare a consolidated profit and loss account, including brought forward reserves, for the Exotic Group for the year ended 31 December 1994 **(12 marks)**

(ii) prepare a consolidated balance sheet as at that date. **(9 marks)**

(b) Show the accounting treatment for Madeira plc in the consolidated profit and loss account of the Exotic Group for the year ended 31 December 1994 in accordance with FRS 3 on the assumption that there has been a discontinuance and that a provision of £500,000 had been created in 1993 in expectation of trading losses.

(3 marks)
(Total: 24 marks)
(ACCA June 95)

4 Wales plc

At 1 January 20X4 Wales plc held 85% of the 141m £1 ordinary shares issued by Miami plc which it had acquired some years ago at a cost of £527m when the reserves of Miami plc showed a credit balance of £359m. The fair value of Miami plc's net assets was equal to their book value.

On 1 April 20X4 Wales plc acquired 75% of the 300m £1 ordinary shares issued by Scotland plc at a cost of £450m and the whole of the £40m 10% debentures issued by Scotland plc at a cost of £60m.

On 1 July 20X4 Wales plc sold shares in Miami plc for £575m leaving it holding a 60% interest.

The profit and loss accounts for the year ended 31 December 20X4 are as follows:

	Wales plc £m	*Miami plc* £m	*Scotland plc* £m
Turnover	8,000	6,000	1,000
Cost of goods sold	(5,000)	(4,112)	(700)
Gross profit	3,000	1,888	300
Administrative expenses	(660)	(530)	(100)
Distribution costs	(1,427)	(1,001)	(80)
Operating profit	913	357	120
Interest paid/payable	(3)		(4)
Interest received from Scotland	4		
Profit on ordinary activities before tax	914	357	116
Tax	(315)	(125)	(36)
Profit on ordinary activities after tax	599	232	80
Dividends	(90)	–	–
Retained profit for the financial year	509	232	80
Profit and loss account b/f	1,000	651	106
Profit and loss account c/f	1,509	883	186

Further information

(1) The group policy is to write off goodwill over five years, with a full year's charge in the year of acquisition.

(2) Wales plc has not yet accounted for the sale of shares in Miami plc. Taxation on the gain is to be ignored.

(3) Scotland plc has made sales of £60m to Wales plc in the period following the acquisition, at cost plus 25%. A quarter of the goods were still in stock at 31 December 20X4.

Required:

(a) (i) Prepare a consolidated profit and loss account disclosing the retained profit for the year for the Wales Group for the year ended 31 December 20X4.

(ii) Calculate the brought forward and carried forward group reserves. Work to the nearest £million.

(21 marks)
(Total: 21 marks)
(ACCA Dec 95)

5 Icing Ltd

Icing Ltd carries on business as a food manufacturer.

Investment in Cake Ltd
On 1 April 1985 it acquired 4m £1 ordinary shares in Cake Ltd at a cost of £4.5m. At the date of acquisition Cake Ltd had an issued capital of 5m £1 ordinary shares and a credit balance on reserves of £1.75m using book values and £1.25m using fair values. It is group policy for subsidiary companies to revalue assets in their own accounts at fair values at the date of acquisition.

Investment in Loaf Ltd
On 1 December 1990 Icing Ltd acquired 336,000 £1 ordinary shares in Loaf Ltd at a cost of £480,000. At the date of acquisition Loaf Ltd had an issued capital of 560,000 £1 ordinary shares and a credit balance on reserves of £70,000 using book values and £80,000 using fair values. The other 224,000 £1 ordinary shares of Loaf Ltd were held by Flour Supplies Ltd which was a major supplier of raw materials to Loaf Ltd.

Until 1993 Loaf Ltd had produced loaves under contract with various supermarkets. In 1993 the company invested in machinery to produce continental style pastries which could be sold at higher gross profit margins. However, trading conditions worsened in 1996 with increased competition from imported frozen products and the directors of Icing Ltd decided to dispose of their holding in Loaf Ltd on a piecemeal basis.

On 31 May 1996 Icing Ltd disposed of 112,000 £1 ordinary shares in Loaf Ltd to the managers of that company for £175,000. At that date the Icing Ltd directors were replaced by Loaf Ltd managers with the exception of the Managing Director of Icing Ltd who was to remain until the final disposal of shares. The Finance Director of Loaf Ltd retired on 31 May 1996 on grounds of ill health and a new Finance Director was appointed on 31 August 1996.

Proposed accounting policy for investment in Loaf Ltd
Icing Ltd proposes to account for its investment in Loaf Ltd as a trade investment in the 1996 accounts and to show the difference on disposal under discontinued operations. The managers of Loaf Ltd were given an option, exercisable by 30 November 1998, to acquire the remainder of the shares held by Icing Ltd. The terms of the option were that the share price would be the higher of three times the profit before tax per share or the price paid by the managers at 31 May 1996. The managers have reached an agreement with the bank that it will not require the overdraft to be reduced pending discussions to raise additional medium term finance in order to reorganise the capital structure of the company. It is group policy to write off goodwill over five years.

Investment in Bun Ltd
On 1 December 1995 Cake Ltd acquired 375,000 £1 ordinary shares in Bun Ltd for £2m. At the date of acquisition Bun Ltd had an issued capital of 500,000 £1 ordinary shares and a credit balance on reserves of £1.5m using book values and £1.2m using fair values.

The draft accounts for Cake Ltd, Bun Ltd and Loaf Ltd for the year ended 30 November 1996 are as follows:

Draft profit and loss accounts for the year ended 30 November 1996

	Cake Ltd	*Bun Ltd*	*Loaf Ltd*
	£'000	£'000	£'000
Operating profit	2,350	800	24
Dividend from subsidiary undertaking	150		
Profit on ordinary activities before tax	2,500	800	24
Tax on profit on ordinary activities	(1,000)	(300)	(8)
Profit on ordinary activities after tax	1,500	500	16
Dividends proposed	(1,000)	(200)	
Retained profit for the financial year	500	300	16

Draft balance sheets as at 30 November 1996

	£'000	£'000	£'000
Fixed assets			
Tangible assets	5,550	1,410	1,425
Investment in Bun Ltd.	2,000		
Current assets			
Debtors	1,800	720	300
Bank	300	700	
Current liabilities			
Trade creditors	(1,150)	(630)	(207)
Proposed dividends	(1,000)	(200)	
Bank overdraft			(742)
	7,500	2,000	776
Ordinary shares of £1 each	5,000	500	560
Profit and loss account	2,500	1,500	216
	7,500	2,000	776

At 30 November 1996 the book values are the same as fair values.

Required:

(a) Calculate the amounts that Icing Ltd would include in its consolidated accounts in respect of Cake Ltd and Bun Ltd for the year ended 30 November 1996 for the following:

(i) Minority interests for inclusion in the consolidated profit and loss account of the Icing Group

(ii) Group profit after tax

(iii) Minority interests for inclusion in the consolidated balance sheet

(iv) The goodwill or negative goodwill prior to their amortisation. **(10 marks)**

(b) Calculate the goodwill figure if Icing Ltd acquired its holding in Cake Ltd by *piecemeal acquisitions* on 1 April 1985 and 1 June 1996 on the following terms:

On 1 April 1985 it acquired 3m ordinary shares in Cake Ltd at a cost of £3.5m at which date Cake Ltd had an issued capital of 5m ordinary shares and a credit balance on reserves of £1.25m using fair values. On 1 June 1996 it acquired 1m ordinary shares for £1m at which date book values were the same as fair values.

(4 marks)

(c) (i) Calculate the gain/(loss) on sale of the shares in Loaf Ltd both in the accounts of Icing Ltd and in the consolidated accounts for the year ended 30 November 1996. Assume a corporation tax rate of 25%.

(ii) Explain how the results of Loaf Ltd will be shown in the consolidated profit and loss account of the Icing Group for the year ended 30 November 1996 assuming that the investment is classified as an associated undertaking after the disposal of shares on 31 May 1996. **(6 marks)**

(Total: 20 marks)

(ACCA Dec 96)

6 Growmoor plc

Growmoor plc has carried on business as a food retailer since 1900. It had traded profitably until the late 1980s when it suffered from fierce competition from larger retailers. Its turnover and margins were under severe pressure and its share price fell to an all time low. The directors formulated a strategic plan to grow by acquisition and merger. It has an agreement to be able to borrow funds to finance acquisition at an interest rate of 10% per annum. It is Growmoor plc's policy to amortise goodwill over ten years.

Investment in Smelt plc

On 15 June 1994 Growmoor plc had an issued share capital of 1,625,000 ordinary shares of £1 each. On that date it acquired 240,000 of the 1,500,000 issued £1 ordinary shares of Smelt plc for a cash payment of £164,000.

Growmoor plc makes up its accounts to 31 July. In early 1996 the directors of Growmoor plc and Smelt plc were having discussions with a view to a combination of the two companies.

The proposal was that:

(a) On 1 May 1996 Growmoor plc should acquire 1,200,000 of the issued ordinary shares of Smelt plc which had a market price of £1.30 per share, in exchange for 1,500,000 newly issued ordinary shares in Growmoor plc which had a market price of £1.20p per share. There has been no change in Growmoor plc's share capital since 15 June 1994. The market price of the Smelt plc shares had ranged from £1.20 to £1.50 during the year ended 30 April 1996.

(b) It was agreed that the consideration would be increased by 200,000 shares if a contingent liability in Smelt plc in respect of a claim for wrongful dismissal by a former director did not crystallise.

(c) After the exchange the new board would consist of 6 directors from Growmoor plc and 6 directors from Smelt plc with the Managing Director of Growmoor plc becoming Managing Director of Smelt plc.

(d) The Growmoor plc head office should be closed and the staff made redundant and the Smelt plc head office should become the head office of the new combination.

(e) Senior managers of both companies were to re-apply for their posts and be interviewed by an interview panel comprising a director and the personnel managers from each company. The age profile of the two companies differed with the average age of the Growmoor plc managers being 40 and that of Smelt plc being 54 and there was an expectation among the directors of both boards that most of the posts would be filled by Growmoor plc managers.

Investment in Beaten Ltd

Growmoor plc is planning to acquire all of the 800,000 £1 ordinary shares in Beaten Ltd on 30 June 1996 for a deferred consideration of £500,000 and a contingent consideration payable on 30 June 2000 of 10% of the amount by which profits for the year ended 30 June 2000 exceeded £100,000. Beaten Ltd has suffered trading losses and its directors, who are the major shareholders, support a takeover by Growmoor plc. The fair value of net assets of Beaten Ltd was £685,000 and Growmoor plc expected that re-organisation costs would be £85,000 and future trading losses would be £100,000. Growmoor plc agreed to offer four year service contracts to the directors of Beaten Ltd.

The directors had expected to be able to create a provision for the re-organisation costs and future trading losses but were advised by their Finance Director that FRS 7 required these two items to be treated as post-acquisition items.

Required:

(a) (i) Explain to the directors of Growmoor plc the extent to which the proposed terms of the combination with Smelt plc satisfied the requirements of the Companies Act 1985 and FRS 6 for the combination to be treated as a merger, and

(ii) If the proposed terms fail to satisfy any of the requirements, advise the directors on any changes that could be made so that the combination could be treated as a merger as at 31 July 1996. **(8 marks)**

(b) Explain briefly the reasons for the application of the principles of recognition and measurement on an acquisition set out in FRS 7 to provisions for future operating losses and for re-organisation costs. **(3 marks)**

(c) (i) Explain the treatment in the profit and loss account for the year ended 31 July 1996 and the balance sheet as at that date of Growmoor plc on the assumption that the acquisition of Beaten Ltd took place on 30 June 1996 and the consideration for the acquisition was deferred so that £100,000 was payable after one year, £150,000 after two years and the balance after three years. Show your calculations.

(ii) Calculate the goodwill to be dealt with in the consolidated accounts for the years ending 31 July 1996 and 1997 explaining clearly the effect of deferred and contingent consideration. **(6 marks)**

(Total: 17 marks)

(ACCA Dec 96)

7 Textures Ltd

Textures Ltd was incorporated in 1985 to manufacture artificial limbs. Its financial year end is 30 November 1996. It manufactures in the United Kingdom and exports more than 60% of its output. It has a number of foreign subsidiary companies.

It has developed a number of arrangements to support its export sales. These include agreements with Pills Plc, Eduaids Ltd and Bracos and Computer Control Ltd. Information on the agreements is as follows:

Agreement with Pills plc

An agreement was made in 1992 with Pills Plc, a pharmaceutical company, to jointly fund on a 50:50 basis an entity, Textures & Pills Joint Venture, to operate a marketing office in Asia which would advertise each of the company's products but not trade in the products. Both Textures Ltd and Pills plc have guaranteed to meet liabilities if the other party fails to meet its share of the costs and risks.

Accounts prepared for Texture & Pills Joint Venture for the year ended 30 November 1996 showed the following:

	£000
Fixed assets	
Premises	300
Current assets	
Bank and cash	30
	330
Capital	
As at 1 December 1995	
Textures Ltd	211
Pills Plc	211
	422
Less: Expenses	92
As at 30 November 1996	330

Agreement with Eduaid Ltd and Bracos

Textures Ltd entered into an agreement on 1 December 1991 with Eduaids Ltd, a company that manufactured educational equipment, and Bracos, a South American lawyer, to set up under their joint control an unincorporated import undertaking in South America to trade as Eurohelp. Textures Ltd had an effective 30% interest in Eurohelp. The balance sheet of Textures Ltd as at 30 November 1996 showed an investment at cost in Eurohelp of £750,000.

The balance sheet of Eurohelp for the year ended 30 November 1996 showed:

	£'000
Fixed assets	7,500
Net current assets	1,100
	8,600
Capital account	
As at 30 November 1995	6,750
Retained profit for the year	1,850
	8,600

Textures Ltd has used proportional consolidation to account for its interest in Eurohelp since entering into the agreement.

Agreement with Computer Control Ltd

Textures Ltd entered into an agreement on 1 December 1993 with Computer Control Ltd to jointly control Afrohelp Ltd, a company in which each company held a 50% interest. Afrohelp Ltd assembled mechanical products from Textures Ltd and automated them with control equipment from Computer Control Ltd.

The joint venture has been equity accounted by each investor company. One of the newly appointed non-executive directors has questioned whether the investment in Afrohelp Ltd should be treated as a quasi subsidiary and consolidated.

On 1 November 1996 Textures Ltd sold stock costing £110,000 to Afrohelp Ltd for £162,000. This stock was unsold at 30 November 1996.

Required::

(a) (i) Explain the advantages of using the gross equity method to account for associates in consolidated accounts.

(ii) Discuss the advantages and disadvantages of using proportional consolidation to account for joint ventures. **(8 marks)**

(b) (i) Explain how the joint activity of Textures & Pills Joint Venture would be dealt with in the accounts of Textures Ltd as at 30 November 1996.

(ii) Calculate the retained profit of Eurohelp as at 1 December 1995 that would be included in the consolidated retained profit brought forward in the accounts of Textures Ltd at 30 November 1996 using proportional consolidation.

(4 marks)

(c) Assuming that you are the Finance Director of Textures Ltd.

(i) Advise the non-executive director of the conditions that would need to be satisfied to avoid Afrohelp Ltd being treated as a quasi subsidiary as at 30 November 1996.

(ii) Contrast the treatment of the unrealised gain on the sale of stock to Afrohelp Ltd on consolidating Afrohelp Ltd as an associate compared to as a quasi-subsidiary. **(8 marks)**

(Total: 20 marks)

(ACCA Dec 96)

8 Walsh plc

Walsh, a public limited company, acquired 80% of the ordinary share capital of Marsh, a public limited company, on 1 April 20X3 when the retained earnings of Marsh were £350 million (credit). The cost of the shares of Marsh was £544 million and the share capital acquired by Walsh was 120 million of the £1 ordinary shares. On 1 July 20X6 Walsh sold 20 million shares of £1 of Marsh for £350 million. There has been no change in the ordinary share capital of Marsh since 1 April 20X3.

On 1 April 20X6 Walsh acquired 85% of the 200 million ordinary shares of £1 of Short, a public limited company at a cost of £900 million.

The draft profit and loss accounts for the year ended 31 December 20X6 are:

	Walsh plc £m	*Marsh plc* £m	*Short plc* £m
Turnover	10,000	8,000	2,000
Cost of sales	(7,000)	(5,500)	(800)
Gross profit	3,000	2,500	1,200
Administrative expenses	(880)	(570)	(180)
Distribution costs	(1,310)	(830)	(240)
Operating profit	810	1,100	780
Interest payable	(7)	-	(4)
Bank interest receivable	5	-	-
Profit on ordinary activities before taxation	808	1,100	776
Tax on profit	(250)	(350)	(200)
Profit on ordinary activities after taxation	558	750	576
Dividends	(85)	-	-
Retained profit for year	473	750	576
Profit and loss reserve at 1 January 20X6	1,500	1,650	675

The following information is relevant to the preparation of the group accounts.

(i) Goodwill is amortised through the profit and loss account over three years, with a full year's charge in the year of acquisition and no charge in the year of disposal.

(ii) The sale of the shares in Marsh plc has not been accounted for in the accounting records of Walsh plc (ignore the taxation aspects of the sale).

(iii) Short plc sold goods to Walsh plc to the selling value of £80 million on 1 August 20X6 at cost plus 20%. Walsh plc had sold £62 million of these goods at the year end.

(iv) Assume that the fair values of the net assets of the subsidiary companies were the same as the book values at the date of acquisition.

(v) Assume that profits accrue evenly and that there are no other reserves than the profit and loss reserve.

Required:

(a) Prepare a consolidated profit and loss account for the Walsh Group plc for the year ended 31 December 20X6 in accordance with the Companies Acts, FRS 2 'Accounting for Subsidiary Undertakings', FRS 3 'Reporting Financial Performance'. Earnings per share and the notes to the accounts are not required. **(15 marks)**

(b) Calculate the balance on the group profit and loss reserve at 31 December 20X6. **(5 marks)**

(Total: 20 marks)

(ACCA 1997 Pilot Paper)

(All calculations should be to the nearest million pounds.)

9 A plc

The following financial statements relate to A plc, B plc, C Ltd and D Ltd for the year ended 31 May 20X7.

	A plc	*B plc*	*C Ltd*	*D Ltd*
	£m	£m	£m	£m
Fixed assets:				
Tangible fixed assets	3,500	550	60	90
Investment in B	900			
Investment in C		90		
Investment in D	50			
	4,450	640		
Net current assets	1,830	400	70	60
Creditors falling due after 1 year	130	30	10	5
	6,150	1,010	120	145
Capital and reserves				
Called up share capital of £1	1,350	100	30	20
Share premium account	1,550	100	10	20
Profit and loss account	3,250	810	80	105
	6,150	1,010	120	145

Profit and loss accounts for the year ended 31 May 20X7

	A plc	*B plc*	*C Ltd*	*D Ltd*
	£m	£m	£m	£m
Turnover	8,000	3,000	325	530
Cost of sales	5,000	2,000	195	320
Gross profit	3,000	1,000	130	210

Administrative and distribution costs	2,000	400	35	125
Income from group companies	13	4	-	
Operating profit before taxation	1,013	604	95	85
Taxation	300	200	40	25
Profit on ordinary activities after tax	713	404	55	60
Dividends paid	30	10	5	5
Retained profit for year	683	394	50	55

(i) The directors of A plc decided to reconstruct the group at 31 May 20X7. Under the scheme the existing group of companies was split into two separate groups in order to separate their different trades. A plc has disposed of its shareholding in B plc to another company E plc. In return the shares in E plc were distributed to the shareholders in A plc. No profit or loss arose on the disposal of the shares in B plc as the 'demerger' simply involved a distribution to the shareholders of A plc of the shares of E plc.

(ii) After the 'demerger', there were two separate groups controlled by A plc and E plc. A plc and D Ltd formed one group. E plc and the B group plc formed another group. E plc issued 300 million ordinary shares of £1 in exchange for A plc's investment in B plc. The transaction took place on 31 May 20X7.

(iii) The following information relates to the dates of acquisition of the investments in group companies:

Holding company account	Co. Acquired	% Acquired	Dates	£m Share premium account	£m Profit/Loss
A plc	B plc	100	1.1.X4	100	250
A plc	D Ltd	60	1.5.X5	20	90
B plc	C Ltd	80	1.6.X5	10	60

(iv) The group's policy is not to amortise goodwill arising on acquisition of a subsidiary unless annual impairment reviews show that a write-down is necessary. No fair value adjustments have been required.

(v) Dividends paid by group companies have been accounted for by the recipient companies. A group plc has decided to show the effect of the distribution of the shares in E plc and the demerger of B group plc in its profit and loss account and not as a movement on reserves.

(vi) The group is to take advantage of the provisions of the Companies Act 1985 regarding group reconstruction relief and the transaction qualifies as a merger.

Required:

(a) Prepare the consolidated balance sheet of the B group plc as at 31 May 20X7.

(5 marks)

(b) Prepare the consolidated profit and loss account and balance sheet of A Group plc for the year ended 31 May 20X7 after accounting for the demerger.

(14 marks)

(Candidates should prepare the financial statements in accordance with FRS 3 'Reporting Financial Performance').

(c) Show the share capital and reserves of E Group plc at 31 May 20X7.

(2 marks)
(Total: 21 marks)
(ACCA June 97)

10 Merge plc

A merger is 'a business combination that results in the creation of a new reporting entity formed from the combining parties, in which the combining entities come together in a partnership for the mutual sharing of the risks and benefits of the combined entity, and in which no party to the combination in substance obtains control over any other, or is otherwise seen to be dominant...' FRS 6 'Acquisitions and Mergers'. The continuity of ownership, control and the sharing of risks and benefits in the combined entity are seen as crucial to a combination being accounted for as a merger. There are certain criteria under FRS 6 which can be verified and substantiated in order to determine whether there is continuity of ownership. Similarly there are certain criteria in FRS 6 which could be said to be circumstantial or implied evidence of a merger and which cannot be exactly determined. This type of evidence is somewhat subjective. Finally FRS 6 has invoked certain criteria which attempt to prevent a company creating the superficial or cosmetic appearance of the occurrence of a merger.

Required:

(a) Analyse and describe the criteria that a business combination must meet under FRS 6 for it to be accounted for as a merger under the following classes:

(i) verifiable and substantive signs of a merger
(ii) implied or circumstantial evidence of a merger
(iii) terms which prevent superficial mergers (anti avoidance criteria). **(9 marks)**

(b) The following abridged financial statements relate to Merge plc and Acquire plc for the year ended 30 November 20X7.

Profit and Loss Account Year Ended 30 November 20X7

	Merge plc £000	*Acquire plc* £000
Turnover	21,285	18,000
Cost of sales	(16,950)	(14,450)
Gross profit	4,335	3,550
Distribution and administrative expenses	(3,310)	(2,730)
Operating profit	1,025	820
Income from investments	200	100
Profit before taxation	1,225	920
Taxation	(365)	(274)
Dividends	(208)	(148)
Retained profit for year	652	498

Balance Sheet at 30 November 20X7

Fixed assets (including cost of investment in Acquire plc)	4,099	3,590
Current assets	5,530	4,350
Creditors: Amounts falling due within one year	(2,502)	(2,530)
Net current assets	3,028	1,820
Total assets less current liabilities	7,127	5,410

Capital and reserves		
Called up share capital -		
ordinary shares of £1	2,500	1,250
Share premium account	400	250
Revaluation reserve	75	185
Other reserves	100	-
Profit and loss account	4,052	3,725
	7,127	5,410

(i) During the year the entire share capital of Acquire plc was acquired following a recommended offer by merchant bankers on 30 April 20X7. Ordinary shares were issued to those shareholders of Acquire plc who accepted the offer and at the same time £36,000 was paid in cash to shareholders who took the cash alternative. The offer was made on the basis of six shares in Merge plc for every five shares in Acquire plc. A fully underwritten cash alternative of £2.25 per share was offered to the shareholders of Acquire plc. The offer became unconditional on 31 May 20X7 when the market value of shares in Merge plc was £2.50 per share. On 31 August 20X7 Merge plc compulsorily acquired 8,000 shares of Acquire plc for cash from shareholders who had not accepted the initial offer under the Companies Act 1985. The above transactions had been incorporated in the financial records of Merge plc at their nominal value.

(ii) Merge plc incurred £156,000 of expenses in connection with the acquisition of Acquire plc. This figure included issue costs of shares of £58,000 and has been included in administrative expenses.

(iii) Acquire plc paid dividends of £48,000 on 31 March 20X7 and has proposed a final dividend of £100,000. Merge plc's dividends are all proposed. The proposed dividend of Acquire plc has been taken into account in Merge plc's financial statements.

(iv) The acquisition fulfils all of the criteria in the Companies Acts and FRS 6 for merger accounting except for the criteria relating to the purchase consideration which has not been tested.

(v) There is no group election for tax purposes in force.

Required:

Prepare the group profit and loss account for the year ended 30 November 20X7 and the balance sheet as at 30 November 20X7 for the Merge Group plc.

(16 marks)
(Total: 25 marks)
(ACCA Dec 97)

11 Wright Group plc

Wright, a public limited company, acquired 80% of the ordinary share capital of Berg, a public limited company, on 1 July 20X6 when the retained earnings of Berg were £300 million. The cost of the shares was £600 million and the share capital and share premium account of Berg at that date were respectively £250 million and £50 million. The fair values of the net assets of Berg at the date of acquisition were equivalent to their book values. Wright sold half of its holding of the shares in Berg on 1 July 20X8 for £350 million.

On 1 April 20X8, Wright acquired 80% of the ordinary share capital of £500 million of Chang, a public limited company, at a cost of £700 million.

The draft profit and loss accounts for the year ended 31 December 20X8 are:

	Wright plc £m	*Berg plc* £m	*Chang plc* £m
Turnover	18,000	1,200	1,600
Cost of sales	(12,000)	(840)	(1,020)
Gross profit	6,000	360	580
Distribution costs	(1,800)	(120)	(140)
Administrative expenses	(180)	(12)	(12)

Operating profit	4,020	228	428
Interest payable	(30)	(8)	(4)
Bank interest receivable	15	10	20
Dividends receivable (all inter company)	112	–	–
Profit on ordinary activities before taxation	4,117	230	444
Tax on profit on ordinary activities	(1,320)	(74)	(80)
Profit on ordinary activities after tax	2,797	156	364
Dividends – proposed	(200)	(80)	(100)
Retained profit for the year	2,597	76	264
Profit and loss reserve at 1.1.X8	8,500	324	249

The following information is relevant to the preparation of the group accounts:

(i) During the period Wright plc closed down 15 of its 100 retail outlets because they were unprofitable and inefficient. These outlets contributed 5% of the turnover and operating costs of Wright plc. The costs of this downsizing included in cost of sales amounted to £14 million.

(ii) The net assets of Chang acquired on 1 April 20X8 and their fair values were as follows:

	Carrying value £m	*Fair value adjustment* £m	*Fair values* £m
Tangible fixed assets	500	(30)	470
Stock and work-in-progress	240	(40)	200
Provision for re-organisation	(30)	(20)	(50)
Other net assets	130		130
	840	(90)	750

The provision for reorganisation of £30 million relates to the reorganisation of the retail outlets of Chang which had been committed and provided for on 31 December 20X7 and a further post acquisition provision of £20 million is required which relates to the reorganisation of the remaining retail outlets as a result of the acquisition. The reduction in the stock value relates to a change in the accounting policy for stocks in order to bring it into line with that of Wright. The required change in the closing stock value of Chang to ensure uniform group accounting policies is a decrease of £30 million. The stock of Chang at 1 January 20X8 was £150 million and at 31 December 20X8 was £350 million.

(iii) Berg sold goods to Wright on 1 September 20X8 which had a selling value of £60 million. The profit made by Berg on these goods was £6 million and Wright had sold half of these goods by the year end.

(iv) Goodwill arising on the acquisition of subsidiaries is amortised through the profit and loss account in cost of sales over four years with a full year's charge being made in the year of acquisition. Depreciation is charged on all group fixed assets at 20% per annum on the carrying value. The depreciation policy of Chang has been the same as the group's policy for several years. The fair value adjustments had not been incorporated into Chang's accounting records.

(v) The sale of the shares in Berg has not been accounted for by Wright, although the dividends receivable reflect the change in Wright's shareholding. Assume that profits accrue evenly and that there are no other expenses or share capital in issue other than those stated in the question. Taxation on any capital gain is to be ignored.

Required:

(a) Prepare a consolidated profit and loss account for the Wright Group plc for the year ended 31 December 20X8 in accordance with the Companies Acts and UK Accounting Standards. (The amount of the consolidated profit dealt with in the holding company's accounts is not required.)

(25 marks)

(b) Show the composition of the balance on the group profit and loss reserve at 31 December 20X8.

(5 marks)
(Total: 30 marks)
(ACCA Dec 98)

12 X Group

X, a public limited company, acquired 100 million ordinary shares of £1 in Y, a public limited company on 1 April 20X6 when the accumulated reserves were £120 million. Y acquired 45 million ordinary shares of £1 in Z, a public limited company, on 1 April 20X4 when the accumulated reserves were £10 million. On 1 April 20X4 there were no material differences between the carrying values and the fair values of Z. On 1 April 20X6, the accumulated reserves of Z were £20 million.

Y acquired 30% of the ordinary shares of W, a limited company, on 1 April 20X6 for £50 million when the accumulated reserves of W were £7 million. Y exercises significant influence over W and there were no material differences between the carrying values and the fair values of W at that date.

There had been no share issues since 1 April 20X4 by any of the group companies. The following balance sheets relate to the group companies as at 31 March 20X9.

		X	*Y*	*Z*	*W*
		£m	£m	£m	£m
Fixed assets	- tangible	900	100	30	40
	- intangible		30		
Investment in Y		320			
Investment in Z			90		
Investment in W			50		
Net Current Assets		640	360	75	73
Creditors: amounts falling due after one year		(200)	(150)	(15)	(10)
		1,660	480	90	103
Share Capital		360	150	50	80
Share Premium		250	120	10	6
Accumulated reserves		1,050	210	30	17
		1,660	480	90	103

(i) The following fair value table sets out the carrying values and fair values of certain assets and liabilities of the group companies together with any accounting policy adjustments required to ensure consistent group policies at 1 April 20X6.

	Carrying value		*Accounting policy adj.*		*Fair value adj.*		*New carrying value*	
	Y	Z	Y	Z	Y	Z	Y	Z
	£m	£m	£m	£m	£m	£m	£m	£m
Tangible fixed assets	90	20			30	10	120	30
Intangible fixed assets	30		(30)				-	
Stocks	20	12	2		(8)	(5)	14	7
Provision for bad debts	(15)				(9)		(24)	

These values had not been incorporated into the financial records. Group companies have consistent accounting policies as at 31 March 20X9.

(ii) During the year ended 31 March 20X9, Z had sold goods to X and Y. At 31 March 20X9, there were £44 million of these goods in the stock of X and £16 million in the stock of Y. Z had made a profit of 25% on selling price on the goods.

(iii) On 1 June 20X6, an amount of £36 million was received by Y from an arbitration award against Q. This receipt was secured as a result of an action against Q prior to Y's acquisition by X but was not included in the assets of Y at 1 April 20X6.

(iv) The group charges depreciation on all tangible fixed assets on the straight line basis at 10% per annum. It capitalises goodwill and amortises it over 11 years from the date of acquisition.

Required:

Prepare a consolidated balance sheet as at 31 March 20X9 for the X group. **(26 marks)**

(All calculations should be rounded to the nearest £ million). **(Total: 26 marks)**
(ACCA June 99)

13 Baden plc

(a) FRS 9 'Associates and Joint Ventures' deals not only with the accounting treatment of associated companies and joint venture operations but covers certain types of joint business arrangements not carried on through a separate entity. The main changes made by FRS 9 are to restrict the circumstances in which equity accounting can be applied and to provide detailed rules for accounting for joint ventures.

Required:

(i) Explain the criteria which distinguish an associate from an ordinary fixed asset investment. **(6 marks)**

(ii) Explain the principal difference between a joint venture and a 'joint arrangement' and the impact that this classification has upon the accounting for such relationships. **(4 marks)**

(b) The following financial statements relate to Baden, a public limited company.

Profit and loss account for year ended 31 December 20X8

	£m	£m
Turnover		212
Cost of sales		(170)
Gross profit		42
Distribution costs	17	
Administrative costs	8	
		(25)
		17
Other operating income		12
Operating profit		29
Exceptional item		(10)
Interest payable		(4)
Profit on ordinary activities before tax		15
Taxation on profit on ordinary activities		(3)
		12
Ordinary dividend - paid		(4)
Retained profit for year		8

Balance Sheet at 31 December 20X8

	£m	£m
Fixed assets - tangible	30	
goodwill	7	
		37
Current assets	31	
Creditors: amounts falling due within one year	(12)	
Net current assets		19
Total assets less current liabilities		56
Creditors: amounts falling due after more than one year		(10)
		46
Capital and Reserves		
Called up share capital –		
Ordinary shares of £1		10
Share premium account		4
Profit and loss account		32
		46

(i) Cable, a public limited company, acquired 30% of the ordinary share capital of Baden at a cost of £14 million on 1 January 20X7. The share capital of Baden has not changed since acquisition when the profit and loss reserve of Baden was £9 million.

(ii) At 1 January 20X7 the following fair values were attributed to the net assets of Baden but not incorporated in its accounting records.

	£m
Tangible fixed assets	30 (carrying value £20m)
Goodwill (estimate)	10
Current assets	31
Creditors: amounts falling due within one year	20
Creditors: amounts falling after more than one year	8

(iii) Guy, an associated company of Cable, also holds a 25% interest in the ordinary share capital of Baden. This was acquired on 1 January 20X8.

(iv) During the year to 31 December 20X8, Baden sold goods to Cable to the value of £35 million. The inventory of Cable at 31 December 20X8 included goods purchased from Baden on which the company made a profit of £10 million.

(v) The policy of all companies in the Cable Group is to amortise goodwill over four years and to depreciate tangible fixed assets at 20% per annum on the straight line basis.

(vi) Baden does not represent a material part of the group and is significantly less than the 15% additional disclosure threshold required under FRS 9 'Associates and Joint Ventures'.

Required:

(i) Show how the investment in Baden would be stated in the consolidated balance sheet and profit and loss account of the Cable Group under FRS 9 'Associates and Joint Ventures', for the year ended 31 December 20X8 on the assumption that Baden is an associate. **(9 marks)**

(ii) Show how the treatment of Baden would change if Baden was classified as an investment in a joint venture. **(6 marks)**

(Total: 25 marks)

(ACCA June 99)

14 A plc

A, a public limited company, has acquired shareholdings in two companies, X and Y, both themselves public limited companies. The following table shows the way in which the current shareholdings in these companies have been acquired:

X plc

Date	*Holding Acquired*	*Fair Value of total net assets*	*Purchase Consideration*
		£m	£m
31.8.X7	10%	30	5
31.10.X8	45%	52	25
31.10.X9	10%	60	8
	65%		

Y plc

Date	*Holding Acquired*	*Fair Value of total net assets*	*Purchase Consideration*
31 October 20X8	60%	70	54

The following balance sheets relate to A, X and Y as at 31 October 20X9:

	A	*X*	*Y*
	£m	£m	£m
Tangible fixed assets	108	50	60
Cost of investments	92		
Net current assets	26	25	15
Long-term liabilities	(6)	(35)	(10)
	220	40	65
Share capital – ordinary shares of £1	80	10	30
Share premium			10
Retained profits brought forward	100	20	15
Profit for year	40	10	10
	220	40	65

(i) Goodwill arising on acquisition is amortised through the profit and loss account over four years with a full year's charge in the year of acquisition. The increase in the fair values is attributable to net current assets.

(ii) A owned 12 million ordinary shares of £1 in Y at 31 October 20X8. On 31 August 20X9, Y issued 10 million ordinary shares of £1 to third parties for a consideration of £20 million.

(iii) A had sold £10 million of goods to Y on 31 August 20X9, making a profit of 25 per cent on cost. All of these goods remained in the stock of Y at 31 October 20X9. X had sold a piece of land to A for £28 million during the year to 31 October 20X9. The land was purchased originally from Y on 1 January 20X9 for £20 million at a profit of £5 million. A had not paid the liability to X as at 31 October 20X9.

(iv) A purchased a five per cent holding on 1 October 20X9 in an overseas company for 42 million krona when the exchange rate was 3·5 krona = £1. This investment is included in tangible fixed assets. It partially financed the investment by borrowing 21 million krona on the same date. This loan is included in long-term liabilities. The company has not repaid any of the loan as at 31 October 20X9 and no adjustments for the change in the exchange rate have been made. The exchange rate at 31 October 20X9 is 3 krona = £1. The company wishes to maximise its reported earnings.

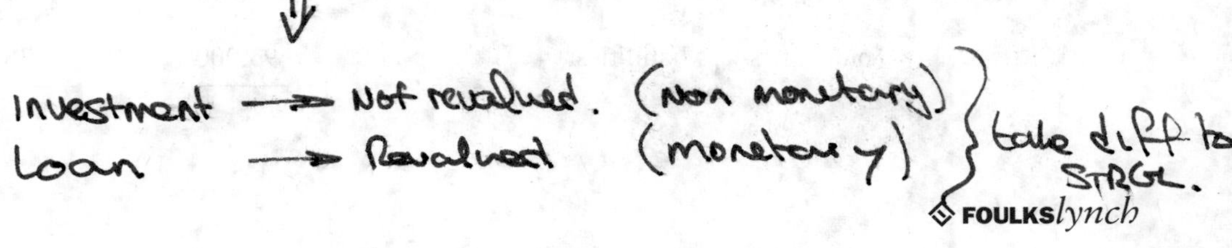

(v) X commenced on 1 November 20X7 manufacturing product Z, and gives a warranty on this product at the time of sale to its customers. Under the terms of the warranty, X undertakes to repair or replace items that fail to perform satisfactorily for two years from the date of sale. The current policy of the company is to charge the cost of claims under the warranty against the profit and loss account in the year in which the claims are settled and this policy has been used to arrive at the fair values of X's net assets. It is estimated that the claims would amount to approximately 5% of sales in a year. Sales of product Z to third parties were £300 million for the year to 31 October 20X8 and £200 million for the year to 31 October 20X9. The charges against profits for the claims were £3 million in 20X8 and £5 million in 20X9. Assume that there is no inflationary adjustment to be made on the provisions.

Required:

(a) Calculate the goodwill arising on the purchase of X and Y which would be shown in the group financial statements for the year ended 31 October 20X8. **(5 marks)**

(b) Prepare the consolidated balance sheet for the A group as at 31 October 20X9. **(25 marks)**

(Total: 30 marks)

(ACCA Dec 99)

15 AB Group

AB, a public limited company, manufactures goods for the aerospace industry. It acquired an electronics company CG, a public limited company on 1 December 20X0 at an agreed value of £65 million. The purchase consideration was satisfied by the issue of 30 million shares of AB, in exchange for the whole of the share capital of CG. The directors of AB have decided to adopt merger accounting principles in accounting for the acquisition, but the auditors have not as yet concurred with the use of merger accounting in the financial statements.

The following summary financial statements relate to the above companies as at 31 May 20X1.

Profit and Loss Accounts for the year ended 31 May 20X1

	AB £'000	*CG* £'000
Turnover	45,000	34,000
Cost of sales	(31,450)	(25,280)
Gross profit	13,550	8,720
Distribution and administrative expenses	(9,450)	(3,820)
Operating profit	4,100	4,900
Interest payable	(200)	(400)
Profit before taxation	3,900	4,500
Taxation	(1,250)	(1,700)
Dividends (proposed)	(250)	
Retained profit for the year	2,400	2,800

Balance Sheets at 31 May 20X1

	AB £'000	*CG* £'000
Tangible fixed assets	36,000	24,500
Cost of investment in CG	30,000	
Net current assets	29,000	17,500
Creditors: amounts due after more than one year	(2,000)	(4,000)
Total assets less liabilities	93,000	38,000

Capital and Reserves		
Ordinary shares of £1	55,000	20,000
Share premium account	3,000	6,000
Revaluation reserve	10,000	
Profit and loss account	25,000	12,000
	93,000	38,000

The following information should be taken into account when preparing the group accounts:

(i) The management of AB feel that the adjustments required to bring the following assets of CG to their fair values at 1 December 20X0 are as follows:

Fixed Assets to be increased by £4 million;
Stock to be decreased by £3 million (this stock had been sold by the year end);
Provision for bad debts increased by £2 million in relation to specific accounts;
Depreciation is charged at 20% per annum on a straight-line basis on tangible fixed assets;
The increase in the provision for bad debts was still required at 31 May 20X1. No further provisions are required on 31 May 20X1.

(ii) CG has a fixed rate bank loan of £4 million, which was taken out when interest rates were 10% per annum. The loan is due for repayment on 30 November 20X2. At the date of acquisition the company could have raised a loan at an interest rate of 7%. Interest is payable yearly in arrears on 30 November.

(iii) CG acquired a corporate brand name on 1 July 20X0. The company did not capitalise the brand name but wrote the cost off against reserves in the Statement of Total Recognised Gains and Losses. The cost of the brand name was £18 million. AB has consulted an expert brand valuation firm who have stated that the brand is worth £20 million at the date of acquisition based on the present value of notional royalty savings arising from ownership of the brand. The auditors are satisfied with the reliability of the brand valuation. Brands are not amortised by AB but are reviewed annually for impairment, and as at 31 May 20X1, there has been no impairment in value. Goodwill is amortised over a 10 year period with a full charge in the year of acquisition.

(iv) AB incurred £500,000 of expenses in connection with the acquisition of CG. The figure comprised £300,000 of professional fees and £200,000 issue costs of the shares. The acquisition expenses have been included in administrative expenses.

Required:

(a) Prepare consolidated profit and loss accounts for the year ended 31 May 20X1 and consolidated balance sheets as at 31 May 20X1 for the AB group utilising:

- Merger accounting
- Acquisition accounting. **(19 marks)**

(b) Discuss the impact on the group financial statements of the AB group of utilising merger accounting as opposed to acquisition accounting. (Candidates should discuss at least three effects on the financial statements.)

(6 marks)
(Total: 25 marks)
(ACCA June 00)

16 Satellite

Satellite, a public limited company has produced the following draft consolidated balance sheet as at 30 November 20X1:

Group Balance Sheet as at 30 November 20X1

	£'000
Fixed Assets	
Intangible Assets	5,180
Tangible Assets	38,120
	43,300
Net Current Assets	27,900
Total Assets less Current Liabilities	71,200
Creditors: amounts falling due after more than one year	(12,700)
Provisions for Liabilities and Charges	(900)
	57,600
Minority Interests	(9,100)
	48,500
Capital and Reserves:	
Called up share capital	16,100
Share premium account	5,000
Profit and Loss account	27,400
Shareholders funds	48,500

The group accountant has asked your advice on several matters. These issues are set out below and have not been dealt with in the draft group financial statements:

1 Satellite has buildings under an operating lease. A requirement of the operating lease for the corporate offices is that the asset is returned in good condition. The operating lease was signed in the current year and lasts for six years. Satellite intends to refurbish the building in six years time at a cost of £6 million in order to meet the requirements of the lease. This amount includes the renovation of the exterior of the building and is based on current price levels. Currently there is evidence that due to severe and exceptional weather damage the company will have to spend £1.2 million in the next year on having the exterior of the building renovated. The company feels that this expenditure will reduce the refurbishment cost at the end of the lease by an equivalent amount. There is no provision for the above expenditure in the financial statement.

An 80% owned subsidiary company, Universe, has a leasehold property (depreciated historical cost £8 million). It has been modified to include a sports facility for the employees. Under the terms of the lease, the warehouse must be restored to its original state when the lease expires in ten years time or earlier termination. The present value of the costs of reinstatement are likely to be £2 million and the directors wish to provide for £200,000 per annum for ten years. The lease was signed and operated from 1 December 20X0. The directors estimate that the lease has a recoverable value of £95 million at 30 November 20X1 and have not provided for any of the above amounts.

Additionally Satellite owns buildings at a carrying value of £20 million which will require repair expenditure of approximately £6 million over the next five years. No provision has been made for this amount in the financial statements and depreciation is charged on leasehold buildings at 10% per annum and on owned buildings at 5% per annum on the straight-line basis.

2 Universe has developed a database during the year to 30 November 20X1 and it is included in intangible fixed assets at a cost of £3 million. The asset comprises the internal and external costs of developing the database. The cost of the database is being amortised over 10 years and one year's amortisation has been charged. The database is used to produce a technical accounting manual which is used by the whole group and sold to other parties. It has quickly become a market leader in this held. Any costs of maintaining the database and the technical manual are written off as incurred. The technical manual requires substantial revision every four years.

3 On 1 December 20X0, Satellite entered into an agreement with a wholly owned overseas subsidiary Domingo, to purchase components at a value of 2.1 million dinars on which Domingo made a profit of 20% on selling price. The goods were to be delivered on 31 January 20X1 with the payment due on 31 March 20X1. Satellite took out a foreign currency contract on 1 December 20X0 to buy 2.1 million dinars on 31 March 20X1 at the forward rate of £1 = 1.4 dinars.

At 30 November 20X1, Satellite had two-thirds of the components in stock. The spot rates were as follows:

	£1 equivalent
1 December 20X0	1.3 dinars
31 January 20X1	1.46 dinars
31 March 20X1	1.45 dinars
30 November 20X1	1.35 dinars

The initial purchase of the stock had been recorded on receipt at the forward rate and the forward rate had been used for the year end valuation of stock The directors are unsure as to how to treat the items above both for accounting and disclosure purposes but they have heard that the simplest method is to translate the asset and liability at the forward rate and they wish to use this method.

4 Satellite purchased a wholly owned subsidiary company, Globe, on 1 December 20W9. The vendors commenced a legal action on 31 March 20X1 over the amount of the purchase consideration which was based on the performance of the subsidiary. An amount had been paid to the vendors and included in the calculation of goodwill but the vendors disputed the amount of this payment. The court made a decision on 30 November 20X1 which requires Satellite to pay an additional £8 million to the vendors. The directors do not know how to treat the additional purchase consideration and have not accounted for the item. Goodwill is written off over five years with no time apportionment in the year of purchase.

(Assume that the effect of the time value of money is not material.)

Required:

(a) Discuss how the above four issues should be dealt with in the group financial statements of Satellite, stating the nature of the accounting entries required. **(22 marks)**

(b) Prepare a revised Group Balance Sheet at 30 November 20X1 taking into account the four issues above. **(8 marks)**

(Total: 30 marks)

(ACCA Dec 00)

17 Bull plc

Bull plc is a company that trades in the United Kingdom manufacturing drugs for animals. Dog Inc has been a wholly owned foreign subsidiary of Bull plc since incorporation carrying on business as a buyer of soya oil which it sells to Bull plc for use as a raw material in its drugs.

Dog Inc has prepared a draft profit and loss account for the year ended 31 October 20X3 and a balance sheet as at that date in dollars ($) as follows:

Profit and loss account for the year ended 31 October 20X3

	$'000	$'000
Sales		3,750
Cost of sales		
Stock at 1.11.X2	115	
Purchases	3,000	
	3,115	
Stock at 31.10.X3	120	
		2,995
Gross profit		755
Administration expenses	100	
Handling charges	200	
Depreciation	150	
		450
Profit before tax		305
Tax		150
Profit after tax		155

Balance sheet as at 31 October 20X3

	$'000	$'000
Fixed assets		
Plant and equipment	1,800	
Less aggregate depreciation	750	
		1,050
Current assets		
Stock	120	
Debtors	80	
Bank	350	
	550	
Current liabilities		
Creditors	175	
Net current assets		375
		1,425
Ordinary share capital		375
Profit and loss account		1,050
		1,425

Additional information is available relating to exchange rates and depreciation:

Exchange rates have been as follows:

	$ to £
At date of incorporation	3.6
At date of acquisition of fixed assets on 1.11.W8	2.2
On 1.11.X2	1.8
On 31.10.X3	1.1
Average rate for financial year ended 31.10.X3	1.5
At date of purchase of stock at beginning of year	1.8
At date of purchase of stock at end of year	1.1

Depreciation is charged on a straight-line basis on cost. No fixed assets have been acquired since 19W8.

Required:

(a) (i) Explain the factors that needed to be taken into account when selecting the appropriate method for translating the financial statements of a foreign subsidiary for consolidation purposes.

(ii) Advise the management on the method that is appropriate for translating the financial statements of Dog Inc in accordance with the provisions of SSAP 20 'Foreign Currency Translation'. **(6 marks)**

(b) On the assumption that the temporal method is appropriate:

Translate the profit and loss account and balance sheet of Dog Inc for consolidation purposes using the temporal method. Show all workings clearly. **(10 marks)**

(c) On the assumption that the closing rate method is appropriate:

(i) Reconcile the sterling profit and loss balance of Dog Inc as at 1 November 20X2 with the sterling profit and loss balance as at 31 October 20X3 using the closing rate of exchange to translate the profit and loss account.

(ii) Calculate the explain how the difference between the retained profit using the closing rate and the retained profit using the average rate of exchange for the profit and loss account would be recorded.

(10 marks)

(d) Assuming that Bull plc borrowed $750,000 on 1 November 20X2 to provide a hedge against the investment, explain the treatment of any gain/loss arising on translating the loan using the closing rate method in the company-only profit and loss account for the year ended 31 October 20X3 and balance sheet as at that date of Bull plc. **(4 marks)**

(Total: 30 marks)

(ACCA Dec 93)

18 UK plc

The balance sheets of UK plc and its subsidiary undertaking Germany gmbh at 31 March 20X6 and their profit and loss accounts for the twelve months then ended are given below:

Balance sheets at 31 March 20X6

	UK plc		*Germany gmbh*	
	£'000	£'000	DM'000	DM'000
Fixed assets:				
Tangible assets	20,000		30,000	
Investments *(notes 1 and 2)*	5,500		-	
		25,500		30,000
Current assets:				
Stocks	10,000		18,000	
Trade debtors	8,500		15,000	
Other debtors *(note 3)*	1,500			
	20,000		33,000	
Current liabilities:				
Trade creditors	4,000		6,000	
Proposed dividends	3,900		4,400	
Bank overdraft	6,100		7,600	
	14,000		18,000	
Net current assets		6,000		15,000
Total assets less current liabilities		31,500		45,000
Creditors falling due after more than one year *(note 4)*		(10,000)		(20,000)
		21,500		25,000
Capital and reserves:				
Called up share capital (£1/1DM shares)		9,000		15,000
Profit and loss account		12,500		10,000
		21,500		25,000

Profit and loss accounts - year ended 31 March 20X6

	UK plc	*Germany gmbh*
	£'000	DM'000
Turnover	50,000	60,000
Cost of sales *(notes 2 and 5)*	(25,000)	(30,000)
Gross profit	25,000	30,000
Other operating expenses	(15,000)	(16,000)
Operating profit	10,000	14,000
Investment income *(note 3)*	1,500	-
Interest payable	(1,000)	(2,000)
Profit before taxation	10,500	12,000
Taxation	(3,600)	(4,200)
Profit after taxation	6,900	7,800
Proposed dividends	(3,900)	(4,400)
Retained profit for the year	3,000	3,400
Retained profit - 1 April 20X5	9,500	6,600
Retained profit - 31 March 20X6	12,500	10,000

Notes to the financial statements

1 On 31 March 20X2, UK plc purchased 11.25 million shares in Germany gmbh. The retained profits of Germany gmbh on this date stood at DM 5 million. Any premium arising on acquisition was capitalised and amortised over its economic life of four years. Germany gmbh operates as a fairly autonomous entity on a day-to-day basis although UK plc does control the long-term strategy of Germany gmbh.

2 Since the date of the investment by UK plc, the £ sterling has depreciated against the DM. Exchange rates at relevant dates have been as follows:

Date	DM to the £
31 March 20X2	3.0
Date on which Germany gmbh acquired its	
- fixed assets	2.8
- opening stock	2.5
- closing stock	2.25
31 March 20X5	2.4
31 March 20X6	2.2

3 UK plc deals with investment income on an accruals basis.

4 The creditors falling due after more than one year represent long-term borrowings. The long-term borrowings of Germany gmbh were raised in Germany and are repayable in DM.

5 The profit and loss account of Germany gmbh includes depreciation as follows:

- DM 5 million included in cost of sales.
- DM 1 million included in other operating expenses.

Required:

(a) Write a short memorandum which explains (with reasons) how Germany gmbh should be dealt with in the consolidated financial statements of UK plc, assuming the provisions of relevant UK accounting standards are followed.

Your memorandum should NOT contain a detailed exposition of the mechanics of the consolidation, but should concentrate on the implications of Germany gmbh being an overseas entity. **(11 marks)**

(b) Translate the balance sheet of Germany gmbh into £ sterling and then prepare the consolidated balance sheet of the UK plc group at 31 March 20X6. **(13 marks)**

(c) Translate the profit and loss account of Germany gmbh into £ sterling and then prepare the consolidated profit and loss account of the UK plc group for the year ended 31 March 20X6, starting with turnover and ending with retained profit for the year. **(6 marks)**

(d) Prepare a statement reconciling the opening and closing balances on consolidated reserves. All figures in the statement should be supported by relevant workings. **(10 marks)**

(Total: 40 marks)

19 Rowen plc

Rowen plc was formed in 1975 to manufacture executive toys. The directors decided to expand their exports and on 1 January 20W9 it acquired investments in an American company, Overseas Inc and a French company, Europe SA, which were to act as selling agencies for the company's products.

The investments consisted of 800,000 shares of US$10 each in Overseas Inc when its reserves were US$25m and of 2,250,000 shares of FF20 each in Europe SA when its reserves were FF230m. At the dates of acquisition, the book values were the same as the fair values.

The directors have instructed their accountant to prepare draft consolidated accounts as at 31 December 20X3 on the basis that Overseas Inc is a subsidiary undertaking due to the fact that they exercise a dominant influence; and that Europe SA is a participating interest but not an associated undertaking.

The balance sheets as at 31 December 20X3 were as follows:

	Rowen £m	*Overseas* US$m	*Europe* FFm
Fixed assets			
Tangible assets	669	458	4,231
Investment in Overseas Inc	12		
Investment in Europe SA	10		
Current assets			
Stocks	675	44	404
Cash	46	113	1,038
Current liabilities			
Creditors	(490)	(31)	(288)
Creditors falling due after more than one year			
Loan	(370)	(103)	(954)
	552	481	4,431
Capital and reserves			
Share capital	185	20	180
Profit and loss account	367	461	4,251
	552	481	4,431

The profit and loss accounts for the year ended 31 December 20X3 are as follows:

	Rowen £m	*Overseas* US$m	*Europe* FFm
Turnover	2,784	1,150	10,615
Cost of sales	1,822	775	7,154
Gross profit	962	375	3,461
Distribution costs	392	90	831
Administrative expenses	370	30	278
Depreciation	35	24	230
Dividend from Overseas Inc	(12)		
Dividend from Europe SA	(11)		
Profit before tax	188	231	2,122
Tax	93	90	831
Profit after tax	95	141	1,291
Dividends paid 31.7.93	37	51	440
Retained profit	58	90	851

Further information

1 The fixed assets in both Overseas Inc and Europe SA were acquired on 1 January 20W5. They are stated at cost less depreciation and there have been no acquisitions or disposals during the year.

2 Stocks

	31 December 20X2		*31 December 20X3*	
	Stock	*Exchange rate at purchase date*	*Stock*	*Exchange rate at purchase date*
Overseas US$m	57	2.0	44	1.6
Europe FFm	523	11.5	404	8.5

3 Exchange rates have been as follows:

	US$ = £1	FF = £1
1 January 20W5	2.4	12.0
1 January 20W9	2.0	12.5
31 December 20X2	1.8	11.0
Average for 20X3	1.7	10.0
31 July 20X3	1.7	10.0
31 December 20X3	1.5	8.0

4 Rowen plc policy is to write off goodwill over ten years.

5 The foreign exchange translation of the foreign subsidiary is to be on the basis that the functional currency of the American operation is sterling.

6 There has been no change in the share capital of Overseas Inc or Europe SA since the date of acquisition.

Required:

(a) Prepare a draft consolidated profit and loss account for the Rowen Group for the year ended 31 December 20X3 and a draft consolidated balance sheet as at that date. **(15 marks)**

(b) (i) Calculate the effect on the consolidated profit and loss account for the year ended 31 December 20X3 if the investment in Europe SA is classified as an associated interest.

(ii) Calculate the carrying value of the investment in the consolidated balance sheet as at 31 December 20X3.

(6 marks)
(Total: 21 marks)
(ACCA June 94)

20 Angol plc

Angol plc acquired 735 million shares of FF1 each in Frank SA on 1 June 20X3 when there was a credit balance of FF126 million on reserves. Frank SA acts as a selling agent for Angol plc. The remaining shares in Frank SA are held by French nationals.

The draft profit and loss accounts for the year ended 31 May 20X6 were as follows:

	Angol plc £'000	*Frank SA* FF'000
Operating profit	821,000	588,000
Income from shares in subsidiary	15,125	
Profit on ordinary activities	836,125	588,000
Tax on profit on ordinary activities before taxation	(320,000)	(229,000)
Profit on ordinary activities after tax	516,125	359,000
Dividend		
Paid	-	(185,000)
Proposed	(262,500)	-
	253,625	174,000

The draft balance sheets as at 31 May 20X6 were as follows:

	£'000	FF'000
Fixed assets		
Land at cost	630,000	1,218,000
Buildings at depreciated cost	529,200	275,520
Plant and machinery	348,600	111,300
	1,507,800	1,604,820
Investment in subsidiary	147,000	

Current assets		
Stock	168,000	134,400
Debtors	426,300	180,600
Bank	176,400	50,400
	770,700	365,400
Current liabilities		
Creditors	(413,700)	(189,000)
Tax	(320,000)	(229,000)
Proposed dividend	(262,500)	
	(996,200)	(418,000)
Net current liabilities	(225,500)	(52,600)
Total assets less current liabilities	1,429,300	1,552,220
Capital and reserves		
Ordinary shares of £1 and FF1 each	525,000	1,050,000
Reserves	904,300	502,220
	1,429,300	1,552,220

The following information is available:

Goodwill
Goodwill arising on the acquisition of the subsidiary undertaking is amortised through the profit and loss account over three years from the date of acquisition.

Depreciation policy
The group follows a uniform depreciation policy and is writing off buildings over 50 years and plant over 10 years in equal instalments. Full depreciation is charged on additions commencing in the year of purchase.

Fixed assets

		Angol plc			*Frank SA*	
Cost:	*Land*	*Buildings*	*Plant*	*Land*	*Buildings*	*Plant*
	£'000	£'000	£'000	FF'000	FF'000	FF'000
At 1.6.X5	630,000	588,000	575,400	1,218,000	504,000	108,150
Additions	-	-	-	-	-	84,000
At 31.5.X6	630,000	588,000	575,400	1,218,000	504,000	192,150
Depreciation:						
At 1.6.X5		47,040	169,260	-	218,400	61,635
Charge for year		11,760	57,540	-	10,080	19,215
At 31.5.X6	-	58,800	226,800	-	228,480	80,850

The additions to plant were made on 1 June 20X5. All other fixed assets had been acquired prior to 1 June 20X3.

Exchange rates

The rates of exchange were as follows:

Prior to 1 June 20X3	FF12	:	£1
1 June 20X3	FF10	:	£1
1 June 20X5	FF9	:	£1
Average for year	FF8	:	£1
31 May 20X6	FF7	:	£1

Assume that closing stock was acquired at the closing rate of exchange.

Required:

(a) Prepare a consolidated profit and loss account for the year ended 31 May 20X6 and a consolidated balance sheet as at that date using the temporal method to translate the financial statements of Frank SA.

(20 marks)
(Total: 20 marks)
(ACCA June 96)

21 Hyper-inflation

SSAP 20 'Foreign Currency Translation' states that the method used to translate financial statements for consolidation purposes should reflect the financial and other operational relationships which exist between an investing company and its foreign enterprises. A key element in determining this relationship is the dependency of the trade of the foreign enterprise on the economic environment of the investing company's currency rather than that of its own reporting currency. Thus it is important to determine the dominant or functional currency in order to determine whether the temporal method should be utilised.

However, where the foreign enterprise operates in a country with a high rate of inflation, the translation process may not be sufficient to present fairly the financial position of the foreign enterprise. Some adjustment for inflation should be undertaken to the local currency financial statements before translation. UITF 9 'Accounting for operations in hyper-inflationary economies' deals with this issue.

Required:

(a) Explain the factors which should be taken into account in determining the dominant or functional currency and how these factors influence the choice of method to be used to translate the financial statements of a foreign enterprise. **(10 marks)**

(b) Discuss the reasons why adjustments for hyper-inflation in the financial statements of foreign enterprises are felt necessary before their translation. **(5 marks)**

(c) On 30 November 20X3, Gold plc, a UK company, set up a subsidiary in an overseas country where the local currency is effados. The principal assets of this subsidiary were a chain of hotels. The value of the hotels on this date was 20 million effados. The rate of inflation for the period 30 November 20X3 to 30 November 20X7 has been significantly high. The following information is relevant to the economy of the overseas country:

	Effados in exchange for		*Consumer Price Index in overseas country*	*Exchange Rate UK£ to US$*
	£UK	*$US*		
30 November 20X3	1.34	0.93	100	£0.69 to $1
30 November 20X7	17.87	11.91	3,254	£0.66 to $1

There is no depreciation charged in the financial statements as the hotels are maintained to a high standard.

Required:

(i) Calculate the value at which the hotels would be included in the group financial statements of Gold plc on the following dates and using the methods outlined below.

(1) At 30 November 20X3 and 30 November 20X7 using the closing rate/net investment method.
(2) At 30 November 20X7 after adjusting for current price levels.
(3) At 30 November 20X7 after remeasuring using the dollar as the stable currency. **(5 marks)**

(Methods (2) and (3) are those outlined in UITF 9 'Accounting for operations in hyper-inflationary economies').

(ii) Discuss the results of the valuations of the hotels commenting on the validity of the different bases outlined above. **(5 marks)**

(Total: 25 marks)

(ACCA Dec 97)

22 XY Group

XY, a public limited company, owns 80% of AG, a public limited company which is situated in a foreign country. The currency of this country is the Kram (KR). XY acquired AG on 30 April 20X6 for £220 million when the retained profits of AG were KR 610 million. AG has not issued any share capital since acquisition. The following financial statements relate to XY and AG:

Balance sheets at 31 December 20X7

	XY *£ million*	*AG* *KR million*
Fixed assets		
Tangible assets	945	1,890
Investment in AG	270	-
Net current assets	735	645
Creditors: falling due after one year	(375)	(1,115)
	1,575	1,420
Share capital	330	240
Share premium	350	80
Profit and loss account	895	1,100
	1,575	1,420

Profit and loss account – year ended 31 December 20X7

	XY *£ million*	*AG* *KR million*
Turnover	1,650	3,060
Cost of sales	(945)	(2,550)
Gross profit	705	510
Administrative and distribution costs	(420)	(51)
Income from AG	8	-
Interest payable	(22)	(102)
Operating profit before taxation	271	357
Taxation	(79)	(153)
Profit on ordinary activities after tax	192	204
Dividends paid	(20)	(52)
Retained profit for year	172	152

(i) During the year AG sold goods to XY for KR 104 million. The subsidiary made a profit of KR 26 million on the transaction. The exchange rate ruling at the date of the transaction was £1 = KR 5.2. All of the goods remained unsold at the year end of 31 December 20X7. XY had paid for the goods on receipt and there were no inter company current balances outstanding at 31 December 20X7. At 31 December 20X6 there were goods sold by AG to XY held in the stock of XY. These goods amounted to £6 million on which AG made a profit of £2 million.

(ii) A loan of £50 million in sterling was raised by AG from XY on 31 May 20X7. The loan is interest free and is repayable in 20Y7. The loan to the subsidiary was translated at the temporal rate in the subsidiary's financial statements and had been included in the investment in AG figure in the balance sheet of XY. An amount of KR 65 million had been paid to XY by AG on 31 December 20X7 in part settlement of the loan. This amount had not been received by XY and was not included in its financial statements.

(iii) The fair value of the net assets of AG at the date of acquisition was KR 1,040 million. Goodwill on consolidation is to be amortised on a straight line basis over three years and is to be calculated using historical cost goodwill. Goodwill is treated as a sterling asset which does not fluctuate with changes in the exchange rate. The increase in the fair value of AG over carrying value is attributable to tangible fixed assets which are depreciated over five years on the straight line basis. Tangible and intangible assets are depreciated without time apportionment in the year of acquisition and the fair value adjustment was not incorporated into the books of AG.

(iv) AG paid the dividend for the year ended 31 December 20X7 on 30 June 20X7. No more dividends were paid or proposed by AG during the year.

(v) The following exchange rates are relevant to the financial statements:

	KRAMS to the £
30 April 20X6	4.0
31 December 20X6	4.6
1 January 20X7	4.7
31 May 20X7	5.3
30 June 20X7	5.2
31 December 20X7	5.0
Weighted Average 20X7	5.1

(vi) The group policy is to use the closing rate/net investment method and translate the profit and loss account at the weighted average rate.

Required:

(a) Prepare a consolidated profit and loss account for the year ended 31 December 20X7 and a balance sheet as at that date for the XY group. (All calculations should be to one place of decimals). **(21 marks)**

(b) Prepare a statement of the movement in consolidated reserves for the financial year ending 31 December 20X7. **(4 marks)**

(c) Discuss why SSAP 20 'Foreign Currency Translation' fails to deal adequately with accounting for foreign currency translation. **(5 marks)**

(Total: 30 marks)

(ACCA June 98)

23 Carver plc

Carver plc is a listed company incorporated in 1958 to produce models carved from wood. In 1975 it acquired a 100% interest in a wood importing company, Olio Ltd; in 20W9 it acquired a 40% interest in a competitor, Multi-products Ltd; and on 1 October 20X3 it acquired a 75% interest in Good Display Ltd. It is planning to make a number of additional acquisitions during the next three years.

The draft consolidated accounts for the Carver Group are as follows:

Draft consolidated profit and loss account for the year ended 30 September 20X4

	£'000	£'000
Operating profit		1,475
Share of profits of associated undertakings		495
Income from fixed asset investment		155
Interest payable		(150)
Profit on ordinary activities before taxation		1,975
Tax on profit on ordinary activities		
Corporation tax	391	
Deferred taxation	104	
Tax attributable to income of associated undertakings	145	
		(640)
Profit on ordinary activities after taxation		1,335
Minority interests		(100)
Profit for the financial year		1,235
Dividends paid and proposed		(400)
Retained profit for the year		835

Draft consolidated balance sheet as at 30 September

	20X3		*20X4*	
	£'000	£'000	£'000	£'000
Fixed assets				
Intangible assets: goodwill				90
Tangible assets				
Buildings at net book value		2,200		2,075
Machinery				
Cost	1,400		3,000	
Aggregate depreciation	(1,100)		(1,200)	
Net book value		300		1,800
		2,500		3,965
Investments in associated undertaking		1,000		1,100
Fixed asset investments		410		410
Current assets				
Stocks		1,000		1,975
Trade debtors		1,275		1,850
Cash		1,820		4,515
		4,095		8,340
Creditors: Amounts falling due within one year				
Trade creditors		280		500
Obligations under finance leases		200		240
Corporation tax		217		462
Dividends		200		300
Accrued interest and finance charges		30		40
		927		1,542
Net current assets		3,168		6,798
Total assets less current liabilities		7,078		12,273

Creditors: Amounts falling due after more than one year		
Obligations under finance leases	170	710
Loans	500	1,460
Provisions for liabilities		
Deferred taxation	13	30
Net assets	6,395	10,073
Capital and reserves		
Called up share capital in 25p shares	2,000	3,940
Share premium account	2,095	2,883
Profit and loss account	2,300	3,135
Total shareholders' equity	6,395	9,958
Minority interest	–	115
Net assets	6,395	10,073

Note 1: There had been no acquisitions or disposals of buildings during the year.

Machinery costing £500,000 was sold for £500,000 resulting in a profit of £100,000. New machinery was acquired in 20X4 including additions of £850,000 acquired under finance leases.

Note 2: Information relating to the acquisition of Good Display Ltd.

	£'000
Machinery	165
Stocks	32
Trade debtors	28
Cash	112
Less: Trade creditors	(68)
Corporation tax	(17)
	252
Less: Minority interest	(63)
	189
Goodwill	100
	289
	£'000
880,000 shares issued as part consideration	275
Balance of consideration paid in cash	14
	289

Goodwill arising on this acquisition is capitalised and amortised through the profit and loss account over its useful economic life. The amortisation charge for the year was £10,000.

Note 3: Loans were issued at a discount in 1994 and the carrying amount of the loans at 30 September 20X4 included £40,000 representing the finance cost attributable to the discount and allocated in respect of the current reporting period.

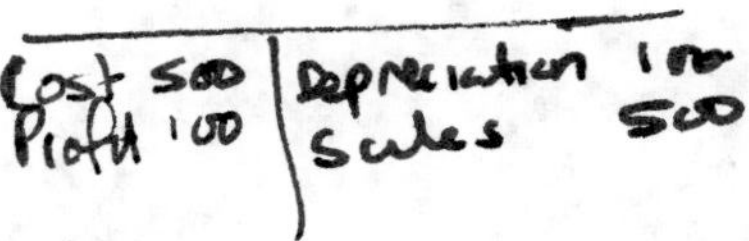

Required:

(a) Prepare a consolidated cash flow statement for the Carver Group for the year ended 30 September 20X4 with supporting notes for:

(i) Reconciliation of operating profit to net cash flow from operating activities
(ii) Reconciliation of net cash flow to movement in net debt
(iii) Analysis of changes in net debt.

(20 marks)

(b) Explain and illustrate any adjustments that you consider the company should make to the cash flow statement prepared in (a) above to take account of the following information:

(i) Carver plc had constructed a laser cutter which is included in the machinery cost figure at £73,000.

The costs comprise:

	£'000
Materials	50
Labour	12
Overheads	6
Interest capitalised	5
	73

(ii) The cash figures comprised the following:

	1.10.X3 £'000	*30.9.X4* £'000
Cash in hand	10	15
Bank overdrafts	(770)	(65)
Bank	1,080	1,890
10% Treasury Stock 20X3	1,500	–
Bank deposits	–	1,125
Gas 3% 20X0–20X5	–	1,550
	1,820	4,515

The 10% Treasury Stock 20X3 was acquired on 1 September 20X3 and redeemed on 31 October 20X3.

The bank deposits were made on 1 January 20X4 for a 12 month term.

The Gas 3% was acquired on 1 June 20X4 and the company proposes to realise this investment on 30 November 20X4.

(5 marks)
(Total: 25 marks)
(ACCA Dec 94)

24 Hebden Group plc

The following draft financial statements relate to the Hebden Group plc.

Draft group profit and loss account for the year ended 31 July 20X6

	£m	£m
Turnover		5,845
Cost of sales		(2,160)
Gross profit		3,685
Distribution costs	510	
Administrative expenses	210	(720)
Operating profit group		2,965
Share of operating profit of associates		990
		3,955
Profit on disposal of tangible fixed assets		300
Income from investments		80
Interest payable		(300)
Profit on ordinary activities before taxation		4,035
Tax on profit on ordinary activities		(1,345)
Profit on ordinary activities after tax		2,690
Minority Interests - equity		(200)
Profit attributable to members of parent company		2,490
Dividends paid and proposed		(800)
		1,690

Draft group balance sheet as at 31 July 20X6

	20X6 £m	*20X5* £m
Fixed assets		
Intangible assets	200	-
Tangible assets	7,750	5,000
Investment in associated undertaking	2,200	2,000
Other fixed asset investments	820	820
	10,970	7,820
Current assets		
Stocks	3,950	2,000
Debtors	3,700	2,550
Cash at bank and in hand	9,030	3,640
	16,680	8,190
Creditors: Amounts falling due within one year	(3,084)	(1,854)
Net current assets	13,596	6,336
Total assets less current liabilities	24,566	14,156

Creditors: Amounts falling due after more than one year	(4,340)	(1,340)
Provision for liabilities and charges		
Deferred taxation	(60)	(26)
Minority interests - equity	(230)	-
	19,936	12,790
Capital and reserves		
Called up share capital	7,880	4,000
Share premium account	5,766	4,190
Profit and loss account	6,290	4,600
Total shareholders funds - equity	19,936	12,790

The following information is relevant to Hebden Group plc.

(a) The Hebden Group plc has two wholly owned subsidiaries. In addition it acquired a 75% interest in Hendry Ltd on 1 August 20X5. It also holds a 40% interest in Sullivan Ltd which it acquired several years ago. Goodwill arising on acquisitions has been capitalised as an intangible fixed asset. No amortisation was charged during the year ended 31 July 20X6.

(b) The following balance sheet recorded at fair values refers to Hendry Ltd at the date of acquisition.

Balance Sheet at 1 August 20X5

	£m	£m
Plant and machinery		330
Current assets		
Stocks	64	
Debtors	56	
Cash at bank and in hand	224	
	344	
Creditors		
Amounts falling due after more than one year (including Corporation tax £34m)	(170)	
		174
		504
Called up share capital		100
Profit and loss account		404
		504

The consideration for the purchase of the shares of Hendry comprised 440 million ordinary shares of £1 of Hebden plc at a value of £550 million and a balance of £28 million was paid in cash.

(c) The taxation charge in the profit and loss account is made up of the following items:

	£m
Corporation tax	782
Deferred taxation	208
Tax attributable to associated undertakings	355
	1,345

(d) The tangible fixed assets of the Hebden Group plc comprise the following:

	Buildings	*Plant and Machinery*	*Total*
	£m	£m	£m
1 August 20X5 cost or valuation	5,100	2,800	7,900
Additions	-	4,200	4,200
Disposals	-	(1,000)	(1,000)
At 31 July 20X6	5,100	6,000	11,100
Depreciation			
At 1 August 20X5	700	2,200	2,900
Provided during year	250	400	650
Disposals		(200)	(200)
At 31 July 20X6	950	2,400	3,350
Net Book Value at 31 July 20X6	4,150	3,600	7,750
Net Book Value at 1 August 20X5	4,400	600	5,000

Assets + financing.

Included in additions of plant and machinery are items totalling £1,700m acquired under finance leases. The plant and machinery disposed of resulted in a profit of £300m. Because of the nature of the industry the finance leases are normally quite short term.

note 1.

(e) Creditors: amounts falling due within one year comprise the following items:

	20X6	*20X5*
	£m	£m
Trade creditors	1,000	560
Obligations under finance leases	480	400
Corporation tax	924	434
Dividends	600	400
Accrued interest and finance charges	80	60
	3,084	1,854

The interest paid on the finance lease rental payments in the year was calculated by the accountant to be £100m.

(f) Creditors: amounts falling due after more than one year included the following items:

	20X6	*20X5*
	£m	£m
Obligations under finance leases	1,434	1,340
6% Debentures repayable 1.8.20Y5	2,906	-
	4,340	1,340

There had been an issue of debentures on 1 August 20X5. The debentures of face value of £3,000 million had been issued at a discount of £100m effectively increasing the yield on the loan to 6.2% approximately.

Required:

Prepare a group cash flow statement for the Hebden Group plc for the year ended 31 July 20X6 in accordance with the requirements of FRS 1 (Revised) 'Cash Flow Statements'. Your answer should only include the following notes:

(i) A reconciliation of operating profit to net cash flow from operating activities.
(ii) A reconciliation of net cash flow to movement in net debt/net funds.
(iii) An analysis of movements in net debt/net funds.

(25 marks)
(Total: 25 marks)
(ACCA 1997 Pilot Paper)

25 Baron Group plc

The following draft financial statements relate to the Baron Group plc.

Draft Group Profit and Loss Account for the Year Ended 30 November 20X7

	£m	£m
Turnover		
Continuing operations	4,458	
Discontinued operations	1,263	
		5,721
Cost of sales		(4,560)
Gross profit		1,161
Distribution costs	309	
Administration expenses	285	
		(594)
		567
Income from interests in joint venture		75
Defence costs of take-over bid		(20)
Operating profit		
Continuing operations	438	
Discontinued operations	184	
		622
Loss on disposal of tangible fixed assets	(7)	
Loss on disposal of discontinued operations (note a)	(25)	(32)
Interest receivable	27	
Interest payable	(19)	8
Profit on ordinary activities before taxation		598
Tax on profit on ordinary activities (note c)		(191)
Profit on ordinary activities after taxation		407
Minority interests — equity		(75)
Profit attributable to members of the parent company		332
Dividends — ordinary dividend		(130)
Retained profit for the year		202

Group Statement of Total Recognised Gains and Losses for the Year Ended 30 November 20X7

	£m
Profit attributable to members of the parent company	332
Deficit on revaluation of land and buildings	(30)
Deficit on revaluation of land and buildings in joint venture	(15)
Gain on revaluation of loan	28
Total recognised gains and losses relating to the year	315

Draft Group Balance Sheet as at 30 November 20X7

	20X7 £m	*20X6* £m
Fixed assets		
Intangible assets	60	144
Tangible fixed assets (note d)	1,415	1,800
Investments (notes b and e)	600	-
	2,075	1,944
Current assets		
Stocks	720	680
Short term investments (note e)	152	44
Debtors (note f)	680	540
Cash at bank and in hand	24	133
	1,576	1,397
Creditors:		
Amounts falling due within one year (note g)	(1,601)	(1,223)
Net current assets	(25)	174
Total assets less current liabilities	2,050	2,118
Creditors: amounts falling due after more than one year	(186)	(214)
Provision for liabilities and charges - bid defence costs	(30)	(15)
Minority interests - equity	(330)	(570)
	1,504	1,319
Capital and reserves		
Called up share capital	440	440
Share premium account	101	101
Revaluation reserve	33	50
Profit and loss account	930	728
Total shareholders' funds - equity	1,504	1,319

The following information is relevant to the Baron Group plc.

(a) The group disposed of a major subsidiary Piece plc on 1 September 20X7. Baron held an 80% interest in the subsidiary at the date of disposal. Piece plc's results are classified as discontinued in the profit and loss account.

The group required the subsidiary Piece plc to prepare an interim balance sheet at the date of the disposal and this is as follows:

Tangible fixed assets (depreciation 30)		310
Current assets		
Stocks	60	
Debtors	50	
Cash at bank and in hand	130	
	240	
Creditors: amounts falling due within one year (including corporation tax - £25m)	(130)	
		110
		420
Called up share capital		100
Profit and loss account		320
		420

The consolidated carrying values of all the assets and liabilities at that date are as above. The depreciation charge in the profit and loss account for the period was £9 million. The carrying amount relating to goodwill in the group accounts arising on the acquisition of Piece plc was £64 million at 1 December 20X6. The loss on sale of discontinued operations in the group accounts comprises:

Sale proceeds	375
Net assets sold (80% × £420m)	(336)
Goodwill	(64)
	(25)

The consideration for the sale of Piece plc was 200 million ordinary shares of £1 in Meal plc, the acquiring company, at a value of £300 million and £75 million in cash. The group's policy is to amortise goodwill arising on acquisition but not in the year of sale of a subsidiary. The amortisation for the year was £20 million on other intangible assets.

(b) During the year, Baron plc had transferred several of its tangible assets to a newly created company, Kevla Ltd which is owned jointly by three parties. The total investment at the date of transfer in the joint venture by Baron plc was £225 million at carrying value comprising £200 million in tangible fixed assets and £25 million in cash. In the draft accounts the group has used equity accounting for the joint venture in Kevla Ltd. No dividends have been received from Kevla Ltd but the land and buildings transferred have been revalued at the year end.

(c) The taxation charge in the profit and loss account is made up of the following items:

	£m
Corporation tax	171
Tax attributable to joint venture	20
	191

(d) The movement on tangible fixed assets of the Baron Group plc during the year was as follows:

	£m
Cost or valuation 1 December 20X6	2,100
Additions	380
Revaluation	(30)
Disposals and transfers	(680)
At 30 November 20X7	1,770
Depreciation	
1 December 20X6	300
Provided during year	150
Disposals and transfers	(95)
At 30 November 20X7	355
Carrying value at 30 November 20X7	1,415
Carrying value at 1 December 20X6	1,800

(e) The investments included under fixed assets comprised the joint venture in Kevla Ltd (£265 million), the shares in Meal plc (£300 million), and investments in corporate bonds (£35 million). The bonds had been purchased in November 20X7 and were deemed to be highly liquid, although Baron plc intended to hold them for the longer term as their maturity date is 1 January 20X9.

The short term investments comprised the following items:

	20X7	*20X6*
		£'m
Government securities (Repayable 1 April 20X8)	51	23
Cash on seven day deposit	101	21
	152	44

(f) A prepayment of £20 million has been included in debtors against an exceptional pension liability which will fall due in the following financial year. Interest receivable included in debtors was £5 million at 30 November 20X7 (£4 million at 30 November 20X6).

(g) Creditors: amounts falling due within one year comprise the following items:

	20X7	*20X6*
	£m	£m
Trade creditors	1,300	973
Corporation tax	181	150
Dividends	80	70
Accrued interest	40	30
	1,601	1,223

Required:

(a) Prepare a group cash flow statement using the 'indirect method' for the Baron Group plc for the year ended 30 November 20X7 in accordance with the requirements of FRS 1 (Revised 1996) 'Cash Flow Statements' and FRS 9 'Associates and Joint Ventures'. Your answer should include the following:

(i) Reconciliation of operating profit to operating cash flows.
(ii) An analysis of cash flows for any headings netted in the cash flow statement.

(Candidates should distinguish net cash flows from continuing and discontinued operations.)**(26 marks)**

The notes regarding the sale of the subsidiary and a reconciliation of net cash flow to movement in net debt are not required.

(b) Explain why the Accounting Standards Board feel that cash flow statements should focus on cash rather than a broader measure such as 'net debt'. **(4 marks)**

(Total: 30 marks)

(ACCA Dec 97)

26 Duke Group plc

The following draft financial statements relate to the Duke Group plc:

Draft Group Balance Sheet at 31 May 20X1

	20X1 £m	*20X0* £m
Fixed Assets:		
Intangible assets – goodwill	90	83
Tangible assets	1,239	1,010
Investments	780	270
	2,109	1,363
Current Assets:		
Stocks	750	588
Debtors	660	530
Cash at bank and in hand	45	140
	1,455	1,258
Creditors: amounts falling due within one year	(1,501)	(1,213)
Net Current Assets	(46)	45
Total assets less current liabilities	2,063	1,408
Creditors: amounts falling due after more than one year	(1,262)	(930)
Minority interests – equity	(250)	(150)
	551	328
Capital and Reserves:		
Called up share capital		
- ordinary shares of £1	100	70
- 7% redeemable preference shares of £1 each	136	130
Share premium account	85	15
Revaluation reserve	30	10
Profit and loss account	200	103
	551	328

Draft Group Profit and Loss Account for the year ended 31 May 20X1

	£m	£m
Turnover - continuing operations	5,795	
- acquisitions	1,515	
		7,310
Cost of sales		(5,920)
Gross profit		1,390
Distribution and administrative expenses		(772)
Share of operating profit in associate		98

Operating profit - continuing operations	598	
- acquisitions	118	
		716
Profit on sale of tangible fixed assets		15
Interest receivable	34	
Interest payable	(22)	
		12
Profit on ordinary activities before taxation		743
Tax on profit on ordinary activities (including tax on income from associated undertakings £15 million)		(213)
Profit on ordinary activities after taxation		530
Minority interests – equity		(97)
Profit attributable to members of the parent company		433
Dividends	153	
Other non-equity appropriations	6	(141)
Retained profit for the year		292

Group Statement of Total Recognised Gains and Losses for the year ended 31 May 20X1

	£m
Profit attributable to members of the parent company	433
Surplus on revaluation of fixed assets	20
Exchange difference on retranslation of foreign equity investment	(205)
Exchange difference on loan to finance foreign equity investment	10
	258

Reconciliation of Shareholders' Funds for the year ended 31 May 20X1

Total recognised gains and losses	258
Dividends	(135)
Other movements:	
New shares issued	100
Total movements during the year	223
Shareholders funds at 1 June 20X0	328
Shareholders funds at 31 May 20X1	551

The following information is relevant to the Duke Group plc:

(i) Duke acquired an eighty per cent holding in Regent plc on 1 June 20X0. The fair values of the assets of Regent on 1 June 20X0 were as follows:

	£m
Tangible fixed assets	60
Stocks	30
Debtors	25
Cash at bank and in hand	35
Trade Creditors	(20)
Corporation Tax	(30)
	100

The purchase consideration was £97 million and comprised 20 million ordinary shares of £1 in Duke, valued at £4, and £17 million in cash. The group amortises goodwill over ten years.

(ii) The tangible fixed asset movement for the period comprised the following amounts at net book value.

	£m
Balance at 1 June 20X0	1,010
Additions (including Regent)	278
Revaluations of properties	20
Disposals	(30)
Depreciation	(39)
Balance at 31 May 20X1	1,239

(iii) There have been no sales of fixed asset investments in the year. The investments included under fixed assets comprised the following items:

	20X1 £m	*20X0* £m
Investment in associated company	300	220
Trade investment (including purchase of foreign equity investment of £400m equivalent during year to 31 May 20X1)	480	50
	780	270

(iv) Interest receivable included in debtors was £15m as at 31 May 20X0 and £17 m as at 31 May 20X1.

(v) Creditors: amounts falling due within one year comprised the following items:

	20X1 £m	*20X0* £m
Trade creditors (including interest payable £9m (20X1) Nil (20X0)	1,193	913
Corporation tax	203	200
Dividends	105	100
	1,501	1,213

(vi) Duke had allotted 10 million ordinary shares of £1 at a price of £2 upon the exercise of directors options during the year.

(vii) Included in creditors: amounts payable after more than one year is a bill of exchange for £100 million (raised 30 June 20X0) which was given to a supplier on the purchase of fixed assets and which is payable on 1 July 20X2.

(viii) The exchange differences included in the Statement of Total Recognised Gains and Loss relate to a transaction involving a foreign equity investment. A loan of £300 million was taken out during the year to finance a foreign equity investment in Peer of £400 million. Both amounts are after retranslation at 31 May 20X1.

(ix) The preference share dividends are always paid in full on 1 July each year and at 31 May 20X1 the preference shares have a par value of £130 million.

Required:

(a) Prepare a group cash flow statement using the indirect method for the Duke Group plc for the year ended 31 May 20X1 in accordance with the requirements of FRS 1 (Revised) 'Cash Flow Statements'. Your answer should include the following:

(i) a reconciliation of operating profit to operating cash flows;
(ii) an analysis of cash flows for any heading netted in the cash flow statement.

(Candidates should distinguish net cash flows from continuing and discontinued operations)

(b) Discuss the nature of the additional information which is provided by the Group Cash Flow Statement of the Duke group in (a) above as compared to the Group Profit and Loss Account and Group Balance Sheet of Duke. **(6 marks)**

(Total: 6 marks)

(ACCA June 00)

27 Yukon plc

Financial Reporting Standard (FRS) 10 addresses the accounting for goodwill and intangible assets. Accounting for goodwill has been a contentious issue in the UK for several years and FRS 10 'Goodwill and Intangible Assets' attempts to eliminate the problems associated with SSAP 22 'Accounting for Goodwill'.

Required:

(a) Describe the requirements of FRS 10 regarding the initial recognition and measurement of goodwill and intangible assets. **(6 marks)**

(b) Explain the approach set out by FRS 10 for the amortisation of positive goodwill and intangible assets. **(5 marks)**

(c) Territory plc acquired 80% of the ordinary share capital of Yukon plc on 31 May 20X6. The balance sheet of Yukon plc at 31 May 20X6 was:

Yukon plc - balance sheet at 31 May 20X6

	£'000
Fixed assets	
Intangible assets	6,020
Tangible assets	38,300
	44,320
Current assets	
Stocks	21,600
Debtors	23,200
Cash	8,800
	53,600
Creditors: amounts falling due within one year	24,000
Net current assets	29,600
Total assets less current liabilities	73,920

Creditors: amounts falling due after more than one year	12,100
Provision for liabilities and charges	886
Accruals and deferred income Deferred government grants	2,700
	58,234
Capital reserves Called up share capital (Ordinary shares of £1)	10,000
Share premium account	5,570
Profit and loss account	42,664
	58,234

Additional information relating to the above balance sheet

(i) The intangible assets of Yukon plc were brand names currently utilised by the company. The directors felt that they were worth £7 million but there was no readily ascertainable market value at the balance sheet date, nor any information to verify the directors' estimated value.

(ii) The provisional market value of the land and buildings was £20 million at 31 May 20X6. This valuation had again been determined by the directors. A valuers report received on 30 November 20X6 stated the market value of land and buildings to be £23 million as at 31 May 20X6. The depreciated replacement cost of the remainder of the tangible fixed assets was £18 million at 31 May 20X6, net of government grants.

(iii) The replacement cost of stocks was estimated at £25 million and its net realisable value was deemed to be £20 million. Debtors and Creditors due within one year are stated at the amounts expected to be received and paid.

(iv) Creditors amounts falling due after more than one year was a long-term loan with a bank. The initial loan on 1 June 20X5 was £11 million at a fixed interest rate of 10% per annum. The total amount of the interest is to be paid at the end of the loan period on 31 May 20X9. The current bank lending rate is 7% per annum.

(v) The provision for liabilities and charges relates to costs of reorganisation of Yukon plc. This provision had been set up by the directors of Yukon plc prior to the offer by Territory plc and the reorganisation would have taken place even if Territory plc had not purchased the shares of Yukon plc. Additionally Territory plc wishes to set up a provision for future losses of £10 million which it feels will be incurred by rationalising the group.

(vi) The offer made to all of the shareholders of Yukon plc was 2.5 £1 ordinary shares of Territory plc at the market price of £2.25 per share plus £1 cash, per Yukon plc ordinary share.

(vii) Goodwill is to be dealt with in accordance with FRS 10. The estimated useful economic life is deemed to be 10 years. The directors of Yukon plc informed Territory plc that as at 31 May 20X7, the brand names were worthless as the products to which they related had recently been withdrawn from sale because they were deemed to be a health hazard.

(viii) A full year's charge for amortisation of goodwill is included in the group profit and loss account of Territory plc in the year of purchase.

Required:

Calculate the amortisation of goodwill in the Group Profit and Loss Account of Territory plc for accounting periods ending on 31 May 20X6 and 31 May 20X7.

(9 marks)
(Total: 20 marks)
(ACCA June 97)

28 Impairment loss

SSAP 12 'Accounting for Depreciation' required that where there has been a permanent diminution in the value of a fixed asset, the carrying amount should be written down to the recoverable amount. The phrase 'recoverable amount' was defined in SSAP 12 as 'the greater of the net realisable value of an asset and, where appropriate, the amount recoverable from its further use'. The issues of how one identifies an impaired asset, the measurement of an asset when impairment has occurred and the recognition of impairment losses were not adequately dealt with by the standard. As a result a new financial reporting standard, FRS 11 'Impairment of Fixed Assets and Goodwill' was issued by the Accounting Standards Board in order to address the above issues.

Required:

(a) (i) Describe the circumstances which indicate that an impairment loss relating to a fixed asset may have occurred. **(7 marks)**

(ii) Explain how Financial Reporting Standard 11 deals with the recognition and measurement of the impairment of fixed assets. **(7 marks)**

(b) AB, a public limited company has decided to comply with FRS 11, as regards the impairment of its fixed assets. The following information is relevant to the impairment review:

(i) Certain items of machinery appeared to have suffered a permanent diminution in value. The product produced by the machines was being sold below its cost and this occurrence had affected the value of the productive machinery. The carrying value at historical cost of these machines was £290,000 and their net realisable value was estimated at £120,000. The anticipated net cash inflows from the machines were £100,000 per annum for the next three years. A market discount rate of 10% per annum is to be used in any present value computations. **(4 marks)**

(ii) AB acquired a car taxi business on 1 January 20X8 for £230,000. The values of the assets of the business at that date based on net realisable values were as follows:

	£000
Vehicles	120
Intangible assets (taxi licence)	30
Debtors	10
Cash	50
Creditors	(20)
	190

On 1 February 20X8, the taxi company had three of its vehicles stolen. The net realisable value (NRV) of these vehicles was £30,000 and because of non-disclosure of certain risks to the insurance company, the vehicles were uninsured. As a result of this event, AB wishes to recognise an impairment loss of £45,000 (inclusive of the loss of the stolen vehicles) due to the decline in the value in use of the income generating unit, that is the taxi business. On 1 March 20X8 a rival taxi company commenced business in the same area. It is anticipated that the business revenue will be reduced by 25% and that a further impairment loss has occurred due to a decline in the present value in use of the business which is calculated at £150,000. The NRV of the taxi licence has fallen to £25,000 as a result of the rival taxi operator. The net realisable values of the other assets have remained the same as at 1 January 20X8 throughout the period. **(7 marks)**

Required:

Describe how AB should treat the above impairments of assets in its financial statements. (In part (b) (ii) candidates should show the treatment of the impairment loss at 1 February 20X8 and 1 March 20X8.)

Please note that the mark allocation is shown after paragraphs (b) (i) and (b) (ii) above.

(Total: 25 marks)
(ACCA Dec 98)

29 Aztech

(a) Accounting practices for fixed assets and depreciation can be said to have developed in a piecemeal manner. The introduction of FRS 11 'Impairment of Fixed Assets' has meant that a standard on the measurement of fixed assets was required to provide further guidance in this area. FRS 15 'Tangible Fixed Assets' deals with the measurement and valuation issue.

Required:

Describe why it was important for a new accounting standard to be issued on the measurement of fixed assets. **(6 marks)**

(b) Aztech, a public limited company, manufacturers and operates a fleet of small aircraft. It draws up its financial statements to 31 March each year.

Aztech also owns a small chain of hotels (carrying value of £16 million), which are used in the sale of holidays to the public. It is the policy of the company not to provide depreciation on the hotels as they are maintained to a high standard and the economic lives of the hotels are long (20 years remaining life). The hotels are periodically revalued and on 31 March 20X0, their existing use value was determined to be £20 million, the replacement cost of the hotels was £16 million and the open market value was £19 million. One of the hotels included above is surplus to the company's requirements as at 31 March 20X0. This hotel had an existing use value of £3 million, a replacement cost of £2 million and an open market value of £2.5 million, before expected estate agents and solicitors fees of £200,000. Aztech wishes to revalue the hotels as at 31 March 20X0. There is no indication of any impairment in value of the hotels.

The company has recently finished manufacturing a fleet of five aircraft to a new design. These aircraft are intended for use in its own fleet for domestic carriage purposes. The company commenced construction of the assets on 1 April 1998 and wishes to recognise them as fixed assets as at 31 March 20X0 when they were first utilised. The aircraft were completed on 1 January 20X0 but their exterior painting was delayed until 31 March 20X0.

The costs (excluding finance costs) of manufacturing the aircraft were £28 million and the company has adopted a policy of capitalising the finance costs of manufacturing the aircraft. Aztech had taken out a three year loan of £20 million to finance the aircraft on 1 April 20W8. Interest is payable at 10% per annum but is to be rolled over and paid at the end of the three year period together with the capital outstanding. Corporation tax is 30%.

During the construction of the aircraft, certain computerised components used in the manufacture fell dramatically in price. The company estimated that at 31 March 20X0 the net realisable value of the aircraft was £30 million and their value in use was £29 million.

The engines used in the aircraft have a three year life and the body parts have an eight year life; Aztech has decided to depreciate the engines and the body parts over their different useful lives on the straight line basis from 1 April 20X0. The cost of replacing the engines on 31 March 20X3 is estimated to be £15 million. The engine costs represent thirty per cent of the total cost of manufacture.

The company has decided to revalue the aircraft annually on the basis of their market value. On the 31 March 20X1, the aircraft have a value in use of £28 million, a market value of £27 million and a net realisable value of £26 million. On 31 March 20X2, the aircraft have a value in use of £17 million, a market value of £18 million and a net realisable value of £18.5 million. There is no consumption of economic benefits in 20X2 other than the depreciation charge. Revaluation surpluses or deficits are apportioned between the engines and the body parts on the basis of their year end carrying values before the revaluation.

Required:

(i) Describe how the hotels should be valued in the financial statements of Aztech on 31 March 20X0 and explain whether the current depreciation policy relating to the hotels is acceptable under FRS 15 'Tangible Fixed Assets'. **(6 marks)**

(ii) Show the accounting treatment of the aircraft fleet in the financial statements on the basis of the above scenario for the financial years ending on:

(a) 31 March 20X0 **(4 marks)**
(b) 31 March 20X1, 20X2 **(6 marks)**
(c) 31 March 20X3 before revaluation. **(3 marks)**

Candidates should use FRS 15 'Tangible Fixed Assets' in answering all parts of the above question.

(Total: 25 marks)
(ACCA June 00)

30 Strained plc

Strained plc supplies office equipment. It has expanded rapidly and its working capital has been under increasing pressure. An extract from the balance sheet as at 31 March 20X4 appeared as follows:

	£m
Ordinary shares	4.95
Share premium	5.50
Profit and loss account	4.40
Loans repayable 1.4.X6	13.75
Net current liabilities	5.50

In order to obtain funds the company has entered into the following transactions:

(a) On 1 April 20X4 the company issued £2,000,000 7% redeemable preference shares at a premium of 20p per share paying issue costs of £100,000. The shares are redeemable on 31 March 20Y4 for £1.25 per share.

(b) On 1 April 20X4 the company borrowed £5m under an agreement to pay interest of 7% on 31 March 20X5, 10% on 31 March 20X6 and a final payment of interest and capital totalling £5,514,000 on 31 March 20X7.

(c) On 1 April 20X4 the company entered into an agreement to sell its vehicles to SFC Finance plc for £10m and to lease the vehicles back on an operating lease for four years at £1m per year, payable in arrears. At the date of the agreement the net book value of the vehicles was £8m and their fair value was £8.5m. Assume an interest rate of 10%.

Annuity table extract: Present value of £1 per year for each of t years = $1/r - 1/[r(1+r)^t]$

Number of years	Interest rate per year 8%	10%	12%
1	0.926	0.909	0.893
2	1.783	1.736	1.713
3	2.577	2.487	2.402
4	3.312	3.170	3.037
5	3.993	3.791	3.605

(d) On 1 March 20X5 the company entered into a factor arrangement with Blue Factors plc whereby Blue Factors plc administered the company's sales ledger. During March 20X5 Blue Factors plc made payments to Strained plc of £45m which represented 90% of the debtors as at 31 March 20X5. Strained plc have eliminated the debtors from the balance sheet and show Blue Factors plc as a debtor for £1m representing the balance of the total debtors for which Strained plc had not received cash.

Required:

(a) (i) Prepare an analysis of shareholders' funds immediately following the issue of the redeemable preference shares with an explanation for the treatment of each of the items included within the shareholders' funds.

(ii) Calculate the *total* finance cost of the redeemable preference shares and explain how this would be allocated to accounting periods in the company's profit and loss account. **(6 marks)**

(Note: You are not required to calculate each year's profit and loss account charge.)

(b) Calculate the carrying amount of the loan of £5m in the balance sheets as at 31 March 20X5 and 20X6 assuming that the overall effective rate of interest was 9% and explain the reasoning for the proposed accounting treatment. **(5 marks)**

(c) Calculate the profit and loss account and balance sheet entries arising from the vehicle sale and leasing transaction for the year ended 31 March 20X5 and explain the reasoning for the entries. **(5 marks)**

(d) Give details of any further information that you would require in order to be able to advise the directors of Strained plc whether the proposed treatment of the transaction with Blue Factors plc is acceptable. **(4 marks)**

(Total: 20 marks)

(ACCA June 95)

31 Timber Products plc

Required:

(a) (i) Explain briefly the objective of FRS 5 *Reporting the substance of transactions*.

(ii) Explain the criteria for ceasing to recognise an asset and give an illustration of the application of each. **(5 marks)**

(b) Explain the appropriate accounting treatment for the following transactions and the entries that would appear in the balance sheet as at 31 October 20X5 for transaction (i) and in the profit and loss account for the year ended 31 October 20X5 and balance sheet as at 31 October 20X5 for transactions (ii) (iii) and (iv).

(i) Timber Products plc supplied large industrial and commercial customers direct on three month credit terms. On 1 November 20X4 it entered into an agreement with Ready Support plc whereby it transferred title to the debtors to that company subject to a reduction for bad debts based on Timber Products plc's past experience and in return received an immediate payment of 90% of the net debtor total plus rights to a future sum the amount of which depended on whether and when the debtors paid. Ready Support plc had the right of recourse against Timber Products plc for any additional losses up to an agreed maximum amount.

The position at the year end, 31 October 20X5, was that title had been transferred to debtors with an invoice value of £15m less a bad debt provision of £600,000 and Timber Products plc was subject under the agreement to a maximum potential debit of £200,000 to cover losses.

(ii) Timber Products plc imports unseasoned hardwood and keeps it for five years under controlled conditions prior to manufacturing high quality furniture. In the year ended 31 October 20X5 it imported unseasoned timber at a cost of £40m. It contracted to sell the whole amount for £40m and to buy it back in five years time for £56.10m.

(iii) Timber Products plc manufactures and supplies retailers with furniture on a consignment basis such that either party can require the return of the furniture to the manufacturer within a period of six months from delivery. The retailers are required to pay a monthly charge for the facility to display the furniture. The manufacturer uses this monthly charge to pay for insurance cover and carriage costs. At the end of six months the retailer is required to pay Timber Products plc the trade price as at the date of delivery. No retailers have yet sent any goods back to Timber Products plc at the end of the six month period.

In the year ended 31 October 20X5, Timber Products plc had supplied furniture to retailers at the normal trade price of £10m being cost plus 33⅓%; received £50,000 in display charges; incurred insurance costs of £15,000 and carriage costs of £10,000; and received £6m from retailers.

(iv) On 1 December 20X4 Timber Products plc sold a factory that it owned in Scotland to Inter plc a wholly owned subsidiary of Offshore Banking plc for £10m. The factory had a book value of £8.5m. Inter plc was financed by a loan of £10m from Offshore Banking plc. Timber Products plc was paid a fee by Inter plc to continue to operate the factory, such fee representing the balance of profit remaining after Inter plc paid its parent company loan interest set at a level that represented current interest rates. If there was an operating loss, then Timber Products plc would be charged a fee that would cover the operating losses and interest payable.

For the year ended 31 October 20X5 the fee paid to Timber Products plc amounted to £3m and the loan interest paid by Inter plc amounted to £1.5m. **(12 marks)**

(c) State what further information you would seek in order to determine the substance of the following transaction:

Timber Products plc has installed computer controlled equipment in its furniture making factory. This has created the need for large extractor fans to remove dust particles. The company has contracted with Extractor-Plus plc for that company to build and install extractor equipment. Timber Products plc will maintain and insure the equipment and make an annual payment to Extractor-Plus plc comprising a fixed quarterly rental and an hourly usage charge.

In the year ended 31 October 20X5 Timber Products plc has paid the fixed quarterly rentals totalling £80,000 and hourly charges totalling £120,000. **(3 marks)**

(Total 20 marks)

(ACCA Dec 95)

Compound interest table

No. of	Interest rate per year				
Years	5%	6%	7%	8%	9%
1	1.050	1.060	1.070	1.080	1.090
2	1.102	1.124	1.143	1.166	1.188
3	1.158	1.191	1.225	1.260	1.295
4	1.216	1.262	1.311	1.360	1.412
5	1.276	1.338	1.403	1.469	1.539
6	1.340	1.419	1.501	1.587	1.677

32 Mortgage Lend Ltd

FRS 5 'Reporting the Substance of Transactions' requires an entity's financial statements to report the substance of transactions in to which it has entered. Once a transaction's commercial purpose has been established, it is necessary under FRS 5 to decide whether the transaction gives rise to new assets or liabilities, or changes the company's existing assets or liabilities.

Required:

(a) Explain briefly how an asset or liability is identified under FRS 5. **(4 marks)**

(b) Explain and comment briefly on the principles behind:

(i) the recognition of an asset or liability in an entity's balance sheet
(ii) the complete derecognition of an asset. **(5 marks)**

(c) Mortgage Lend Ltd, a subsidiary of Lendco plc, has sold a portfolio of mortgages to Borrow Ltd. Borrow Ltd has financed this purchase by issuing floating rate loan notes that are secured on all of the assets of Borrow Ltd. Borrow Ltd was set up for the purpose of this transaction and has issued a small amount of equity share capital.

Discuss the criteria which would determine how the above transaction would be treated in the financial statements of:

(i) Borrow Ltd
(ii) Mortgage Lend Ltd
(iii) Lendco Group plc

(Students should discuss whether the transaction should be treated as a linked or separate transaction or derecognised in the financial statements of the companies.)
(11 marks)
(Total: 20 marks)
(ACCA 1997 Pilot Paper)

33 Tall plc

You are the Chief Accountant of Tall plc. The company is planning a number of acquisitions in 20X0 and so you are aware that additional funding will be needed. Today's date is 30 November 20W9. The balance sheet of the company at 30 September 20W9 (the financial year-end of Tall plc) showed the following balances:

	£m
Equity share capital	100.0
Share premium account	35.8
Profit and loss account	89.7
	225.5
Net assets	225.5

On 1 October 20W9 Tall plc raised additional funding as follows:

- Tall plc issued 15 million £1 bonds at par. The bonds pay no interest but are redeemable on 1 October 20X4 at £1.61 – the total payable on redemption being £24.15m. As an alternative to redemption, bondholders can elect to convert their holdings into £1 equity shares on the basis of one equity share for every bond held. The current price of a £1 share is £1.40 and it is reckoned that this will grow by at least 5 per cent per annum for the next five years.

- Tall plc issued 10 million £1 preference shares at £1.20 per share, incurring issue costs of £100,000. The preference shares carry no dividend and are redeemable on 1 October 20X5 at £2.35 per share – the total payable on redemption being £23.5m.

Your assistant is unsure how to reflect the additional funding in the financial statements of Tall plc. He expresses the opinion that both of the new capital instruments should logically be reflected in the shareholders' funds section of the balance sheet. He justifies this by saying that:

- the preference shares are legally shares and so shareholders' funds is the appropriate place to present them

- the bonds and the preference shares seem to have very similar terms of issue and it is quite likely that the bonds will *become* shares in five years' time, given the projected growth in the equity share price.

He has no idea how to show the finance costs of the capital instruments in the profit and loss account. This is because he has never before encountered a capital instrument where no payments will be made to the holders of the instrument until the date of redemption.

Required:

(a) Write a memorandum to your assistant which evaluates the comments he has made and explains the correct treatment where necessary. Your memorandum should refer to the provisions of relevant accounting standards.
(8 marks)

(b) Prepare the relevant balances in the balance sheet of Tall plc immediately after the issue of the bonds and the preference shares.
(4 marks)

(c) Calculate the finance cost that will be required to be shown in the profit and loss account of Tall plc for the year ended 30 September 20X0 for the bonds and the preference shares. You should state where in the profit and loss account the costs should be shown. **(8 marks)**

(Total: 20 marks)

34 Financial instruments

Standard setters have been struggling for several years with the practical issues of the disclosure, recognition and measurement of financial instruments. The ASB has issued a Discussion Paper on 'Derivatives and Other Financial Instruments' and Financial Reporting Standard 13 on the disclosure of such instruments. The dynamic nature of international financial markets has resulted in the widespread use of a variety of financial instruments but present accounting rules in this area do not ensure that the financial statements portray effectively the impact and risks of the instruments currently being used.

Required:

(a) (i) Discuss the concerns about the accounting practices used for financial instruments which led to demands for an accounting standard. **(7 marks)**

(ii) Explain why regulations dealing with disclosure alone cannot solve the problem of accounting for financial instruments. **(4 marks)**

(b) (i) Discuss three ways in which gains and losses on financial instruments might be recorded in the financial statements commenting on the relative merits of each method. **(8 marks)**

(ii) AX, a public limited company, issued a three year £30 million 5% debenture at par on 1 December 20W8 when the market rate of interest was 5%. Interest is paid annually on 30 November each year. Market rates of interest on debentures of equivalent term and risk are 6% and 4% at the end of the financial years to 30 November 20W9 and 30 November 20X0. (Assume that the changes in interest rates took place on 30 November each year.)

Show the effect on 'profit' for the three years to 30 November 20X1 if the debenture and the interest charge were valued on a fair value basis. **(6 marks)**

(Total: 25 marks)

(ACCA Dec 99)

35 Flow Ltd

Flow Ltd prepares financial statements to 31 March each year. On 1 April 20X8, Flow Ltd sold a freehold property to another company, River plc. Flow Ltd had purchased the property for £500,000 on 1 April 20X8 and had charged total depreciation of £60,000 for the period 1 April 20X8 to 31 March 20X8.

River plc paid £850,000 for the property on 1 April 20X8, at which date its true market value was £550,000.

From 1 April 20X8 the property was leased back by Flow Ltd on a ten-year operating lease for annual rentals (payable in arrears) of £100,000. A normal annual rental for such a property would have been £50,000.

River plc is a financial institution which, on 1 April 20X8, charged interest of 10.56% per annum on ten-year fixed rate loans.

Required:

(a) Explain what is meant by the terms 'finance lease' and 'operating lease' and how operating leases should be accounted for in the financial statements of lessee companies. **(6 marks)**

(b) Show the journal entries which Flow Ltd will make to record

- its sale of the property to River plc on 1 April 20X8,
- the payment of the first rental to River plc on 31 March 20X9.

Justify your answer with reference to appropriate Accounting Standards. **(14 marks)**

(Total: 20 marks)

36 AB plc

(a) The development of conceptual frameworks for financial reporting by accounting standard setters could fundamentally change the way in which financial contracts such as leases are accounted for. These frameworks identify the basic elements of financial statements as assets, liabilities, equity, gains and losses and set down their recognition rules. In analysing the definitions of assets and liabilities one could conclude that most leases, including non-cancelable operating leases, qualify for recognition as assets and liabilities because the lessee is likely to enjoy the future economic benefit embodied in the leased asset and will have an unavoidable obligation to transfer economic benefits to the lessor. Because of the problems of accounting for leases, there have been calls for the capitalisation of all non-cancellable operating leases so that the only problem would be the definition of the term 'non-cancellable'.

Required:

(i) Explain how leases are accounted for in the books of the lessee under SSAP 21 'Accounting for leases and hire purchase contracts'. **(7 marks)**

(ii) Discuss the current problems relating to the recognition and classification of leases in corporate financial statements. (Candidates should give examples where necessary.) **(8 marks)**

(b) (i) During the financial year to 31 May 20X8, AB plc disposed of electrical distribution systems from its electrical power plants to CD plc for a consideration of £198m. At the same time AB plc entered into a long-term distribution agreement with CD plc whereby the assets were leased back under a 10-year operating lease. The fair value of the assets sold was £98m and the carrying value based on the depreciated historic cost of the assets was £33m. The lease rental payments were £24m per annum which represented twice the normal payment for leasing this type of asset. **(5 marks)**

(ii) Additionally on 1 June 20X7, AB plc sold plant with a book value of £100m to EF plc when there was a balance on the revaluation reserve of £30m which related to the plant. The fair value and selling price of the plant at that date was £152m. The plant was immediately leased back over a lease term of four years which is the asset's remaining useful life. The residual value at the end of the lease period is estimated to be a negligible amount. AB plc can purchase the plant at the end of the lease for a nominal sum of £1. The lease is non-cancellable and requires equal rental payments of £43.5m at the commencement of each financial year. AB plc has to pay all of the costs of maintaining and insuring the plant. The implicit interest rate in the lease is 10% per annum. The plant is depreciated on a straight line basis. (The present value of an ordinary annuity of £1 per period for three years at 10% interest is £2.49.) **(5 marks)**

Required:

Show and explain how the above transactions should be dealt with in the financial statements of AB plc for the year ending 31 May 20X8 in accordance with SSAP 21 'Accounting for leases and hire purchase contracts' and FRS 5 'Reporting the substance of transactions'.

(Total: 25 marks)

(ACCA June 98)

37 Leese

Leese, a public limited company and a subsidiary of an American holding company operates its business in the services sector. It currently uses operating leases to partly finance its usage of land and buildings and motor vehicles. The following abbreviated financial information was produced as at 30 November 20X0:

Profit and Loss Account for the year ending 30 November 20X0

	£m
Turnover	580
Profit on ordinary activities before taxation	88
Taxation on profit on ordinary activities	(30)
Profit on ordinary activities after taxation	58

Balance Sheet as at 30 November 20X0

Fixed assets	200
Net current assets	170
Creditors: amounts falling due after more than one year (interest free loan from holding company)	(50)
	320
Share Capital	200
Profit and Loss Account	120
	320

Notes

Operating lease rentals for the year – paid 30 November 20X0:

	£m
Land and buildings	30
Motor vehicles	10

Future minimum operating lease payments for leases payable on 30 November each year were as follows:

	Land and Buildings £	*Motor Vehicles* £
Year		
30 November 20X1	28	9
30 November 20X2	25	8
30 November 20X3	20	7
Thereafter	500	-
Total future minimum operating lease payments (non-cancellable)	573	24

The company is concerned about the potential impact of bringing operating leases onto the balance sheet on its profitability and its key financial ratios. The directors have heard that the Accounting Standards Board (ASB) is moving towards this stance and wishes to seek advice on the implications for the company.

For the purpose of determining the impact of the ASB's proposal, the directors have decided to value current year and future operating lease rentals at their present value.

The appropriate interest rate for discounting cash flows to present value is 5% and the current average remaining lease life for operating lease rentals after 30 November 20X3 is deemed to be 10 years.

Depreciation on land and buildings is 5% per annum and on motor vehicles is 25% per annum with a full year's charge in the year of acquisition. The rate of corporation tax is 30% and depreciation rates equate to those of capital allowances. Assume that the operating lease agreements commenced on 30 November 20X0.

Required:

(a) Discuss the reasons why accounting standard setters are proposing to bring operating leases onto the balance sheets of companies. **(7 marks)**

(b) (i) Show the effect on the Profit and Loss Account for the year ending 30 November 20X0 and the Balance Sheet as at 30 November 20X0 of Leese capitalising its operating leases. **(10 marks)**

(ii) Discuss the specific impact on key performance ratios as well as the general business impact of Leese capitalising its operating leases. **(8 marks)**

(Total: 25 marks)

(ACCA Dec 00)

38 AZ plc

(a) For enterprises that are engaged in different businesses with differing risks and opportunities, the usefulness of financial information concerning these enterprises is greatly enhanced if it is supplemented by information on individual business segments. It is recognised that there are two main approaches to segmental reporting. The 'risk and returns' approach where segments are identified on the basis of different risks and returns arising from different lines of business and geographical areas, and the 'managerial' approach whereby segments are identified corresponding to the enterprises' internal organisation structure.

Required:

(i) Explain why the information content of financial statements is improved by the inclusion of segmental data on individual business segments. **(5 marks)**

(ii) Discuss the advantages and disadvantages of analysing segmental data using

- the 'risk and returns' approach **(4 marks)**
- the 'managerial' approach. **(3 marks)**

(b) AZ, a public limited company, operates in the global marketplace.

(i) The major revenue-earning asset is a fleet of aircraft which are registered in the UK and its other main source of revenue comes from the sale of holidays. The directors are unsure as to how business segments are identified. **(3 marks)**

(ii) The company also owns a small aircraft manufacturing plant which supplies aircraft to its domestic airline and to third parties. The preferred method for determining transfer prices for these aircraft between the group companies is market price, but where the aircraft is of a specialised nature with no equivalent market price the companies fix the price by negotiation. **(2 marks)**

(iii) The company has incurred an exceptional loss on the sale of several aircraft to a foreign government. This loss occurred due to a fixed price contract signed several years ago for the sale of secondhand aircraft and resulted through the fluctuation of the exchange rates between the two countries. **(3 marks)**

(iv) During the year the company discontinued its holiday business due to competition in the sector. **(2 marks)**

(v) The company owns 40% of the ordinary shares of Eurocat Ltd, a specialist aircraft engine producer with operations in China and Russia. The investment is accounted for by the equity method and it is proposed to exclude the company's results from segment assets and revenue. **(3 marks)**

Required:

Discuss the implications of each of the above points for the determination of the segmental information required to be prepared and disclosed under SSAP 25 'Segmental Reporting' and FRS 3 'Reporting Financial Performance'.

Please note that the mark allocation is shown after each paragraph in part (b).

(Total: 25 marks)
(ACCA: June 99)

39 C Ltd

You are the financial controller of C Ltd a company which has recently established a pension scheme for its employees. It chose a defined benefit scheme rather than a defined contribution scheme.

C Ltd makes payments into the pension scheme on a monthly basis as follows:

- Employer's contribution of 12% of the gross salaries of the participating employees.
- Employees' contribution (via deduction from salary) of 6% of gross salary.
- Payments are made on the twentieth day of the month following payment of the salary.

C Ltd makes up financial statements to 30 June each year. On 30 June 20X5 the scheme was subject to its first actuarial valuation. The valuation revealed a deficit of £2.4 million. The deficit was primarily caused by a change in the assumptions made by the actuary since the scheme was originally established. The deficit was extinguished by a one-off lump sum payment of £2.4 million into the scheme by C Ltd on 30 September 20X5. The annual salaries of the scheme members for the year ended 31 December 20X5 totalled £15 million, accruing evenly throughout the year.

Required:

(a) Write a memorandum to your Board of Directors which explains:

- the difference between a defined contribution scheme and a defined benefit scheme
- the requirements of FRS 17 *Retirement benefits* concerning the determination of the amounts to be included in the financial statements of the employing company
- why these requirements are more difficult to satisfy for an employer with a defined benefit scheme. **(12 marks)**

(b) Determine the total charge in the profit and loss account for pensions (EXCLUDING amounts deducted from employees' gross salaries) AND any balance sheet amounts in respect of pensions, explaining clearly where exactly on the balance sheet the amounts would be included.

Assume the provisions of FRS 17 are followed by C Ltd.

You ascertain that for the year ended 30 June 20X5 the net finance cost of the scheme was £600,000 and the actuarial loss was £2,000,000.

Ignore deferred taxation. **(8 marks)**

(Total: 20 marks)

40 Diverse plc

Diverse plc has established a defined benefit pension scheme for all the company's full-time employees. The scheme receives contributions from the company and the participating employees. The scheme was originally established on 31 December 20X1 and was actuarially valued at 31 December 20X7. The scheme showed a deficit of £6 million. This deficit was caused by a reassessment of the original actuarial assumptions (an experience deficiency). No change to contribution levels was made as a result of the 20X7 valuation. However, the deficit was funded by a one-off lump sum payment of £6 million into the scheme on 30 June 20X8.

The scheme was actuarially valued at 31 December 20X8. The results of this second valuation showed a surplus of £4 million. The actuaries advised that £3 million of this surplus was caused by a significant reduction in the number of scheme members because of a redundancy programme. No change was made to the normal contribution levels for 20X8 other than the lump sum payment noted above. Total contributions payable to the scheme for 20X8 were £5 million. The current service cost and net finance income relating to the scheme were £6.5 million and £0.7 million respectively for the year ended 31 December 20X8.

Required:

(a) Explain the principles outlined in FRS 17 – Accounting for retirement benefits, under which the amounts to be recognised in the financial statement of employing companies is determined. You should indicate why this is more complicated in the case of defined benefit schemes than defined contribution schemes. **(7 marks)**

(b) Compute the amounts to be recognised in the profit and loss account and the statement of total recognised gains and losses of Diverse plc in respect of the scheme for the year to 31 December 20X8. **(8 marks)**

(c) Compute the pension asset or liability which would appear in the balance sheet of Diverse plc at 31 December 20X8 and explain how it would be disclosed on the balance sheet. **(5 marks)**

(Total: 20 marks)

41 Harmonise plc

Harmonise plc is a plastic toy manufacturer. Its toy sales have been adversely affected by imports and it has been changing towards the supply of plastic office equipment. Profits are expected to continue to fall for the next four years when they are expected to stabilise at the 20X9 level. There will be a regular programme of plant renewal.

The following information is available:

Year ended 30 April	Profit before depreciation and tax	Capital allowances	Depreciation
	£	£	£
20X6	1,250,000	400,000	80,000
20X7	1,200,000	80,000	160,000
20X8	1,100,000	80,000	240,000
20X9	1,000,000	560,000	160,000

Assume a corporation tax rate of 33%. On 1 March 20X5 there was a nil balance on the deferred tax account.

Required:

(a) Prepare the profit and loss and balance sheet extracts for corporation tax and deferred taxation for the four years 20X6-X9 using the following methods

(i) Flow-through
(ii) Full provision
(iii) Partial provision. **(10 marks)**

Notes to the profit and loss account and balance sheet are *not* required.

(b) Discuss arguments for and against each of the three methods in (a) above. **(6 marks)**

(c) Assuming that all of the shares in Harmonise plc were acquired for cash by Grab plc on 1 May 20X5, explain the factors that would be taken into account in determining the fair value of deferred tax as at the date of acquisition. Grab plc applies the partial provision method. **(4 marks)**

(Total: 20 marks)

(ACCA June 96)

42 XL plc

The Accounting Standards Board (ASB) faced a dilemma. IAS 12 (revised), 'Income Taxes' published by the International Accounting Standards Committee (IASC) recommends measures which significantly differ from current UK practice set out in SSAP 15 'Accounting for Deferred Tax'. IAS 12 requires an enterprise to provide for deferred tax in full for all deferred tax liabilities with only limited exceptions whereas SSAP 15 utilised the partial provision approach. The dilemma faced by the ASB was whether to adopt the principles of IAS 12 (revised) and face criticism from many UK companies who agree with the partial provision approach. FRS 19 'Deferred Tax' eliminates the partial provision method and requires full provision.

The different approaches are particularly significant when acquiring subsidiaries because of the fair value adjustments and also when dealing with revaluations of fixed assets as the IAS requires companies to provide for deferred tax on these amounts.

Required:

(a) Explain the main reasons why SSAP 15 has been criticised. **(8 marks)**

(b) Discuss the arguments in favour of and against providing for deferred tax on:
(i) fair value adjustments on the acquisition of a subsidiary
(ii) revaluations of fixed assets. **(7 marks)**

(c) XL plc has the following net assets at 30 November 20X7.

	£'000	*Tax value* £'000
Fixed assets		
Buildings	33,500	7,500
Plant and equipment	52,000	13,000
Investments	66,000	66,000
	151,500	86,500
Current assets	15,000	15,000
Creditors: Amounts falling due within one year		
Creditors	13,500	(13,500)
Liability for health care benefits	300	-
	(13,800)	
Net current assets	1,200	1,500
Provision for deferred tax	(9,010)	(9,010)
	143,690	78,990

XL plc has acquired 100% of the shares of BZ Ltd on 30 November 20X7. The following statement of net assets relates to BZ Ltd on 30 November 20X7.

	Fair value £'000	*Carrying value* £'000	*Tax value* £'000
Buildings	500	300	100
Plant and equipment	40	30	15
Stock	124	114	114
Debtors	110	110	110
Retirement benefit liability	(60)	(60)	-
Creditors	(105)	(105)	(105)
	609	389	234

There is currently no deferred tax provision in the accounts of BZ Ltd. In order to achieve a measure of consistency XL plc decided that it would revalue its land and buildings to £50 million and the plant and equipment to £60 million. The company did not feel it necessary to revalue the investments. The liabilities for retirement benefits and healthcare costs are anticipated to remain at their current amounts for the foreseeable future.

The land and buildings of XL plc had originally cost £45 million and the plant and equipment £70 million. The company has no intention of selling any of its fixed assets other than the land and buildings which it may sell and lease back. XL plc currently utilises the full provision method to account for deferred taxation. The projected depreciation charges and tax allowances of XL plc and BZ Ltd are as follows for the years ending 30 November:

	20X8 £'000	*20X9* £'000	*20Y0* £'000
Depreciation			
(Buildings, plant and equipment)			
XL plc	7,010	8,400	7,560
BZ Ltd	30	32	34
Tax allowances			
XL plc	8,000	4,500	3,000
BZ Ltd	40	36	30

The corporation tax rate had changed from 35% to 30% in the current year. Ignore any indexation allowance or rollover relief and assume that XL plc and BZ Ltd are in the same tax jurisdiction.

Required:

Calculate the deferred tax expense for XL plc which would appear in the group financial statements at 30 November 20X7 using:

(i) the full provision method incorporating the effects of the revaluation of assets in XL plc and the acquisition of BZ Ltd.

(ii) the partial provision method. **(10 marks)**

(Total: 25 marks)

(ACCA Dec 97)

(Candidates should not answer in accordance with IAS 12 (Revised) 'Income Taxes'.)

43 DT

(a) The partial provision method of accounting for deferred tax has lost favour internationally mainly because it anticipates future events, which is considered inconsistent with other aspects of accounting. Major international standard setters have moved to methods which require full provision for deferred tax.

Financial Reporting Standard (FRS) 19 'Deferred Tax' has been issued in order to facilitate the process of harmonisation of accounting for deferred tax. However, full provision for deferred tax under FRS 19 is entirely different to that of equivalent accounting standards internationally. Under these standards full provision is based on 'temporary differences' whereas FRS 19 uses a system based on 'timing differences'. There is strong opposition within the Accounting Standards Board (ASB) to accounting for deferred tax using temporary differences and not timing differences. Additionally the ASB is suggesting that deferred tax balances may be discounted but internationally this is currently not normally allowable.

Required:

(a) (i) Explain the differences between accounting for deferred tax using timing differences as opposed to temporary differences. **(6 marks)**

(ii) Discuss the arguments for and against discounting long-term deferred tax balances. **(6 marks)**

(b) DT a public limited company has decided to determine the impact that the provisions of FRS 19 will have on its financial statements for the year ending 30 November 20X0. The amounts of deferred taxation provided and unprovided in the group financial statements for the year ending 30 November 20W9 were as follows:

	Provided	*Unprovided*
	£m	£m
Capital allowances in excess of depreciation	38	12
Other timing differences	11	14
Pensions and other post retirement benefits	62	–
Losses available for offset against future taxable profits	(34)	(42)
Corporation tax on capital gains arising on the disposal of property which has been deferred under the roll-over provisions	–	165
Tax that would arise if properties were disposed of at their revalued amounts	–	140
	77	289

The following notes are relevant to the calculation of the deferred tax provision under FRS 19 as at 30 November 20X0:

(i) DT acquired a 100% holding in an overseas company several years ago. The subsidiary has declared a dividend for the financial year to 30 November 20X0 of £8 million. The dividend has been accrued but no account has been taken of the tax liability on this dividend of £2 million payable 30 November 20X1. During the year DT had supplied the subsidiary with stock amounting to £30 million at a profit of 20% on selling price. This stock had not been sold by the year-end and the tax rate applied to the subsidiary's profit was 25%. No other adjustments to deferred taxation are required for the subsidiary other than those required by this note.

(ii) The excess of capital allowances over depreciation is £180 million as at 30 November 20X0. It is anticipated that the timing differences will reverse according to the following schedule:

	30 Nov 20X1	*30 Nov 20X2*	*30 Nov 20X3*
	£m	£m	£m
Depreciation	1,100	1,100	1,100
Capital Allowances	1,050	1,040	1,030
	50	60	70

Other timing differences amount to £90 million as at 30 November 20X0. It is anticipated that they will all reverse in the year to 30 November 20X1.

(iii) The amount of the deferred tax provision required for pensions and other post retirement benefits has risen to £90 million as at 30 November 20X0. DT has an actuarial valuation of the pension fund every three years.

(iv) It is envisaged that any unrelieved tax losses will be offset in equal proportion against taxable profits for the years ending 30 November 20X1 and 20X2. The auditors have concurred with the directors of the company as regards the future recovery of the unrelieved tax losses. No further losses arose in the year to 30 November 20X0. The tax losses provided for at 30 November 20W9 were offset against profits for the year ended 30 November 20X0.

(v) Corporation tax on the property disposed of becomes payable on 30 November 20X3 under the roll-over relief provisions. There had been no sales or revaluations of property during the year to 30 November 20X0.

(vi) Corporation tax is assumed to be 30% for the foreseeable future and the company wishes to discount any deferred tax liabilities at a rate of 4%.

Required:

Calculate the provision for deferred tax required in the Group Balance Sheet of DT plc at 30 November 20X0 using FRS 19, commenting on the effect that the application of FRS 19 will have on the financial statements of DT plc. **(13 marks)**

(Total: 25 marks)

(ACCA Dec 00)

44 Brachol plc

Brachol plc is preparing its accounts for the year ended 30 November 20X2.

The following information is available from the previous year's balance sheet:

At 30 November 20X1 there were credit balances on the share premium account of £2,025,000, the revaluation reserve of £4,050,000 and the profit and loss account of £2,700,000.

During 20X2 the following transactions occurred:

(a) One million shares of £1 each were issued in exchange for net assets that had a fair value of £3,755,000.

(b) A factory property that had been revalued from £500,000 to £1,310,000 in 20X0 was sold for £2,525,000.

(c) A fixed asset investment was revalued from £1,305,000 to £900,000.

(d) There was a currency translation loss of £270,000 arising on foreign currency net investments.

(e) A warehouse property was revalued from £1,000,000 to £1,540,000.

A prior period adjustment of £1,350,000 was required which had arisen from a change in accounting policy that had overstated the previous year's profit.

The profit and loss account for the year ended 30 November 20X2 showed a profit attributable to members of the company of £810,000 and a dividend of £675,000.

Required:

(a) (i) Draft a note showing the movements on reserves as at 30 November 20X2.

(ii) Draft a statement of total recognised gains and losses to show the net deduction from or addition to net assets as at 30 November 20X2. **(6 marks)**

(b) Explain briefly

(i) the purpose of the statement of total recognised gains and losses

(ii) the extent to which a user of the accounts will be better able to make decisions by referring to a statement of total recognised gains and losses rather than the statement of movements on reserves that is produced to comply with the Companies Act 1985. **(7 marks)**

(c) Explain briefly

(i) the nature of the adjustments that would be required to reconcile the profit on ordinary activities before tax to the historical cost profit.

(ii) the possible use that can be made of such information by a potential investor. **(7 marks)**

(Total: 20 marks)

(ACCA June 93)

45 Shiny Bright plc

Shiny Bright plc was incorporated in 1980 to provide cleaning services for hotel, hospital and catering clients; it diversified into hotel ownership in the 1990s. In the early 1990s the company acquired a chain of 20 country hotels from Retort Hotels Ltd, a company then in receivership. 15 of the hotels were located in the South of England and five were located in Ireland. Since 20X4 the directors have been preparing to seek a listing on the Alternative Investment Market and part of their strategy has been to dispose of operations that did not achieve an adequate return on capital employed.

At a recent seminar on reporting financial performance attended by the Managing Director, the seminar leader had briefly explained that exceptional items needed to be disclosed by virtue of their size or incidence; emphasised the importance of the operating profit figure and commented that it seemed that the market was often too easily misled by some companies' innovative use of FRS 3's layered approach to the profit and loss account to divert attention from the overall total result for which management was accountable.

When Shiny Bright plc was finalising its accounts for the year ended 31 October 20X6 the Managing Director requested the Finance Director to make a brief presentation to the Board explaining exceptional items and innovative uses of the layered approach for the profit and loss account and advising on the accounting treatments that would produce the highest operating profit and on the presentation format that would concentrate attention on the EPS figure that was most favourable to the company.

The operating profit was £4m from continuing operations and £0.1m from its hospital cleaning services, which were discontinued in 20X6, before taking account of the following information.

1 The company had acquired a restaurant in Central London for £1m in 20X1. It was revalued at £1.5m in 20X3. No depreciation had been provided on the property as it was company policy to maintain properties to a high standard.

The restaurant was sold on 30 September 20X6 for £2.5m.

2 All of the hotels acquired from Retort Hotels Ltd which were located in Ireland were sold on 31 August 20X6 for £12.5m. They were the only hotels operated by the company in Ireland and the directors decided that they were too distant for them to exercise effective management. They had been acquired for £16m at the date they were purchased from the receiver. No depreciation has been provided by the company.

3 Shiny Bright plc has incurred costs of £1.4m arising from the reorganisation of the hotel administration. This comprised £0.5m for the centralisation of the accounting and booking function, £0.3m for refurbishing the reception area to a common plan, £0.4m for retraining staff and £0.2m for redundancy payments.

4 The fixed assets used for cleaning were estimated to have fallen in value by £0.75m following the discovery that cleaning equipment had suffered damage due to staff failing to follow the manufacturers' instructions.

5 There was an item on the agenda for the October 20X6 Board meeting proposing the closure in the following financial year of a loss making hotel. The Finance Director had prepared estimates for the following year for this hotel showing turnover £350,000, cost of sales £400,000, write down of equipment £50,000 and redundancy costs £40,000. The proposal was to complete the closure by May 20X7.

Required

Assuming that you are the Finance Director, you are required to:

(a) (i) Explain the terms *size* and *incidence* in relation to exceptional items and the major difficulties in applying these terms. **(4 marks)**

(ii) Explain how companies might be able to make use of FRS 3's layered approach to the profit and loss account to direct attention to a result other than the overall total result for which management was accountable. **(4 marks)**

(b) (i) Describe the accounting treatments in the profit and loss account for the year ended 31 October 20X6 that would produce the highest operating profit figure, giving reasons to support your advice in respect of items 1 - 5 above

(ii) Calculate the operating profit from continuing and discontinued operations for 20X6 assuming that your advice was followed

(iii) Describe the presentation of profit and loss account that would best direct attention to the profit figure most favourable to the company. **(12 marks)**

(Total: 20 marks)

(ACCA Dec 96)

46 Reporting Financial Performance

The Accounting Standards Board has published FRED 22 'Revision of FRS 3 'Reporting Financial Performance'. The proposals in FRED 22 build upon the strengths of, and are a progression from FRS 3 'Reporting Financial Performance'. It proposes that a single performance statement should replace the profit and loss account and the Statement of Total Recognised Gains and Losses, effectively combining them in one statement. FRED 22 also takes the view that gains and losses should be reported only once and in the period when they arise, and should not be reported again in another component of the financial statements at a later date, a practice which is sometimes called 'recycling'.

Required:

(a) (i) Explain the reasons for presenting financial performance in one statement rather than two or more statements. **(8 marks)**

(ii) Discuss the views for and against the recycling of gains and losses in the financial statements. **(6 marks)**

(b) Describe how the following items are dealt with under current Financial Reporting Standards, and how their treatment would change if FRED 22 were adopted:

(i) Gains and losses on the disposal of fixed assets **(4 marks)**

(ii) Revaluation gains and losses on fixed assets **(4 marks)**

(ii) Foreign currency translation adjustments arising on the net investment in foreign operations. **(3 marks)**

(Total: 25 marks)

(ACCA Dec 00)

47 X plc

In 20X6 the Accounting Standards Board (ASB) issued a Discussion Paper on 'Earnings per Share' which was essentially an exposure draft on the same subject published by the International Accounting Standards Committee (IASC) (E52 'Earnings per Share' published by IASC). The ASB has now issued FRS 14 'Earnings per share', which replaces SSAP 3.

(a) FRS 14 states that only those financial instruments that would dilute basic EPS should be taken into account when calculating diluted EPS. FRS 14 additionally states that the order in which potential ordinary shares are considered can affect the dilution of basic EPS and that the sequence of each issue of shares should be considered from the most to the least dilutionary in order to determine whether potential ordinary shares are anti dilutive.

(b) FRS 14 requires a new method of calculation to deal with the dilutive effects of share options and warrants. The assumed proceeds should be considered to have been received from the issue of shares at fair value. The difference between the actual number of shares issued and the number that would have been issued at fair value to generate the proceeds is treated as the amount of the dilution.

Required:

(a) Explain why the ASB issued Exposure Drafts of the IASC as Discussion Papers (students should refer to Earnings per Share in their answer). **(3 marks)**

(b) Discuss why there is a need to disclose diluted earnings per share. **(3 marks)**

(c) Calculate the diluted EPS according to FRS 14 given the following information.

X plc - Accounting Data Year Ended 31 May 20X7

Net profit after tax and minority interest	£18,160,000
Ordinary shares of £1 (fully paid)	£40,000,000
Average fair value for year of ordinary shares	£1.50

(1) Share Options have been granted to directors giving them the right to subscribe for ordinary shares between 20X8 and 20Y0 at £1.20 per share. The options outstanding at 31 May 20X7 were 2,000,000 in number.

(2) The company has £20 million of 6% convertible loan stock in issue. The terms of conversion of the loan stock per £200 nominal value of loan stock at the date of issue (1 May 20X6) were

Conversion Date	*Number of Shares*
31 May 20X7	24
31 May 20X8	23
31 May 20X9	22

No loan stock has as yet been converted. The loan stock had been issued at a discount of 1% and the company has complied with FRS 4 'Capital Instruments' as regards the treatment of the discount.

(3) There are 1,600,000 convertible preference shares in issue. The cumulative dividend is 10p per share and each preference share can convert into two ordinary shares. The preference shares can be converted in 20X9.

(4) Assume a corporation tax rate of 33%.

(5) The price of 2.5% Consolidated Stock on 1 June 20X6 for the purpose of this question is to be taken as £25.

(9 marks)
(Total: 15 marks)
(ACCA 1997 Pilot Paper)

48 Mayes plc

Earnings per share is one of the most quoted statistics in financial analysis, coming into prominence because of the widespread use of the price earnings ratio as an investment decision making yardstick. In 1972 SSAP3 'Earnings per share' was issued and revised in 1974, and the standard as amended was operating reasonably effectively. In fact the Accounting Standards Board (ASB) has stated that a review of earnings per share would not normally have been given priority at this stage of the Board's programme. However, in June 1997 FRED16 'Earnings Per Share' was issued which proposed amendments to SSAP3 and subsequently in October 1998 FRS 14 'Earnings Per Share' was published.

Required:

(a) Explain why there is a need to disclose diluted earnings per share in financial statements. **(5 marks)**

(b) The following financial statement extracts for the year ending 31 May 20X9 relate to Mayes, a public limited company.

	£'000	£'000
Operating profit		
Continuing operations	26,700	
Discontinued operations	(1,120)	
	25,580	
Continuing operations		
Profit on disposal of tangible fixed assets		2,500
Discontinued operations		
(Loss) on sale of operations		(5,080)
		23,000
Interest payable		(2,100)
Profit on ordinary activities before taxation		20,900
Tax on profit on ordinary activities		(7,500)
Profit on ordinary activities after tax		13,400
Minority interest – equity		(540)
Profit attributable to members of parent company		12,860

Dividends:		
Preference dividend on non-equity shares	210	
Ordinary dividend on equity shares	300	
	—	(510)
Other appropriations – non equity shares (note iii)		(80)
Retained profit for year		12,270

Capital as at 31 May 20X9	£'000
Allotted, called up and fully paid ordinary shares of £1 each	12,500
7% convertible cumulative redeemable preference shares of £1	3,000
	15,500

Additional Information

(i) On 1 January 20X9, 3·6 million ordinary shares were issued at £2·50 in consideration of the acquisition of June Ltd for £9 million. These shares do not rank for dividend in the current period. Additionally the company purchased and cancelled £2·4 million of its own £1 ordinary shares on 1 April 20X9. On 1 July 20X9, the company made a bonus issue of 1 for 5 ordinary shares before the financial statements were issued for the year ended 31 May 20X9.

(ii) The company has a share option scheme under which certain directors can subscribe for the company's shares. The following details relate to the scheme.

Options outstanding 31 May 20X8:
(i) 1·2 million ordinary shares at £2 each
(ii) 2 million ordinary shares at £3 each
both sets of options are exercisable before 31 May 20Y0.

Options granted during year 31 May 20X9
(i) One million ordinary shares at £4 each exercisable before 31 May 20Y2, granted 1 June 20X8.
During the year to 31 May 20X9, the options relating to the 1·2 million ordinary shares (at a price of £2) were exercised on 1 March 20X9.

The average fair value of one ordinary share during the year was £5.

(iii) The 7% convertible cumulative redeemable preference shares are convertible at the option of the shareholder or the company on 1 July 20Y0, 20Y1, 20Y2 on the basis of two ordinary shares for every three preference shares. The preference share dividends are not in arrears. The shares are redeemable at the option of the shareholder on 1 July 20Y0, 20Y1, 20Y2 at £1·50 per share. The 'other appropriations – non equity shares' item charged against the profits relates to the amortisation of the redemption premium and issue costs on the preference shares.

(iv) Mayes issued £6 million of 6% convertible bonds on 1 June 20X8 to finance the acquisition of Space Ltd. Each bond is convertible into 2 ordinary shares of £1. Assume a corporation tax rate of 35%.

(v) The interest payable relates entirely to continuing operations and the taxation charge relating to discontinued operations is assessed at £100,000 despite the accounting losses. The loss on discontinued operations relating to the minority interest is £600,000.

Required:

Calculate the basic and diluted earnings per share for the year ended 31 May 20X9 for Mayes plc utilising FRS 14 'Earnings per Share'. **(14 marks)**

(Candidates should show a calculation of whether potential ordinary shares are dilutive or anti-dilutive).

(Total: 19 marks)

(ACCA June 99)

49 Worldwide Nuclear Fuels

Provisions are particular kinds of liabilities. It therefore follows that provisions should be recognised when the definition of a liability has been met. The key requirement of a liability is a present obligation and thus this requirement is critical also in the context of the recognition of a provision. However, although accounting for provisions is an important topic for standard setters, it is only recently that guidance has been issued on provisioning in financial statements. In the UK, the Accounting Standards Board has recently issued FRS 12: 'Provisions, Contingent Liabilities and Contingent Assets'.

Required:

(a) (i) Explain why there was a need for more detailed guidance on accounting for provisions in the UK. **(7 marks)**

(ii) Explain the circumstances under which a provision should be recognised in the financial statements according to FRS 12: 'Provisions, Contingent Liabilities and Contingent Assets'. **(6 marks)**

(b) Discuss whether the following provisions have been accounted for correctly under FRS 12: 'Provisions, Contingent Liabilities and Contingent Assets'.

World Wide Nuclear Fuels plc disclosed the following information in its financial statements for the year ending 30 November 20X9:

Provisions and long-term commitments

(i) Provision for decommissioning the Group's radioactive facilities is made over their useful life and covers complete demolition of the facility within fifty years of it being taken out of service together with any associated waste disposal. The provision is based on future prices and is discounted using a current market rate of interest.

Provision for decommissioning costs

	£m
Balance at 1.12.X8	675
Adjustment arising from change in price levels charged to reserves	33
Charged in the year to profit and loss account	125
Adjustment due to change in knowledge (charged to reserves)	27
Balance at 30.11.X9	860

There are still decommissioning costs of £1,231m (undiscounted) to be provided for in respect of the group's radioactive facilities as the company's policy is to build up the required provision over the life of the facility.

Assume that adjustments to the provision due to change in knowledge about the accuracy of the provision do not give rise to future economic benefits. **(7 marks)**

(ii) The company purchased an oil company during the year. As part of the sale agreement, oil has to be supplied for a five year period to the company's former holding company at an uneconomic rate. As a result a provision for future operating losses has been set up of £135m which relates solely to the uneconomic supply of oil. Additionally the oil company is exposed to environmental liabilities arising out of its past obligations, principally in respect of remedial work to soil and ground water systems, although currently there is no legal obligation to carry out the work. Liabilities for environmental costs are provided for when the Group determines a formal plan of action on the closure of an inactive site and when expenditure on remedial work is probable and the cost can be measured with reasonable certainty. However in this case, it has been decided to provide for £120m in respect of the environmental liability on the acquisition of the oil company. World Wide Nuclear Fuels has a reputation for ensuring that the environment is preserved and protected from the effects of its business activities. **(5 marks)**

(Total: 25 marks)

(ACCA Dec 99)

50 Maxpool plc

The Companies Act 1985 and the Stock Exchange Listing rules contain requirements for disclosure of some related party transactions. The Accounting Standards Board has however, published FRS 8 'Related Party Disclosures' in order to give users of financial information a more detailed insight into transactions. FRS 8 adopted the proposals of FRED 8 'Related Party Disclosures' with a few amendments which came about as a result of comments made on the exposure draft. Without disclosure to the contrary, there is a general presumption that transactions reflected in financial statements have been conducted on an arms length basis between independent parties. However, this presumption is not justified when related party transactions exist because the requisite conditions of competitive, free market dealings may not exist.

Required:

(a) (i) Explain the reasons why the ASB felt that FRS 8 'Related Party Disclosures' was required when disclosure of such transactions was already deemed necessary under the Companies Act 1985 and the Stock Exchange Listing Rules. **(6 marks)**

(ii) Explain the reasons why the ASB feel that it is important to obtain comment on Financial Reporting Exposure Drafts prior to their acceptance as Financial Reporting Standards. **(3 marks)**

(b) Maxpool plc, a listed company, owned 60% of the shares in Ching Ltd. Bay plc, a listed company, owned the remaining 40% of the £1 ordinary shares in Ching Ltd. The holdings of shares were acquired on 1 January 20X6. Ching Ltd sold a factory outlet site to Bay at a price determined by an independent surveyor on 30 November 20X6. On 1 March 20X7 Maxpool plc purchased a further 30% of the £1 ordinary shares of Ching Ltd from Bay plc and purchased 25% of the ordinary shares of £1 of Bay plc. On 30 June 20X7 Ching Ltd sold the whole of its fleet of vehicles to Bay plc at a price determined by a vehicle auctioneer.

Explain the implications of the above transactions for the determination of related party relationships and disclosure of such transactions in the financial statements of Maxpool Group plc, Ching Ltd and Bay plc for the years ending 31 December 20X6 and 31 December 20X7. **(11 marks)**

(Total: 20 marks)

(ACCA June 97)

51 RP Group plc

Related party relationships and transactions are a normal feature of business. Enterprises often carry on their business activities through subsidiaries and associates and it is inevitable that transactions will occur between group companies. Until relatively recently the disclosure of related party relationships and transactions has been regarded as an area which has a relatively low priority. However, recent financial scandals have emphasised the importance of an accounting standard in this area.

Required:

(a) (i) Explain why the disclosure of related party relationships and transactions is an important issue. **(6 marks)**

(ii) Discuss the view that small companies should be exempt from the disclosure of related party relationships and transactions on the grounds of their size. **(4 marks)**

(b) Discuss whether the following events would require disclosure in the financial statements of the RP Group plc under FRS 8 'Related Party Disclosures'.

RP Group plc, merchant bankers, has a number of subsidiaries, associates and joint ventures in its group structure. During the financial year to 31 October 20X9, the following events occurred:

(i) The company agreed to finance a management buyout of a group company, AB, a limited company. In addition to providing loan finance, the company has retained a twenty-five per cent equity holding in the company and has a main board director on the board of AB. RP received management fees, interest payments and dividends from AB. **(6 marks)**

(ii) On 1 July 20X9, RP sold a wholly owned subsidiary, X, a limited company, to Z, a public limited company. During the year RP supplied X with second hand office equipment and X leased its factory from RP. The transactions were all contracted for at market rates. **(4 marks)**

(iii) The pension scheme of the group is managed by another merchant bank. An investment manager of the group pension scheme is also a non-executive director of the RP Group and received an annual fee for his services of £25,000 which is not material in the group context. The company pays £16m per annum into the scheme and occasionally transfers assets into the scheme. In 20X9, fixed assets of £10m were transferred into the scheme and a recharge of administrative costs of £3m was made. **(5 marks)**

(Total: 25 marks)

(ACCA Dec 99)

52 Industrial Estates plc

Industrial Estates plc is a company that was formed in 1962 to build and sell industrial units. Its share capital and reserves totalled £500m at 31 December 20X2.

During the three years 20X0/20X2, sales turnover fell as a result of financial lending institutions restricting the amount they were prepared to lend to prospective purchasers to 60% of the sales price of an industrial unit.

In 20X3 the company was building standard units to be sold for £1,250,000 each and in order to overcome the decline in sales it introduced a new scheme which was to be offered as an option to outright purchase whereby:

(i) the company transferred the legal ownership of an industrial unit on payment by the purchaser of £750,000 being 60% of the sales price

(ii) the purchaser gave a second charge over the industrial unit as security for the amount outstanding of £500,000 being 40% of the sales price

(iii) the purchaser paid no annual interest on the £500,000 but, in the event of a re-sale to a third party, would pay the company 40% of the market value as at the date of the re-sale in full settlement of the amount outstanding

(iv) the company agreed to repurchase the unit in the event that the purchaser ceased trading on payment of the market price as at the date of cessation less the £500,000 balance unpaid.

The following information was available at 31 December 20X3:

(a) Industrial units under construction

There were three units which were each 75% complete. At the commencement of building, the estimated total construction cost had been £1,000,000 per unit. The costs incurred on two of the units was in accordance with the original estimate but additional costs of £300,000 had been incurred on the third unit as a result of defective workmanship.

Reservation deposits of £50,000 had been received on each of these units from potential purchasers interested in an outright purchase for £1,250,000 per unit but no formal sales contracts had been entered into by 31 December 20X3.

The directors are proposing to show these units at cost plus attributable profit in the balance sheet.

(b) Industrial units sold under the new scheme on payment of 60% of the selling price.

Five units had been built in 20X3. The total cost of each unit had been £1,000,000 and the selling price £1,250,000. The sales contracts required a payment of 60% on signing the contract and a charge for the remaining 40%.

(c) A further unit had been sold under the new scheme at the standard selling price of £1,250,000 and payment of £750,000. Later in the year the company repurchased the unit at an agreed repurchase price of £1,350,000. This unit was unsold at the year end.

Required:

(a) Explain how the industrial units under construction should be treated in the balance sheet. Show workings to support the entry or entries. **(5 marks)**

(b) As the chief accountant, write a memo to explain to your assistant how you are proposing to treat the five industrial units which have been sold under the new scheme in the profit and loss account and balance sheet for the year ended 31 December 20X3.

Assume that the transactions are to be treated in accordance with the legal position. **(5 marks)**

(c) Draft journal entries to record the accounting treatment of the unit repurchased during the year. **(4 marks)**

(d) The conditions relating to repurchase were not as the company had stated in the information given in the question.

The actual terms were that on a repurchase the company would pay the original purchaser 60% of the market value.

Explain the effect of this on the treatment of the five units built and sold in 20X3 in the profit and loss account and balance sheet of Industrial Estates plc as at 31 December 20X3. **(6 marks)**

(Total: 20 marks)

(ACCA June 94)

53 Badger Plc

You are the Chief Accountant of Badger plc. The draft profit and loss account of the company for the year ended 31 October 20X8 showed a profit before taxation of £66 million. Your assistant (who has prepared the draft accounts) is unsure about the treatment of three transactions which have taken place during the year. She has written you a memorandum which explains the key principles of each transaction and also the treatment adopted in the draft accounts.

Required:

Draft a reply to your assistant which reviews the treatment suggested by your assistant and recommends changes where relevant. In each case your reply should refer to the provisions of relevant Accounting Standards.

Transaction 1

On 1 May 20X8 Badger plc purchased a large item of machinery for a total cost of £15 million. The machinery was leased to Cub Ltd for a 5-year primary period at an annual rental of £3.2 million, payable in advance. The expected useful life of the machinery was 5 years and Cub Ltd had the option to continue to lease the machine at the end of the primary period for a further 5 years at a rental of £1 per annum. The purchaser of the machine qualified for a tax-free grant of £3 million, payable on 1 May 20X8.

Your assistant has capitalised the machine at its total cost of £15 million and charged depreciation of £1.5 million. Rental income of £1.6 million has been credited to the profit and loss account. The tax-free grant has been credited to a deferred income account and released to the profit and loss account over the lease term. For the year ended 31 October 20X8, 10% of the grant was released to the profit and loss account. The tax-free amount released — £300,000 — was grossed up by the rate of corporation tax of 31%, and the notional taxation shown as part of the tax charge. **(9 marks)**

Transaction 2

The company has operated a defined benefit pension scheme since 31 October 20X2. The scheme was actuarially valued at 31 October 20X7 and a deficit of £20 million was revealed. In the year ended 31 October 20X8, the company took no action in respect of this deficit and paid its normal contributions of £2.5 million. The actuarial valuation was reviewed at 31 October 20X8 and the actuary reported that the deficit was now £25 million. This increase largely arose as a result of an actuarial loss of £4 million.

In the draft financial statements your assistant has charged the profit and loss account with the contributions paid of £2.5 million. This treatment was based on the fact that the company has not yet decided what action to take in respect of the deficit. However, a note to the financial statements has highlighted the potential deficit of £25 million. **(6 marks)**

Transaction 3

One of the major corporate objectives of Badger plc is to ensure that the company conducts its business in such a way as to minimise any damage to the environment. It is committed in principle to spending extra money in pursuit of this objective but has not as yet made any firm proposals. The directors believe that this objective will prove very popular with customers and are anxious to emphasise their environmentally-friendly policies in the annual report.

Your assistant suggests that a sum should be set aside from profits each year to create a provision in the financial statements against the possible future costs of environmental protection. Accordingly, she has charged the profit and loss account for the year ended 31 October 20X8 with a sum of £100,000 and proposes to disclose this fact in a note to the financial statements. **(5 marks)**

(Total: 20 marks)

54 Portfolio plc

You are the Chief Accountant of Portfolio plc, a listed company with a number of subsidiaries located throughout the United Kingdom. Your assistant has prepared the first draft of the financial statements of the group for the year ended 31 July 20X0. The draft statements show a group profit before taxation of £50 million. The statements are due to be approved by the Directors on 15 December 20X0. Your assistant has written you a memorandum concerning three transactions that have arisen during the year. The memorandum outlines the key elements of each transaction and suggests the appropriate treatment.

Transaction 1

During the year ended 31 July 20X0, the company entered into an arrangement with a finance company to factor its debts. Each month 90% of the value of the debts arising from credit sales that month was sold to the factor, who assumed legal title and responsibility for collection of all debts. Upon receipt of the cash by the factor, the remaining 10% was paid to Portfolio plc less a deduction for administration and finance costs. Any debtor who did not pay the factor within three months of the debt being factored was transferred back to Portfolio plc and the amounts advanced by the factor recovered from Portfolio plc. In preparing the draft financial statements, your assistant has removed the whole of the factored debts from trade debtors at the date the debts are factored. The net amount receivable from the factor has been shown as a sundry debtor. **(5 marks)**

Transaction 2

One of the subsidiaries is operating a chemical reprocessing plant. The plant is due to close on 31 July 20X4 but will be fully operational up to that date. On 15 July 20X0, government passed new environmental legislation. This legislation requires that companies operating chemical reprocessing plants leave the site environmentally safe when the plant is closed. Given the expected date of closure, it is estimated that the legislation will require the group to spend £40 million on rendering the plant environmentally safe. Your assistant proposes to make no entries in the financial statements for the year ended 31 July 20X0 but to set aside £10 million from the profits of each of the years ending 31 July 20X1-20X4 inclusive. This would build up a provision of £40 million by the date the expenditure is likely to be incurred. A suitable discount rate for evaluating investments of this nature (appropriately adjusted for risk) is 12% per annum. **(8 marks)**

Transaction 3

On 1 August 20W9, the company raised finance of £80 million by issuing 80 million £1 loan stock. On this date £80 million was credited to creditors. The loan stock was quoted on the UK stock exchange. The loan stock pays no interest but is redeemable on 31 July 20X4 at a price £1.61 per £1. This represents an effective interest rate of 10% each year. On 31 July 20X0, the stock had a quoted price of £1.18 per £1. Your assistant proposes to make no further entries in the financial statements since nothing is due to be paid until 20X4. She expresses the view that the quoted price of the stock is of no relevance to the company, only to the stockholders. **(7 marks)**

Required:

Draft a reply to your assistant that appraises her suggested treatments and recommends changes where relevant. In each case, your reply should refer to the provisions of relevant Accounting Standards and explain the rationale behind such provisions. **(Total: 20 Marks)**

55 Dragon plc

You are the Chief Accountant of Dragon plc. Today's date is 15 October 20X9. Your assistant has prepared the first draft of the financial statements of the company for the year ended 31 August 20X9. The draft statements show a group profit before taxation of £50m. He has a good general accounting knowledge but is not up to date with recent changes in the regulatory framework. Therefore he has written to you asking for advice regarding the appropriate accounting treatment of the three items shown below.

- **Item 1**. Dragon plc owns a chain of hotels. These hotels have been purchased at various dates over the last 30 years and are maintained to a very high standard. Your assistant notes that no depreciation appears ever to have been charged on any of the hotels, even though they are classified as fixed assets. He wonders whether it is because the hotels are likely to be increasing in value given the buoyant state of the property market.

- **Item 2**. On 10 August 20X9 the board of directors met and agreed the outline of a rationalisation programme. The programme will involve some redundancies and is due to commence on 1 January 20Y0. The reorganisation costs are likely to total £15m. A further board meeting on 9 September 20X9 finalised the plan and a public announcement was made on 14 September 20X9. Your assistant is unsure whether or not to provide for the £15m in the 20X9 financial statements.

- **Item 3**. The company is due to borrow a substantial sum – £100m – for three months on 15 November 20X9. The treasurer has been concerned that interest rates may rise, and on 15 August 20X9 covered the position by selling 200 three-month interest rate futures. Interest rates have indeed risen since 15 August and the interest futures look likely to yield a profit to the company. Given that no cash has been laid out, other than the initial deposit on the futures contract, your assistant is uncertain as to what action, if any, to take.

Required:

Prepare a response to your assistant which explains the correct treatment of each item. In each case your reply should refer to the provisions of relevant accounting standards and explain the rationale behind such provisions. The allocation of marks is as follows:

- Item 1 **(7 marks)**
- Item 2 **(6 marks)**
- Item 3 **(7 marks)**

(Total: 20 marks)

56 Finaleyes plc

The following questions relate to Finaleyes plc, a car seat manufacturer. The company is pursuing a policy of growth by acquisition and it has targeted a number of specific companies for takeover during the next three years.

For the year ended 30 April 20X6 its turnover was £100m; post tax profits £13m applying a tax rate of 33%; net assets £80m and issued share capital £10m in 25p shares. At 30 April 20X6 its share price was £6 per share and at 31 May 20X6 its share price was £7 per share.

The financial director is reviewing the accounting treatment of various items prior to the signing of the 20X6 accounts which is planned for July 20X6.

The items are:

(1) **A share issue**

On 31 January 20X6 it was announced that the company was raising £14m before expenses by the issue of shares for cash. The issue took place on 31 May 20X6 at market share price.

(2) **Acquisition of a plant**

On 1 May 20X5 the company acquired a factory in Norway for £4m. On 30 April 20X6 they obtained professional advice that the building had an expected life of 40 years with no residual value but that the heating systems would require replacing every 15 years at an expected cost of £450,000.

Depreciation on the buildings has been charged following the company's normal accounting policy of using the straight-line method.

A charge of £30,000 has been made to the profit and loss account to create a provision for the replacement of the heating system assuming a 15 year life. The initial reasoning for making the charge for the heating system replacement was that it complied with the ASB definition of a liability ie, 'Liabilities are an entity's obligations to transfer economic benefits as a result of past transactions or events'.

(3) **Sale and lease back**

At 30 April 20X6 the balance sheet included the main offices of the company at a figure of £10m. On 15 May 20X6 the company exchanged contracts with the Helpful Friendly Society Ltd for the sale of the main offices for £12m with lease back for an initial period of 20 years at market rentals. The company intended to use the proceeds to invest in office property in Kuala Lumpur. The contract provided that the cash consideration would be paid to Finaleyes plc on 14 June 20X6.

(4) **Stock valuation errors**

The company's policy on stock valuation was to value stock in accordance with SSAP 9 at the lower of cost and net realisable value. The company discovered in May 20X6 that there had been an omission for three years to apply this policy to stock held in a warehouse in Cyprus; the provisions required to bring the stock down to net realisable values were £63,000 for 20X3, £70,000 for 20X4, £105,000 for 20X5 and £115,000 for 20X6.

The adjustment has been treated as a prior period adjustment and reduced the profit and loss account balance brought forward at 1 May 20X5 and the stock by £238,000 being the total of the provisions required for the years ended 30 April 20X3 to 20X5.

Required:

For each of the items (1) to (4) above:

(a) State your view on the appropriate treatment in the financial statements as at 30 April 20X6 giving your reasons; and

(b) Draft an appropriate note to the accounts and/or state the adjustment that would be made to items in the accounts as required.

Each of the items (1) to (4) carries equal marks.

(20 marks)
(Total: 20 marks)
(ACCA June 96)

Preparation of reports and current issues

57 Look Ahead & Co

Look Ahead & Co were instructed to value as at 31 December 20X2 a minority holding of 10,000 25p shares in Arbor Ltd held by D Dodd who is considering disposing of his shareholding.

Arbor Ltd is a private company with an issued share capital of £125,000. The shareholdings are as follows:

Shareholder	*Shareholding*
A Arny	61,250
B Brady	30,000
D Brady	20,000
E Brady	11,250
D Dodd	2,500

The following are extracts from the profit and loss accounts of Arbor Ltd for the four years ended 31 December 20X2:

	20W9	*20X0*	*20X1*	*20X2*
	£'000	£'000	£'000	£'000
Sales	4,200	5,600	8,470	11,700
Cost of sales	1,825	2,920	5,205	7,810
Gross profit	2,375	2,680	3,265	3,890
Administration expenses	900	1,000	1,200	1,400
Distribution costs	1,345	1,500	1,800	2,100
Profit before tax	130	180	265	390
Taxation	40	60	90	136
Profit after tax	90	120	175	254
Ordinary dividend	21.6	22.7	23.8	25.0

The following additional information is available:

The gross dividend yields on quoted companies operating in the same sector were 12% and the firm estimated that this yield should be increased to 18% to allow for lack of marketability.

Assume tax credits are available at $\frac{1}{3}$ of net dividends paid.

Required:

(a) Discuss the relevance of dividends in the valuation of D Dodd's shareholding on the assumption that it is sold to his son W Dodd. Illustrate your answer from the data given in the question. **(4 marks)**

(b) Explain briefly the factors that the firm would take into account when:

(i) estimating the future net dividends
(ii) estimating the investor's required gross yield. **(8 marks)**

(c) Explain how the approach adopted by the firm when valuing a minority interest might be influenced by the size of the shareholding or its relative importance to the other shareholdings. **(8 marks)**

(Total: 20 marks)

(ACCA June 93)

58 Old Parcels Ltd

(a) The administrative and legislative burdens which have been imposed on small companies have been the subject of debate for several years. The application of accounting standards to small companies has been the subject of considerable research. It is the view of some accountants that accounting standards should apply to all financial statements whilst others feel that small companies should have a completely different set of accounting standards. In response to the continuing debate in this area, the Accounting Standards Board has issued a Financial Reporting Standard 'Financial Reporting Standard for Smaller Entities'.

Required:

Discuss the main issues in the development of an accounting framework for small companies with reference to the Financial Reporting Standard 'Financial Reporting Standard for Smaller Entities'.

(6 marks)

(b) The directors of the Old Parcels Limited, an unlisted company, have drawn up their financial statements in accordance with the Financial Reporting Standard 'Financial Reporting Standard for Smaller Entities' (FRSSE) for the year ended 31 May 20X8. All exemptions from compliance with accounting standards given to small companies by the FRSSE have been utilised by the company. They have been approached by a publicly quoted company, New Parcels plc, with a view to selling the whole of the share capital of Old Parcels Ltd to this company. New Parcels plc is in the same industry as Old Parcels Ltd and has a Price Earnings ratio of 14. The shares in Old Parcels Ltd are held by one family who have agreed to sell all of the shares to New Parcels plc subject to an independently agreed valuation of the shares. Following the purchase of the shares, the two companies are to be joined together to form a single company.

Financial Information — Old Parcels Ltd
Balance Sheet at 31 May 20X8

	£'000
Fixed Assets	
Intangible asset	12
Tangible assets	278
	290
Current Assets	835
Creditors: amounts falling due within one year	(365)
Net Current Assets	470
Total Assets less Current liabilities	760
Creditors: amounts falling due after more than one year	(119)
Provisions for liabilities and charges	(12)
	629
Capital and Reserves	
Share capital	204
Profit and Loss Account	425
	629

Profits and Dividends 20X4 to 20X9

Year ended 31 May	*Profit/(Loss) on ordinary activities after tax (£)*	*Dividends (include Pref Dividend) declared (£)*	*Preference Share Redemption- Additional finance cost (£)*
20X4	60,000	6,000	-
20X5	66,000	6,500	-
20X6	75,000	8,000	510
20X7	45,000	2,100	554
20X8	(30,000)	Nil	603
20X9 (projected)	35,000	6,200	654

The profit/loss amounts are before dividend payments.

(1) The intangible asset is a license to distribute a product and is estimated to generate net income before tax in the future of £10,000 per annum for the period of the license which expires on 31 May 20Y0. The carrying value in the balance sheet represents the original cost of £20,000 less amortisation and it is estimated that the market value of the license is £15,000.

(2) The tangible fixed assets were revalued on 31 May 20X7 by an independent valuer. The assets are depreciated at 10% per annum. The directors estimate that the market price of the fixed assets has increased by approximately 5% of their current carrying value during the year and that the net realisable value of the assets is £250,000.

(3) The company has an employee share ownership scheme which is run by trustees with rules which prevent transfer of the schemes assets to the company. The assets of the scheme amount to £150,000 at 31 May 20X8 and have not been included in the balance sheet. The costs of the scheme have been charged to the profit and loss account for the year.

(4) The current assets and liabilities are felt to be worth their balance sheet amounts. The creditors falling due after more than one year are 6% Debentures which are repayable at a premium of 25% on 31 May 20X9. The original debenture loan was £100,000. Interest is payable on 31 May of each year and the finance cost has been allocated at a constant rate on the carrying amount.

(5) The provision for liabilities and charges in the accounts of Old Parcels Ltd represents the provision for deferred taxation. The calculation is based on accumulated net timing differences of £52,000. These timing differences are anticipated to rise by £70,000 per annum from 31 May 20X8 until the millennium.

(6) The share capital comprises the following elements:

	£
30,000 7% cumulative redeemable preference shares of £1	33,767
170,000 ordinary shares of £1	170,000
	203,767

There are one year's arrears of preference dividends at 31 May 20X8 included in the above figure for preference shares and the shares are redeemable at 31 May 20Y0 at a premium of 10%. There were no issue costs or premiums paid on the original issue of the preference shares on 1 June 20X5. The share capital is owned by the directors of Old Parcels Ltd. Share options have been granted to certain senior employees and these will be exercised in the event of a sale or stock market flotation of the company if it is financially beneficial. There are options outstanding at 31 May 20X8 to subscribe for 30,000 shares at £1 per share.

(7) The company operates a computer system which will require adjustment for the effects of the new millennium. The costs of a new system would be £100,000 and the cost of adjusting the existing system would be £30,000 as at 31 May 20X8.

(8) During the current financial year, the company discontinued part of its business activities. The operating loss after tax of these activities was £6,000 and the loss on the disposal of the sale of the operation was £3,000. This part of the business normally contributed 20% of the annual post tax profit or loss of Old Parcels Ltd.

(9) The appropriate discount rate to be used in any calculations is a rate of 8% per annum. Corporation Tax is 23%. Assume any future dividend payments are made at the year end.

Required:

Calculate and discuss the range of share values which may be placed on the ordinary shares of Old Parcels Ltd utilising the following methods of valuation:

(i) Net assets valuation (going concern basis) **(11 marks)**

(ii) Earnings based valuation **(8 marks)**

(Total: 25 marks)

(ACCA June 98)

59 Prospect plc

You are an accountant who provides financial planning advice to a range of individual and corporate clients. One of your clients, Mr Green, owns 1,000 shares in Prospect plc, a mining company with a listing on the London Stock Exchange. Prospect plc has interests all over the world through a number of wholly-owned subsidiaries. Extracts from the consolidated financial statements of Prospect plc for the year ended 30 June 20X9 are given below. Mr Green has read these extracts and is dissatisfied with the performance of Prospect plc because profits and dividends have fallen even though turnover has increased. He is wondering whether he should sell his shares in the company.

Extracts from the consolidated financial statements of Prospect plc

Profit and loss accounts for the year ended	*30 June 20X9*	*30 June 20X8*
	£ million	£ million
Turnover (Note 1)	1,300	1,000
Cost of sales	(700)	(450)
Gross profit	600	550
Distribution costs	(100)	(90)
Administrative expenses	(250)	(180)
Operating profit	250	280
Interest payable	(90)	(75)
Profit before taxation (Note 2)	160	205
Taxation	(50)	(60)
Profit after taxation	110	145
Equity dividends	(70)	(80)
Retained profit for the year	40	65
Retained profit brought forward	470	315
Foreign currency translation differences	140	90
Retained profit carried forward	650	470

Balance sheets at	*30 June 20X9*		*30 June 20X8*	
	£ million	£ million	£ million	£ million
Fixed assets:				
Intangible assets (Note 4)	200		100	
Tangible assets	1,100		950	
		1,300		1,050
Current assets:				
Stocks	380		300	
Debtors	460		400	
Cash at bank and in hand	35		35	
	875		735	

Creditors falling due within one year:				
Trade creditors	115		95	
Taxation	50		60	
Proposed dividend	70		80	
Bank overdraft	90		80	
	325		315	
Net current assets		550		420
Creditors falling due after more than one year:				
Loan stock		(1,000)		(800)
		850		670
Capital and reserves:				
Called-up share capital (£1 shares)		100		100
Share premium account		100		100
Profit and loss account		650		470
		850		670

Selected notes to the financial statements:

Note 1 – geographical analysis of turnover:

	Europe		*Africa*		*Far East*		*Total*	
	20X9	*20X8*	*20X9*	*20X8*	*20X9*	*20X8*	*20X9*	*20X8*
	£ million	£ million	£ million	£ million	£ million	£ million	£ million	£ million
Total sales	520	500	390	200	460	360	1,370	1,060
Inter-segment sales	(40)	(35)	(10)	(10)	(20)	(15)	(70)	(60)
Sales to third parties	480	465	380	190	440	345	1,300	1,000

Note 2 – geographical analysis of profit before tax:

	Europe		*Africa*		*Far East*		*Total*	
	20X9	*20X8*	*20X9*	*20X8*	*20X9*	*20X8*	*20X9*	*20X8*
	£ million	£ million	£ million	£ million	£ million	£ million	£ million	£ million
Segment operating profit	70	145	100	55	100	100	270	300
Common costs							(20)	(20)
Group operating profit							250	280
Interest payable							(90)	(75)
Group profit before tax							160	205

Note 3 – geographical analysis of net assets:

	Europe		*Africa*		*Far East*		*Total*	
	20X9	*20X8*	*20X9*	*20X8*	*20X9*	*20X8*	*20X9*	*20X8*
	£ million	£ million	£ million	£ million	£ million	£ million	£ million	£ million
Segment net assets	675	620	540	300	585	500	1,800	1,420
Unallocated assets							50	50
							1,850	1,470

Note 4 – intangible fixed assets

It is group policy to capitalise some direct costs of locating new mineral sources. These costs are amortised over the expected period during which the source will provide economic benefits for the group.

Required:

Write a report to Mr Green which:

- highlights the major reasons for the decline in profits and dividends despite the increase in turnover;
- indicates the other factors which Mr Green may wish to take into account in making a hold or sell decision.

While your report should include some analysis of the segmental data which has been provided in Notes 1 to 3, it is not necessary to compute any financial ratios based on that data. **(Total: 24 marks)**

60 Heavy Goods plc

Heavy Goods plc carries on business as a manufacturer of tractors. In 20X4 the company was looking for acquisitions and carrying out investigations into a number of possible targets. One of these was a competitor, Modern Tractors plc.

The company's acquisition strategy was to acquire companies that were vulnerable to a takeover and in which there was an opportunity to improve asset management and profitability.

The chief accountant of Heavy Goods plc has instructed his assistant to calculate ratios from the financial statements of Modern Tractors plc for the past three years and to prepare a report based on these ratios and the industry average ratios that have been provided by the trade association. The ratios prepared by the assistant accountant and the industry averages for 20X4 are set out below:

Required:

(a) Assuming the role of the Chief Accountant, draft a brief report to be submitted to the managing director based on the ratios of Modern Tractors plc for 20X2–X4 and the industry averages for 20X4. **(12 marks)**

(b) Draft a brief memo to management explaining:

(i) in general terms why the comparison of the 20X4 ratios with the ratios of previous years and other companies might be misleading **(3 marks)**

(ii) how specific ratios might be affected and the possible implications for the evaluation of the report. **(5 marks)**

(Total: 20 marks)
(ACCA Dec 94)

		20X2	20X3	20X4	Industry average 20X4
Sales growth	%	30.00	40.00	9.52	8.25
Sales/total assets		1.83	2.05	1.60	2.43
Sales/net fixed assets		2.94	3.59	2.74	16.85
Sales/working capital		–21.43	–140.00	38.33	10.81
Sales/debtors		37.50	70.00	92.00	16.00
Gross profit/sales	%	18.67	22.62	19.57	23.92
Profit before tax/sales	%	8.00	17.62	11.74	4.06
Profit before interest/interest		6.45	26.57	14.50	4.95
Profit after tax/total assets	%	9.76	27.80	13.24	8.97
Profit after tax/equity	%	57.14	75.00	39.58	28.90
Net fixed assets/total assets	%	62.20	57.07	58.54	19.12
Net fixed assets/equity		3.64	1.54	1.75	0.58
Equity/total assets	%	18.29	37.07	33.45	32.96
Total liabilities/total assets	%	81.71	62.93	66.55	69.00
Total liabilities/equity		4.47	1.70	1.99	2.40
Long-term debt/total assets	%	36.59	18.54	29.27	19.00
Current liabilities/total assets	%	45.12	44.39	37.28	50.00
Current assets/current liabilities		0.84	0.97	1.11	1.63
(Current assets – Stock)/Current liabilities		0.43	0.54	0.72	0.58
Stock/total assets	%	17.07	18.54	14.63	41.90
Cost of sales/stock		8.71	8.55	8.81	4.29
Cost of sales/creditors		6.10	6.25	6.17	12.87
Debtors/total assets	%	4.88	2.93	1.70	18.40
Cash/total assets	%	15.85	21.46	25.08	9.60

Note

Total assets = Fixed assets at net book value + Current assets
Net fixed assets = Fixed assets at net book value.

61 Lewes Holdings plc

Lewes Holdings plc is an international group whose principal activities are the manufacture of air-conditioning systems, the supply of packaging products and automated manufacturing systems. The draft consolidated financial statements for the year ended 31 December 20X4 together with supporting extracts are set out below.

Consolidated profit and loss account of the Lewes Group for the year ended 31 December

		20X4	20X3
	£m	£m	£m
Turnover (Note 1)			
Continuing operations		2,928.6	1,966.3
Acquisitions		453.2	–
		3,381.8	1,966.3
Operating costs		(3,168.7)	(1,843.7)
Operating profit			
Continuing operations	183.2		
Acquisitions	29.9		
		213.1	122.6
Costs of restructuring UK subsidiaries		(18.9)	–

Profit on ordinary activities before interest	194.2	122.6
Income from associated undertakings	6.0	4.6
Interest	(23.9)	(5.6)
Profit on ordinary activities before tax	176.3	121.6
Tax on profit on ordinary activities	(42.4)	(25.4)
Profit on ordinary activities after tax	133.9	96.2
Dividends		
On preference shares	(4.2)	(4.2)
On ordinary shares	(61.1)	(35.0)
Retained profit transferred to reserves	68.6	57.0
EPS	16p	14p

Consolidated balance sheet of the Lewes Group as at 31 December

	20X4 £m	20X3 £m
Fixed assets		
Intangible assets	252.5	0.5
Tangible assets	438.5	277.0
Investments		
Associate	6.7	1.3
Other listed investments	7.4	0.5
	705.1	279.3
Current assets		
Stocks	259.8	129.5
Debtors	966.9	574.7
Investments	31.6	28.5
Cash at bank	165.1	108.7
	1,423.4	841.4
Creditors: Amounts falling due within one year	(1,186.2)	(691.4)
Net current assets	237.2	150.0
Total assets less current liabilities	942.3	429.3
Creditors: Amounts falling due after more than one year	(212.4)	(97.3)
Provisions for liabilities and charges	(36.5)	(6.8)
	693.4	325.2
Capital and reserves		
Called up share capital		
Ordinary shares (20p each)	172.7	148.0
9% Preference shares (£1 each)	47.0	47.0
Share premium account	9.9	9.2
Revaluation reserve	33.5	27.0
Other reserve – distributable	43.9	43.9
Merger reserve	247.4	–
Capital redemption reserve	0.6	0.6
Profit and loss account (Note 2)	138.4	49.5
	693.4	325.2

Notes

(1) Group turnover and profit on ordinary activities before tax

(a) Analysis by geographical area by destination

	20X4		*20X3*	
	Turnover	*Profit*	*Turnover*	*Profit*
	£m	£m	£m	£m
United Kingdom	1,892.3	133.3	1,191.5	137.5
Continental Europe	260.8	21.4	201.9	15.4
North America				
USA	1,002.2	36.9	396.2	(15.3)
Canada	160.1	6.8	121.3	(3.9)
Other areas	66.4	3.5	55.4	3.1
	3,381.8	201.9	1,966.3	136.8
Central items, including interest and investment income		(25.6)		(15.2)
	3,381.8	176.3	1,966.3	121.6

(b) Analysis by class of business

	20X4		*20X3*	
	Turnover	*Profit*	*Turnover*	*Profit*
	£m	£m	£m	£m
Manufacturing	1,041.4	65.5	533.4	60.1
Distribution	489.0	51.0	268.5	34.7
Automated manufacturing systems				
UK and Europe	889.2	48.3	666.7	56.3
North America	962.2	37.1	497.7	(14.3)
	3,381.8	201.9	1,966.3	136.8
Central items, including interest and investment income		(25.6)		(15.2)
	3,381.8	176.3	1,966.3	121.6

(2) Profit and loss account

	£m
Opening balance	49.5
Retained profit for year	68.6
Foreign exchange adjustments	20.3
Profit and loss account	138.4

(3) Goodwill

Goodwill arose on the acquisitions in the year as follows:

	£m
Fair value of consideration	385.4
Fair value of assets (Note 4)	(133.6)
Total goodwill	251.8

(4) Values of assets and liabilities of companies acquired on 1 January 20X4

	£m
Fixed assets	
Intangible assets	0.3
Tangible assets	92.5
	92.8
Current assets	
Stocks	117.8
Debtors	197.0
Cash at bank	23.8
	338.6
Creditors: Amounts falling due within one year	
Bank overdrafts	(35.6)
Other creditors	(245.7)
Net current assets	57.3
Total assets less current liabilities	150.1
Creditors: Amounts falling due after more than one year	(11.4)
Provisions for liabilities and charges	(5.1)
	133.6

Note that no acquisitions in 20X4 have been merger accounted.

Required:

(a) (i) Explain briefly the principal aim of the financial review section of an operating and financial review prepared in accordance with the ASB Statement *Operating and financial review.*

(ii) Explain briefly the matters that should be considered when discussing capital structure and treasury policy. **(5 marks)**

(b) (i) Draft a brief report for an existing shareholder who was concerned that earnings per share in 20X4 had risen by only 14% although turnover had increased by more than 70% and who is considering whether to sell his shareholding in Lewes plc.

(ii) State any additional information arising from a review of the information given in the question that would assist the investor in making a hold or sell decision. **(18 marks)**

(Total: 23 marks)

(ACCA June 95)

62 Bewise plc

Bewise plc had carried on business as a furniture retailer since 1954 operating from a number of stores under short-term annual rental leases. In 20X2 the company extended its product range to include domestic electrical goods. Each store was regarded as a separate profit centre and had authority to agree its own credit terms with customers including the amount of deposit required and the length of the repayment period.

In order to improve the sales per square metre of stores area, it was company policy that all store managers were paid a basic salary plus a commission based on sales.

The profit and loss accounts and balance sheets for the four years ended 31 December 20X5 were as follows (note 20X5's figures are a forecast):

Profit and loss accounts for the years ended 31 December

	20X2	20X3	20X4	20X5
Forecast				
	£m	£m	£m	£m
Turnover	1,706	1,867	2,233	2,512
Cost of sales	(1,138)	(1,257)	(1,519)	(1,731)
Gross profit	568	610	714	781
Administrative expenses	(140)	(163)	(166)	(177)
Selling/distribution costs	(338)	(378)	(461)	(534)
Depreciation	(13)	(14)	(16)	(18)
	77	55	71	52
Investment income	2	2	2	2
Interest paid	(28)	(24)	(30)	(107)
Bad debts			(27)	(28)
Finance income from credit sales	42	45	66	101
Profit before tax	93	78	82	20
Tax	(43)	(35)	(34)	(4)
Profit after tax	50	43	48	16
Dividends	(28)	(28)	(28)	(28)
Profit/(loss) retained	22	15	20	(12)
EPS	59p	51p	56p	19p

Balance sheets as at 31 December

	20X2		20X3		20X4		20X5	
	£m	£m	£m	£m	£m	£m	£m	£m
Fixed assets		82		104		123		136
Investments		32		43		49		59
Stock	351		404		540		609	
Debtors	483		551		633		730	
Cash	47		67		41		63	
		881		1,022		1,214		1,402
		995		1,169		1,386		1,597
Share capital	85		85		85		85	
Reserves	277		292		312		300	
		362		377		397		385
Long-term loans – repayment date 20Y0		62		194		194		323
Creditors	239		277		269		278	
Liability to company's bank								
Short-term loans	135		135		324		324	
Overdraft (unsecured)	197		186		202		287	
		571		598		795		889
		995		1,169		1,386		1,597

The company had an agreed overdraft limit of £240m which was to be reviewed at 31 December 20X5.

Required:

Prepare, as independent accountants, a report to the bank on 30 June 20X5 to assist it in making a decision relating toa requested increase in short-term loans to Bewise plc. The report is to be supported by appropriate financial data.

(20 marks)
(Total: 20 marks)
(ACCA Dec 95)

63 Thermo Ltd

Mike Ried and Jane Thurby were refrigeration engineers who were made redundant in 20X3. Whilst working together they had often discussed the idea of setting up on their own. They believed that there was a niche in the market for the manufacture of low temperature thermometers. Following their redundancy, they agreed to attempt to put their idea into practice.

They prepared a business plan which showed that after start up losses the business would be profitable. They estimated that they would need £350,000 to finance the business. They presented their plan to the bank which agreed to provide an overdraft facility of £175,000 for two years on condition that they raised share capital of £175,000.

A company, Thermo Ltd was formed and commenced trading on 1 July 20X4. It was financed by the issue of 100,000 shares at par value to Mike and Jane and 75,000 shares at par value to their relatives and friends.

The accounts for the period to 31 March are set out below:

Profit and loss account for the period ending 31 March

	20X5	*20X6*
	£	£
Sales	304,500	549,500
Cost of sales	(252,787)	(443,170)
Gross profit	51,713	106,330
Administrative expense	(15,100)	(18,050)
Selling expenses	(36,490)	(39,368)
Operating profit	123	48,912
Interest payable	(3,922)	(18,455)
(Loss)/profit before tax	(3,799)	30,457
Taxation	-	(6,637)
(Loss)/profit after tax	(3,799)	23,820

Balance sheets as at 31 March

	20X5			20X6		
	Cost	*Depreciation*		*Cost*	*Depreciation*	
	£	£	£	£	£	£
Fixed assets						
Premises 105,000	1,600	103,400	105,000	3,200	101,800	
Machinery 87,500	8,750	78,750	122,500	21,000	101,500	
Office furniture	3,500	700	2,800	5,250	1,750	3,500
Motor vehicles	21,000	3,937	17,063	21,000	9,187	11,813
		202,013			218,613	
Current assets						
Stock	47,775			138,375		
Debtors	151,200			190,539		
Prepayments				8,750		
Cash				1,253		
	198,975			338,917		
Current liabilities						
Creditors	(93,445)			(125,675)		
Accruals	(43,775)			(25,962)		
Tax				(5,851)		
Overdraft	(74,567)			(188,235)		
	211,787			345,723		
Net current liabilities			(12,812)			(6,806)
Total assets less current liabilities			189,201			211,807
Provisions for liabilities and charges						
Deferred income: Grants			(18,000)		(16,000)	
Deferred tax					(786)	
					(16,786)	
		171,201			195,021	
Capital and reserves						
Share capital	175,000			175,000		
Profit and loss account		(3,799)			20,021	
		171,201			195,021	

Note: Agreed credit terms were 90 days for collection and payment.

In April 20X5 Mike and Jane presented their first period's draft accounts to the bank. At the meeting the bank manager produced ratios which he used to analyse the year's results during their discussion.
The ratios prepared by the bank for 20X5 were as follows:

Profitability	
Gross profit %	17.00%
Operating profit %	0.04%
Profit before tax %	(1.25%)
Profit after tax %	(1.25%)
Return on share capital and reserves	(2.22%)
Net asset turnover	1.78

Liquidity

Current ratio	0.94
Liquid ratio	0.71
Collection period (days)	136
Stock period (days) based on cost of sales	52
Payment period (days) based on purchases	85

Leverage

Total liabilities/tangible net worth	1.24
Bank debt/tangible net worth	0.43
Profit cover for interest	0.03

It was agreed that Mike and Jane would discuss the position with the bank in May 20X6. At that meeting they proposed to request a restructuring of the bank facility to take the form of a term loan of £200,000 repayable over three years. They were intending to suggest a repayment schedule of £100,000, £50,000 and £50,000 on 31 March 20X7, 31 March 20X8 and 31 March 20X9 respectively.

They produced projected profit and loss accounts and balance sheets for three years as follows:

	20X7	*20X8*	*20X9*
	£'000	£'000	£'000
Sales	670	750	960
Cost of sales	(545)	(600)	(760)
Gross profit	125	150	200
Administrative expenses	(18)	(20)	(21)
Selling expenses	(37)	(40)	(42)
Operating profit	70	90	137
Interest payable	(27)	(14)	(5)
Profit before tax	43	76	132
Taxation	(9)	(20)	(33)
Profit after tax	34	56	99

	20X7		*20X8*		*20X9*	
	£'000	£'000	£'000	£'000	£'000	£'000
Fixed assets		230		230		230
Current assets						
Stock	120		170		190	
Debtors	145		126		200	
Prepayments	10		10		10	
	275		306		400	
Current liabilities						
Creditors	(140)		(150)		(180)	
Accruals	(8)		(9)		(10)	
Tax	(4)		(16)		(27)	
Overdraft	(5)		(5)		(5)	
	(157)		(180)		(222)	
Net current assets		118		126		178

Total assets less current liabilities		348		356		408
Less:						
Term loan	(100)		(50)		-	
Deferred tax	(5)		(9)		(14)	
Deferred income	(14)		(12)		(10)	
		(119)		(71)		(24)
		229		285		384
Share capital		175		175		175
Profit brought forward		20		54		110
Profit for year		34		56		99
		229		285		384

Mike and Jane have asked you, as their accountant, to assist them in drafting a report to the bank, requesting the restructuring of the bank facility. The report to the bank is to be presented in two sections:

(i) a review of the company's performance in the two periods: from incorporation to 31 March 20X5 and from 1 April 20X5 to 31 March 20X6

(ii) the case for the request for restructuring of the bank facility, supported by the projected accounts.

Required:

(a) Draft the first section of the report on the company's performance in the two periods from incorporation to 31 March 20X6 that Mike and Jane are to present to the bank. **(9 marks)**

(b) Draft a report to Mike and Jane commenting on the projected accounts and their request for a restructuring of the bank facility. **(16 marks)**

(Total: 25 marks)

(ACCA June 96)

64 Language-ease Ltd

Language-ease Ltd is a company incorporated by Peter Wong and Daphne Hillier in 1975 to provide English language teaching to foreign students. Peter and Daphne are the directors and each holds 50% of the issued shares. Since 1975 40 colleges have been opened in city centre locations in the UK and abroad. Each college is owned by a separate company of which Peter and Daphne are the directors and shareholders.

Each college has approximately 400 students for 30 weeks per year. Language-ease Ltd employs staff centrally to market the courses at all of the colleges. Peter and Daphne have appointed a different firm of auditors to audit each separate company and there are different dates for the financial year ends.

In 1990 Student-Food Ltd was incorporated to sell food, mainly in long-life packs priced at approximately £5 per pack, to college students either to eat on the premises or to take away. The directors were Peter Wong's son and Daphne Hillier's sister who had previously taught at a college. Each held 30% of the issued share capital with the remaining shares being held by private business investors.

In some of the colleges, Student-Food Ltd sold to the college and the college itself operated the sales outlet; in the other colleges, Student-Food Ltd operated the sales outlet under a license granted by a college whereby it was permitted to rent space on the college premises for a period of eight years from 1 November 1992 at a rental of £1 per square metre; the market rental was £6.50 per square metre. As at 31 October 20X4 the company had fixed assets with a gross cost of £650,000 and a book value of £400,000 consisting of motor vehicles £96,000, storage equipment £200,000 and fixtures and fittings £104,000. The company planned to sell 4 pre-packed units per week to at least 15% of the student population for the year ended 31 October 1995.

In 1995 the company incurred fixed asset expenditure to encourage students to remain on the premises for meals so that the company could achieve its planned sales: by installing a freezer unit costing £5,000 at each college to satisfy health and safety regulations; by installing fittings costing £7,500 per college and storage equipment costing £4,000 per college.

In 1996 it incurred expenditure of £12,500 per college for additional fittings. This fixed asset expenditure was considered to be necessary in order for the company to be able to compete with local city centre restaurants.

The directors considered that the fixed asset expenditure had been successful and they consequently revised their target for 1996 to achieving sales of 4 packs per week to 30% of the student population. On the basis of this estimated increase in turnover, the company undertook further improvements to the college locations. It is company policy not to charge depreciation in the year of acquisition and to charge depreciation in the year of disposal. The bank overdraft and loan increased steadily during 1995 and 1996. Interest of 20% per annum was charged on the bank overdraft. The market rate of interest on loans was 12% per annum.

In 1996 the shareholders decided to dispose of their shares in Student-Food Ltd. The audit of the accounts for the year ended 31 October 1996 was to be completed by January 1997. Extracts from the accounts of Student-Food Ltd for years ended 31 October were as follows:

Profit and Loss Accounts for year ended 31 October

		1994		*1995*		*1996 (draft)*
	£'000	£'000	£'000	£'000	£'000	£'000
Sales		900		1,200		1,240
Gross profit		252		272		320
Less:						
Expenses	66		138		146	
Rent	6		6		6	
Depreciation	60		60		100	
Interest	-		28		84	
		(132)		(232)		(336)
Profit/(Loss) before tax		120		40		(16)
Tax		(28)		(7)		
		92		33		(16)
Dividends		(48)		(36)		
		44		(3)		(16)

Balance sheets as at 31 October

1994		1995		1996 (draft)		
	£'000	£'000	£'000	£'000	£'000	£'000
Ordinary shares of £1 each		400		400		400
Profit and loss account		320		317		301
		720		717		701
Loan				240		760
		720		957		1,461
Fixed assets		400		1,000		1,400

Current assets						
Stock	240		360		400	
Debtors	160		360		480	
Bank	80		-		-	
	480		720		880	
Current liabilities						
Trade creditors	112		431		518	
Expense creditors	48		29		18	
Bank overdraft	-		303		283	
	160		763		819	
Net current assets/ (liabilities)		320		(43)		61
		720		957		1,461

Tan, Wether & Co, a firm of Certified Accountants, was informed by a client, Cold Pack Ltd, that the company was having preliminary discussions to acquire the issued share capital of Student-Food Ltd. Cold Pack Ltd has been following a strategy of growth by acquisition. It has been valuing its acquisitions using a Price Earnings multiple of between 10 and 15 applied to earnings after interest. It has been able to improve results by obtaining better terms from suppliers to the acquired companies through centralised purchasing and increasing the gross profit to 42.5% of sales.

On 25 November 1996 Cold Pack Ltd instructed Tan, Wether & Co to prepare a report based on the accounts of Student-Food Ltd for the 3 years ended 31 October 1996 and to prepare a valuation of the business. The valuation was to take into account Cold Pack Ltd's estimate that Student-Food Ltd could maintain its 1996 level of sales and achieve a gross profit of 42.5% under new management.

Joseph Tan, the partner in Tan, Wether & Co responsible for the assignment, has requested Joyce Asprey, a trainee accountant with the firm, to draft a report and a share valuation.

Required:

(a) Assuming that you are Joyce Asprey,

(i) Comment on the financial position of Student-Food Ltd as at 31 October 1996 and on the changes that have occurred during the three years to that date for inclusion in a report to Cold Pack Ltd. Please include appropriate financial data. **(13 marks)**

(ii) Comment on the action that Cold Pack Ltd might need to take to improve the company's profitability. **(4 marks)**

(b) Assuming that you are Joseph Tan,

Prepare an initial valuation of the shares in Student-Food Ltd based on the information available at 25 November 1996. **(5 marks)**

(Total: 22 marks)

(ACCA Dec 96)

65 Accounting ratios

There has been widespread debate for several years concerning the declining value of traditional methods of measuring corporate performance and the ability to predict corporate failure. Earnings per share, return on capital employed and other investment ratios are seemingly out of step with the needs of investors. The analysis of financial ratios is to a large extent concerned with the efficiency and effectiveness of management's use of resources and also with the financial stability of the company. Researchers have developed models which attempt to predict business failure. Altman's 'Z score', and Argenti's failure model are examples of such research.

However, many analysts feel that financial statements require several adjustments before any meaningful evaluation of corporate performance can be made. Analysts often make amendments to corporate profit and net assets before calculating even the most basic of ratios because of their disapproval of certain generally accepted accounting principles and in an attempt to obtain comparability.

Required:

(a) Evaluate the usefulness of traditional accounting ratios, calculated by reference to published financial statements, in providing adequate information for analysts and investors. **(8 marks)**

(b) Discuss the value and usefulness of the corporate failure prediction models such as those developed by Altman and Argenti. **(8 marks)**

(c) Describe, with reasons, an accounting adjustment which analysts might wish to make to financial statements before evaluating corporate performance in the case of each of the following elements:

(i) [Not reproduced as no longer valid due to technical developments.]
(ii) [Not reproduced as no longer valid due to technical developments.]
(iii) Depreciation

(9 marks)
(Total: 25 marks)
(ACCA June 98)

66 Changeling plc

An assistant accountant of Changeling plc has been requested to prepare a profit and loss account using the CPP model for the year ended 31 March 20X3. He has calculated the net operating profit for the year and the remaining entries are yet to be completed.

The profit and loss accounts for the year ended 31 March 20X3 are set out below, comprising the historic cost profit and loss account and partially completed CPP profit and loss account.

	Historic cost £'000	*Index factor*	*CPP units as at 31.3.X3* 000
Sales	6,500	2,000/1,875	6,933
Opening stock	700	2,000/1,700	824
Purchases	4,250	2,000/1,875	4,533
	4,950		5,357
Closing stock	(900)	2,000/1,937	(929)
	4,050		4,428
Gross profit	2,450		2,505
Expenses	1,150	2,000/1,875	1,227
Depreciation:			
Original equipment	500	2,000/1,025	976
New equipment	50	2,000/1,813	55
Net Operating profit	750		247
Tax	338		
Profit (loss) after tax	412		
Gain(loss) on net monetary assets	-		
Gain(loss) on long-term loans	-		

Net profit (loss) for year	412
Dividends	187
Retained profit (loss) for year	225
Retained profit brought forward	750
Retained profit carried forward	975

The balance sheets as at 31 March 20X2 and 20X3 are set out below

	Historic cost	*Index factor*	*CPP units as at 31.3.X2*	*Index factor*	*CPP units as at 31.3.X3*
	£'000		000		000
Capital	2,500	$\frac{1,750}{950}$	4,605	$\frac{2,000}{1,750}$	5,263
Retained profit	750		1,142		1,305
	3,250		5,747		6,568
Fixed assets					
Equipment	5,000	$\frac{1,750}{1,025}$	8,537	$\frac{2,000}{1,750}$	9,757
Depreciation	(1,500)	$\frac{1,750}{1,025}$	(2,561)	$\frac{2,000}{1,750}$	(2,927)
Current assets					
Stock	700	$\frac{1,750}{1,700}$	721	$\frac{2,000}{1,750}$	824
Debtors	1,050	-	1,050	$\frac{2,000}{1,750}$	1,200
Current liabilities					
Trade creditors	(875)	-	(875)	$\frac{2,000}{1,750}$	(1,000)
Non-current liabilities					
Loan	(1,125)	-	(1,125)	$\frac{2,000}{1,750}$	(1,286)
	3,250		5,747		6,568

Balance sheet as at 31 March 20X3:

	Historic cost £'000	*Index factor*	*CPP units as at 31.3.X3* 000
Capital	2,500	$\frac{2,000}{950}$	5,263
Retained profit	975	-	1,142
	3,475		6,405
Fixed assets			
Equipment	5,000	$\frac{2,000}{1,025}$	9,757
Depreciation	(2,000)	$\frac{2,000}{1,025}$	(3,903)
New equipment	500	$\frac{2,000}{1,813}$	552
Depreciation	(50)	$\frac{2,000}{1,813}$	(55)
Current assets			
Stock	900	$\frac{2,000}{1,938}$	929
Debtors	1,150	-	1,150
Current liabilities			
Trade creditors	(400)	-	(400)
Non-current liabilities			
Loan	(1,625)	-	(1,625)
	3,475		6,405

Assume that inflation index increased evenly through the year ended 31 March 20X3; the tax and dividends were paid on 31 March 19X3, and that the loan was raised at the same time that the additional fixed assets were acquired.

Required:

(a) To calculate the retained profit (loss) for the year using the CPP model for the year ended 31 March 20X3. **(5 marks)**

(b) To explain what the method of indexing is attempting to deal with and discuss the process from the viewpoint of both the entity and the proprietors. **(5 marks)**

(c) To write a brief report to the principal shareholder of Changeling Ltd who holds 20% of the issued share capital on the management of the company commenting on profitability, liquidity and financial structure. **(10 marks)**

(Total: 20 marks)

67 Air Fare plc

Air Fare plc is the subsidiary of an American parent company. It had been incorporated in the United Kingdom in 1985 to provide in-flight packed meals for American airlines on return flights from the United Kingdom.

The fixed assets in the annual accounts have been carried at cost less depreciation but the directors have been considering the production of supplementary statements that are based on current values and show a profit after maintaining the operating capital and also a profit that encompassed gains on holding assets to the extent that these were real gains after allowing for general/average inflation.

The following information (1) to (6) was available when preparing the supplementary statements for the year ended 31 December 20X3.

(1) Draft profit and loss account for the year ended 31 December 20X3 prepared under the historic cost convention.

	£'000
Sales	11,441
Cost of sales	10,292
	1,149
Loan interest	625
	524
Tax	124
	400
Less: Proposed dividend	100
	300

(2) The current cost values of the net assets representing shareholders' funds was £25m at 1 January 20X3.

(3) Freehold premises had cost £8m in 1985 and were being depreciated over 40 years which was the group policy specified by the American parent. The current gross replacement cost was £14m at 31 December 20X3 and £13.8m at 1 January 20X3.

Equipment had cost £12m in 20X1 and was being depreciated over 15 years. The gross replacement cost was £12.6m at 31 December 20X3 and £12.5m at 1 January 20X3.

(4) The cost of sales had increased by £412,000 during the year due to price increases. The costs and price increases occurred evenly during the year.

(5) The retail price index had risen by 3% during the year.

(6) Stock at the beginning of the year was £660,000 at cost and £670,000 at current replacement cost and stock at the end of the year was £750,000 at cost and £795,000 at current replacement cost.

The following information relates to a consideration not to provide for depreciation on the freehold property.

The freehold property consisted of the premises where the meals were prepared and packed. When the directors were reviewing the information prepared for the current value supplementary statements, they noted that the current value of the freehold property exceeded the book value and decided that it was appropriate not to provide for depreciation.

The chief accountant advised them that it was probable that the auditor would qualify the accounts if depreciation were not provided in accordance with the provisions of FRS 15 *Tangible fixed assets*.

The directors had been discussing the problem over lunch at the local hotel and were surprised when the owner of the hotel informed them that the auditor of the company that owned the hotel had not required depreciation to be provided on the hotel premises. Further enquiry by the directors established that there were a number of companies that were not providing depreciation on freehold properties from a range of industries that included hotels, retail shops and banks. They even discovered that the Financial Reporting Review Panel had accepted one company's policy on non-depreciation of freehold buildings in respect of the accounts of Forte plc. They had therefore formed the view that non-depreciation was acceptable provided the auditors were offered and accepted the company's reasons.

They accordingly requested the chief accountant to prepare a brief report for the board of reasons to support a decision by the company to adopt an accounting policy of non-depreciation which they could subsequently discuss with the auditors.

Required:

(a) (i) Prepare a profit and loss account that shows a result after maintaining the operating capital and also a result that encompasses the gains for the year on holding assets to the extent that these are real gains after allowing for inflation.

(ii) Write a brief memo to the directors explaining the results disclosed in the profit and loss account prepared in (i). **(10 marks)**

(b) As chief accountant, prepare a brief report for the board giving reasons to support a decision by the company to adopt an accounting policy of non-depreciation of the freehold property.

(10 marks)
(Total: 20 marks)
(ACCA June 94)

68 Measurement systems

There are several measurement systems which can be used in accounting. The most important single characteristic which distinguishes them is whether they are based on historical cost or current value. A further related issue is that of general price changes which affect the significance of reported profits and the ownership interest. It is often stated that a measurement system based on current values is superior to one based on historical cost and that accounting practice should develop by greater utilisation of current values. Current value systems can utilise replacement cost accounting and net realisable value techniques which use entry and exit values respectively. If general inflation is a problem, it is possible to eliminate the effect by producing a 'real terms' measure of total gains and losses, where a current value system of accounting is adjusted for the effects of changes in current purchasing power (CPP).

Required:

(a) Describe the problems associated with replacement cost accounting and net realisable value accounting when used as an alternative to historical cost accounting. **(7 marks)**

(b) The following summary financial statements relate to AB, a public limited company, for its first year of trading to 30 November 20X8:

Profit and loss account

	£m
Turnover	4,500
Cost of sales (including depreciation)	(3,000)
Gross profit	1,500
Distribution and administrative expenses	(500)
Profit before taxation	1,000
Taxation	(300)
Profit after taxation	700

Balance sheet

	£m
Fixed assets (net of depreciation £600m)	2,000
Current assets	
Stock	1,200
Debtors	2,400
Cash	300
	3,900
Creditors: amounts falling due within one year	(1,200)
Net current assets	2,700
Creditors: amounts falling due after more than one year	(1,500)
	3,200
Capital and reserves	
Share capital	2,500
Reserves	700
	3,200

The company has decided to adjust its financial statements for the impact of changing prices and has generated the following information to assist in these adjustments for the period.

		£m
Turnover	– amount in terms of current purchasing power (CPP)	4,950
Cost of sales	– cost of goods sold in terms of CPP	3,300
	– current cost of goods sold	3,750
Distribution & administrative expenses	– historical cost in terms of CPP	550
Depreciation	– cost of depreciation in terms of CPP	660
	– current cost depreciation	720
Gain on loan (CPP)		20
Monetary working capital adjustment		400
Gearing adjustment		423
Stock – current value		1,600
– in terms of CPP		1,320
Fixed Assets – current value (replacement cost)		3,120
– in terms of CPP before depreciation		2,860

Assume a rate of inflation of 20% per annum

Prepare a balance sheet as at 30 November 20X8 and a profit and loss account for the year ended 30 November 20X8 showing the impact of changing prices for each of the following models:

(i) Current purchasing power accounting (CPP) **(7 marks)**

(ii) Current cost accounting incorporating a gearing adjustment. **(6 marks)**

(c) Describe the principal features of a 'Real Terms' system of accounting for inflation by reference to the financial statements of AB in part (b) of this question. **(5 marks)**

(Total: 25 marks)

(ACCA Dec 98)

69 CIC plc

CIC plc is a multinational chemical company that is registered in the United Kingdom and quoted on the London Stock Exchange.

The company is a member of an inter-company comparison scheme for companies that operate in the United Kingdom and it receives an annual comparison report including information such as returns on capital employed, returns on investment, asset utilisation and liquidity. The information relates to CIC plc and 32 other chemical companies that operate in the United Kingdom market. However, the directors are not finding the report as useful as they wished because CIC plc has over 90% of the United Kingdom market and the other 32 companies are United Kingdom registered marketing subsidiaries of major multinational companies which are based in other countries such as America, France, Germany, Italy, Japan and South America.

They have requested the accountant to produce an inter-company comparison report based on the statements of the other multinational companies rather than on the financial statements of the marketing subsidiaries and also to advise them of any problems that may arise in extracting and interpreting ratios from the consolidated financial statements of foreign multinational competitors.

Required:

(a) to draft a memorandum to the directors to explain the problems that may arise in:

- collecting the relevant data
- interpreting the data when it has been prepared to satisfy different disclosure requirements
- interpreting the data when there may be differing attitudes to financing and risk
- interpreting the data when there may have been differing user requirements.

(10 marks)

(b) to comment on the suggestion that all countries should abandon their domestic accounting standards and follow standards laid down by the International Accounting Standards Committee. **(5 marks)**

(Total: 15 marks)

(ACCA June 91)

70 AHS SA

You are the Chief Accountant of XYZ plc. The Managing Director has provided you with the financial statements of XYZ plc's main competitor, AHS SA, a French company. He finds difficulty in reviewing these statements in their non-UK format, presented below.

AHS SA - Balance sheet at 31 March 20X5 (in FFr million)

	31.03.X5	31.03.X4		31.03.X5	31.03.X4
Assets				**Capital and liabilities**	
Tangible fixed assets				Capital & reserves	
Land	1,000	750	Share capital	850	750
Buildings				750	500
	Share premium		100	-	
Plant	200	150	Legal reserve	200	200
			Profit & loss b/fwd	590	300
	1,950	1,400	Profit & loss for year	185	290
			Net worth	1,925	1,540
Current assets					
Stock	150	120			
Trade debtors		180	100	Creditors	
Cash	20	200	Trade creditors	170	150
			Taxation	180	150
	350	420	Other creditors	75	50
				425	350
Prepayments and accrued income					
Prepayments		50	70		
	2,350	1,890		2,350	1,890

AHS SA - Income statement for the year ended 31 March 20X5 (in FFr million)

	20X5	20X4		20X5	20X4
Expenses			**Income**		
Operating expenses:			Operating income:		
Purchase of raw materials	740	400	Sale of goods produced	1,890	1,270
Variation in stocks thereof	90	40	Variation in stock of		
Taxation 190	125		finished goods & WIP 120	80	
Wages 500	285		Other operating income	75	50
Valuation adjustment on					
fixed assets:			Total operating income 2,085	1,400	
Depreciation	200	150			
Valuation adjustment on					
current assets:					
Amounts written off	30	20			
Other operating expenses	50	40			
Total operating expenses	1,800	1,060			
Financial expenses:					
Interest	100	50			
Total financial expenses	100	50			
Total expenses	1,900	1,110	**Total income**	2,085	1,400
Balance - Profit	185	290			
Sum total 2,085	1,400		2,085	1,400	

Required:

Prepare a report for the managing director,

(a) analysing the performance of AHS SA using the financial statements provided. **(20 marks)**

(b) explaining why a direct comparison of the results of XYZ plc and AHS SA may be misleading. **(10 marks)**

(Total: 30 marks)

71 Badgo plc

You are Chief Accountant of Badgo plc, a company with subsidiaries all over the world. The draft consolidated financial statements of the group for the year ended 31 December 20X9 are given below.

Consolidated profit and loss account for The year ended December

	20X9 *£ million*	*20X8* *£ million*
Turnover	2,000	1,900
Cost of sales	(1,400)	(1,330)
Gross profit	600	570
Other operating expenses	(400)	(300)
Share of operating profit of associate	35	-
Operating profit	235	270
Investment income	-	4
Interest payable	(65)	(50)
Profit before taxation	170	224
Taxation		(53) (69)
Profit after taxation	117	155
Dividends	(60)	(80)
Retained profit	57	75

Consolidated statement of total recognised
Gains and losses for the year ended 31 December

	20X9	20X8
	£ million	£ million
Profit for the financial year	117	155
Currency translation difference on foreign currency		
Net investments	5	(4)
Total gains and losses for the year	122	151

Consolidated balance sheet
At 31 December

	20X9		20X8	
	£ million	£ million	£ million	£ million
Fixed assets				
Intangible assets	4		5	
Tangible assets	380		360	
Investments (see note)	400		-	
		784		365
Current assets				
Stocks	235		222	
Debtors	300		285	
Short-term investments	-		100	
Cash in hand and at bank	1		1	
	536		608	
Current liabilities				
Trade creditors	135		128	
Taxation	53		69	
Proposed dividends	60		80	
Bank overdraft	170		80	
	418		357	
Net current assets		118		251
Long-term loans		(181)		(157)
		721		459
Capital and reserves				
Called-up share capital (£1 shares)		300		200
Share premium account		100		-
Profit and loss account		321		259
		721		459

Note – investment in associate:

During the year the group invested in 35% of the equity share capital of Stateside Inc, a company incorporated in the United States of America. No other investments appear in the consolidated balance sheet.

Required:

A Non-Executive Director has recently received a copy of the draft consolidated financial statements. His attendance at Board meetings has been irregular over the last year and he plays no part in the day-to-day running of the group. He has sent you a memorandum that contains a number of questions and asks you to draft a reply. The questions are as follows:

(a) We have raised more money from our shareholders this year and our turnover has gone up. Even so, profit and dividends have fallen. How do you explain this? **(8 marks)**

(b) I don't understand why the retained profit for the year is £57 million when the balance of retained profits shown in the balance sheet has increased by a different amount. Is this a mistake? **(5 marks)**

(c) I am pleased to see that we made an investment in Stateside this year. I was told we paid £380 million for it but it's in the consolidated balance sheet at £400 million. Why is this? Have we paid for it out of the money we raised from our shareholders this year? **(6 marks)**

(d) A few weeks ago I saw a set of account for Stateside Inc that had been sent over by their accountants. The accounts were drawn up in US $. They showed that the company had made a loss in the year ended 31 December 20X9. We have shown our share of Stateside's results in our accounts as a profit. I know the results have to be translated into £ before we can consolidate them but I don't see how this process can turn a loss into a profit. Have we made a mistake? **(6 marks)**

(Total: 25 marks)

72 Stateside plc

(a) Discuss the potential benefits of greater harmonisation of international accounting policies and disclosure requirements, and comment on the obstacles hindering its progress.

(6 marks)

(b) (i) Explain why you think each of the adjustments has been made in the statement for Stateside plc reconciling UK to US GAAP as at 31 May20X5:

Income statement adjustments

	£m
Net profit per UK GAAP	100
US GAAP Adjustments (assumed net of tax)	
Capitalised interest amortised	(5)
Elimination of results prior to merger	(150)
Acquisition accounting – additional depreciation and amortisation of goodwill	(200)
Estimated reported loss as adjusted to accord with US GAAP	(255)

(ii) Explain whether the equity as reported per UK GAAP will be increased or decreased when reconciled to the equity as adjusted to accord with US GAAP for the items in (b)(i).

(iii) Explain the effect on the equity of a proposed final dividend which under US GAAP has to be included in the year in which the directors propose to pay the dividends. **(9 marks)**

(c) Assuming that the fixed assets were revalued from £20m to £30m on 1 June 20X3 at which date they had a remaining life of 10 years and disposed of for £40m on 31 May 20X5.

(i) Show the accounting treatment in the accounts for 20X4 and 20X5 of the revaluation and disposal of fixed assets in accordance with FRS 3 (note that a full year's depreciation is charged in 20X4 and 20X5)

(ii) Explain the reasons why the ASB required such accounting treatment. **(5 marks)**

(Total: 20 marks)

(ACCA June 95)

73 Morgan plc

Morgan plc is considering the acquisition of one of two companies. Their investment advisers have prepared a report on the acquisition of the companies, one of which is situated in the United Kingdom, UK Group plc, the other is situated overseas. The overseas company, Overseas Group Inc prepares its financial statements in accordance with local accounting standards. The following financial ratios had been prepared for discussion at a board meeting of Morgan plc based on the financial statements for the year ending 31 May 20X7.

	UK Group plc	*Overseas Group Inc*
Current ratio - $\frac{\text{Current assets}}{\text{Current liabilities}}$	1.75 to 1	1.2 to 1
Stock turnover - $\frac{\text{Cost of goods sold}}{\text{Closing stock}}$	6.5 times	2.6 times
Debtors collection period - $\frac{\text{Closing debtors}}{\text{Sales per day}}$	41.7 days	85.5 days
Interest cover - $\frac{\text{Earnings before interest and tax}}{\text{Interest charges}}$	6 times	1.8 times
Profit margin - $\frac{\text{Net profit before tax}}{\text{Sales}}$	5.4%	0.6%
Return on total assets - $\frac{\text{Earnings before interest and tax}}{\text{Total assets}}$	7.4%	0.8%
Return on net worth - $\frac{\text{Net profit before tax}}{\text{Shareholders funds (including minority interests)}}$	12.2%	1.6%
Gearing ratio - $\frac{\text{Total long - term debt}}{\text{Total assets}}$	27.7%	43.3%
Price earnings ratio - $\frac{\text{Market price per share}}{\text{Earnings per share}}$	15	81.6

The financial statements of Overseas Group Inc are as follows:

Consolidated profit and loss account for year ending 31 May 20X7

		$'000
Sales		132,495
Operating costs (see below)		(130,655)
Operating profit		1,840
Interest		(1,020)
Profit before tax		820
Income taxes		(200)
Profit after tax		620
Minority interests		(80)
Net profit for the year before extraordinary item		540
Extraordinary profit	72	
Taxation	(18)	
		54
Net profit		594

Note: Operating costs comprise cost of goods sold of $110,100,000 and other expenses of $20,555,000.

Consolidated balance sheet at 31 May 20X7

	$'000
Assets	
Current assets	
Cash and deposits	22,230
Debtors	31,050
Stock	42,020
	95,300
Long-term assets	135,200
Total assets	230,500
Liabilities and shareholders equity	
Current liabilities	79,400
Long-term liabilities	99,700
Minority interests in subsidiaries	8,200
Shareholders equity	
Ordinary shares	30,000
Retained earnings	13,200
	43,200
Total liabilities and shareholders equity	230,500

At the board meeting the financial director questioned the validity of the financial ratios in view of the differences in the accounting practices of the UK and Overseas countries. She requested that the ratios be recalculated on a common basis using UK Generally Accepted Accounting Practice. The following information is relevant to these calculations.

(i) Overseas Inc had purchased a 60% holding in a subsidiary on 1 June 20X6. For accounting purposes the purchase consideration was taken as $10 million to be satisfied by the issue of 8 million ordinary shares of $1 and $2 million in cash. Overseas Inc's shares were valued at $2 each on 1 June 20X6. If the subsidiary makes profits in excess of the profit for the year ended 31 May 20X7 in the financial year to 31 May 20X8, then a further cash sum of $200,000 is payable on 1 June 20X8. Preliminary indications suggest that the subsidiary will exceed this target profit.

(ii) Overseas Inc had taken account of the above transaction by proportionately reducing the fixed assets of the subsidiary by the negative goodwill figure of $2 million which was calculated by using the book value of the net assets acquired of $20 million. The fair value of the net assets of the subsidiary at the date of acquisition was $25 million. The difference between the book value and fair value of the assets comprised the increase in the value of buildings which are depreciated at 2% per annum on cost. No adjustment to the depreciation charge is required for the treatment of negative goodwill. The current borrowing cost in the overseas country is 10%. UK plc capitalises goodwill and amortises it through the profit and loss account over five years.

(iii) Overseas Inc had capitalised the costs of developing computer software products totalling $1 million incurred in 20X7. The product's first revenues were received in the year to 31 May 20X7 and were expected to have an economic life of four years. Overseas Inc amortises such costs based on the economic life of the product. UK plc charges all such costs in the year in which they are incurred.

(iv) Overseas Inc has a share option scheme under which options are granted to certain directors. On 1 December 20X6 100,000 ordinary shares were allotted for $175,000 upon the exercise of options. The company had accounted for the full market price of $250,000 of the shares with the discount on the share price being treated by Overseas Inc as directors' remuneration. Additionally the company had included an employee share ownership trust in its balance sheet at a cost of $7 million. The assets of the trust had been deducted from the reserves of Overseas Inc.

(v) The share capital of UK plc is 50 million ordinary shares of £1 and of Overseas Inc 30 million shares of $1 at 31 May 20X7. The earnings per share calculation used in the Price Earnings ratio calculations had utilised the above share capital figures. The market price of Overseas Inc's shares at 31 May 20X7 was $1.47.

(vi) The extraordinary item in the profit and loss account of Overseas Inc is the profit on the repayment of long-term debt in the accounts of a subsidiary.

(vii) Part of the stock of Overseas Inc has been valued at market value. Overseas Inc does not trade in commodities but purchases precious metals which it uses in the production process. The stock of these precious metals and related values are as follows:

	Market value	*Cost*
	$'000	$'000
Year end 31 May 20X6	30,000	21,000
Year end 31 May 20X7	10,000	7,500

There is no tax impact of any change in policy regarding stock. Because of the poor quality of the initial report by the investment analyst, the financial director has asked the auditor to prepare another report on the potential acquisition taking into account the above factors.

Required:

(a) Recalculate the financial ratios of Overseas Inc so that they can be compared to UK plc's ratios. (Candidates should describe the reasons for the adjustments to the financial statements of Overseas Inc.) **(16 marks)**

(b) Discuss the implications of the revision of the financial ratios on the decision to acquire UK plc or Overseas Inc. **(5 marks)**

(c) Explain what considerations other than differences in accounting practice should be taken into account when analysing the financial ratios of an overseas company, such as Overseas Inc. **(5 marks)**

(Total: 26 marks)

(ACCA June 97)

(All workings should be to the nearest thousand units of currency.)

74 Pailing

(a) There is a wide variety of accounting practices adopted in different countries and it seems that no two countries have identical accounting systems. At present overseas companies preparing financial statements utilising International Accounting Standards (IAS) can obtain a listing on the London Stock Exchange. However, UK companies cannot use IAS to obtain an equivalent listing but have to use UK Generally Accepted Accounting Practice ('UK GAAP'). Many UK companies feel that there are several advantages in preparing financial statements in accordance with IAS which outweigh the disadvantages of changing from UK GAAP.

Required:

(i) Describe the main reason why multi-national companies might wish International Accounting Standards to be adopted as the only standards of accounting **(6 marks)**

(ii) Describe the problems with International Accounting Standards which may act as a barrier to their widespread acceptance. **(7 marks)**

(b) Pailing, a public limited company, is a company registered in Europe. Under the local legislation, it is allowed to prepare its financial statements using International Accounting Standards (IAS) and local GAAP. Klese, a UK registered company, is considering buying the company but wishes to restate Pailing's group financial statements so that they are consistent with UK GAAP before any decision is made, as the company is also considering the purchase of a UK company.

The Pailing group's net profit for the period drawn up utilising IAS and local GAAP is £89 million for the year ending 31 March 20X0, and its group capital and reserves under IAS and local GAAP is £225 million as at 31 March 20X0.

The following accounting practices under IAS and local GAAP have been determined.

(1) A change in accounting policies has been dealt with by a cumulative catch up adjustment which is included in the current year's income. During the year, depreciation on buildings was charged for the first time. The total cumulative depreciation charge for the buildings was computed at £30 million, of which £3 million relates to the current year.

(2) Pailing had acquired a subsidiary company, Odd, on 31 March 20X0. The minority interest (25%) and related assets stated in the balance sheet were based on the carrying value of the net assets of the subsidiary before any fair value adjustments. Pailing's interest was based on fair values. The fair value and the carrying value of the net assets of Odd at the date of acquisition were £28 million and £24 million respectively.

(3) Pailing had paid £16 million for the subsidiary, Odd, on 31 March 20X0. The payment reflected the fact that Odd was likely to make losses in the current year and it had recognised all of the negative goodwill in the profit and loss account in the current year. Klese does not carry any trading stock and writes off its non-monetary assets on average over a five year period. The fair value of the non-monetary assets is £7 million.

(4) Pailing had sold a 100% owned overseas subsidiary on 1 April 20W9 for £40 million, resulting in a gain on sale of £8 million when comparing the sale proceeds with the cost of the investment. Pailing had excluded all of the results of the subsidiary from its financial statements other than reporting the gain on sale of £8 million in its group profit and loss account for the year. The net asset value of the subsidiary at the date of sale was £36 million. The cumulative exchange gain held in the Group Exchange Reserve was £3 million on 31 March 20W9 and this was transferred to the group profit and loss account together with the gain on sale of £8 million. There was no goodwill arising on the original purchase of the subsidiary.

Required:

(i) Restate the net profit for the year ending 31 March 20X0 and the capital and reserves of Pailing as at 31 March 20X0 in accordance with UK GAAP. **(9 marks)**

(ii) Briefly, state the effect that the restatement of Pailing's financial statements might have on the decision to purchase the company. **(3 marks)**

(Total: 25 marks)

(ACCA June 00)

75 Daxon plc

Daxon plc is a listed company that carries on business as a book wholesaler. In the financial year ended 31 October 20X5, the growth in sales turnover to £25m has continued to match the rate of inflation; costs have been contained by reducing staff from 96 to 90; the asset turnover rate has been maintained at five times.

The Daxon plc accountant has prepared draft accounts for the year ended 31 October 20X5, and included the following directors' responsibilities statement:

'The directors are required by UK company law to prepare financial statements for each financial period which give a true and fair view of the state of affairs of the group as at the end of the financial period and of the profit and loss for that period. In preparing the financial statements, suitable accounting policies have been used and applied consistently, and reasonable and prudent judgements and estimates have been made. Applicable accounting standards have been followed. The directors are also responsible for maintaining adequate accounting records, for safeguarding the assets of the group, and for preventing and detecting fraud and other irregularities.'

On receiving the statement, one of Daxon plc's directors commented that the statement included aspects that he had always assumed were the responsibility of the auditor and complained about the apparent proliferation of irrelevant new rules.

He requested that the accountant should prepare a memo for the board to explain certain of the items.

Required:

(a) Assuming that you are the accountant of Daxon plc, draft a memo to the board of directors explaining:

(i) The background to the inclusion in the annual report of a directors' responsibilities statement. **(6 marks)**

(ii) What is meant by true and fair and how the board can determine whether the financial statements give a true and fair view. **(5 marks)**

(iii) [Not reproduced as this part is no longer within the syllabus.] **(5 marks)**

(b) Discuss the proposal that Daxon plc should be exempt from the requirement to apply some or all accounting standards on the grounds that it is a relatively small company. **(4 marks)**

(Total: 20 marks)

(ACCA Dec 95)

Section 8

ANSWERS TO PRACTICE QUESTIONS

1 FSR Group

(a) (i) The Companies Act contains permissive exclusions and a required exclusion. One of the permissive exclusions in S229 is where the parent company interest is exclusively with a view to subsequent resale and the undertaking has not previously been included in consolidated group accounts by the parent company.

Depending on the parent company's choice, the investment might be dealt with by consolidation or by treating it as a current asset valued at the lower of cost and net realisable value.

(ii) FRS 2 'Accounting for Subsidiary Undertakings' issued by the ASB in 1992 recognises that the Act permits exclusion if the group's interest is held exclusively with a view to a subsequent resale but goes further by requiring exclusion in para 25b.

FRS 2 para 29 stipulates that subsidiaries excluded from consolidation because they are held for resale are to be included as current assets at the lower of cost and net realisable value.

The reasoning followed by the ASB FRS 2 para 79b in requiring the subsidiary to be treated as an investment in the consolidated accounts was that such an undertaking did not form part of the continuing activities of the group and the control was not used to deploy the underlying assets and liabilities of the subsidiary as part of the continuing group's activities for the benefit of the parent company. The valuation at the lower of cost and net realisable value recognises the temporary nature of the parent company's interest.

(b) (i) FRS 2 para 39 requires the elimination of profits relating to intra-group transactions by setting against the interests held by the group and the minority interest in respective proportion to their holdings in the undertaking whose individual financial statements recorded the eliminated profits.

This means that the stock sold by GBH plc must be reduced to a cost figure of £200,000 and the minority interest will be reduced by £5,000.

The elimination of £12,000 on the stock sold by FSR plc was correctly treated.

(ii) FRS 2 para 38 provides that the assets and liabilities of a subsidiary undertaking should be attributable to the minority on the same basis as those attributable to the interests held by the parent. However, goodwill arising on acquisition should only be recognised with respect to the part of the subsidiary undertaking that is attributable to the interest held by the parent and its other subsidiary undertakings. No goodwill should be attributed to the minority.

(iii) The profit on the sale by Short plc need not be eliminated because Short plc is not to be consolidated under the exclusion provision of FRS 2 para 25b if it is assumed that the investment in Short plc is an interest held exclusively with a view to a subsequent resale.

That means obtaining additional information that a purchaser has been identified or is being sought; that there is a reasonable expectation that the investment will be disposed of within approximately one year of its date of acquisition; and Short plc has not previously been consolidated by FSR.

This means ascertaining the date of acquisition and intended disposal and whether Short plc has been previously consolidated.

The situation would be different if the non-consolidation arose because the subsidiary was excluded on the basis of its different activities in that elimination would be required.

(c) (i) The reason for the elimination of the £20,000 from the stock held by FSR plc is that the accounts are presented from a group perspective as a single entity. No increase or decrease has occurred in the group's net assets as a result of the transfer of stock from GBH plc to FSR plc. In addition transactions between undertakings included within the consolidation are wholly within the control of the parent company, even though they may not be wholly owned.

The profit has been realised as far as the minority interest are concerned and will properly appear in the accounts of GBH plc but the transaction has not changed the net assets under the parent's control.

(ii) The reasoning is that the effect of the existence of minority interests on the returns to investors in the parent undertaking is best reflected by presenting the net identifiable assets attributable to minority interests on the same basis as those attributable to group interests.

The goodwill treatment on an entity basis requires the extrapolation of an amount for goodwill attributable to the whole entity. The Explanatory Notes para 82 states that the resulting figure is however hypothetical because the minority is not a party to the transaction by which the subsidiary is acquired.

In addition the goodwill might be a valuation attaching to the obtaining of control rather than a pro rata value attaching to each share in the subsidiary company.

(iii) The Explanatory Notes to FRS 2 state that profit arising on a sale effected by a subsidiary undertaking excluded on the basis that it is held exclusively with a view to sale need not be eliminated.

It then goes on to say that it is, however, important to consider whether it is prudent to record any profits arising from transactions in these circumstances.

How can a judgement be made as to whether it is prudent? The implication is that the ASB wish to raise a flag that although the profit need not normally be eliminated there may be circumstances where this should happen. If the transactions were presented in a manner that led to a reader misinterpreting the consolidated accounts they would presumably be regarded as failing to satisfy the true and fair test. The implication in the Explanatory Notes to FRS 2 is that there should be vigilance to possible risks. The ASB's *Statement of Principles* explains that the exercise of prudence results in a degree of caution under conditions of uncertainty.

2 Complex plc

MEMORANDUM

To: Assistant Accountant

From: Chief Accountant

Subject: Complex transactions **Date:** 24 November 20X9

Thank you for your memorandum outlining the key elements of two transactions. I would like to recommend some changes to your proposed treatments and I explain these changes below.

Transaction 1

In your workings, the fair values of the net assets of Easy Ltd acquired on 1 March 20X9 include a provision for reorganisation costs of £4 million. FRS 7 Fair values in acquisition accounting states that provisions for reorganisation costs expected to be incurred as a result of an acquisition are post-acquisition items and should not affect fair values at the date of acquisition. It seems clear that the costs of the group reorganisation fall into this category and therefore should not be included in the goodwill calculation. The provision should be reversed and the reorganisation costs should be charged to the profit and loss account for the year.

The purchased goodwill that you have recognised on the acquisition includes goodwill relating to the minority interests. This is incorrect. The minority interest recognised in the balance sheet consists of the minority's share of the net assets and liabilities of the subsidiary at the balance sheet date. FRS 2 *Accounting for subsidiary undertakings* states that goodwill arising on acquisition should only be recognised with respect to that part of the subsidiary undertaking that is attributable to the interest held by the parent. No goodwill should be attributed to the minority interest. The minority interests were not a party to the purchase of the subsidiary and therefore the amount of any goodwill attributable to them is hypothetical.

Therefore the goodwill on the acquisition of Easy Ltd is calculated as follows:

	£m
Fair value of investment	60
Less: group share of fair value of net assets acquired (75% × 72)	(54)
	6

Transaction 2

FRS 2 *Accounting for subsidiary undertakings* states that profits or losses on the disposal of subsidiary undertakings should be calculated as the proceeds received less the carrying amount of the subsidiary's net assets attributable to the group's interest before cessation. However, it also states that the net assets should include any related goodwill that has not previously been written off through the profit and loss account. Therefore the loss on disposal should be calculated as follows:

	£m	£m
Sales proceeds		15
Less: net assets at the date of disposal	25	
Goodwill not previously written off	5	
		(30)
Loss on disposal		(15)

The loss on disposal will be shown as an exceptional item on the face of the profit and loss account. However, Redundant Ltd does not meet the definition of a discontinued operation in FRS 3 *Reporting financial performance*. Although its results are clearly identifiable and the disposal has taken place, the group has reorganised the retail distribution of its products and the overall output of the group has not been significantly affected. For the disposal to be a discontinued operation, FRS 3 also requires that it should have a material effect on the nature and focus of the group's operations and that it should represent a material reduction in its operating facilities resulting either from its withdrawal from a particular market or from a material reduction in turnover in continuing markets. It does not appear that these criteria have been met and therefore the disposal (and the operating results of Redundant Ltd for the period up to the disposal) must be included in continuing operations.

3 Exotic Group

Key answer tips

Read the requirement carefully. Part (a) concerns the main group; part (b) concerns the discontinued operation. You are not required to include Madeira (the discontinued operation) in the consolidated financial statements in part (a).

The requirement for part (b) was to show how Madeira would appear in the financial statements. This answer shows both the accounting entries in the profit and loss account and the actual presentation required by FRS 3 Example Format 1. It would also have been possible to use Example Format 2.

(a) (i)

Consolidated profit and loss account of the Exotic Group for the year ended 31 December 20X4

	£'000	£'000
Turnover		92,120
Cost of sales	(27,915)	
Gross profit	64,205	
Distribution costs	(7,362)	
Administrative expenses		(6,325)
Operating profit	50,518	
Interest	(325)	
Profit on ordinary activities before tax		50,193
Taxation		(17,931)
Profit on ordinary activities after tax		32,262
Minority interest	(3,714)	
Profit available for distribution		28,548
Dividends proposed		(9,500)
Retained profit for the year		19,048
Retained profits brought forward		
Exotic plc	20,013	
Melon plc	10,701	
Kiwi plc	6,846	
		37,560
		56,608

(ii)

Consolidated balance sheet for the Exotic Group as at 31 December 20X4

	£'000
Fixed assets	72,787
Current assets	19,446
Current liabilities	(23,134)
Minority interest	(8,454)
	60,645
Share capital and reserves	
Ordinary shares	8,000
Profit and loss account (56,608,000 – 2,667,000 – 1,296,000)	52,645
	60,645

Workings For Consolidated Profit And Loss Account

	Exotic plc £'000	Melon plc £'000	Kiwi plc £'000		(Dr)/Cr £'000	CPL £'000
Turnover	45,600	24,700	22,800	**(a)**	(740)	
				(c)	(240)	92,120
Cost of sales	(18,050)	(5,463)	(5,320)	**(a)**	740	
				(c)	200	(27,893)
Provision/stock		(15)	(15)	**(b)**		(30)
Depreciation adjustment		8		**(d)**		8
Gross profit	27,510	19,230	17,465			64,205
Distribution costs	3,325	2,137	1,900			(7,362)
Administrative expenses	3,475	950	1,900			(6,325)
Operating profit	20,710	16,143	13,665			50,518
Interest paid	325					(325)
Profit before tax	20,385	16,143	13,665			50,193
Tax on profit on ordinary activities	8,300	5,390	4,241			(17,931)
Profit on ordinary activities after tax	12,085	10,753	9,424			32,262
Minority interest			[10% + 28%]		**(e)**	3,714
	(3,714)					
						28,548
Dividends – proposed	9,500					(9,500)
Retained profit for year	2,585	10,753	9,424			19,048
Retained profit brought forward	20,013	13,315	10,459	**(f)**		37,560
Retained profit carried forward	22,598	24,068	19,883			56,608

(a)

Elimination of inter-company sales from turnover and cost of sales

	£'000
Kiwi 480	
Melon 260	
	740

(b)

Elimination of unrealised profit on stock

	£'000
Kiwi 20% of £75,000	15
Melon 25% of £60,000	15
	30

(c)

Elimination of unrealised profit on fixed asset

	£'000
Sale price to Melon plc	240
Cost price to Exotic plc	(200)
Unrealised profit	40

(d)

Adjust for depreciation on inter-company fixed asset sale

	£'000
20% of sales price	48
20% of cost price	(40)
Excess depreciation	8

(e)

Minority interest

	£'000
Melon 10% of £10,753,000	1,075
Kiwi 28% of £9,424,000	2,639
	3,714

(f)

Profit and loss account balance brought forward

	£'000
Exotic plc	20,013
Melon plc 90% of (13,315,000 – 1,425,000)	10,701
Kiwi plc 90% of 80% of (10,459,000 – 950,000)	6,846
	37,560

Workings For Consolidated Balance Sheet

	Exotic plc £'000	*Melon plc* £'000	*Kiwi plc* £'000		*(Dr)/Cr* £'000	*CBS* £'000
Fixed assets (NBV)	35,483	24,273	13,063	**(c)**	(40)	
				(d)	8	72,787
Investments						
Shares in Melon plc	6,650			**(g)**		2,667
Shares in Kiwi plc		3,800		**(g)**		1,296
Current assets	1,568	9,025	8,883	**(b)**	(30)	19,446
Current liabilities	13,063	10,023	48	**(h)**	(9,500)	(13,634)
Exotic plc dividend				**(h)**		(9,500)
Minority interest				**(i)**		(8,454)
30,638	27,075	21,898			64,608	
Share capital and reserves						
Ordinary shares	8,000	3,000	2,000			8,000
Profit and loss account	22,638	24,075	19,898			56,608
	30,638	27,075	21,898			64,608

(g)

Goodwill on acquisition

Melon plc investment in Kiwi plc

(*Note:* Exotic's indirect investment in Kiwi plc is 90% × 80% = 72% minority interest is 28%.)

	£'000	£'000
Investment 90% of £3,800,000		3,420
Less: Shares (72% of £2,000,000)	1,440	
Preacquisition reserves (72% of £950,000)	684	
		2,124
Goodwill		1,296

Exotic plc investment in Melon plc

	£'000	£'000
Investment		6,650
Less: Shares (90% of £3,000,000)	2,700	
Preacquisition reserves (90% of £1,425,000)	1,283	
		3,983
Goodwill		2,667
Goodwill – Melon in Kiwi		1,296
Goodwill – Exotic in Melon		2,667
		3,963

(h)

Current liabilities

	£'000	£'000	£'000	£'000
Current liabilities	13,063	10,023	48	
Less: Dividends	9,500		—	
	3,563	10,023	48	
Total			13,634	
Dividends			9,500	

(i)

Minority interest

In Kiwi plc (28%)

	£'000
Ordinary share capital 28% of £2,000,000	560
Reserves 28% of (19,898,000 –15,000)	5,567
	6,127
Less: Cost of investment 10% of £3,800,000	(380)
	5,747

In Melon plc (10%)

	£'000
Ordinary share capital 10% of £3,000,000	300
Reserves 10% of (24,075,000 + 8,000 – 15,000)	2,407
	2,707
Total minority interest (5,747,000 + 2,707,000) =	8,454

(b)

Madeira plc

The results will appear under discontinued operations.

The entries will be as follows:

	Discontinued operations	
	£'000	
Turnover	2,000	
Cost of sales		(2,682)
Less: 1993 provision		500
Gross loss	(182)	
Operating expenses		(118)
Operating loss		(300)
Loss on termination of discontinued operations	(348)	
Loss on ordinary activities before tax	(648)	

Applying the FRS 3 Example 1 format, the results would appear as follows:

	£'000
Turnover	2,000
Operating loss	
Discontinued operations	(800)
Less 1993 provision	500
	(300)
Loss on termination of discontinued operations	(348)
Loss on ordinary activities before tax	(648)

(Tutorial note

The Examiner's answer calculates retained profit carried forward in three stages: retained profit brought forward, plus retained profit for the year, less goodwill. It is possible to 'prove' the calculation as follows:)

	£'000	£'000
Exotic plc (22,638 – 40)		22,598
Melon plc: At the year-end (24,075 – 15 + 8)	24,068	
At acquisition	(1,425)	
Group share (90%)	22,643	20,379
Kiwi plc: At the year-end (19,898 – 15)	19,883	
At acquisition	(950)	
Group share (72%)	18,933	13,631
		56,608
Less: goodwill (fully amortised) (2,667 + 1,296)		(3,963)
		52,645

4 Wales plc

Key answer tips

Notice the format of the answer to part (a) (ii). Although the question did not explicitly ask for a statement of reserves, this is the obvious way to answer the question.

(a) (i)

Consolidated profit and loss account for the year ended 31 December 20X4

	£m
Turnover (W1)	14,690
Cost of goods sold (W1)	(9,580)
Gross profit	5,110
Administration expenses [660 + 530 + 75 + 30 (W5)]	(1,295)
Distribution costs [1,427 + 1,001 + 60]	(2,488)
Operating profit	1,327
Profit on part disposal of shares in subsidiary undertaking (W2)	348
Income from other fixed asset investments	
Interest payable	(3)
Profit on ordinary activities before tax	1,672
Tax on profit on ordinary activities [315 + 125 + 27]	(467)
Profit on ordinary activities after tax	1,205
Minority interest (W3)	(78)
Profit on ordinary activities attributable to members of Wales Ltd	1,127
Dividends	(90)
Retained profit for the financial year	1,037

(ii)

Consolidated profit and loss account

	£m	£m
Wales	1,000	
Miami 85% × (883m – 232m – 359m)	248	
	1,248	
Less: Goodwill written off – Miami (W4)	(102)	
Consolidated profit and loss b/f		1,146
Retained for year (above)		1,037
Consolidated profit and loss c/f		2,183

Consolidated profit and loss account c/f

Proof for information only:

	£m
Wales [1,509m – 1m debenture interest]	1,508
Profit on sale of Miami shares (W2)	420
Miami 60% [883m – 359m Pre-acquisition]	314
Scotland 75% [186 – (106 + 20) – 3 Unrealised]	43
	2,285
Less: Goodwill re Miami: (W4)	(72)
Goodwill re Scotland: (W5)	(30)
	2,183

Workings

(W1) Turnover

	£m
Wales 8,000	
Miami6,000	
Scotland	750
	14,750
Less: Elimination	(60)
	14,690

Cost of goods sold

Wales	5,000
Miami	4,112
Scotland	525
	9,637
Less: Elimination	(57)
	9,580

Turnover elimination

	£m
Scotland turnover eliminated	60
Wales stock – unrealised profit [20% of £15m]	(3)
Cost of sales eliminated	57

(W2) Profit on sale of shares in Miami plc

	£m	
Proceeds	575	
Cost of shares [25/85 × 527m]		(155)
Parent company's exceptional item		420

In consolidated profit and loss account:

	£m	£m
Proceeds	575	
Net assets of Miami plc		
At 31 December 20X4 [883 + 141]	1,024	
Less: Retained profit for six months	(116)	
At 30.6.X4	908	
Disposed of 25%		(227)
		348

(***Note:*** No adjustment for goodwill is required since all the goodwill relating to Miami plc has already been charged through the consolidated profit and loss account.)

(W3) Minority interest

	£m
Miami plc	
15% × £232m × 6/12	17
40% × £232m × 6/12	47
	64
Scotland plc	
25% × (60 – 3 unrealised profit)	14
Total	78

(W4) Goodwill in Miami

	£m
On original purchase:	
Cost	527
Share of net assets (85% × 500m)	(425)
	102

On 60% remaining:

$$\frac{60}{85} \times 102\text{m} = £72\text{m}$$

All goodwill in Miami is fully amortised by 20X4 since the acquisition was made some years ago.

(W5) Goodwill in Scotland

Ordinary shares

		£m	£m
Cost			450
Less:	Share capital	300	
	Reserves		
	At 1.1.X4	106	
	Three months to 31.3.X4	20	
		426	
	75% thereof		320
Goodwill			130

Debentures	£m
Cost [60m – 1m]	59
Less: Nominal value	(40)
Premium	19
Total [130 + 19]	149

$$\text{Amortisation charge for year} = \frac{149}{5} = £30\text{m}.$$

5 Icing Ltd

Key answer tips

Read the question carefully. Part (a) relates to Cake and Bun, part (b) concerns Cake only and part (c) concerns Loaf only.

Your answer to part (c) (ii) should not only consider the treatment of the results of Loaf Ltd, but also the disclosure of the profit or loss on disposal. It should be an explanation, not simply a set of extracts from the financial statements.

(Tutorial note: Minor changes have been made to the wording of the answer to part (c) (ii) to reflect the new presentation requirements introduced by FRS 9 Associates and joint ventures. Under FRS 9 associates continue to be consolidated using the equity method).

(a) (i) Minority interests for the consolidated profit and loss account are as follows

	Cake Ltd		*Bun Ltd*	*CPL*
£'000		£'000	£'000	
Profit after tax	1,500		500	
Inter company dividends	(150)		-	
	1,350		500	
Minority interest		[100% - (80% × 75%)]		
20% of £1,350,000	270	40% of £500,000	200	470

Note: Minority interest in Bun Ltd is 40% made up as follows:

Shares held by outside shareholders of Bun Ltd	25%
Indirect interest of Cake Ltd's outside shareholders 20% × 75%	15%
	40%

(ii) **Group proportion of profit after tax is as follows:**

	Cake Ltd		*Bun Ltd*	*CPL*
	£'000		£'000	£'000
Profit after tax	1,500		500	
Inter company dividends	(150)		-	
	1,350		500	
Group interest		[100% – 40%]		
80% of £1,350,000	1,080	60% of £500,000	300	1,380

(iii) **Minority interests for the consolidated balance sheet:**

		Cake Ltd		*Bun Ltd*	*CBS*
		£'000		£'000	£'000
Ordinary shares	[20%]	1,000	[25%]	125	
Ordinary shares - indirect interest [20% of £375,000]				75	
Cost of shares in Bun Ltd [20% of £2m]		(400)			
P & L Account	[20% of £2.5m]	500			
[40% of £1.5m]				600	
		1,100		800	1,900

Shown separately under current liabilities:

	Cake Ltd	*Bun ltd*	*CBS*
	£'000	£'000	£'000
Dividends [20% of £1m]	200		200
Creditor [25% of £200,000]		50	50

(iv) **Goodwill on acquisition:**

	Cake Ltd		*Bun Ltd*		*CBS*
	£'000	£'000	£'000	£'000	£'000
Cost of shares		4,500		1,600	
Less: Ordinary shares	5,000		500		
Reserves	1,250		1,200		
	6,250		1,700		
	[80%]	5,000	[60%]	1,020	
Negative goodwill		(500)			(500)
Goodwill				580	580

(b) Calculation of goodwill following piecemeal acquisition

	(60%)		(20%)		CBS
	£'000	£'000	£'000	£'000	£'000
Cost of investment		3,500	1,000		
Net assets at the date of investment:					
Share capital			5,000	5,000	
Reserves		1,250		2,250	
		6,250		7,250	
Group share (60%/20%)(3,750)		(1,450)			
Accrual for pre-acquisition dividend (20% × $\frac{6}{12}$ × £1,000,000)			(100)		
Negative goodwill		(250)	(550)	(800)	

(c) (i) Calculate the gain/(loss) on sale of the shares in Loaf Ltd in both the accounts of Icing Ltd and in the consolidated accounts for the year ended 30 November 20X6. Assume a tax rate of 25%.

In parent accounts:	£	£
Sales proceeds		175,000
Less: Cost 112,000/336,000 × £480,000		160,000
		15,000
Less: Tax at 25%		3,750
Gain	11,250	
In consolidated accounts:		
Sales proceeds		175,000
Less: Share of net assets at date of disposal		
Share capital	560,000	
Reserve at 1 December 1995 [216,000 - 16,000]	200,000	
In year of disposal [16,000 / 2]	8,000	
768,000		
Proportion 112,000/560,000 i.e. 20%		(153,600)
21,400		
Less: Tax		(3,750)
Gain on disposal		(17,650)

(*Note:* Since all the goodwill purchased on acquiring Loaf Ltd will have been amortised through the consolidated profit and loss account by the disposal date, no further adjustment is required for goodwill in the disposal calculation.)

(ii) The disclosure treatment of the gain on disposal of £17,650 will be dependent on the classification of the investment. It will be disclosed as a gain on disposal under continuing operations if the investment in Loaf Ltd is classified as an associated undertaking. The reason is that, as an associated undertaking, Loaf Ltd would be contributing to profits on ordinary activities before taxation and to net assets in Icing Ltd's consolidated accounts on an equity accounting basis. Therefore from the group's point of view, the cessation of operation is not complete and no operation has been discontinued.

It will be disclosed as a gain on disposal under discontinued operations only in cases where the former subsidiary becomes merely an investment rather than an associated undertaking and could not be equity accounted for and there are no other subsidiaries within the group involved in the same activity as the subsidiary that has been sold.

The results i.e. turnover, cost of sales and expenses should be consolidated for the first six months. In the second six months, the operating profit will be apportioned - £12,000 arising prior to the disposal will be included in operating profit and 40% of £12,000 will be included as income from interests in associated undertakings.

Taxation will include £4,000 within the group tax figure and 40% of £4,000 as share of tax of associated undertaking.

6 Growmoor plc

Key answer tips

Your answer to part (a) should not simply state the FRS 6 criteria, but apply them to this combination, explaining the way in which they are applied.

When answering part (c) you should not only calculate the amounts to be included in the accounts, but explain the reasoning behind your calculations.

(a) (i) FRS 6 requires that to determine whether a business combination meets the definition of a merger, it should be assessed against certain specified criteria; failure to meet any of these criteria indicates that the definition was not met and thus that merger accounting is not to be used for the combination.

This entails considering the following 5 criteria:

Criterion 1: No party to the combination is portrayed as either acquirer or acquired, either by its own board or management or by that of another party to the combination.

Para 61 of FRS 6 elaborates on this stating that where the terms of a share-for-share exchange indicate that one party has paid a premium over the market value of the shares acquired, this is evidence that that party has taken the role of acquirer unless there is a clear explanation for this apparent premium other than its being a premium paid to acquire control.

This is relevant in the present situation where the value of the Growmoor plc shares issued as consideration was [1,500,000 × £1.20p] £1,800,000 to acquire Smelt plc shares valued at £1,560,000 resulting in a premium of £240,000.

This indicates *prima facie* that it was an acquisition. However, the exchange price was within the range [£1.20 - £1.50] of market prices for Smelt plc during the previous year. This could well be a clear explanation for this apparent premium other than its being a premium paid to acquire control.

The circumstances surrounding the transaction also support the view that this is a merger. For example, the closure and redundancy programme applied to Growmoor plc and not to Smelt plc.

Criterion 2: All parties to the combination, as represented by the boards of directors or their appointees, participate in establishing the management structure for the combined entity and in selecting the management personnel, and such decisions are made on the basis of a consensus between the parties rather than by an exercise in voting.

The need for re-application for posts and appearance before an interview panel indicates that there will be a consensus decision on appropriate personnel which would satisfy Criterion 2 even though the final result might be that the posts are largely filled by Growmoor plc managers.

Criterion 3: The relative sizes of the combining entities are not so disparate that one party dominates the combined entity by virtue of its relative size.

This requires a consideration of the proportion of the equity of the combined entity attributable to the shareholders of each of the combining parties to test if one is more than 50% larger than the other. This 50% is a rebuttable presumption. In this case, Growmoor plc shareholders hold 1,625,000 shares and Smelt plc 1,500,000 shares. This indicates that the criterion is satisfied even though the 1,500,000 shares are in consideration of only 80% of Smelt plc's capital.

Criterion 4: Under the terms of the combination or related arrangements, the consideration received by equity shareholders in relation to their shareholding comprises primarily equity shares in the combined entity; and any non-equity consideration, or equity shares carrying substantially reduced voting or distribution rights, represents an immaterial proportion of the fair value of the consideration received by the equity shareholders. Where one of the combining entities has, within the period of two years before the combination, acquired equity shares in another of the combining entities, the consideration for this acquisition should be taken into account in determining whether this criterion has been met.

This indicates that the cash payment made on 15 June 20X4 should be taken into account being less than two years before the combination on 1 May 20X6. Appendix 1 of FRS 6 refers to the Companies Act requirements for a transaction to be treated as a merger. This includes the provision that the fair value of any consideration other than the issue of equity shares given pursuant to the arrangement by the parent company did not exceed 10% of the nominal value of the equity shares issued.

The transaction does not comply with this requirement and would be required to be treated as an acquisition.

Criterion 5: No equity shareholders of any of the combining entities retain any material interest in the future performance of only part of the combined entity.

This criterion is concerned with situations where the allocation depended to any material extent on the post-combination performance of the business. In the present case, the allocation is dependent on the determination of the eventual value of a specific liability as opposed to the future operating performance and the criterion is satisfied.

(ii) Change of terms

The Companies Act requirement is not met because the cash payment of £164,000 in 20X4 is more than 10% of the nominal value of the shares issued which was £1,500,000.

The company has acquired 16% of the shares of Smelt plc in 20X4 and 80% in 1995. The company could require the holders of the remaining 4% to sell their shares on the same terms as those offered to the holder of the 80% but, even if it did this, the new shares issued as consideration would be 1,575,000 and the Companies Act requirement would still not be satisfied with the cash payment of £164,000 being 10.4%.

A further, and more common, possibility is that Growmoor plc could make a small bonus issue, say 1 for 10, prior to the exchange thus increasing the nominal value of the equity given from £1,500,000 to £1,650,000. The cash payment of £164,000 is then reduced to less than 10% of the nominal value.

(b) The following reasons could be put forward for the approach taken by the ASB in formulating the FRS 7 requirements concerning provisions on acquisition.

The practice of companies creating provisions or accruals for future operating losses and/or reorganisation costs expected to be incurred as a result of an acquisition was abused. Companies created provisions which gave rise to a larger goodwill figure that could be written off immediately against reserves and a provision against which expenses could be charged in subsequent accounting periods resulting in a higher profit figure. The effect of this was to prevent the accounts showing a true and fair view of the substance of commercial activities that had taken place in an accounting period.

(c) (i) FRS 7 para 77 states that when settlement of cash consideration is deferred, fair values are obtained by discounting to their present value the amounts expected to be payable in the future.

The appropriate discount rate is the rate at which the acquirer could obtain a similar borrowing, taking into account its credit standing and any security given.

For the Beaten Ltd acquisition the appropriate rate is 10% as stated in the question.

Treatment in the balance sheet of Growmoor plc as at 31 July 20X6

The discounted deferred consideration payable is a form of debt instrument. It is this amount that will appear as the investment's cost in the acquiring company's balance sheet i.e. £402,685. The same amount would appear as a creditor for the deferred consideration. [100,000 × .9090 + 150,000 × .8264 + 250,000 × .7513]. The liability would be split into £90,900 payable within 1 year and £311,785 payable in more than one year.

Treatment in the profit and loss account of Growmoor plc for the year ended 31 July 20X6

Because the deferred consideration is a form of debt instrument, the difference of £97,315 between the discounted amount of the payments and the total cash amount [500,000 - 402,685] is treated as a finance cost to be charged as an interest expense in Growmoor plc's profit and loss account over the period the liability is outstanding so that the annual cost gives a constant rate on the liability's carrying amount. The finance cost charged in the accounts to 31 July 20X6 is £3,355 representing 1 month's charge on £402,685 at 10% finance charge.

(ii) Goodwill calculation

Goodwill is calculated as at the date of acquisition based on the discounted amount of the cash payments. This results in a negative goodwill figure of £282,315 [402,685 - 685,000].

Effect of deferred consideration

There is no adjustment to this figure on the stage payments of the consideration. Growmoor plc has obtained the benefit of deferring the payment of the consideration and the cost of this benefit is charged in the profit and loss account over the period of the deferral.

Effect of contingent consideration

The terms of the agreement are such that it is impossible to say whether and how much additional consideration will be paid and the appropriate treatment is to deal with the matter by disclosure rather than provision.

Enquiries would be needed to establish whether the service agreement with the directors of Beaten Ltd constitutes a payment for the business acquired or an expense for services. If the substance of the agreement is payment for the business acquired the payments would be accounted for as a part of the purchase consideration and, as they are quantified, they would be included within the goodwill calculation.

7 Textures Ltd

Key answer tips

In part (a) you should do more than just state that the gross equity method gives more information. You should explain how the extra information helps users to assess gearing and the group's financial position.

Your answer to part (c) should not simply repeat the definitions of joint venture, subsidiary and quasi-subsidiary. Instead, you should *advise* on the aspects of the agreement that would influence the way in which Afrohelp is treated in practice.

(a) (i) *Explain the advantages of using the gross equity method to account for associates in consolidated accounts*

been argued that expanded equity information allows a user to calculate the correct debt: equity ratio. Without the expanded equity information the debt: equity ratio would be understated when there was a significant debt in the associate.

The existence of such loans have been a form of Off Balance Sheet financing as far as the Group were concerned.

Problem of significant debt - ROCE

In so far as the value of the associate in the consolidated balance sheet is represented by the investor's share of the net assets of the associate, the investor's share of any debt is not separately included in the balance sheet. This means that the existence of significant debt reduces the net assets and produces a higher ROCE. This can be adjusted for if expanded equity information is disclosed.

The amount of detail is of course debatable and there will be a compromise between providing a complete balance sheet of the associate to providing selected key totals.

Treatment of assets that are not controlled by parent company

The gross equity method allows a user to understand the assets that underlie the investment in associates. The method does not require consolidation on a line by line basis which would involve the aggregation of assets that were not under the control of the parent company management. The gross equity method therefore overcomes the disadvantages of the one line equity method whilst still distinguishing between assets under the control of the group and those held through strategic alliances.

(ii) Discuss the advantages and disadvantages of using proportional consolidation to account for joint ventures.

The discussion could include advantages and disadvantages such as the following:

Advantages

- Proportional consolidation includes the investor's share of its joint activity assets and liabilities under each format heading, not merely summary or net amounts. This gives an indication of the size of, and liabilities related to, the investor's interests in its joint venture. Including the investor's share of both assets and liabilities also helps users to take account of the structure and financing of the group and its joint ventures. In total the information provided is useful in assessing the investor's past performance and future prospects

- The best way to present an investor's interest in the results and assets of its joint venture is to treat it as having sole control over its proportionate share of these even though, in fact, it shares control over the whole.

- Joint activities amounting to a sharing of facilities are proportionally consolidated and consistency would require the same treatment for all joint ventures with each participant accounting for its share of the results, assets and liabilities directly in its individual financial statements.

Disadvantages

- Unless a clear distinction is maintained between assets and liabilities that are, directly or indirectly, within the control of the investor and those that are not, the performance and resources of the group are obscured and the usefulness of financial statements that aggregate consolidated amounts with proportionally consolidated amounts on a line-by-line basis is questionable.

- the results, assets and liabilities do not satisfy the criteria set out in the Statement of Principles e.g. assets require the ability to control rights or other access to benefits and in a joint venture the control does not exist. The investor should account for what it does control which is the net investment.

- including fractions of underlying items could make understanding of the financial statements difficult.

(b) (i) Textures & Pills Joint Venture would be dealt with in the accounts of Textures Ltd as at 30 November 20X6 as follows:

This joint activity amounts only to a sharing of facilities with the joint venturers deriving their benefit from services rather than by receiving a share in the profits of trading from the joint activity.

This means that each of the joint venturers should account for their share of the costs, assets and liabilities arising from those activities in their individual financial statements.

For Textures Ltd there would be assets in its balance sheet comprising premises £150,000 and Bank £15,000 and an expense charge to the profit and loss account of £46,000.

(ii) The retained profit of Eurohelp that appears in the consolidated profit and loss account as at 30 November 20X6 as a brought forward figure is calculated as follows:

	£'000
Net assets at 1 December 1995 were	6,750
Capital introduced was £750,000/30 × 100	2,500
Accumulated profit at 1 December 1995	4,250
Attributable to Textures Ltd - 30%	1,275

(c) (i) Advise the non-executive director of the conditions that would need to be satisfied to avoid Afrohelp Ltd being treated as a quasi subsidiary as at 30 November 20X6.

Where there is a 50:50 situation, the joint venture can still be 'off balance sheet', in so far as the disclosure is restricted to that required by the gross equity method, for both investor companies provided the two companies are genuine equals in terms of ability to control the venture and their interests in its underlying assets and its profits.

This would initially seem to be the situation with Computer Control Ltd because each is a trading company and it is not a situation where one is a trading company and the other a financial institution which would bring it within the FRS 5 *Reporting the Substance of Transactions* classification of a quasi subsidiary.

However, there are other criteria and it would be necessary to confirm that:

- the risks and rewards of ownership of the Afrohelp Ltd assets are to be shared equally between its two shareholders; and
- one company does not exert dominant influence over Afrohelp Ltd which would create a subsidiary relationship;
- profits and losses are to be shared equally between Textures Ltd and Computer Control Ltd with no arrangement for differential dividend rights or payments such as management charges that had the effect of stripping out the profits in favour of one of the investor companies.

(ii) Contrast the treatment of the unrealised gain on sale of equipment to Afrohelp Ltd on the consolidation of Afrohelp as an associate compared to as a quasi-subsidiary.

Treatment if an associate

The gain of £26,000 [50% of (£162,000 - £110,000)] that cannot be treated as realised should be deducted from the net assets of Afrohelp Ltd.

Treatment as a quasi-subsidiary

If Afrohelp Ltd results are consolidated turnover would be reduced by £162,000; cost of sales by £110,000; stock would be reduced by £52,000 thus eliminating the whole of the unrealised gain.

(Tutorial note: At the time this question was originally set, there was no accounting standard which dealt with joint ventures. The ASB subsequently issued FRS 9 *Associates and joint ventures.* Minor changes have been made to the question and answer as a result. The question contained no specific requirement to apply FRS 9. However, there are several points to note:*)*

1 Despite the fact that there is a separate entity, Textures & Pills Joint Venture is effectively a joint arrangement under FRS 9, rather than a joint venture. This is because it is a sharing of facilities. Textures Ltd would account for its own assets, liabilities and cash flows. The answer to part (b) (i) would be unchanged.

2 It is unclear whether Eurohelp is a joint arrangement or a joint venture under FRS 9 although the fact that there are retained profits suggests that the undertaking is trading on its own and is therefore a joint venture. Under the Companies Act, unincorporated joint ventures can be proportionally consolidated (which is the treatment followed in the answer). Under FRS 9 (assuming that Eurohelp meets the definition of a joint venture), the gross equity method would be used. The retained profit of Eurohelp included in the consolidated profit and loss account would be 30% × (6,750 – 2,500) and the answer to part (b) (ii) would be unchanged.

3 The status of Afrohelp Ltd is unclear. If it were a joint venture under FRS 9 it would be included in the consolidated financial statements using the gross equity method and the answer to part (c) (ii) would be unchanged.

The original answer has also been amended slightly to reflect the introduction of FRS 10 *'Goodwill and intangible assets')*.

8 Walsh plc

Key answer tips

Notice the format of the profit and loss account working below. It has been drawn up so that it produces sub-totals for continuing operations and acquisitions, (as required by the question) and is the best form of working to use where there have been changes to a group during the year.

(a)

Walsh Group
Group Profit and Loss Account for the Year Ended 31 December 20X6

	£m	£m
Turnover		
Continuing operations		
Ongoing	18,000	
Acquisitions	1,420	
	19,420	
Cost of sales		(13,023)
Gross profit		6,397
Distribution costs	2,320	
Administrative expenses	1,596	
	(3,916)	
Operating profit		
Continuing operations		
Ongoing	1,899	
Acquisitions	582	
	2,481	
Profit on disposal of shares in subsidiary		60
Bank interest receivable		5
Interest payable		(10)
Profit on ordinary activities before tax		2,536
Tax on profit on ordinary activities		(750)

Profit on ordinary activities after taxation	1,786
Minority interests - equity	(264)
Profit attributable to members of the parent company	1,522
Dividends	(85)
Retained profit for the year	1,437

(b)

Profit and loss reserve as at 31 December 20X6

	£m
Walsh plc balance at 1 January 20X6	1,500
Post acquisition reserves of Marsh plc	
80% × (1,650 - 350)	1,040
Retained profit for year	1,437
	3,977
Less Goodwill adjustments	
Goodwill - Marsh plc	
(544 - 80% (150 + 350))	(144) ✓
Group profit and loss reserve at 31 December 20X6	3,833

Alternative calculation

Walsh retained profits		1,973
Profit on sale of shares in Walsh plc accounts		
$(350 - \frac{20}{120} \times 544)$		259
Marsh retained profits		1,367
$\frac{100}{150} \times (2400 - 350)$		
Short retained profits		
85% × ($\frac{9}{12}$ of 576) 3		365
Less goodwill amortised		
Marsh $\frac{100}{120} \times 144$		(120)
Short	(11)	
	3,833	

Workings (all in £ million)

	Walsh plc	*Marsh plc*	*Goodwill*	*Sub Total*	*Short plc*	*InterCo*	*InterCo profit*		*Sub Total*	*Grand Total*
Turnover		10,000	8,000	-	18,000	1,500	(80)	-	1,420	19,420
Cost of sales		(7,000)	(5,500)	-	(12,500)	(600)	80	(3)	(523)	(13,023)
Gross profit	3,000		2,500	-	5,500	900	-	(3)	897	6,397
Admin expenses	(880)	(570)	(11)	(1,461)	(135)		-	-	(135)	(1,596)
Distribution costs	(1,310)	(830)	-	(2,140)	(180)				(180)	(2,320)
Operating profit		810	1,100	(11)	1,899	585	-	(3)	582	2,481

Profit on sale of shares in Marsh plc			
Proceeds of sale			
less net assets sold - Marsh plc			350
Net assets at 31 December 20X6			
Ordinary share capital		150	
Profit and Loss Reserve (750 + 1,650)		2,400	
	2,550		
Less six months profit		(375)	
Net assets at 1 July 20X6		2,175	
Net assets disposed of $\frac{20}{150} \times 2,175$			(290)
			60

(*Note:* No adjustment for goodwill is required since all the goodwill relating to Marsh plc has already been charged through the consolidated profit and loss account.)

Minority interests	
Marsh plc	
20% × 750 × 6/12	75
$33\frac{1}{3}$% × 750 × 6/12	125
	200
Short plc	
15% of $\left[(\frac{9}{12} \text{ of } 576) - 3\right]$	64
(The £3 million is the unrealised profit)	
	264

(***Tutorial note***
This question and answer have been amended to reflect the issue of FRS 10 *Goodwill and intangible assets*. Goodwill on the acquisition of Short plc is calculated as follows:

	£m	£m
Cost of investment		900
Less:Share capital	200	
Profit and loss account reserve b/f	675	
Profit 1.1.X6 - 31.3.X6 ($^3/_{12}$ × 576)	144	
	1,019	
Group share (85%)		(866)
		34
Amortisation (34 ÷ 3)		11

)

9 A plc

Key answer tips

Notice that the profit and loss account in part (b) follows Example Format 2 of FRS 3. Although this gives more information than is strictly required, using this format saves time here because it replaces the columnar working that might otherwise be necessary.

(a)

Consolidated balance sheet of B Group plc at 31 May 20X7

	£m
Intangible assets: goodwill	10
Tangible assets	610
Net current assets	470
Creditors due after one year	(40)
Minority interest	(24)
	1,026
Called up share capital	100
Share premium account	100
Profit and loss account	826
	1,026

Workings (all in £ million)

Adj a/c

Inv in C	90	Share capital C	24
		Share premium C	8
	90	Profit/Loss a/c	48
		Goodwill	10
			90

Minority interest

Bal	24	Share Capital	6
		C Res	18
	24		24

Group Res

Goodwill amortisation	-	Bal	810
Bal c/d	826	C Res	16
	826		826

Share premium

		Bal	100

C Reserves

Adj a/c - Sh premium	8	Bal P/L a/c	80
- P/L a/c	48	Sh Premium	10
Minority Int	18		
20% of (80 + 10)			
Group res	16		
	90		90

(b)

A Group plc
Consolidated profit and loss account for the year ended 31 May 20X7

	£m *Continuing operations*	£m *Discontinued operations*	£m *Total*
Turnover	8,530	3,325	11,855
Cost of sales	(5,320)	(2,195)	(7,515)
Gross profit	3,210	1,130	4,340
Net operating expenses	(2,125)	(435)	(2,560)
Operating profit	1,085	695	1,780
Goodwill on discontinued operations		(460)	(460)
Profit on ordinary activities before taxation	1,085	235	1,320
Taxation			(565)
Profit on ordinary activities after taxation			755
Minority interests			(35)
Profit for financial year			720
Dividends			(1,046)
Retained loss for financial year			(326)

A Group plc (after demerger)
Consolidated balance sheet at 31 May 20X7

	£m
Intangible assets: negative goodwill	(28)
Tangible assets	3,590
Net current assets	1,890
Creditors due after one year	(135)
Minority interest	(58)
	5,259
Called up share capital	1,350
Share premium account	1,550
Profit and loss account	2,359
	5,259

Workings (all in £ million)

Adj a/c

Inv in D	50	Share capital D	12
		Share premium D	12
		Profit/Loss a/c D	54
		Negative goodwill	(28)
	50		50

D Res

Adj a/c	12	Share premium	20
MI	8	Profit and loss account	105
Adj a/c	54		
MI	42		
Group Res	9		
	125		125

Minority interest

Bal	58	Share cap	8
		Sh premium	8
		Profit/Loss a/c D	42
	58		58

Group res

Demerger of B	900	Bal	3,250
Bal	2,359	D Res	9
	3,259		3,259

Minority Interest - A Group Profit/Loss account	
Minority interest in D 40% of 60	24
Minority interest in C 20% of 55	11
	35

Goodwill		
Cost of investment - B plc	900	
Net assets acquired - B plc (100 + 100 + 250)	(450)	
	450	
Goodwill on acquisition of C		10
Goodwill on discontinued operations		460

Demerged assets

DR Profit/loss a/c (dividend in specie)	1,016
CR Separable net assets of B group plc (1,026 – 10) BEFORE demerger	1,016

There will be no profit or loss on the demerger of B group plc as the demerger involves simply a distribution of assets effectively to existing shareholders in the form of a dividend in specie.

Dividends - dividend paid	30
- dividend in specie	1,016
	1,046

Consolidated reserves (for information only)	
At 1 June 20X6	2,685
Loss for period	(326)
at 31 May 20X7	2,359

Opening balance on reserves	
A (3,250 – 683)	2,567
B (810 – 394 – 250)	166
C 80% of (80 – 50 – 60)	(24)
D 60% of (105 – 55 – 90)	(24)
	2,685

(c)

E Group plc
Share Capital and Reserves at 31 May 20X7

		£m
Ordinary shares of £1		300
Profit and loss account		716
		1,016
Profit and loss account		
B Group's Profit and loss account (826 – 10)		816
Less difference on consolidation		
E's share capital	300	
B's share capital	(100)	
B's share premium	(100)	
		100
		716

(***Tutorial note***: It would be possible to present the consolidation workings in part (a) and (b) as schedules rather than as T accounts. The workings below follow the approach described in the Textbook and the Lynchpin.)

Part (a)

	£m	£m
Goodwill		
Cost of investment		90
Less: Share of net assets acquired:		
Share capital	30	
Share premium	10	
Profit and loss account	60	
	100	
Group share (80%)		(80)
		10
Minority interest		
Share capital	30	
Share premium	10	
Profit and loss account	80	
	120	
MI share (20%)		24
Group profit and loss account		
B plc	810	
C Ltd:		
At year-end	80	
At acquisition	(60)	
	20	
Group share (80%)		16
Less: goodwill amortisation to date		(-)
		826

Part (b)

	£m	£m
Goodwill		
Cost of investment		50
Less: Share of net assets acquired:		
Share capital	20	
Share premium	20	
Profit and loss account	90	
	130	
Group share (60%)		(78)
		(28)
Minority interest		
Share capital	20	
Share premium	20	
Profit and loss account	105	
	145	
MI share (40%)		58
Group profit and loss account		
A plc	3,250	
D Ltd:		
At year-end	105	
At acquisition	(90)	
	15	
Group share (60%)		9
Less: demerger (cost of investment in B plc)		(900)
		2,359

10 Merge plc

Key answer tips

Your answer to part (a) should not simply restate the conditions for merger accounting but analyse them into three classes, as required.

Start part (b) by calculating the non-equity proportion of the consideration for the purchase of Acquire. This will tell you whether to use acquisition or merger accounting.

(a) FRS 6 requires that to determine whether a business combination meets the definition of a merger it should be assessed against five criteria. If one analyses these criteria, it can be seen that it is possible to categorise these criteria into the three elements set out in the question.

(i) *Verifiable signs of a merger*

FRS 6 states that an essential feature of a merger is a genuine combining of interests. No one party should have a dominant role as an acquirer or subservient role of being acquired. Therefore no acquirer should be identifiable. For example, where one party has paid a premium over the market value of the shares acquired, this is evidence of that party having taken the role of an acquirer.

The consideration received by equity shareholders of each party to the combination should comprise primarily equity shares in the combined entity. All but an immaterial proportion of the fair value of the consideration must be in the form of equity shares. FRS 6 utilises company legislation to state that the value of consideration other than equity shares should not exceed 10% of the nominal value of the shares issued. A business combination may not be accounted for as a merger if a material part of the consideration is in the form of shares with substantially reduced rights. This latter offer would be contrary to the mutual sharing of the risks and rewards of the combined entity.

The above criteria are verifiable and show substantive signs of continuity of ownership.

(ii) *Implied evidence of a merger*

An essential feature of a merger is that all parties to the merger are involved in determining the management structure of the combined entity and reach consensus on the appropriate structure and personnel. If one party dominates this process, possibly by the exercise of majority voting rights, then it is not a genuine pooling of interests. Where the senior management structure and personnel are essentially those of one of the combining parties, then the criterion will not have been met unless all parties to the merger have genuinely participated in the decision.

Where one party is substantially larger than the other parties, this will not be consistent with the equal partnership view of a merger. A party would be presumed to dominate if it is more than 50% larger than each of the other parties to the combination (by reference to ownership interests). This presumption may be rebutted if it can be clearly shown that there is no such dominance.

The circumstances surrounding the transaction may provide evidence as to the role of the parties to the combination. Certain characteristics although not conclusive would need to be considered. For example, the plans for the entity's future operations and the proposed corporate image.

(iii) *Anti-avoidance terms*

FRS 6 utilises general anti-avoidance provisions. All arrangements made in conjunction with the combination must be taken into account. Equity shareholders will be considered to have disposed of their shareholding for cash where they have been able to exchange or redeem the shares for cash or other non-equity consideration. For example a vendor placing is treated as giving rise to non-equity consideration. Also if one entity has acquired an interest in exchange for non-equity consideration or equity shares with reduced rights within two years of the combination, then such consideration is deemed to be part of the total consideration for the use of determining the non-equity consideration.

Finally, merger accounting cannot be used where one party has been created as a result of divestment from a larger party as the divested business will not be sufficiently independent until it has established a track record of its own. FRS 6 does not quantify divestment time limits.

(b)

Merge Group plc
Profit and Loss Account for the Year Ended 30 November 20X7

	£'000
Turnover	39,285
Cost of sales	(31,400)
	7,885
Distribution and administration expenses	(5,884)
Operating profit	2,001
Reorganisation expenses of merger	(156)
Income from investments	200
Profit before taxation	2,045
Taxation	(639)
	1,406

Dividends	
Pre-merger dividend	(48)
Proposed dividend	(208)
Retained profit for year	1,150

Merge Group plc
Balance Sheet at 30 November 20X7

	£'000
Fixed assets	6,164
Current assets	9,780
Creditors: Amounts falling due within one year	(4,932)
Net current assets	4,848
Total assets less current liabilities	11,012
Called up share capital	2,500
Share premium account	342
Revaluation reserve	260
Other reserves	75
Profit and loss account	7,835
	11,012

Workings

Purchase consideration	*Nominal value* £'000	*Fair value* £'000
Shares issued	1,471	3,678
Cash - initial offer	36	36
Compulsorily acquired (8,000 × 2.25)	18	18
	1,525	3,732

Shares issued	
Share capital - Acquire plc	1,250
Less: Shares - cash equivalent taken £54,000 divided by £2.25	(24)
	1,226
× factor 6:5	1,471

The Companies Act 1985 requires that non-equity consideration should not exceed 10% of the nominal amount of shares issued. FRS 6 requires that all but an immaterial portion of the fair value of the consideration should be in the form of equity shares. The above cash consideration is 3.5% of the nominal value of shares issued and 1.4% of the fair value of the consideration. Therefore the criteria are both met for merger accounting.

Distribution and administrative expenses	£'000
Per question (3,310 and 2,730)	6,040
Less: Expenses	(156)
	5,884

Income from investments	
Per question (200 + 100)	300
Less: Inter company dividend	(100)
	200

Taxation

Per question (365 + 274)	639

Dividends

The pre-merger dividends of the parent and subsidiary are shown in the profit and loss account but after the date of the merger only those of the parent are shown.

Current assets and creditors

Current assets per question (5,530 + 4,350)	9,880
Less: Inter co div	(100)
	9,780
Creditors per question (2,502 + 2,530)	5,032
Less: Inter co div	(100)
	4,932

Fixed assets

Balance per question (4,099 + 3,590)	7,689
Less: Cost of investment in Acquire plc	(1,525)
	6,164

Share premium account - Merge plc

Balance per question	400
Less: Issue costs	(58)
	342

Profit and loss account

Balance per question (4,052 + 3,725)	7,777
Add: Issue costs to share premium	58
	7,835

Equity elimination

Cost of investment	1,525
Less: Share capital - Acquire plc	(1,250)
Share premium account - Acquire plc	(250)
To other reserves	25

Other reserves

Balance per question	100
less equity elimination	(25)
Other reserves	75

11 Wright Group plc

Key answer tips

Start by drawing up the group structure, paying particular attention to the dates on which changes took place. Use a columnar profit and loss account working (W1).

The restructuring should not be treated as a discontinued operation (there is no evidence that it meets the FRS 3 definition).

(a)

Wright Group plc
Group profit and loss account for the year ended 31 December 20X8

	£m	£m	£m
Turnover			
Continuing operations			
Ongoing		18,600	
Acquisition – Chang plc		1,200	
	19,800		
Cost of sales			(13,232)
Gross profit			6,568
Distribution costs		1,965	
Administrative expenses		195	
	(2,160)		
Operating profit			
Continuing operations			
Ongoing		4,112	
Acquisitions		296	4,408
Profit on disposal of shares in subsidiary		47	
Costs of restructuring		(34)	13
	4,421		
Share of operating profit in associate			37
Bank interest receivable – group	35		
– associates	2	37	
Interest payable – group	37		
– associates	2	(39)	
	(2)		
Profit on ordinary activities			4,456
*Tax on profit on ordinary activities			(1,432)
Profit on ordinary activities after taxation			3,024
Minority interests – equity			(61)
Profit attributable to members of the parent company			2,963
Dividends			(200)
Retained profit for the year			2,763
*Tax relates to the following:			
Parent and Subsidiaries			1,417
Associate			15
			1,432

(b)

Balance on Wright Group reserves 31 December 20X8

	£m
Wright's reserves – 1.1.X8	8,500
Berg's reserves – 1.1.X8 (324 – 300) × 80%	19
Profit for period	2,763
Goodwill written off	(60)
Balance at 31.12.X8	11,222

Alternative calculation

Wright's retained profits	11,097
Profit on sale of shares (in Wright's accounts)	50
Berg's retained profits (40% × (400 – 300 – 38))	39
Chang's retained profits	102
Goodwill written off (60 + 44 – 38)	(66)
	11,222

Workings

(W1)

	Wright	*Berg (1/2)*	*Chang (3/4)*	*Ass Co*	*Goodwill*	*Adj*	*Total*
Turnover	18,000	600	1,200				19,800
Cost of sales	12,000	420	795		36		13,251
Fixed assets dep'n			(5)				(5)
Restructuring costs	(14)						(14)
	11,986	420	790		36		13,232
Distribution costs	1,800	60	105				1,965
Admin. expenses	180	6	9				195
Associated Co				(45)	8		(37)
Interest payable	30	4	3	2			39
Bank interest receivable	(15)	(5)	(15)	(2)			(37)
Exceptional item	14		20				34
Taxation	1,320	37	60				1,417
Associates taxation				15			15
	3,329	102	182	(30)	8		3,591
Profit for period	2,685	78	228	30	(44)		2,977
Profit on disposal	50				(3)		47
Inter group div	112	(32)	(80)				-
Minority interests		(15)	(46)				(61)
Dividend	(200)						(200)
	2,647	31	102	30	(44)	(3)	2,763

(W2) The depreciation on the fixed assets of Chang needs adjustment for the revaluation adjustment This amounts to £30m × 20% × 9/12, i.e. £4.5 million.

Downsizing can only be classified under discontinued operations where there is a material effect on the nature and focus of the operations. Therefore the main effect of this restructuring is to show the costs (£14m) as a non-operating exceptional item and to eliminate them from the cost of sales. Therefore the total adjustment to cost of sales is £18.5m.

(W3) *Chang plc stock* – the cost of sales of Chang will be calculated as follows:

	£m
Stock at acquisition (240 – 40)	200
Purchases 3/4 × (1,020 – 150 + 350)	915
less closing stock (350 – 30)	(320)
	795

(W4) Goodwill

	£m
Chang plc	
Purchase consideration	700
less net assets acquired 80% × (750 + 20)	(616)
Goodwill	84
Charge for year ÷ 4	21

The post acquisition provision of £20 million will be eliminated from the goodwill calculation and charged to post acquisition profits. It is assumed that this provision will be accrued for in the group profit and loss account and included as a non-operating exceptional item.

(W5) Profit on sale of shares of Berg

	£m	£m
Proceeds of sale		350
Less net assets sold		
Equity share capital	250	
Share premium	50	
Retained profit (b/f)	324	
add 1/2 year profit	78	
	702 × 40%	(280.8)
		69.2
Goodwill relating to disposal not written off (60 – 15) × 40/80		(22.5)
Profit on sale of shares		46.7

Alternative calculation

		£m
Proceeds		350 ✓
Cost of inv. (40/80 of 600)		(300) ✓
Profit in Wright's account		50 ✓
less		
Opening reserves	324 ✓	
Profit for six months	78 ✓	
less profits at acquisition	(300) ✓	
	102 × 40%	(40.8)
		9.2
add goodwill written off (120 × 40/80 – 22.5)		37.5
		46.7

(W6) Minority interest

Berg – 20% × 78	15.6
Chang – 20% × 228	45.6
	61.2

(W7) Associated Company profit

	£m
Operating profit for the year - Berg	228
Operating profit for the half year	114
Less: Inter company profit	(3)
	111
Operating profit relating to associate (40%)	44.4
Less: Goodwill	(7.5)
	36.9
Less: Interest payable (4 × .4)	(1.6)
Add: Bank interest receivable (5 × .4)	2.0
Less: Tax on profit (74 × 40% × 1/2)	(14.8)
	22.5

The inter company sales of £60 million would not affect the turnover in the group profit and loss account as they occurred when Berg was an associate. The goodwill charged on associates would be disclosed.

(W8) Berg

	£m	£m
Purchase consideration		600
Less net assets acquired		
Share capital	250	
Share premium	50	
Retained earnings	300	
	600 × 80%	(480)
Goodwill		120
Less: Written off (two years)		(60)
Balance at 1.1.X8		60
Less: Written off 20X8		
Goodwill		(15)
(as an associate) 1.7.X8 – 31.12.X8		(7.5)
Less: Written off on sale of shares		(22.5)
		15

The charge for goodwill amortisation in the consolidated profit and loss account in cost of sales is Berg £15m and Chang (working 4) £21m i.e. £36m.

(W9) It is assumed that the exceptional item is material and that the costs of restructuring would be shown in the financial statements.

12 X Group

Key answer tips

Read the information in the question carefully; it is particularly important to establish the group structure. The main complication here is that the group includes an associate owned by a subsidiary.

(a)

X Group
Balance Sheet as at 31 March 20X9

	£m
Tangible fixed assets	1,058
Investment	47
Goodwill	40
Net current assets	1,060
Creditors due more than one year	(365)
	1,840
Share capital	360
Share premium	250
Reserves	1,071
Minority interest	159
	1,840

Consolidation Schedule (£m)

Working			*Total*	*Adj (Cost of Control)*	*Goodwill*	*M.I.*	*Cd. Res.*	*B /S*
(1)	Tangible fixed assets		1,030✓	40 ✓	(26)	(14)		
			(12)		4	8	1,058	
	Intangible fixed assets		30		20	10		–
	Inv in W		50✓	(3)		1	2	47
	Inv in Y		320		320			
	Inv in Z		90		60	30		
(2)	Net C.A.		1,075 ✓	(15) ✓		6	9	1,060
					7		(7)	
(3)					(24)		24	
(4)					6		(6)	
	Creditors: due more 1 yr.		(365)					(365)
	Share capital	– X	360					360
		– Y	150		(100)	(50)		
		– Z	50		(30)	(20)		
	Share premium	– X	250					250
		– Y	120		(80)	(40)		
		– Z	10		(6)	(4)		

Profit/loss a/c	– X	1,050			(1,050)
	– Y	210	(80)	(70)	(60)
	– Z	30	(12)	(12)	(6)
			55		(1,086)
Goodwill write off (3/11)			(15)		15
			40	(159)	(1,071)

The holding of X in Y and Z is as follows:

	Y	*Z*	
X	2/3	6/10 (2/3 of 90%)	
MI		1/3	4/10

Goodwill is calculated at 1 April 20X6 when X gained control of Y and hence Z.

Workings

1 **Tangible fixed assets**

	X	*MI*	*Total*
	£m	£m	£m
Fair value adj. – Y	20	10	30
Fair value adj. – Z	6	4	10
	26	14	40

Depreciation – additional depreciation of 40 × 10% × 3 years needs to charged ie £12m. This will be split between the consolidated reserves and the minority interest as follows.

	X	*MI*	*Total*
	£m	£m	£m
Y 1/3 : 2/3	6	3	9
Z 4/10 : 6/10	2	1	3
	8	4	12

Accounting entries	£m
DR Fixed assets	40
CR Cost of control	26
Minority interest	14
DR Consolidated reserves	8
Minority interest	4
CR Depreciation	12

2 **Stocks – Inter company profit and fair values**

	Cd res	*MI*	*Total*
	£m	£m	£m
Inter co. profit			
Sales to X	44		
Sales to Y	16		
60 × 25%	9	6	15

Profit will be eliminated by reference to the relative shareholdings of X and the minority interest in Z (4/10).

DR	Consolidated reserves	9
	Minority Interest	6
CR	Stock	15

Fair value and change in accounting policy

On acquisition of Y net decrease is £6m
X's share of this decrease is 2/3 ie £4m
On acquisition of Z net decrease is £5m
X's share of this decrease is 6/10 ie £3m

DR	Cost of control	£7m
CR	Consolidated reserves	£7m

3 **Arbitration receipts**

The amount of £36m received on 1 June 20X6 is an amount which relates to the preacquisition period and as such was the crystallisation of a contingent asset as at 1 April 20X6. Therefore it should be included in the fair value exercise. The group's share of the debtor is 2/3 of £36m ie £24m.

	£m
DR Consolidated reserves	24
CR Cost of control	24

4 **Provision for bad debts**

The increase in the provision on acquisition is £9m

	£m
DR Cost of control	6
CR Post acquisition profits	6

The increase in the provision moves profits from the post acquisition period into the pre-acquisition period (£9m × $^2/_3$).

5 The associated company of Y is also deemed to be an associate of X and therefore is equity accounted. In practice the group would be consolidated using the indirect method and W would be equity accounted in the group accounts of Y. Therefore in the group accounts of X, using the direct method, W should be equity accounted. The investment in W will be debited with 30% (£17m - £7m) ie £3m and the consolidated reserves and minority interest credited with £2m and £1m respectively. The goodwill arising on acquisition will be

	£m
Cost of investment	50
Net assets acquired 30% of (80 + 6 + 7)	(28)
Goodwill	22

Therefore goodwill would be amortised over eleven years with three years having elapsed.

Goodwill written off associate 3/11 × 22 = £6m.

Thus the total adjustment to the investment in W would be (in £m).

	Investment	MI	Cd Res
Post acquisition Reserves	DR3	CR1	2
Goodwill	CR(6)	DR(2)	(4)
	(3)	(1)	(2)

(***Tutorial Note:*** The Examiner's Answer presents the workings in a columnar format, but it would be possible to present the main consolidation workings as schedules. The workings below follow the approach described in the Textbook and the Lynchpin.)

Goodwill

	£m	£m	£m
In Y			
Cost of investment			320
Less: share of net assets acquired:			
Share capital		150	
Share premium		120	
Reserves	120		
Adjustments (30 – 8 – 9 – 30 + 2 + 36)	21		
	141		
		411	
Group share (2/3)			(274)
			46
In Z			
Cost of investment (2/3 × 90)			60
Less: share of net assets acquired:			
Share capital		50	
Share premium		10	
Reserves	20		
Adjustments (10 – 5)	5		
	25		
	85		
Group share (60%)			(51)
			9
Total goodwill			
Y	46		
Z	9		
	55		
Less amortisation (55 × 3/11)	(15)		
	40		

Minority interest

	£m	£m	£m
In Y			
Share capital		150	
Share premium		120	
Reserves	210		
Fair value adjustments (30 – 30)	–		
Additional depreciation	(9)		
		201	
W (50 – 47)		(3)	
		468	
MI share (1/3)			156

In Z

Share capital		50	
Share premium		10	
Reserves	30		
Fair value adjustment	10		
Additional depreciation	(3)		
Provision for unrealised profit	(15)		
		22	
		82	
MI share (40%)			33
Less: cost of investment (1/3 × 90)			(30)
			159

Group reserves

	£m	£m
X		1,050
Y:		
At year-end	201	
At acquisition	(141)	
	60	
Group share (2/3)		40
Z:		
At year-end	22	
At acquisition	(25)	
	(3)	
Group share (60%)		(2)
W:		
At year-end	17	
At acquisition	(10)	
	7	
Group share (30%)		2
Less: amortisation of goodwill		
Group	15	
W (2/3 × 22 × 3/11)	4	
		(19)
		1,071

13 Baden plc

Key answer tips

Your answer to part (a) should not simply restate the definitions and requirements of FRS 9 but *explain* them.

Start part (b)(i) by dealing with the fair value adjustments, then calculate goodwill. You should then be able to calculate the amount at which the investment in Baden will be included in the consolidated balance sheet. Then calculate the amounts to be included in the consolidated profit and loss account.

Calculate the group's share of turnover, gross assets and gross liabilities to answer part (b)(ii). You are not required to make the additional disclosures for material associates and joint ventures (see point (vi) in the question).

(a) (i) The principal difference between an associate and an ordinary fixed asset investment is that in the latter case the investor takes on a relatively passive role whereas an associate is a medium through which an investor conducts its business. Thus an associate will normally implement accounting policies that are consistent with those of the investor. The investor must be able to exercise a significant influence over the investee and maintain a participating interest, which is an interest in shares held on a long term basis for the purpose of securing a contribution to the investor's activities by the exercise of control or influence.

FRS 9 'Associates and Joint Ventures' states that a holding of 20% or more of the voting rights suggests but does not ensure that the investor exercises significant influence. The FRS also suggests that the attitude towards the investee's dividend policy may indicate the status of the investment. In the case of an ordinary fixed asset investment, the investor may press for a high dividend but in the case of an associate the investor will be more interested in reinvestment of cash flows and less with dividend. FRS 9 indicates that associate status is achieved where the investor has board representation or equivalent participation in the decision making process combined with at least 20% voting rights. Additionally the investor must not merely have the ability to exercise significant influence but must actively exercise it.

(ii) A joint venture must be an 'entity' whereas a joint arrangement is not. An entity is essentially a body corporate, partnership or incorporated association carrying on a trade or business of its own and where all significant matters of operating and financial policy are predetermined by the participants. For example several oil companies may own a pipeline, the throughput of which is sold separately by the companies rather than the joint venture. FRS 9 states that there are indicators of a joint arrangement and these are:

(a) the participants derive their benefit from products or services taken in kind rather than by receiving a share in the trading results.

(b) each participant's share of output or result is determined by its supply of key inputs to the production process.

A joint arrangement is accounted for by each participant accounting for their own 'assets, liabilities and cash flows' within the arrangement. In many cases this will generate the same numbers that would have been obtained using proportional consolidation. FRS 9 states that this is not proportional consolidation but a reporting entity recording its own transactions, and therefore requires such arrangements to be accounted for at the individual entity level and on consolidation.

(b) (i) In the consolidated balance sheet, the group's share of the net assets will be shown as a single line under FRS 9 'Associates and Joint Ventures'.

At 1 January 20X7 – fair value of assets.

	£m
Tangible fixed assets	30
Current assets	31
Creditors – within one year	(20)
Creditors – more than one year	(8)
Fair value of net assets	33
Shareholding 30% – value of assets purchased	9.9
Cost of investment	14
Goodwill	4.1

In calculating goodwill FRS 9 (para 31) states that 'any goodwill carried in the balance sheet of the investee should not be included in the calculations'.

At 31 December 20X8 – Balance Sheet amount

	£m
Cost of investment	14
Post acquisition profits 30% of (32 – 9 – URP 10)	3.9
Less	
Goodwill written off (2 years)	(2)
Increased depreciation of tangible fixed assets due to fair values	
2 × 20% × (30 – 20) × 30%	(1.2)
Investment in associate	14.7

Alternative presentation

Net assets 30% x (46 – URP 10)		10·8
Fair value increase (net assets 31/12/X8)	46	
less profit 20X7 + 20X8	23	
Net assets at acquisition	23	
Fair value	33	
Increase in fair value	10 × 30%	3
		13·8
Goodwill		4·1
		17·9
less goodwill written off		(2)
Depreciation		(1·2)
Investment in associate		14·7

FRS 9 states that goodwill should be treated in accordance with FRS 10 'Goodwill and Intangible Assets' that inter company profit should be eliminated and that depreciation should be based on fair values.

The investment in the associate should be included as a fixed asset investment and goodwill of £2·1million should be included in the carrying amount and disclosed separately.

The following amounts would be shown in the consolidated profit and loss account.

Profit and Loss account for year ended 31 December 20X8

	£m
Share of operating profit in associate	4·1
[(30% of 29) – goodwill 1– interco. profit 3 – depreciation 0·6]	
Exceptional item – associate	(3)
Interest payable – associate	(1·2)
*Taxation on profit on ordinary activities	
*Tax relates to the following:	
Associate	(0·9)

Note: that the amount of goodwill written off will be disclosed. The investors share of group turnover may be shown as a memorandum item in the profit and loss account.

Note: any interest held by associates or joint ventures are ignored (such as those held by Guy).

The intercompany profit on stock will be treated as follows:

(i) in the consolidated profit and loss account, the profit will be eliminated from the share of the associates profit as the associate recorded the profit.

(ii) in the consolidated balance sheet the profit will be eliminated from stock as this is the asset subject to the transaction which is held by the holding company.

(b) (i) Joint ventures are accounted for under FRS 9 using the 'gross' equity method. This is the same as the equity method for associates but with two exceptions

(ii) In the consolidated profit and loss account the group's share of turnover must be shown, but as a memorandum item separate from group turnover.

	£m
Turnover: group and share of joint ventures (212 – 35) × 30%	y + 53.1
Less share of joint ventures turnover	(53.1)
Where y = group turnover	y

(iii) In the consolidated balance sheet, the share of net assets of joint ventures must be sub analysed into the group's share of assets and liabilities and included as a fixed asset investment. Any goodwill (£2·1 million) should be disclosed separately.

Investment in joint ventures	
Share of gross assets (working 1)	21·3
Share of gross liabilities (30% of 12 + 10).	(6·6)
	14·7

Groups may give memorandum information on the face of the consolidated profit and loss account and balance sheet of the amount of each line item.

Working 1

Fixed assets	37	
Current assets (31–10)	21	
58 × 30%	17·4	
Increase in fair value	3	
Goodwill	4·1	
less goodwill write off	(2)	
Depreciation	(1·2)	
		21·3

14 A plc

Key answer tips

Remember to include the warranty provision when calculating goodwill in part (a).

The issue of shares by Y results in a 'deemed disposal'. Y changes from a subsidiary to an associate and therefore should be consolidated using the equity method.

(a) A acquired a controlling interest in X in two stages and FRS 2 'Accounting for subsidiary undertakings' recommends that goodwill be computed in a single computation by reference to the fair value of the net assets of the subsidiary when it becomes part of the group. This complies with the Companies Act 1985 (Sch4A paragraph 9).

X plc

Date	Holding	Net Assets £m	Consideration £m
31.8.97	10%		5
31.10.98	45%	52	25
		52	
less provision for warranty ((5% of 300)–3)		(12)	
	55%	40	30

Goodwill = £30 million – (55% of 40 million)
= £8 million

Y plc

Purchase consideration	54
Fair value of assets acquired (60% of 70)	(42)
Goodwill	12
Total Goodwill (8 + 12 =)	20
Amortisation	5
Goodwill	15

(b) Where a group increases its interest in an undertaking that is already a subsidiary, the subsidiary's assets should be revalued to fair value on consolidation. Goodwill arising on the increased interest in the company should be calculated by reference to those values.

A Group
Consolidated Balance Sheet as at 31 October 20X9

Tangible fixed assets	150
Associated company	51·2
Goodwill	7·4
Net current assets (26 + 25 + 20)	71
Long-term liabilities (6 + 35 + 1)	(42)
Provision for warranties	(17)
	220.6
Share Capital	80
Retained Profits	128·35
Minority Interest	12·25
	220.6

Workings (£m)

Consolidation of A and X including previous years' balances for illustration
Cost of Control

Cost of Investment	30	Share Capital – X	5·5
Provision	6·6	Reserves	11
		Revaluation (55% 52 – 30)	12·1
		Goodwill	8
	36·6		36·6
Goodwill	8	Transfer to grp. res	2
		Balance c/d (31.10.X8)	6
	8		8
Balance b/d	6	Share Capital from MI	1
Cost of investment (10%)	8	Reserves from MI	2
Provision	1·7	X – profit for 20X9	1
(10% of 5 + 1·2 MI)		Minority Interest revaluation	2·2
Inter company profit	0·8	Revaluation	(0·2)
		Goodwill c/d	10·5
	16·5		16·5
Goodwill b/d	10·5	Goodwill written off (2 + 1·1)	3·1
		Balance	7·4
	10·5		10·5

Inter group profit X

X has made a profit on the sale of land to A and it needs to be eliminated

DR	Minority Interests 35% of 8	2·8
	Group Reserves 55% of 8	4·4
	Cost of Control 10% of 8	0·8
CR	Tangible fixed assets	8

Group Reserves

Goodwill X 20X8	2	Balance (31.10.X8)	100
X 20X9	3·1	Profit for year	40
Y (20X8/X9)	6	X Reserves	5·5
Provision (55% 5)	2·75	Exchange gain	1
Revaluation Reserves	1·1	Associated Co – post acqn profit	4
Inter group profit – X	4·4		
– Y (2 + 0·8)	2·8		
Balance	128·35		
	150·5		150·5

Minority Interest

Provision	5	·4Share Capital	4·5
Balance c/d	18	X Reserves	9
		Revaluation (45% 52 – 30)	9·9
	23·4		23·4
To Cost of Control – Share Capital (10% of 10)	1	Balance (31.10.X8)	18
To Cost of Control – Reserves (10% of 20)	2	X Reserves	3·5
To Cost of Control – Revaluation (10% of 22)	2·2	Provision – Cost of Control	1·2
Provision (35% 5)	1·75		
Revaluation Reserves	0·7		
Inter group profit	2·8		
Balance	12·25		
	22·7		22·7

X Reserves

Cost of Control (55% of 20)	11	Balance(31.10.X8)	20
Minority Interest (45% of 20)	9		
	20		20
To Cost of Control (10% of 10)	1	Profit for 20X9	10
Minority Interest	3·5		
Group Reserves	5·5		
	10		10

Group Revaluation Reserves

Cost of Control	12·1	Revaluation of X (31.10.X8)	22
Minority Interest	9·9		
	22		22
Revaluation deficit (60 – (52 + 10))	2	Minority Interest (35% 2)	0·7
		Cost of Control (10% 2)	0·2
		Group Reserves (55% 2)	1·1
	2		2

Provision for Warranties

Balance c/f	17	Balance	12
		Additional provision (5% of 200) – 5	5
	17		17

Overseas Investment

Equity shares recorded at $\frac{42m}{3.5} = £12m$

Loan recorded at $\frac{21m}{3.5} = £6m$

Loan retranslated at 31.10.X9 $\frac{21m}{3} = £7m$

Equity shares retranslated at 31.10.X9 $\frac{42m}{3} = £14m$

Therefore there is an exchange gain of £2m on the investment and an exchange loss on the loan of £1m. The exchange gain and loss can be taken to reserves under SSAP20 'Foreign Currency Translation'.

Y Deemed Disposal

A owns 12 million ordinary shares of £1 of Y and this amounted to a 60% holding on 1.11.X8. However Y has issued a further 10 million ordinary shares of £1 to third parties. Thus A's holding is now

$$\frac{12 \text{ million}}{20 \text{ million} + 10 \text{ million}} \text{ ie } \underline{40\%}.$$

Thus it would appear that Y is now an associated company.

	£m
Cost of investment	54
Add post acquisition profit (10 × 40%)	4
less – intercompany profit in stock (2 × 40%)	(0·8)
Less goodwill 12 ÷ 4 × 2 years	(6)
Associated Company	51·2

Tangible Fixed Assets

	£m
A	108
X	50
Inter group profit – X	(8)
Inter group profit – Y	(2)
(land £5m × 40%)	
Foreign currency gain	2
	150

Note: not all of the inter group profit arising on transactions with the associate Y has been eliminated. Only the investors share has been eliminated. FRS 9 'Associates and Joint Ventures' states that profits on inter company trading should be made in the balance sheet against the carrying amount of the asset if it is still held by the group.

Provision for warranty		£m	£m Expense	£m Provn
20X8 5% × 300	=	15	(3)	12
20X9 5% × 200	=	10	(5)	5
				17

Pre acqn 12 × 55%	=	6·6
Pre acqn 17 × 10%	=	1·7
Post acqn 5 × 55%	=	2·75
Minority 17 × 35%	=	5·95

(5·4 – 1·2 + 1·75)

Proof of Minority Interest and goodwill on purchase of 10% holding in X on 31.10.X9

		£m
Minority Interest:	Share of net assets 60 × 35%	21
	Provision (above)	(5·95)
	Inter company	(2·8)
		12·25
Goodwill (10% purchase)	Cost of acqn	8
	Share of net assets (60 – 17 – 8) × 10%	(3·5)
	Goodwill	4·5

15 AB Group

Key answertips

Your answer to part (b) must do more than simply restate the differences between acquisition accounting and merger accounting; it must be related to the scenario in part (a). The fair value adjustments are central to the difference between the two methods in this case.

(a)

Consolidated Profit and Loss Account for the year ending 31 May 20X1
AB Group plc

	Merger Accounting £'000	*Acquisition Accounting* £'000	
Turnover		79,000	62,000
Cost of sales		(56,730)	(42,482)
Gross profit		22,270	19,518
Distribution and administrative expenses		(15,070)	(10,860)
Operating profit		7,200	8,658
Interest payable		(600)	(348)
Profit before taxation		6,600	8,310
Taxation		(2,950)	(2,100)
	3,650	6,210	
Dividends (proposed)		(250)	(250)
	3,400	5,960	

Consolidated Balance Sheet as at 31 May 20X1
AB Group plc

	Merger Accounting £'000	*Acquisition Accounting* £'000
Fixed assets	60,500	64,100
Intangible assets	18,000	28,925
Net current assets	44,500	44,552
Creditors: amounts due after more than one year	(6,000)	(6,217)

	117,000	131,360
Ordinary shares of £1	55,000	55,000
Share premium account	2,800	37,800
Revaluation reserve	10,000	10,000
Profit and loss account	49,200	28,560
	117,000	131,360

Workings

Acquisition Accounting

In the profit and loss account, the consolidated figures are the addition of the holding company's figures and the time apportioned figures of the subsidiary (that is AB's profit and loss account plus ½ of CG's profit and loss account). However, the following adjustments are made to certain categories of expense.

(i)	Cost of Sales	£'000
	Cost of Sales - CG	12,640
	- AB	31,450
	Stock adjustment	(3,000)
	Depreciation adjustment (4,000 × 20% × ½)	400
	Goodwill write off	992
		42,482
(ii)	Distribution and Administrative Expenses	
	AB	9,450
	Acquisition costs	(500)
	CG	1,910
		10,860
(iii)	Interest payable	
	AB	200
	CG	148
		348

Under FRS 7 the fair value of the loan of CG would be as follows (in £'000) (400 ÷ 1.07) + [4,400 + (1.07 Squared)] = £4,217

The profit and loss charge for the six month period for the loan of CG would be

$$\frac{4{,}217 \times 0.07}{2} \text{ i.e. } \underline{£148}$$

Therefore there would be a loan interest adjustment in the balance sheet of 200 – 148 52

(iv) Balance Sheet

Cost of control

Cost of investment	65,000	Ordinary shares	20,000
Stock	3,000	Share premium	6,000
Provision for BD	2,000	CG reserves	28,600
Acquisition costs	300	Revaluation of FA	4,000
Revaluation of loan	217	Brand name - increase in value	2,000
		Goodwill	9,917
	70,517		70,517

AB Reserves

Depreciation on revaluation	400	Balance	25,000
Goodwill written off	992	CG reserves	1,400
Balance	28,560	Stock	3,000
		Acquisition - loan interest adjustment	52
		expenses	500
	29,952		29,952

CC Reserves

Cost of control	28,600	Balance	12,000
Post acquisition profits	1,400	Brand name	18,000
	30,000		30,000

Share Premium

Issue costs	200	Balance - AB	3,000
Balance	37,800	Premium on issue shares	35,000
	38,000		38,000

(v) *Fixed assets*

AB	36,000
CG	24,500
Revaluation	4,000
Depreciation	(400)
	64,100

Intangible assets

Goodwill (9,917 – 992)	8,925
Intangible asset – brand	20,000
	28,925

Net current assets

AB	29,000
CG	17,500
Provision for BD	(2,000)
Interest adj	52
	44,552

An intangible asset acquired as part of a business should be capitalised separately from goodwill if its value can be measured reliably on initial recognition. (FRS 10).

Post acquisition reserves reconciliation

AB retained profits brought forward (25,000 – 2,400)	22,600
Profit for year	5,960
Balance in consolidated balance sheet	28,560

Merger Accounting

	£'000
(vi) Cost of Sales	
AB	31,450
CD	25,280
	56,730

Share Premium account - AB

Balance per question	3,000	
Less: issue costs	(200)	
		2,800

Profit and Loss Account		£'000	
Balance per question (25,000 + 12,000)		37,000	
Add:	issue costs	200	
	brand written off	18,000	
Less:	equity elimination	(4,000)	
	provision for bad debts	(2,000)	
			49,200

Equity elimination

Cost of investment	30,000
Less: share capital - CG	(20,000)
Share premium - CG	(6,000)
Profit and Loss Account	4,000

As regards eliminating the balance of £4,000 there are no particular rules on the matter. If the subsidiary had capitalised £4,000 of its distributable profits then no difference would have emerged, therefore the charge has been made against retained profits.

Distribution and Administrative Expenses		
AB		9,450
CD		3,820
Provision for bad debts	2,000	
Issue costs		(200)
		15,070

Net Current Assets		
AB		29,000
CD		17,500
Provision for bad debts	(2,000)	
		44,500

The provision for bad debts will be provided for under both methods as the provision is still required. The brand name had been written off to reserves by CG but should have been capitalised at cost (FRS 10 'Goodwill and Intangible Assets').

(b) There are several effects of utilising merger accounting rather than acquisition accounting

When using merger accounting, there is no restatement of asset values to fair values, no restatement of the purchase consideration to fair value, no concept of pre and post acquisition profits and no calculation of goodwill. As a result the effect on the financial statements can be significant

If the financial statements of AB under the two methods are compared then the following effects become apparent

(i) The profit before taxation is lower in this case using merger accounting. The main reason for this is that although a whole year's profit is included in the profit and loss account when using merger accounting, the fair value adjustment for stock (£3 million) using acquisition accounting has boosted post acquisition profits and also under merger accounting, the expenses of the merger have to be charged in the profit and loss account thus reducing the disparity between reported profits under merger and acquisition accounting. Additionally the increase in the bad debts provision has been charged under both methods.

(ii) The fair value adjustments under acquisition accounting will cause a drag on future profits. Goodwill and the increase in the depreciation charge due to the increase in the value of fixed assets will cause an increase in the post acquisition cost of sales totalling £1,392,000 in the current year and £1,792,000 per annum in future years. Offsetting this increased cost will be the reduction of the interest charge payable by CG under acquisition accounting (£400,000 – merger: £295,000 – acquisition). Thus in the short term, it appears that the net impact on profits will be quite significant. However goodwill is being written off over 10 years and the increase in the fair value of the assets over five years so that the impact on profits will be greater in the longer term as the loan raised by CG is repayable on 30 November 20X2.

(iii) Under acquisition accounting, an intangible asset acquired as part of the purchase of subsidiary should be capitalised in the balance sheet if its value can be measured reliably. Thus AB would have to recognise the brand name on the acquisition of CG at fair value and the company may not wish to recognise the true value exchanged in the transaction. Although brands are not currently amortised but reviewed annually for impairment, the impairment test is quite comprehensive and involves an annual cost to the company. Additionally, the brand's value may become impaired with the resultant charge against profits. Under merger accounting the brand need only be recognised at its cost with less chance of impairment occurring and the subsequent charge against profits.

(iv) The fair value of the long-term loan in CG will have an adverse effect on the gearing of the company. Essentially under acquisition accounting, part of the future interest charge is being rolled up in the balance sheet.

Thus the balance sheet position will be adversely affected by acquisition accounting. The accumulated profits will be greater under merger accounting because there is no concept of pre acquisition profits (£492m - merger accounting £2856m acquisition accounting). Thus, again merger accounting strengthens the balance sheet position.

(v) The true cost of the transaction is ignored under merger accounting. The share premium account does not record the true premium received on the issue of the shares. This factor can have an adverse effect if the company wishes to issue bonus shares from a share premium account but has a positive effect on Return on Capital Employed (ROCE).

Candidates need only discuss three of the above.

16 Satellite

Key answer tips

Remember to account for the minority interest element of the adjustments where this is appropriate.

(a) (i) **Operating Lease**

The requirement of the lease that the building be returned in good condition means that there is an obligation to a third party which has occurred because of a past event which is the signing of the lease. The obligation cannot be avoided. However FRS 12 'Provisions, Contingent Liabilities and Contingent Assets' states that future repairs and maintenance costs are not present obligations resulting from past events as they relate to the future operation of the business and therefore should be capitalised as assets or written off as operating expenses when incurred. FRS 12 does additionally state that in the case of operating leases, the lessee may have to incur periodic charges for maintenance or make good dilapidations or other damage during the rental period. The recognition of such liabilities is not precluded by the standard if the event giving rise to the obligation under the lease has occurred. Thus in the case of Satellite, due to the severe weather damage, a provision for £1.2 million should be set up.

However, there is a further complication as there is still a need to determine whether a more general provision should be built up over the six years for the dilapidation costs. It could be argued that the event giving rise to the obligation under the lease is the passage of time and, therefore, £1 million ought to be provided for. A stricter interpretation could be that a specific event has to occur and there has to be specific dilapidation before any provision can be made. (For example, where there has been weather damage.) In conclusion, there should be provision of £1.2 million for the renovating due to the exceptional weather damage and a further provision of say (£6 million – £1.2 million divided by 6, i.e. £800,000) for the obligation under the lease as it cannot be avoided. If the operating lease was terminated immediately then some expenditure would be required on the interior of the building and the exterior would require complete renovation. Thus the total provision required is £2 million.

It is possible that if the spirit of FRS 12 were adopted that the provision required could be based on the actual dilapidation in the year. This would be difficult to estimate and may not be more accurate than the arbitrary allocation made.

Leasehold property

In this case an obligation to restore the building to its original state arose when the sports facility was created. It appears that the company cannot avoid the reinstatement costs and, therefore, full provision of £2 million should be made. The company should set up a corresponding asset as the sports facility represents access to future economic benefits that are to be enjoyed over more than one period. The amount will be added to the finance lease costs and additional depreciation of 10% of £2 million will be charged as follows:

		£'000
DR	Group retained profits	160
	Minority Interest	40
CR	Depreciation	200

The Balance Sheet value of the leased building is (£8 million + £2 million – £200,000) £9.8 million. However the recoverable amount of the lease is £9.5 million and, therefore, the asset is impaired and requires writing down to this amount:

		£'000
DR	Group retained profits	240
	Minority Interest	60
CR	Leased asset	300

Owned Assets

Major periodic repairs to fixed assets are not provided for under FRS 12. These repairs are not present obligations of the company as they relate to the future operations of the company. If there is declining service potential then the asset should be depreciated to reflect this and expenditure on repairs and maintenance should be capitalised to reflect the restoration of service potential. Also the repairs in the case of Satellite could be avoided by selling the buildings. Thus no provision for the £6 million is made.

(ii) Database

FRS 10 'Goodwill and Intangible Assets states that internally generated intangible assets may only be capitalised if they have a readily ascertainable market value. A readily ascertainable market value has to be established by reference to a market where:

(a) the asset belongs to a homogeneous population of assets that are equivalent in all material aspects, and

(b) an active market evidenced by frequent transactions, exists for that population of assets.

The database clearly falls to meet the above criteria for capitalisation as only if the database were sold to other companies and there is an established market for such databases would it meet the criteria. However the cost of the database would appear to meet the criteria for being treated as development costs. SSAP 13 'Accounting for Research and Development' defines development costs as 'use of scientific or technical knowledge in order to produce new or substantially improved materials, devices, products or services, to install new processes or systems prior to the commencement of commercial production or commercial applications, or to improving substantially those already produced or installed'.

Capitalisation is only permitted if recovery of the costs is assured and as the publication has quickly become a market leader', then this would seem to be the case. The conditions in SSAP 13 (clearly defined project expenditure separately identifiable, outcome of project assessed with reasonable certainty future revenue exceeds costs, and adequate resources exist) would have to be met and at each balance sheet date, the unamortised balance should be reviewed to ensure that it still fulfils the criteria of SSAP 13.

The most suitable treatment appears to be to regard the costs as development expenditure so that it will remain as an intangible asset. Thus the cost should be written off over four years as the data will require substantial revision at this time and not ten years as for intangible assets. This will mean the following entries should be made as regards the increased amortisation:

		£'000
DR	Group reserves	360
	Minority Interest	90
CR	Intangible fixed assets	450

(iii) Satellite, being a listed company, will have to comply with the disclosure requirements of FRS 13 'Derivatives and other Financial Instruments: Disclosures' and disclose its accounting policy in respect of hedge accounting, which will be to translate its foreign currency assets and liabilities at the forward rate (SSAP 20) at the date of delivery. Under this method no exchange gain or loss is recognised and this reflects the fact that the company has eliminated all currency risks by entering into the contract. The forward premium inherent in the currency contract (the difference between the forward rate and the spot rate at 1 December 20X0) is not separately identified.

The inter company profit in stock will need to be eliminated as two thirds of the stock remains unsold. The value of the stock in Satellite's books is £1 million (2/3 of 2.1 million dinars ÷ 1.4) of which the inter company element is £200,000. The accounting entries will be:

		£'000
DR	Profit and Loss account	200,000
CR	Stock	200,000

Additionally the company will have to disclose certain information about the hedge accounting gains and losses. This information is required by FRS 13 (paragraph 59). In taking out the forward contract and accounting for the foreign currency assets and liabilities in this way the company has fixed the cost of the stock at £1.5 million based on the forward contract rate (2.1 million dinars ÷ 1.4).

Satellite has paid nothing to enter into the forward contract and, therefore, its book and fair value at the inception date is zero. At 31 March 20X1, the settlement date, there is a loss on the hedging contract of (2.1 million dinars at 1.45 – 2.1 million dinars at 1.4) i.e. £51,724. Part of this loss relating to the stock sold (one third) is essentially recognised in the profit and loss account for the year (£17,241). The balance represents a deferred loss of £34,483 which is carried forward in the value of stock. However; it would seem logical that this could be reduced by the inter company element, i.e. 20% on selling price, and only £27,586 be disclosed under FRS 13 as being a deferred loss carried forward in the balance sheet pending recognition in the profit and loss account. Also, based on the assumption that the remaining stock will be sold in the next year this figure should be shown as a loss which is expected to be recognised in the profit and loss account in the next accounting period.

(iv) The time limit for fair value adjustments imposed by FRS 7 'Fair Values in Acquisition Accounting' applies only to the acquired assets and liabilities. There is no time limit on the recognition of goodwill relating to contingent consideration (paragraph 27 FRS 7). Therefore, an additional amount of goodwill of £8 million is recognised and a liability of £8 million shown. The increase in goodwill should be written off over the remaining useful life of four years, it is an adjustment to a prior period's accounting estimate. Due credit will be given to those candidates who argue that the adjustment could be taken back to the date of acquisition of the subsidiary

		£m
DR	Group Reserves	2
	Goodwill	6
CR	Creditors	8

(b) **Revised Group Balance Sheet as at 30 November 20X1**

	£'000
Fixed Assets	
Intangible Assets (5,180 – 450 + 6,000)	10,730
Fixed Assets (38,120 + 2,000 – 200 – 300)	39,620
	50,350
Net current assets (27,900 – 200 – 8,000)	19,700
Total Assets less Current Liabilities	70,050
Creditors: amounts falling due after more than one year	(12,700)
Provisions for liabilities and charges (900 + 2,000 + 2,000)	(4,900)
Minority Interests (9,100 – 40 – 60 – 90)	(8,910)
	43,540

Capital and Reserves	
Called up share capital	16,100
Share Premium account	5,000
Profit and Loss account (27,400 – 2,000 – 160 – 240 – 360 – 200 – 2,000)	22,440
	43,540

17 Bull plc

(a) (i) The question requires a knowledge of the considerations that influence the choice of translation method; an understanding of dominant currency; an ability to apply the criteria of the standard to the particular circumstances given.

Choice of translation method

The standard requires that the method to be used for translating the financial statements of a foreign enterprise should reflect the financial and other operational relationship which exists between the holding company and its foreign enterprise: SSAP 20 para 13. In most cases this means that the consolidated accounts will be prepared using the closing rate/net investment method. However, the temporal method is to be used where the trade of the foreign enterprise is more dependent on the economic environment of the investing company's currency than that of its own reporting currency.

Dominant currency

The determination of the dominant currency requires other factors to be taken into account SSAP 20 para 23 including:

- The extent to which the cash flows of the enterprise have a direct impact upon those of the investing company e.g. whether there is a regular and frequent movement of cash between the holding company and the foreign enterprise.

- The extent to which the functioning of the enterprise is dependent directly upon the investing company e.g. whether management is based locally.

- The currency in which the majority of the trading transactions are denominated e.g. whether invoicing and payment of expenses are in the foreign currency.

- The major currency to which the operation is exposed e.g. whether the company is dependent on local financing.

Examples of situations where the temporal method may be appropriate are:

- Where enterprise acts as a selling agency for holding company products.
- Where enterprise supplies raw materials for inclusion in the holding company products.
- Where the enterprise is located overseas for tax purposes.

Application to facts given in the question

(ii) Advising management

The question states that Dog Inc supplies soya oil to be used as a raw material in the drugs manufactured by Bull plc. This indicates that the appropriate method is the temporal method under the example listed above.

(b) Translate the profit and loss account and balance sheet of Dog Inc for consolidation purposes using the temporal method.

The first stage is to establish the equity interest at 1 November 20X2 as follows:

	$'000	*Exchange rate*	£
Fixed assets			
Plant and equipment			
Cost	1,800	2.2	818,182
Aggregate depreciation	600	2.2	272,727
	1,200	2.2	545,455
Current assets			
Stock	115	1.8	63,889
Net monetary assets (balance)	(45)	1.8	(25,000)
	1,270		584,344
Ordinary share capital	375	3.6	104,167
Profit and loss account	895	balance	480,177
	1,270		584,344

The second stage is to translate the balance sheet as at 31 October 20X3 as follows:

	$'000	*Exchange rate*	£
Fixed assets			
Plant and equipment			
Cost	1,800	2.2	818,182
Aggregate depreciation	750	2.2	340,909
	1,050	2.2	477,273
Current assets			
Stock	120	1.1	109,091
Net monetary assets (balance)	255	1.1	231,818
	1,425		818,182
Ordinary share capital	375	3.6	104,167
Profit and loss account	1,050	balance	714,015
	1,425		818,182

The third stage is to translate the profit and loss account excluding the exchange difference as follows:

Profit and loss account for the year ended 31 October 20X3

	$'000	$'000	*Exchange rate*	£
Sales	3,750		1.5	2,500,000
Cost of sales				
Stock at 1.11.X	2115		1.8	63,889
Purchases	3,000		1.5	2,000,000
	3,115			2,063,889
Stock at 31.10.X3	120		1.1	109,091
		2,995		1,954,798

Gross profit		755		545,202
Administration expenses	100		1.5	66,667
Handling charges	200		1.5	133,333
Depreciation	150		2.2	68,182
		450		
Profit before tax		305		277,020
Tax		150	1.5	100,000
Profit after tax		155		177,020

The fourth stage is to identify the exchange difference as follows:

	£
Profit and loss as at 1.11.X2	480,177
Add retained profits	177,020
	657,197
Less profit and loss as at 31.10.X3	714,015
Exchange gain	56,818

The profit before tax is revised:

	£
Profit pre-exchange loss	277,020
Exchange gain	56,818
Profit before tax	333,838
Less: Tax	100,000
Profit after tax	233,838

(c) (i) There is an exchange gain of £448,990 calculated as follows:

	$'000
Net assets at 1.11.X2	1,270
	£
At rate at 1.11.X2 [1,270,000/1.8]	705,555
At rate at 31.10.X2 [1,270,000/1.1]	1,154,545
Exchange gain	448,990

The exchange gain will be recorded as movement on reserves. If exchange differences were introduced into the profit and loss account, the results from trading operations, as shown in the local currency financial statements would be distorted.

The question requires a further analysis to quantify the profit for the year and the opening and closing profit and loss account balance in the balance sheet.

First, establish the profit and loss account balance as at 1 November 20X2 as follows:

	$'000	*Exchange rate*	£
Net assets	1,270	1.8	705,556
Ordinary share capital	375	3.6	104,167
Profit and loss account	895	balance	601,389
	1,270		705,556

Second, establish the profit and loss account balance as at 31 October 20X3.

	$'000	*Exchange rate*	£
Net assets	1,425	1.1	1,295,455

Third, translate the profit for the year ended 31 October 20X3 at the closing rate:

$155,000/1.1 = £140,909

Finally, reconcile the profit and loss account balances as follows:

		£
Profit and loss account as at 31.10.X2	601,389	
Add: Profit for the year	140,909	
		742,298
Add: The exchange gain	448,990	
Profit and loss account as at 31.10.X3	1,191,288	

(ii) The profit for the year using the average rate of exchange would be $155,000/1.5 = £103,333.

The difference of £37,576 [£140,909-£103,333] would be recorded as a movement on reserves.

(d) This requires an understanding of the effect of financing foreign equity investments by borrowings on the company-only accounts.

In the company-only accounts, there will be a gain on the investment and a loss on the loan. These are calculated as follows:

	£
Investment in Dog Inc	
1.11.X2 $375,000 at 1.8 =	208,333
31.10.X3 $375,000 at 1.1 =	340,909
Exchange gain	132,576
Loan	
1.11.X2 $750,000 at 1.8 =	416,667
31.10.X3 $750,000 at 1.1 =	681,818
Exchange loss	265,151

The exchange gain on the investment would be set against the exchange loss on the loan and the net difference of £132,575 would be debited to the profit and loss account.

18 UK plc

(a)

MEMORANDUM

To: Recipient

From: An accountant

Subject: Accounting treatment of Germany gmbh **Date:** XX XX XX

UK plc has purchased 75% of the shares in Germany gmbh. As UK plc's investment in Germany gmbh is greater than 20% and is for the long term, it qualifies as a participating interest (as defined by FRS 2 *Accounting for subsidiary undertakings*). As UK plc can control the long-term strategy of Germany gmbh, it exercises a dominant influence over it. Germany gmbh is therefore a subsidiary undertaking of UK plc and must be consolidated.

In order to include the financial statements of Germany gmbh in the consolidation, it is necessary to translate them into sterling. SSAP 20 *Foreign currency translation* describes two methods of translation. These are the closing rate or net investment method and the temporal method. The choice of method is dictated by the relationship between the parent and the subsidiary. Generally speaking, the closing rate method is appropriate where the subsidiary is an autonomous business and the temporal method is appropriate where the subsidiary is a direct extension of the operations of the parent company.

Germany gmbh operates as a fairly autonomous entity on a day-to-day basis. Its operations are partly financed by a loan in the local currency, meaning that it is not dependent on the reporting currency of UK plc. These factors suggest that the closing rate method is appropriate.

The closing rate method recognises that the parent's investment is in the net worth of its subsidiary. All items in the balance sheet, other than share capital and pre-acquisition reserves are translated at the rate of exchange ruling at the balance sheet date. Share capital and pre-acquisition reserves are translated using the rate of exchange ruling at the date on which the investment was acquired. All items in the profit and loss account are translated at either the rate of exchange ruling at the balance sheet date or at the average rate for the period. Exchange differences will arise on the retranslation of opening net assets each year and these will be taken directly to reserves. These exchange differences do not form part of the results for the year because they would distort the subsidiary's own results for the period and they do not affect cash flows.

(b)

Balance sheet of Germany gmbh at 31 March 20X6

	DM'000	*Rate*	£'000
Fixed assets	30,000	2.2	13,636
Stocks	18,000	2.2	8,182
Trade debtors	15,000	2.2	6,819
Trade creditors	(6,000)	2.2	(2,727)
Proposed dividends	(4,400)	2.2	(2,000)
Bank overdraft	(7,600)	2.2	(3,455)
Long-term liabilities	(20,000)	2.2	(9,091)
	25,000		11,364
Called up share capital	15,000	3.0	5,000
Pre-acquisition reserves	5,000	3.0	1,667
Post-acquisition reserves	5,000	balancing figure	4,697
	25,000		11,364

Consolidated balance sheet of UK plc at 31 March 20X6

	£'000	£'000
Tangible fixed assets (20,000 + 13,636)		33,636
Current assets:		
Stocks (10,000 + 8,182)	18,182	
Trade debtors (8,500 + 6,819)	15,319	
	33,501	
Creditors: amounts falling due within one year		
Bank overdraft (6,100 + 3,455)	9,555	
Trade creditors (4,000 + 2,727)	6,727	
Proposed dividends:		
parent undertaking	3,900	
minority interest (25% × 2,000)	500	
	20,682	
Net current assets		12,819
Total assets less current liabilities		46,455
Creditors: amounts falling due after more than one year:		
Loans (10,000 + 9,091)		(19,091)
		27,364
		£'000
Capital and reserves:		
Called up share capital		9,000
Profit and loss account (W2)		15,523
		24,523
Minority interest (W3)		2,841
		27,364

(c)

Profit and loss account of Germany gmbh for the year ended 31 March 20X6

	DM'000	*Rate*	£'000
Turnover	60,000	2.2	27,273
Cost of sales	(30,000)	2.2	(13,636)
Gross profit	30,000		13,637
Operating expenses	(16,000)	2.2	(7,273)
Operating profit	14,000		6,364
Interest payable	(2,000)	2.2	(909)
Profit before taxation	12,000		5,455
Taxation	(4,200)	2.2	(1,909)
Profit after taxation	7,800		3,546
Dividend proposed	(4,400)	2.2	(2,000)
Retained profit for the year	3,400		1,546

Consolidated profit and loss account of UK plc for the year ended 31 March 20X6

	£'000
Turnover (50,000 + 27,273)	77,273
Cost of sales (25,000 + 13,636)	(38,636)
Gross profit	38,637
Operating expenses (15,000 + 7,273 + 125 (W1))	(22,398)
Operating profit	16,239
Interest payable (1,000 + 909)	(1,909)
Profit on ordinary activities before taxation	14,330
Tax on profit on ordinary activities (3,600 + 1,909)	(5,509)
Profit on ordinary activities after taxation	8,821
Minority interest (25% × 3,546)	(886)
Profit attributable to the group for the year	7,935
Proposed dividend	(3,900)
Retained profit for the year	4,035

(d)

Reconciliation of consolidated reserves

	£'000	£'000
Opening balance		
UK plc		9,500
Germany gmbh (75% × 2,333 (W4))		1,750
Less: goodwill amortised (500 × ¾) (W1)		(375)
Consolidated reserves at 1 April 20X5		10,875
Add: group retained profit for the year		4,035
Exchange differences on re-translation of opening net assets of Germany gmbh:		
At rate on 1 April 20X5 (21,600 ÷ 2.4)	9,000	
At rate on 31 March 20X6 (21,600 ÷ 2.2)	(9,818)	
Exchange gain	818	
Group share (75%)		613
Consolidated reserves at 31 March 20X6 (W2)		15,523

Workings

(W1) **Goodwill**

	£'000	£'000
Cost of investment		5,500
Less: Share of net assets acquired:		
Share capital	5,000	
Profit and loss account	1,667	
	6,667	

Group share (75%)	(5,000)
	500
Annual amortisation charge (500 ÷ 4)	125

(W2) **Consolidated profit and loss account**

	£'000
UK plc:	12,500
Germany gmbh: group share of post-acquisition profits (75% × 4,697)	3,523
Less: Goodwill amortised (W1)	(500)
	15,523

(W3) **Minority interest**

	£'000
Minority share of net assets at 31 March 20X6: (25% × 11,364)	2,841

(W4) **Opening post-acquisition reserves in Germany gmbh**

	DM'000	*Rate*	£'000
Called up share capital	15,000	3.0	5,000
Pre-acquisition reserves	5,000	3.0	1,667
Post-acquisition reserves	1,600	balancing figure	2,333
	21,600	2.4	9,000

19 Rowen plc

(a)

Consolidated profit and loss account of the Rowen Group for the year ended 31 December 20X3

	Rowen £m	*Overseas* £m	*Consolidated* £m
Turnover	2,784	676.5	3,460.5
Cost of sales	1,822	449.2	2,271.2
Gross profit	962	227.3	1,189.3
Distribution costs	392	53.0	445.0
Administrative expenses	370	17.7	387.7
Depreciation and amortisation	35	12.0	47.3
Dividends received	(23)		(11.0)
Exchange differences		6.5	6.5
Profit before tax	188	138.1	313.8
Tax	93	53.0	146.0
Profit after tax	95	85.1	167.8

Minority interests	60% of 85.1	51.0
		116.8
Dividends paid		37.0
		79.8

Consolidated balance sheet as at 31 December 20X3

	Rowen £m	*Overseas* £m	*Consolidated* £m
Fixed assets			
Intangible assets: goodwill			1.5
Tangible assets	669	229.0	898.0
Investment in Europe	10		10.0
Current assets			
Stock	675	27.5	702.5
Cash	46	75.3	121.3
Current liabilities			
Trade creditors	(490)	20.7	(510.7)
Creditors due after more than one year			
Loans	(370)	68.7	(438.7)
			783.9
Capital and reserves			
Share capital			185.0
Profit and loss account			453.5
Minority interest (60% of 242.4)			145.4
			783.9

Statement of group reserves for the year ended 31 December 20X3

Profit and loss account at 31 December 20X2	373.7
Retained profit for the year	79.8
Profit and loss account at 31 December 20X3	453.5

Workings

(W1) Goodwill to be recognised on Overseas Inc acquisition

		US$m	£m
Cost			12
Less:	Share of net assets acquired		
	Share capital	20	
	Profit and loss account	25	
		45	
Translated at \$2 × 40%			9
Goodwill			3

∴ annual amortisation charge = £0.3m.

(W2) Translation of Overseas Inc balance sheet at 31 December 20X3

	Overseas **US$m**	*Exchange rate*	**£m**
Fixed assets			
Tangible assets	458	2.0	229.0
Current assets			
Stocks	44	1.6	27.5
Cash	113	1.5	75.3
Current liabilities			
Creditors	(31)	1.5	(20.7)
Creditors falling due after more than one year			
Loan	(103)	1.5	(68.7)
	481		242.4
Capital and reserves			
Share capital	20	2.0	10.0
Pre-acquisition profit	25	2.0	12.5
Post-acquisition profit	436	Balance	219.9
	481		242.4

(W3) Group reserves at 31 December 20X3

	£m
Rowen plc	367.0
Overseas Inc (40% of 219.9)	88.0
	455.0
Less goodwill amortised to date	(1.5)
	453.5

(W4) Translation of the profit and loss account of Overseas Inc for the year ended 31 December 20X3

The profit and loss accounts for the year ended 31 December 20X3 are as follows:

	Overseas US$m	*Rate*	£m	£m
Turnover	1,150	1.7		676.5
Opening stock	57	2.0	28.5	
Purchases	762	1.7	448.2	
Closing stock	(44)	1.6	(27.5)	
Cost of sales	775			449.2
Gross profit	375			227.3
Distribution costs	90	1.7	53.0	
Admin. expenses	30	1.7	17.7	
Depreciation	24	2.0	12.0	
				82.7
Exchange differences				6.5
Profit before tax	231			138.1
Tax	90	1.7		53.0

Profit after tax	141		85.1
Dividends paid 31.7.93	51	1.7	30.0
Retained profit	90		55.1
Profit and loss a/c b/f (W5)	346		164.8
Profit and loss a/c c/f (W2)	436		219.9

(W5) (a) Calculating net assets/liabilities at 31 December 20X2 in US$

		US$m
Share capital		20
Pre-acquisition profit		25
Post-acquisition profit (436 – 90)		346
		391
Less: Fixed assets (458 + 24)	482	
Stock	57	
		539
Net monetary liabilities		148

(b) Calculate the opening post-acquisition profit and loss account balance

	US$m	Rate	£m
Fixed assets	482	2.0	241.0
Stock	57	2.0	28.5
Net monetary liabilities	(148)	1.8	(82.2)
			187.3
Less: Share capital	20	2.0	(10.0)
Pre-acquisition profit	25	2.0	(12.5)
Post-acquisition profit (436 – 90)	346		164.8

(W6) Group reserves at 31 December 20X2

Rowen plc (367-58)		309.0
Overseas Inc [40% of 164.8]	65.9	
		374.9
Less: Goodwill amortised to date		1.2
		373.7

(W7) Exchange difference carried to profit and loss account

On opening net monetary liabilities of US$148m

Translated at US$1.5 exchange rate at 31.12.X3	(98.7)	
Translated at US$1.8 exchange rate at 31.12.X2	82.2	
		(16.5)

On profit and loss items expressed at average rate

	US$m	
Balance retained	90.0	
Stock change	13.0	
Depreciation	24.0	
	127.0	
Translated at US$1.5 rate at 31.12.X3	84.7	
Translated at US$1.7 rate at average	(74.7)	
		10.0
Exchange loss		(6.5)

(b) (i) The profit and loss account for the year ended 31 December 20X3 will be translated using the closing rate to arrive at the profit before tax; tax and profit after tax figures.

	Europe **FFm**	***Exchange rate*** **£m**	***Included in the consolidation***
Turnover	10,615		
Cost of sales	7,154		
Gross profit	3,461		
Distribution costs	831		
Administrative expenses	278		
Depreciation	230		
Profit before tax	2,122	8.0	265.3
Tax	831	8.0	103.9
Profit after tax	1,291	8.0	161.4
Dividends paid 31.7.X3	440		
Retained profit	851		

		£m
Profit before tax per draft consolidated accounts		313.8
Less: Dividends received from Europe SA		11.0
Amortisation charge (W)		0.2
		302.6
Add: 25% share of associated undertaking's profit (25% of 265.3)		66.3
Amended profit before tax		368.9
Tax per consolidated accounts	146.0	
Add 25% of Europe's tax	26.0	
		172.0
Amended profit after tax		196.9

(ii) Carrying value of investment in Europe if treated as an associated undertakingz

	£m
Share of net assets	
$25\% \times \frac{\text{FF4,431m}}{8}$	138.5
Premium on acquisition (W)	0.9
	139.4

Working

Goodwill arising on acquiring 25% of Europe SA

	FFm	£m
Cost		10.0
Net assets acquired		
Share capital	180	
Reserves	230	
	410	
$25\% \times \frac{410}{12.5}$		8.2
		1.8

∴ annual amortisation charge = £0.2m.

After 5 years the NBV of goodwill = $\frac{5}{10}$ × £1.8m = £0.9m.

20 Angol plc

Key answer tips

Read the question carefully. The subsidiary's fixed assets must be translated at the date of purchase; not all the fixed assets were purchased before 1 June 1993.

Consolidated profit and loss account for the Angol plc Group for the year ended 31 May 20X6

		£'000	
Operating profit		W7	867,567
Less: Tax		W8	(348,625)
Profit after tax			518,942
Less: Minority interest	W9	(11,851)	
Profit attributable to Angol plc shareholders	N1	507,091	
Less: Proposed dividend		(262,500)	
		244,591	

N1 **The profit before dividend dealt with in the accounts of the company is £516,125,000.**

Consolidated balance sheet as at 31 May 20X6

		Angol plc	*Frank SA*	*Consolidated*
		£'000	£'000	£'000
Fixed assets				
Land at cost		630,000	121,800	751,800
Buildings at depreciated cost		529,200	27,552	556,752
Plant and machinery		348,600	11,970	360,570
		1,507,800	161,322	1,669,122
Investment in Frank SA		147,000		
Current assets				
Stock		168,000	19,200	187,200
Debtors		426,300	25,800	452,100
Bank		176,400	7,200	183,600
		770,700	52,200	822,900
		Angol plc	*Frank SA*	*Consolidated*
		£'000	£'000	£'000
Current liabilities				
Creditors		(413,700)	(27,000)	(440,700)
Tax		(320,000)	(32,714)	(352,714)
Proposed dividend		(262,500)		(262,500)
		(996,200)	(59,714)	(1,055,914)
Net current liabilities		(225,500)	(7,514)	(233,014)
Total assets less current liabilities		1,429,300	153,808	1,436,108
Capital and reserves				
Ordinary shares of £1		525,000		525,000
Reserves	(W11)	904,300		864,966
Shareholders' funds		1,429,300		1,389,966
Minority interests	(W10)			46,142
		1,429,300		1,436,108

(W1)

Translate balance sheet of Frank SA as at 31 May 20X6

	FF'000	*Rate*	£'000
Fixed assets			
Land at cost	1,218,000	10	121,800
Buildings at depreciated cost	275,520	10	27,552
Plant and machinery	111,300	W2	11,970
Current assets			
Stock	134,400	7	19,200
Debtors	180,600	7	25,800
Bank	50,400	7	7,200
	365,400		52,200
Current liabilities			
Creditors	(189,000)	7	(27,000)
Tax	(229,000)	7	(32,714)
	(418,000)		(59,714)

Net current liabilities	(52,600)		(7,514)
	1,552,220		153,808
Capital and reserves			
Ordinary shares of FF1	1,050,000	10	105,000
Reserves at acquisition	126,000	10	12,600
Reserves	376,220	balance	36,208
	1,552,220		153,808

(W2)

Translating plant

		£'000
Cost:of existing plant	FF108,150/10	10,815
of new plant	FF84,000/9	9,333
		20,148
Aggregate depreciation		
Purchased in year	FF8,400/9	933
At 1.6.X5	FF72,450/10	7,245
		8,178
Net book value	FF111,300	11,970

(W3)

Translate profit and loss account

	Frank SA FF'000		£'000
Operating profit	588,000	W4	74,139
Tax on profit	(229,000)	W8	(28,625)
Profit after tax	359,000		45,514
Dividend paid	(185,000)	15,125/70 × 100	(21,607)
Retained profit	174,000		23,907

Note that the closing rate is also acceptable for translating the tax figure. This would give a figure of £32,714,285.

(W4)

Frank SA operating profit translated

		FF'000
Per Frank SA profit and loss account		588,000
Add back depreciation:		
on buildings	[FF504,000/50 years]	10,080
on plant	[FF192,150/10 years]	19,215
		617,295

		£'000	£'000
Translated at average rate	[617,295/8]		77,162
Less depreciation:			
on buildings	[FF10,080/10]	1,008	
on plant existing at date of acquisition	[FF10,815/10]	1,082	
acquired on 1.6.X5	[FF8,400/9]	933	
			3,023
			74,139

(W5)

Translate balance sheet of Frank SA as at 1 June 20X5

	FF'000	FF'000	Rate	£'000
Fixed assets				
Land at cost		1,218,000	10	121,800
Buildings				
Cost	504,000			
Depreciation	218,400			
		285,600	10	28,560
Plant and machinery				
Cost	108,150			
Depreciation	61,635			
		46,515	10	4,652
		1,550,115		
Net current liabilities [balance]		(171,895)	9	(19,099)
		1,378,220		135,913
Share capital		1,050,000	10	105,000
Reserves:				
at date of acquisition		126,000	10	12,600
post acquisition		202,220	balance	18,313
[1,552,220 – 174,000]		1,378,220		135,913

(W6)

Exchange difference

Post acquisition reserves at 31.5.X6	W1	36,208
Post acquisition reserves at 1.6.X5	W5	18,313
Increase		17,895
Retained profit for year	W3	23,907
Exchange loss		(6,012)

(W7)

Operating profits

		£'000
Angol plc		821,000
Frank SA	W4	74,139
Exchange loss		(6,012)
Goodwill amortisation (64,680 ÷ 3)		(21,560)
		867,567

(W8)

Tax

	£'000
Angol plc	320,000
Frank SA	28,625
	348,625

(W9)

Minority interest

	£'000
30% of [£45,514,000 – £6,012,000] =	11,851

(W10)

Minority interest

Calculate as 30% of £153,808,000 = £46,142,400

(W11)

Consolidated reserves

	£'000
Angol plc reserves	904,300
Frank SA post acquisition reserves	
70% of £36,208,000	25,346
	929,646
Less goodwill written off W12	64,680
	864,966

(W12)

Goodwill

	£'000	£'000
Cost of shares in Frank SA		147,000
Less shares		
70% of £105,000,000	73,500	
pre-acquisition reserves		
70% of £12,600,000	8,820	
		82,320
Goodwill		64,680

21 Hyper-inflation

Key answer tips

Care must be taken with part (a) as this is *not* the usual question about the choice of translation method. You are required to explain the factors determining the *functional currency* as well as how *these factors* influence the choice of method.

In part (c) your answer should not just compare the results of the three calculations, but should also discuss the validity of the different approaches to adjusting for the effects of inflation.

(a) For most investments in foreign enterprises from the UK, the foreign companies will normally be separate or quasi independent entities. The normal operations will be based in local currency and are likely to be at least partly financed locally and are unlikely to be totally dependent upon the reporting currency of the holding company. The foreign enterprise will probably be managed in such a way as to maximise the local currency profits attributable to the holding company.

If as described above, the foreign entity's operations are relatively self contained and integrated within a foreign country, its functional or dominant currency would ordinarily be its local one and therefore the closing rate method would be used to preserve the financial statement ratios.

The financial statements expressed in local currency will be the best indicator of the performance of the foreign enterprise. Thus in order to preserve the inter relationships of the items in the financial statements denominated in local currency, a single rate of exchange ought to be used when translating them into the holding company's currency. If however the trade of the foreign enterprise is more dependent on the economic environment of the investing company's currency and is merely an extension of the holding company's operations, then its functional or dominant currency would be that of the holding company. In this case the temporal method should be used as this method reflects the transaction as if they had been carried out by the investing company itself.

No single factor would indicate when the temporal method should be used but the following factors should be taken into account:

(i) The extent to which the cash flows of the enterprise have an impact on those of the investing company.

(ii) The extent to which the functioning of the enterprise is dependent directly upon the investing company.

(iii) The currency in which the majority of the trading transactions are denominated.

(iv) The major currency to which the operation is exposed in its financing structure.

It is possible to summarise the factors which might determine the functional currency into:

(i) Cash flow indicators.
(ii) Sales price and market indicators - is the price and market determined locally?
(iii) Expense indicators - local costs or imported labour/parts.
(iv) Financing indicators - locally or from parent company.
(v) Intercompany transactions - low volume or high volume of transactions.

The functional currency determines the translation method used. As the two main methods are so diverse in their application and effect on the financial statements, this decision is the key feature as the disposition of exchange gains and losses is determined by it.

(b) Failure to adjust for hyper-inflation before translating the financial statements of a foreign enterprise can cause significant distortion in the group accounts. Profits may be inflated either from high interest income on deposits in a rapidly depreciating currency or from trading at unrealistic levels of profitability. Additionally a significant exchange loss may be taken to reserves.

More generally, adjusting for hyper-inflation enables management to gauge better the performance of the subsidiary's financial assets within the environment in which the subsidiaries assets are domiciled. Financial statements can be assessed in terms of local currency as well as the impact of inflation on these results. Additionally if devaluation of a currency occurs, the full effects of the devaluation and the hyper-inflation can be assessed.

Foreign currency translation methods under SSAP 20 ignore the effects of hyper-inflation in the consolidation process. With many of the emerging economies suffering from high inflation, it is important that local currency financial statements are adjusted to reflect current price levels.

(c) (i) (1)

	Value E million	Exchange *rate*	£ million
30 November 20X3	20	1.34	14.93
30 November 20X7	20	17.87	1.12

Therefore on 30 November 20X3, the value of the hotels would be £14.93 million but would drop to £1.12 million on 30 November 20X7.

(2)

	Value E million	*Index*	*Exchange rate £*		*£ million*
30 November 20X7	20 ×	$\frac{3,254}{100}$	17.87	=	36.42

Therefore the value of the hotels would be £36.42 million after adjusting for current price levels.

(3)

	Value E million	Dollar rate	Value $ million	Pound rate per $	Value £ million
30 November 20X7	20	0.93	21.51	0.66	14.2

The asset is remeasured using the historical rate of exchange for US dollars at 30 November 20X3. The original cost of the asset is therefore $21.51 million. This is then translated into sterling at the US dollar exchange rate at 30 November 20X7 i.e. £14.2 million.

(ii) Part (1) of the answer illustrates the disappearing assets' problem associated with foreign enterprises in hyper-inflationary economies. The value of the hotels has dropped due to exchange rate movements and not necessarily due to local factors. In the country concerned the value may have increased. This point is illustrated in answer (2) where on adjustment for the consumer price index, it appears that the asset may be worth substantially more than on acquisition.

Answer (3) utilises a method which uses the movement between the original currency of record and a stable currency as a surrogate for an inflation index. However, if one looks at the underlying principles of methods (2) and (3) it can be argued that the translation of an inflation adjusted foreign currency amount could result in a double charge for inflation as exchange rates also reflect the increase in inflation in a country. Additionally historical amounts translated into a stable currency are seldom perfectly negatively correlated with price level changes whereas balance sheet amounts may be adjusted for inflation effects. Thus all three methods have underlying faults not least of which being that they produce significantly different valuations. UITF 9 does however state that if either of methods (2) and (3) are inappropriate, then alternative methods to eliminate the distortions should be adopted.

Method (3) treats the investment in property as if it were a dollar monetary investment. The effect therefore is that the value of the hotel is based on the movement of the dollar/pound sterling exchange rate which may not be affected by the pound/effados rate and the value of the property.

22 XY Group

Key answer tips

Your answer to part (c) should cover a range of shortcomings of SSAP 20, rather than concentrating on one or two (meeting the requirement to *discuss why*).

(a)

Consolidated Balance Sheet at 31 December 20X7
XY Group

	£m
Tangible fixed assets	1,340
Goodwill	4
Net current assets	872
Long-term creditors	(558)
Minority interests	(60)
	1,598
Share capital	330
Share premium	350
Reserves	918
	1,598

It is acceptable to show the consolidated balance sheet/profit and loss account as per working (iii)/(v) although candidates will not gain maximum marks for presentation.

Workings

(W1) *Translation of subsidiary's balance sheet*

	KR	*rate*	*£m*
Net assets	1,420	5	284
Share capital	240	4	60
Share premium	80	4	20
Pre acquisition reserves	610	4	152.5
Post acquisition reserves	490	Balance	51.5
	1,420		284

(W2) Consolidated balance sheet workings

	£m			
	Group			
	Total	*Preacq*	*Postacq*	*MI*
Share capital	60	48		12
Share premium	20	16		4
Reserves at acquisition	152.5	122		30.5
Reserves since acquisition	51.5		41.2	10.3
Revaluation	27.5	22		5.5
Cost of investment (270-50)		220		
Goodwill		12	(8)	
			33.2	62.3

(Revaluation = 1040 – (240 + 80 + 610) divided by 4 = £27.5m)

(W3) Consolidated balance sheet

XY Group at 31 December 20X7

	XY	*AG*	*Fair Value Adj*	*Inter Co*	*Cash in Trans*	*Depr*	*Trans Gains/ Losses*	*Total*
Tangible fixed assets	945	378	27.5			(11)		1,339.5
Goodwill (W2)								4
Loan to AG	50			(37)	(13)			-
Net current assets	735	129		(5)	13			872
Long-term creditors	375	223		(40)				(558)
Minority interest (W2)		62.3		(1)		(2.2)	0.6	(59.7)
								1,597.8
Share capital	330							330
Share premium	350							350
Reserves (W2)	895	33.2		(4)		(8.8)	2.4	917.8
								1,597.8

Consolidated profit and loss account for the year ended 31 December 20X7
XY Group

	£m
Turnover	2,230
Cost of sales (including extra depreciation)	(1,434)
Gross profit	796
Administrative and distribution expenses	(430)
Exchange gains	3
Amortisation of goodwill	(4)
Interest payable	(42)
Profit before tax on ordinary activities	323
Taxation	(109)
Profit after tax on ordinary activities	214
Minority interest	(7)
Dividends	(20)
	187

Workings

(W4) *Translation of subsidiary AG's Profit and Loss account*

	KR	*Rate*	*£m*
Turnover	3,060		600
Cost of sales	(2,550)		(500)
Administrative and distribution costs	(51)	5.1	(10)
Interest payable	(102)		(20)
Taxation	(153)		(30)
Dividends	(52)	5.2	(10)
	152		30

(W5)

Consolidated Profit and Loss Account
XY Group for year ended 31 December 20X7

	XY	*AG*	*Inter Co*	*Minority Interest*	*Goodwill*	*Con*
Turnover	1,650	600	(20)			2,230
Cost of sales	(945)	(500)	20			(1,428)
Stock adj			(3)			
Gross profit	705	100	(3)			802
Administrative & distribution exp	(420)	(10)				(430)
Exchange gain		3				3
Additional depreciation		(5.5)				(5.5)
Goodwill amortisation					(4)	(4)
Interest payable	(22)	(20)				(42)
Taxation	(79)	(30)				(109)
	184	37.5	(3)		(4)	214.5
Minority interest (37.5 – 3) × 20%)				(6.9)		(6.9)
Inter group div	8	(8)				
Dividends paid	(20)					(20)
	172	29.5	(3)	(6.9)	(4)	187.6

The inter group dividend has been translated at the same rate as that of the holding company in order to eliminate it on consolidation. If the weighted average rate is used, then exchange differences will arise.

(W6) Total exchange difference on translation of subsidiary

	KR	*Rate*	*£m*
AG – net assets at 31 December 20X6	1,268	4.6	275.7
Share capital	240		60
Share premium	80	4	20
Pre acquisition reserves	610		152.5
Post acquisition reserves	338	Balance	43.2
	1,268		275.7

	£m
Post acquisition reserves at 31 December 20X6	(43.2)
Post acquisition reserves at 31 December 20X7	51.5
	8.3
Retained profit (W4)	(30)
Exchange difference – loss	(21.7)

Movement on reserves 80% of £21.7m i.e. £17.4m

(W7) *Exchange difference – analysis*

	£m
Equity interest at 31 December 20X6	275.7
Loss on retranslation at closing rate (1,268 ÷ 4.6 – 1,268 ÷ 5)	(22.1)
Equity interest at 31 December 20X6 restated at closing rate (5 KR = £1)	253.6
Retained profit for year (W4)	30
Exchange difference – profit and loss at weighted average rate compared with closing rate $\frac{152}{5}$ - 30	0.4
	284

Total exchange difference (22.1 – 0.4) × 80% = £17.4m

Explanatory notes

(i) Where the weighted average rate is used to translate the results of foreign subsidiaries then the rate ruling on the date of the transaction is used to eliminate inter company profit in stock. In this case £20m (104 KR divided by 5.2) has to be eliminated from turnover and purchases and additionally £2m has to be eliminated from opening stock and £5m from closing stock giving a net adjustment of £3m. The amount of profit to be eliminated is the amount of profit in the holding company's financial statements.

(ii) The loan from XY to AG is not a permanent loan as it is intended that it will be repaid. Evidence of this is the fact that an amount of KR 65 million has been repaid at the year end. As a result the loan should be restated at the closing rate and the resulting exchange differences taken to the profit and loss account.

	KR
Loan	265
Less paid 31 December	(65)
	200
translated at closing rate (KR5 = £1)	£40m

The loan in the parent company's books is £50m.
The cash in transit is KR 65 million divided by 5 i.e. £13m.
Therefore there is an exchange gain of £40m - £37m i.e. **£3 million** in the books of AG.

(iii) *Goodwill – historical cost rate*

This method regards goodwill as the excess of the price paid over the fair value of the net assets of the subsidiary expressed in the foreign currency translated into the holding company's currency at the date of acquisition. The asset is not deemed to fluctuate with changes in the exchange rate. Although not specifically dealt with by SSAP 20, it would appear by inference to be the method adopted by the standard. Under this method the fair value of the net assets of AG has been translated into sterling at the date of acquisition and therefore as the revaluation has not been incorporated into the records of AG, there is no requirement to retranslate the fair value of the net assets of AG at subsequent year ends.

Calculation (see also W2)	£m
XY - investment	220
less	
AG (80%)	
Share capital (£1 = KR 4.0)	(48)
Share premium (£1 = KR 4.0)	(16)
Pre acquisition reserves (£1 = KR 4.0)	(122)
Revaluation (£1 = KR 4.0)	(22)
Goodwill	12
Goodwill amortisation 20X6	4
Goodwill amortisation 20X7	4
Balance in consolidated balance sheet	4

(iv) *Tangible fixed assets*

The tangible assets in the consolidated balance sheet will be stated as follows:

	KR	*Rate*	*£m*
Balance per AG accounts	1,890	5	378
Increase to fair value (KR (1,040 – (240 + 80 + 610)))	110	4	27.5
Less: Increase in depreciation (2 years)	(44)	4	(11)
			394.5
XY's tangible assets			945
			1,339.5

(v) *Net current assets*

	£m
XY	735
AG (645 divided by 5)	129
Less: Inter company profit in stock	(5)
Cash in transit	13
	872

(vi) *Long-term creditors*

	£m
XY	375
AG	223
	598
Less: Inter company loan (explanatory note (ii))	(40)
	558

(vii) *Minority interest*

	£m
Balance per (W2)	62.3
Less inter company profit in stock	(1)
Additional depreciation on fair value	(2.2)
Add gain on exchange on loan (20% × 3)	0.6
	59.7

(b)

Movement on consolidated reserves

	£m *XY*	£m *AG*	£m *Total*
Profit and loss account at 1 January 20X7	723	34.6 (80% of 43.2)	757.6
Adjustments: Fair value depreciation (80% × 5.5)			(4.4)
Inter company profit on opening stock (80% × 2)			(1.6)
Goodwill written off			(4)
Retained profit for year			187.6
Exchange loss (W6)			(17.4)
Profit and loss account at 31 December 20X7			917.8

(c) SSAP 20 'Foreign currency translation' fails to deal adequately with certain issues relating to overseas transactions. The following issues are a cause for concern as they can lead to subjective judgement being used in the preparation of financial statements.

(i) The basic requirement of SSAP20 is that transactions should be recorded at the rate ruling at the date the transaction occurred but there is little guidance as to what that date should be. For example should this date be the order date, the shipping date, the date of receipt, or the date of the invoice.

(ii) Average rates can be used if rates do not fluctuate significantly. However little guidance is given on the calculation and use of the average rate. For example over what period should average rates be calculated? Should average rates be used for large transactions where the exchange rate is known?

(iii) A problem arises where there are two or more exchange rates for a currency or there has been a suspension of an exchange rate. SSAP20 does not give guidance on these matters. Fundamental accounting concepts such as prudence and conservatism would prevail in these circumstances.

(iv) There are certain areas where SSAP20 does not give definitive guidance on the accounting treatment of certain items.

(a) Not all items neatly fall into monetary or non monetary categories for translation purposes and problems arise where this distinction is not clear: for example debt securities held as investments.

(b) Little reference is made in SSAP20 to hedge accounting and forward contracts. The only specific reference to hedge accounting is to borrowings in a foreign currency used as a hedge against foreign currency equity investments. Similarly forward contracts are only mentioned briefly. These complex areas are partially dealt with in a standard on financial instruments and derivatives (FRS 13 'Derivatives and other financial instruments: Disclosures').

(c) SSAP20 does not specifically deal with cumulative exchange differences and the net investment in a foreign subsidiary when all or part of it is sold. There are problems over which method should be used to calculate goodwill on consolidation, i.e. the historical rate or current rate. Additionally the rate to be used when eliminating inter group profits could be either the closing rate or average rate.

In conclusion, there is concern over the inadequacy of present accounting rules in this area. Hedge accounting has not been effectively dealt with by the ASB and there is an urgent need to deal with the problem areas of SSAP20 as the volume and complexity of overseas transactions significantly increase.

23 Carver plc

Note: this question and answer have been amended to reflect the changes introduced by FRS 1 (Revised), which was issued in October 20X6, and other technical developments including the issue of FRS 10 and the abolition of ACT.

(a)

Consolidated cash flow statement for the year ended 30 September 20X4

		£'000	£'000
Operating activities	Note 1		
Net cash inflow from operating activities			372
Dividends received from associates	W5		250
Returns on investments and servicing of finance			
Interest paid (150 + 30 – 40) – 40 discount		(100)	
Dividends received from fixed asset investments		155	
Dividends paid to minority interest	W6	(48)	
Net cash from returns on investments and servicing of debt			7
Taxation			
UK corporation tax paid	W7		(250)
Capital expenditure			
Purchase of tangible fixed assets			
Machinery	W8	(1,085)	
Sale of tangible fixed assets			
Machinery		500	(585)
Acquisitions and disposals			
Purchase of subsidiary undertaking	W9	98	
		98	
Equity dividends paid (400 + 200 – 300)			(300)

Financing		
Issue of ordinary share capital	W102,453	
Issue of loan stock	W11 920	
Capital payments under leases	W12(270)	
Net cash inflow from financing		3,103
Increase in cash		2,695

Notes to cash flow statement

1 Reconciliation of operating profit to net cash flow from operating activities

	£'000	
Operating profit	1,475	
Depreciation charges	335	(W1)
Profit on sale of machinery	(100)	
Increase in stocks	(943)	(W2)
Increase in trade debtors	(547)	(W3)
Increase in trade creditors	152	(W4)
Net cash inflow from operating activities	372	

2 Reconciliation of net cash flow to movement in net funds (Note 3)

	£'000
Increase in cash in the period	2,695
Cash outflow from lease financing	270
Cash inflow from issue of loan stock	(920)
Change in net funds resulting from cash flows	2,045
Accrued interest on loan	(40)
New finance leases	(850)
Movement in net funds in the period	1,155
Net funds at 1 October 20X3	950
Net funds at 30 September 20X4	2,105

3 Analysis of changes in net funds

	At 1 Oct 20X3	*Cash flows*	*Other changes*	*At 30 Sept 20X4*
	£'000	£'000	£'000	£'000
Cash at bank and in hand	1,820	2,695		4,515
Loans	(500)	(920)	(40)	(1,460)
Obligations under finance leases	(370)	270	(850)	(950)
Tota	950	2,045	(890)	2,105

Workings

(W1) *Depreciation charges*

	£'000	£'000
Buildings		125
Machinery		
Closing aggregate amount	1,200	
Less opening aggregate amount	(1,100)	
	100	
Add depreciation on disposal	100	
		200
		325
Add: Amortisation of goodwill		10
		335

(W2) *Stock*

	£'000	£'000
Closing balance		1,975
Less: Opening balance	1,000	
Arising from the acquisition	32	
	(1,032)	
Cash outflow	943	

(W3) *Trade debtors*

	£'000	£'000
Closing balance		1,850
Less: Opening balance	1,275	
Arising from the acquisition	28	
		(1,303)
Cash outflow		547

(W4) *Trade creditors*

	£'000	£'000
Closing balance		500
Less: Opening balance	280	
Arising from the acquisition	68	
		(348)
Cash inflow		152

(W5) *Dividends received from associate*

	£'000	£'000
Opening balance		1,000
Add share of profit	495	
Less tax	(145)	
		350
		1,350
Closing balance		(1,100)
Cash inflow		250

(W6) *Minority*

	£'000
Opening balance	–
Add profit for year	100
Add arising from acquisition	63
	163
Less closing balance	(115)
Cash outflow	48

(W7) *Tax*

	£'000
Opening balances	
Corporation tax	217
Deferred tax	13
Transfer from profit and loss account	495
Closing balances	
Corporation tax	(462)
Deferred tax	(30)
	233
Acquisition tax	17
Cash outflow	250

(W8) *Investment in machinery*

		£'000
Cost at 30.9.X4		3,000
Less cost at 1.10.X3		(1,400)
		1,600
Add disposal		500
		2,100
Less: Arising from acquisition		(165)
Leased	(850)	
Cash outflow		1,085

(W9) *Cash*

	£'000
Cash acquired from acquisition	112
Less cash consideration	(14)
Cash inflow	98

(W10) Shares

	£'000
Closing balance	
Shares	3,940
Premium	2,883
	6,823
Less: Opening balance	
Shares	(2,000)
Premium	(2,095)
Non-cash consideration	
Shares	(220)
Premium	(55)
Cash inflow	2,453

(W11) *Loans*

	£'000
Closing balance	1,460
Less: Opening balance	(500)
	960
Less increase – finance cost	(40)
Cash inflow	920

(W12) *Lease – capital payments*

	£'000
Opening balances (200 + 170)	370
Add new lease commitment	850
	1,220
Less closing balances (240 + 710)	(950)
Cash outflow	270

(b) (i) The treatment of capitalised interest

FRS 1 requires capitalised interest to be shown within the interest paid heading in the Returns on Investments and Servicing of Finance section of the cash flow statement.

The effect of this will be to increase the interest paid from £140,000 to £145,000. The purchase of tangible fixed assets will be reduced by the same amount from £1,085,000 to £1,080,000.

(***Tutorial note***: interest paid in the cash flow statement is net of the discount; the figure shown will increase from £100,000 to £105,000.)

(ii) The treatment of cash and cash equivalents

We have noted that the cash figures comprised the following:

	1.10.X3	**30.9.X4**
	£'000	£'000
Cash in hand	10	15
Bank overdrafts	(770)	(65)
Bank 1,080	1,890	
10% Treasury Stock 20X3	1,500	–
Bank deposits	–	1,125
Gas 3% 20X0–20X5	–	1,550
	1,820	4,515

FRS 1 (revised) converts the cash flow statement into a statement of movements in pure cash only. What used to be called 'cash equivalents' are now dealt with in the statement under a separate heading 'Management of liquid resources'.

The cash in hand, bank overdrafts and bank figures comprise the balance of cash. The other three components of the cash figure satisfy the FRS 1 (revised) definition of liquid resources, so the cash flow statement for the year ended 30 September 20X4 would show cash received from the sale of the Treasury Stock and cash paid to acquire the deposits and the Gas Stock in the 'Management of liquid resources' section.

24 Hebden Group plc

Key answer tips

Suggested procedure:

1 Complete the reconciliation of operating profit to net cash flow from operating activities.

2 Calculate the cash flows from: dividends received from associates; dividends paid to minority interests; tax paid; payments for tangible fixed assets.

3 Complete the cash flow statement as far as net cash flow before financing.

4 Calculate the cash flows from the issue of share capital, the issue of loans and the finance leases.

5 Complete the financing section. Add up the statement and complete the totals.

6 Complete the analysis note. Then use this to complete the reconciliation of net cash flow to movements in net debt/funds.

Hebden Group plc
Group statement of cash flows for the year ended 31 July 20X6

(i) Reconciliation of operating profit to net cash flow from operating activities

	£m
Operating profit	2,965
Depreciation charges	650
Increase in stocks (3,950-2,000-64)	(1,886)
Increase in debtors (3,700-2,550-56)	(1,094)
Increase in creditors (1,000-560-(170-34))	304
Net cash inflow from operating activities	939

Cash flow statement

	£m
Net cash inflow from operating activities	939
Dividends received from associates	435
Returns on investments and servicing of finance	
Interest paid (300 - discount 6 - 80 + 60 - 100)	(174)
Interest element of finance lease rental payments	(100)
Dividends from fixed asset investments	80
Dividends paid to minority interests	(96)
Net cash outflow from returns on investments and servicing of finance	(290)
Taxation	
Corporation tax paid	(500)
Capital expenditure	
Payments to acquire tangible fixed assets	(2,170)
Receipts from sale of tangible fixed assets	1,100
Net cash outflow from capital expenditure	(1,070)
Acquisitions and disposals	
Purchase of subsidiary undertaking	(28)
Cash at bank and in hand acquired	224
Net cash inflow from acquisitions and disposals	196
Equity dividends paid	(600)
Net cash outflow before financing	(890)
Financing	
Issue of ordinary share capital	4,906
New long-term loans	2,900
Repayments of capital element of finance lease rentals	(1,526)
Net cash inflow from financing	6,280
Increase in cash	5,390

(ii) **Reconciliation of net cash flow to movement in net funds (Note)**

	£m
Increase in cash in the period	5,390
Cash outflow from lease financing	1,526
Cash inflow from new long term loans	(2,900)
Change in net funds resulting from cash flows	4,016
Accrued interest on loans	(6)
New finance leases	(1,700)
Movement in net funds in the period	2,310
Net funds at 1 August 20X5	1,900
Net funds at 31 July 20X6	4,210

(iii) **Note to the group cash flow statement**

Analysis of changes in net funds

	At 1 Aug 20X5	*Cash flows*	*Other changes 20X6*	*At 31 July*
	£m	£m	£m	£m
Cash at bank and in hand	3,640	5,390		9,030
Debentures	–	(2,900)	(6)	(2,906)
Obligations under finance leases	(1,740)	1,526	(1,700)	(1,914)
Total	1,900	4,016	(1,706)	4,210

Workings (all in £m)

(W1) Dividends from associated undertakings

Opening balance 1 August 20X5	2,000
add share of profit	990
less taxation	(355)
less closing balance 31 July 20X6	(2,200)
Cash inflow	435

(W2) Dividends paid to minority interest

Opening balance 1 August 20X5	-
add profit for year	200
Acquisition of Hendry Ltd (504 × 25%)	126
less closing balance	(230)
	96

(W3) Taxation paid

Opening balances 1 August 20X5		
Corporation tax	434	
Deferred tax	26	
		460
Profit and loss account (782 + 208)		990
Tax on acquisition of Hendry Ltd		34
less closing balances		
Corporation tax	924	
Deferred tax	60	
		(984)
Cash outflow		500

(W4) Payments for tangible fixed assets

Acquisitions in period	4,200
less arising from acquisition	(330)
leased assets	(1,700)
Cash outflow	2,170

(W5) Purchase of subsidiary

Cash acquired from acquisition	224
less cash in consideration	(28)
Cash inflow	196

(W6) Issue of ordinary share capital

Balance 31 July 20X6 -ordinary shares	7,880
share premium	5,766
Non cash consideration -ordinary shares	(440)
share premium	(110)
less opening balance 1 August 20X5	
ordinary shares	(4,000)
share premium	(4,190)
	4,906

(W7) New long-term loans

Balance 31 July 20X6	2,906
less finance cost - discount	(6)
(6.2% - 6%) × 3,000	
Cash inflow	2,900

(W8) Repayments of capital lease rentals

Balance 1 August 20X5 (1,340 + 400)	1,740
New lease commitments	1,700
less closing balance 31 July 20X6 (1,434 + 480)	(1,914)
	1,526

(***Tutorial note*** This question and answer have both been updated to reflect the changes introduced by FRS 1 (Revised) and FRS 10).

25 Baron Group plc

Key answer tips

Remember that you must analyse the components of the reconciliation between continuing and discontinued operations.

Read the requirement carefully; you are not required to prepare the reconciliation of net cash flow to movement in net debt or the note regarding the sale of the subsidiary.

(a)

Baron Group plc Cash Flow Statement for the year ended 30 November 20X7

	£m
Cash flow from operating activities (note 1)	875
Returns on investments and servicing of finance (note 2)	(214)
Taxation (working 5)	(115)
Capital expenditure (note 2)	(312)
Acquisitions and disposals (note 2)	(80)
Equity dividends paid (working 2)	(120)
Cash inflow before use of liquid resources and financing	34
Management of liquid resources (note 2)	(143)
Decrease in cash in the period	(109)

(i) ***Note 1:*** Reconciliation of Operating Profit to Operating Cash flows

	Continuing £m	*Discontinued* £m	*Total* £m
Operating profit (working 1)	383	184	567
Depreciation charges	141	9	150
Goodwill	20		20
Increase in stocks	(40)	(60)	(100)
Increase in debtors (working 4)	(119)	(50)	(169)
Increase in creditors	327	105	432
Net cash inflow from continuing operating activities	712		
Net cash inflow in respect of discontinued activities		188	
Net cash inflow from operating activities			900
Bid defence cash outflow	(5)		(5)
Pension prepayment	(20)		(20)
	687	188	875

(ii) ***Note 2:*** Analysis of cash flows for headings netted in the cash flow statement

Returns on investments and servicing of finance	£m	£m
Interest received (4 + 27 – 5)	26	
Interest paid (30 + 19 – 40)	(9)	
Minority interest – equity dividend (working 2)	(231)	
Net cash outflow for returns on investments and servicing of finance		(214)

Capital expenditure		
Purchase of tangible fixed assets	(380)	
Sale of tangible fixed assets (working 3)	68	
Net cash outflow for capital expenditure		(312)
Acquisitions and disposals		
Purchase of interest in joint venture	(25)	
Cash disposed of with subsidiary	(130)	
Disposal proceeds of subsidiary	75	
Net cash outflow for acquisitions and disposals		(80)
Management of liquid resources		
Purchase of corporate bonds	(35)	
Purchase of government securities	(28)	
Cash deposited on seven day deposit	(80)	
		(143)

Workings

(W1)

Operating profit — continuing activities	438
less income from joint venture*	(75)
add bid defence costs	20
Per cash flow statement	383

(***Tutorial note*** FRS 9 requires that the share of a joint venture's operating profit should not be included in the group operating profit).

(W2)

Minority interest - opening balance	570	
- Sale of Piece plc (20% of 420)	(84)	
Profit for year	75	
- Closing balance	(330)	
Minority interest - equity dividend		231
Dividends paid to equity (130 + 70 – 80)		120

(W3)

Cost/valuation - disposals	680	
Depreciation	(95)	
Carrying value		585
Less: Subsidiary disposed of		(310)
		275
Less: Transfer to joint venture		(200)
Carrying value disposed of		75
Loss on disposal		(7)
Cash proceeds		68

(W4)

Debtors

Debtors - 30.11.X7	680
Less: Prepayment - pension	(20)
Less: Interest receivable	(5)
	655
Debtors - 30.11.X6	540
Less: Interest receivable	(4)
	536
Increase in debtors	119

(W5)

Taxation on profit	191
Tax on subsidiary disposed of	(25)
Opening balance on taxation account	150
Closing balance on taxation account	(181)
Taxation on joint venture	(20)
	115

(W6)

Intangible assets - opening balance	144
Written off to profit/loss account on disposal	(64)
Amortisation for year	(20)
Closing balance 30.11.X7	60

(b) FRS 1 (Revised 20X6) focuses on cash rather than an alternative measure such as net debt for the following reasons.

(i) The cash flow statement highlights the significant components of cash which is useful for informational purposes.

(ii) Certain cash flow movements would not be captured by a broader measure. If two transactions fell within that broader measure then they would not be reported individually.

(iii) Comparison of the cash flow performances of different entities is facilitated.

(iv) Internationally the focus of such statements is cash and therefore international comparability is made easier.

The standard does in fact recognise that movements in net debt can give useful information and requires an analysis of the movement in net debt or net funds in the period. This is particularly important in the UK where management, shareholders and investment analysts pay close attention to measures of indebtedness, such as the gearing ratio.

(***Tutorial note*** The examiner's answer to part (a) of this question has been amended to reflect the changes to cash flow statements required by FRS 9).

26 Duke Group plc

Key answer tips

Your answer to part (b) must be specifically related to the financial statements of the Duke Group. It must not simply be a list of the general benefits of producing a cash flow statement.

(a)

Duke Group plc
Cash Flow Statement for the Year Ended 31 May 20X1

		£m
Cash flow from operating activities (note 1)		683
Dividends received from associates (working 2)		3
Returns on investments and servicing of finance		(7)
Taxation		(225)
Capital expenditure and financial investment		(708)
Acquisitions and disposals		18
Equity dividends paid		(121)
Cash flow before use of liquid resources and financing		(357)
Financing - issue of shares	20	
- increase in debt	242	
		262
Decrease in cash in the period		(95)

(i) **Note 1**

Reconciliation of Operating Profit to Operating Cash Flows

		£m
Operating Profit (1,390 – 772)		618
Depreciation		39
Amortisation of goodwill		10
Increase in stocks (750 – 588 – 30)	(132)	
Increase in debtors (660 – 530 – 25 – 17 + 15)	(103)	
Increase in creditors (1,193 – 913 – 20 – 9)	251	
		16
Net cash inflow from operating activities		683

(ii) **Note 2**

Analysis of Cash Flows for Headings Netted in the Cash Flow Statement

Returns on investments and servicing of finance:		£m
Interest received (15 + 34 – 17)		32
Interest paid (22 – 9)		(13)
Preference dividend paid		(9)
Minority interest – equity dividend		(17)
Net cash outflow for returns on investments and servicing of finance	(7)	
Capital expenditure and financial investment		
Purchase of tangible fixed assets (278 – 60 – 100)		(118)
Sale of tangible fixed assets (30 + 15)		45
Purchase of trade investments		(635)
Net cash outflow for capital expenditure and financial investment		(708)

Acquisitions and disposals:	
Purchase of subsidiary (17 – 35)	18
Net cash inflow from acquisitions and disposals	18
Financing	
Issue of ordinary share capital	20
Debt due beyond a year - new loan	310
- repaid	(68)
	262

Note as the purchase of fixed assets is being financed by the supplier in part, and the bill of exchange of £100m has not been paid, then the purchase of fixed assets in terms of its cash effect is reduced.

Workings

(W1)	*Purchase of subsidiary*		*£m*
	Net assets acquired		100
	Groups share of net assets (80%)		80
	Purchase consideration (£80m ordinary shares plus £ 17m cash) 97		
	Goodwill		17
	Goodwill Account: Opening balance		83
	Goodwill on Regent	17	
			100
	Amortisation		(10)
	Closing balance		90
(W2)	*Associated Company*		
	Balance as at 1 June 20X0		220
	Income for the period (98 – 15) (net of tax)		83
	Dividends received - cash flow		(3)
	Balance as at 31 May 20X1		300
(W3)	*Dividends paid*		
	Preference dividend		9
	Non equity appropriation		6
	Dividends - ordinary		126
		141	
	Balance dividends payable - 31 May 20X0		100
	Dividends - ordinary for year		126
	Dividends paid - ordinary		(121)
	Balance - dividends payable 31 May 20X1		105
	Minority interest - equity dividend (150 + 97 – 250 + 20)		17

(W4) *Taxation*

		£m
Balance at 31 May 20X0		200
Profit and loss account (213 – 15)		198
Taxation - Regent		30
Tax paid		(225)
Balance at 31 May 20X1		203

(W5) *Investments and Creditors due after more than one year*

Trade investments - balance 31 May 20X0		50
Foreign equity investment	605	
Exchange difference	(205)	
		400
Purchased in year - other		30
Trade investments - balance 31 May 20X1		480
Therefore purchase of trade investments is (605 + 30)		635
Creditors due more than one year-balance at 31 May 20X0		930
Loan taken out to finance equity investment	310	
Exchange difference	(10)	
		300
Bills of Exchange		100
Cash paid		(68)
Creditors due mere than one year - balance at 31 May 20X1		1,262

(b) When interpreting financial statements, it is essential that all the elements of such statements are scrutinised in conjunction with each other. Therefore, the balance sheet and profit and loss account must be analysed in conjunction with the cash flow statements. The additional information provided by the cash flow statement over and above that of the balance sheet and profit and loss account of Duke is as follows:

(i) The cash flow statement shows the cash generated from operations of £683m. This information is not readily available from the other elements of the financial statements.

(ii) The true cash flow effect of the taxation charge (£225m) as compared to the cash generated from operations (£683m) can be calculated easily from the statement (34.7%)

(iii) The amounts expended on capital and financial investment are nearly as great as the total cash generated from operations (Capital expenditure £708m, cash generated £683m).

(iv) Duke has financed its cash outflows on capital expenditure and investments partly out of cash generated from operations, partly out of the issuance of share capital (£20m) and partly out of the proceeds from long-term debt (£242m). The cash impact of the finance raised is not readily apparent from the profit and loss account and balance sheet.

(v) The cash payments to the minority interests (£17m) and the cash receipts from associates (£3m) and the resultant impact can be readily ascertained.

(vi) The acquisition of the subsidiary has not had a significant impact on the liquidity of the company. In fact the acquisition has had a positive impact on cash flows (£18m).

The cash flow statement gives the user a detailed insight into the reasons why there has been a significant decline in cash in the period. The purchase of tangible fixed assets (£118m) and trade investments (£635m) has been financed from cash generated from operations (£683m) and the issuance of share capital (£20m) and long-term debt (£242m). The other significant elements are the amounts of cash expended on dividend payments (dividends £121m, minority interest £17m) and taxation £225m. The cash flow statement is a key aid in understanding financial statements and the cash activities of the company.

27 Yukon plc

(*Note:* At the time that this question was originally set, FRS 10 had not been issued. Minor amendments have been made to the question and answer to reflect the change from FRED 12.)

Key answer tips

The requirement for part (b) is to explain the approach, so your answer must do more than just state the requirements of FRS 10.

(a) FRS 10 'Goodwill and Intangible Assets' sets out the following recommendations for the initial recognition and measurement of goodwill and intangible assets.

(i) Positive purchased goodwill should be capitalised and shown as an asset on the balance sheet. Negative purchased goodwill should be disclosed separately on the balance sheet, immediately below the goodwill heading.

(ii) Internally generated goodwill should not be recognised.

(iii) An intangible asset purchased separately from a company should be capitalised at its cost.

(iv) An intangible asset acquired as part of the acquisition of a business should be recognised separately from goodwill if its value can be reliably measured. The intangible asset should be measured at its fair value, subject to the constraint that, unless the asset has a readily ascertainable market value, the fair value should be limited to an amount that does not create or increase any negative goodwill arising on the acquisition.

(v) If its value cannot be measured reliably, an intangible asset acquired on the acquisition of a business should be subsumed within the value of goodwill.

(vi) An internally developed intangible asset may be recognised only if it has a readily ascertainable market value.

(b) The required approach seeks to charge goodwill to the profit and loss account only to the extent that the carrying value of goodwill is not supported by the current value of the goodwill within the acquired business. Amortisation is a practical means of recognising the reduction in value of goodwill that has a limited useful economic life. The useful economic life of purchased goodwill is the period over which the value of an acquired business is expected to exceed the values of its identifiable assets and liabilities.

There is a rebuttable presumption in FRS 10 that the useful economic life of purchased goodwill and intangible assets are limited and do not exceed 20 years. If there are valid grounds for the life of the asset to exceed 20 years (for example where the benefit of the intangible asset is achieved through renewable legal rights), then the longer period may be used but the tone of FRS 10 indicates that a 20 year life should normally be considered to be the maximum life. However there may be grounds for rebutting that presumption and treating the asset's life as indefinite.

Where the useful economic life of goodwill or an intangible asset is believed to be 20 years or less, the carrying value should be amortised in the profit and loss account over the estimated useful economic life. If the useful economic life is believed to exceed 20 years but the value is insignificant and is not capable of future measurement, then a deemed economic life of 20 years should be used. If the economic life of goodwill or an intangible asset is believed to exceed 20 years and the value is significant and expected to be capable of future continued measurement, then:

(i) If the useful economic life can be estimated, then the goodwill or the intangible asset should be amortised in the profit and loss account over that life.

(ii) If the useful economic life is indefinite, the goodwill or intangible asset should not be amortised.

The goodwill or intangible asset should be reviewed for impairment each period. In amortising an intangible asset, a residual value may be assumed only if such a value can be measured reliably. No residual value may be assumed for goodwill. A straight line method should be used unless inappropriate. The useful economic lives of goodwill and intangible assets should be reviewed at the end of each reporting period and revised if necessary.

(c) Fair values of net assets acquired at 31 May 20X6 by Territory plc

	£'000	
Intangible assets (subsumed within goodwill)		
Land and buildings	20,000	
Other tangible fixed assets	18,000	
Stocks	20,000	
Debtors	23,200	
Cash	8,800	
Creditors due within 1 year	(24,000)	
Creditors due more than 1 year	(13,147)	
Provisions for liabilities and charges	(886)	
Fair value	51,967	
Purchase consideration		
25 million × 2.25 per share	56,250	
Cash	10,000	
	66,250	
Goodwill (66,250 – 51,967) × 80%	11,426	
Charge to profit and loss account		
Year to 31 May 20X6	$\frac{11,426}{10 \text{ years}}$	1,143
Year to 31 May 20X7		
Net book value at 1 June 20X6	10,283	
Adjustment for fair value of tangible asset (3,000 × .8 × .9)	(2,160)	
Intangible assets written off (6,020 × .8 × .9)	(4,334)	
	3,789	
Amortisation (÷9)	421	
Write off of intangible assets	4,334	
Charge to profit/loss account	4,755	
Adjustment for fair value - goodwill (2,400 – 2,160)	(240) CREDIT	

Where an impairment in value arises, such as in the case of the intangible asset, the loss should be charged in the profit and loss account. The fair value adjustment is in relation to the revision of the value of the land and buildings.

Notes:

(i) FRS 7 'Fair values in acquisition accounting' allows adjustments to fair values up to the accounts for a full financial year following an acquisition. Therefore as a valuation of land and buildings by an independent valuer was received within this period, then this value £23 million will be taken into account for the fair value exercise in the accounts for the year ended 31 May 20X7.

(ii) Where an intangible asset cannot be measured reliably on acquisition, its value should be subsumed within purchased goodwill.

(iii) Stocks are stated for fair value purposes at current replacement cost. However the fair value should not exceed the recoverable amount which is its net realisable value i.e. £20 million.

(iv) Creditors: amounts falling due more than one year.

Amount due on 31 May 20X9 £11 million × 1.464	£16,105,100
Fair value 31 May 20X6	£13,146,559

$$\left(\frac{£16{,}105{,}100}{1.07^3}\right)$$

Current market interest rates should be taken into account when calculating the fair value of the long-term loan.

(v) As the reorganisation of Yukon plc would have taken place irrespective of the acquisition, the provision is included in the fair value exercise. The provision for future losses however is deemed to be post acquisition.

(vi) The deferred government grants will be ignored as the fair value of the assets to which they relate has already been included in the fair value exercise.

28 Impairment loss

Key answer tips

The key requirement word in part (a) (i) is *describe* and so your answer must be more than simply a list of 'bullet points'.

Answer part (a)(ii) by explaining how impairment is measured and then how it is recognised. (This is the logical order in which to tackle the two aspects of the requirement, even though the question says 'recognition and measurement'.)

Remember that the carrying amount of assets should not be reduced below their net realisable value.

(a) (i) A review for impairment of a fixed asset should be carried out if events or changes in circumstance indicate that the carrying amount may not be recoverable. In identifying whether an impairment of a tangible fixed asset may have occurred an enterprise should consider the following indications:

- there has been a significant decrease in the market value of the asset in excess of the normal process of depreciation
- there has been a significant adverse change in either the business or the market in which the asset is involved. This will include changes in the technological, economic or legal environment in which the enterprise operates and changes in market interest rates or other market rates of return
- there has been a significant adverse change in the manner in which the asset has been used
- evidence is available that indicates that the economic performance of the asset will be worse than expected
- the asset has suffered considerable physical change, or obsolescence or physical damage
- there has been an accumulation of costs significantly in excess of those originally expected in the acquisition or construction of an asset so that it may affect profitability
- the management is committed to a significant reorganisation programme or redundancy of key employees

- where an asset is valued in terms of value in use and the actual cash flows are less than the estimated cash flows before discounting

- there has been a significant adverse change in any value indicator used to measure the fair value of the fixed asset or acquisition

- a current period operating loss and net cash outflow combined with similar past and predicted occurrences

(ii) FRS 11 'Impairment of Fixed Assets and Goodwill' says that if there is an indication of impairment, then a review must be undertaken to confirm this fact and establish the extent of the impairment. The Statement of Principles states that an asset should not be valued at an amount greater than its cost or recoverable amount in a historical cost system. The recoverable amount is defined as the higher of net realisable value (if known and based on market value) and value in use (net present value of future cash flows). The above rule applies, also, to assets which have been revalued to replacement cost. The FRS 11 approach is to compare the carrying value of the asset with its recoverable amount. If the NRV or value in use exceeds the carrying value then no write down is necessary and there is no need to estimate the other amount. If the recoverable amount is lower than the carrying value, the asset is impaired. Impairment is measured on a post-tax basis.

If no reliable estimate of NRV can be made, the recoverable amount is determined by value in use alone. If the NRV is lower than the carrying amount, one should consider whether the value in use is lower still. If it is not then the recoverable amount is based on value in use not NRV.

Impairment can often be tested only for groups of assets because the cash flows used for the calculation do not arise from the use of a single asset. In these cases impairment is measured for the smallest income generating unit that produces independent income streams. To the extent that the carrying amount exceeds the value in use of the income generating unit, the unit is impaired and in the absence of impairment of specific assets, the impairment should be allocated first to goodwill, then to capitalised intangible assets and finally to tangible assets in the unit.

The consideration of past impairment losses should be recognised when the recoverable amount of a tangible fixed asset has increased because of a change in economic conditions. There must be a demonstrable reversal of the economic event which caused the impairment and this must not have originally been foreseen.

Impairment losses are recognised in the profit and loss account unless they arise on revalued assets. In the latter case they are recognised in the statement of total recognised gains and losses until the carrying value falls below depreciated historical cost. If the impairment is due to a reduction in the service potential of the asset, it is recognised in the profit and loss account. Impairments below depreciated historical cost are recognised in the profit and loss account. Where an impairment loss on a fixed asset is recognised, the remaining useful economic life should be reviewed and revised if necessary. A reversal of an impairment loss should be recognised in the profit and loss account but in the case of a revalued asset only to the extent that the original impairment loss was so recognised.

(b) (i) AB will have undertaken an impairment review because of the effect of the stock losses and the problems associated with the taxi business. FRS 11 first requires an assessment of whether there was a reliable estimate of NRV and value in use. The next step would be to determine whether the value in use is less than or equal to the NRV. In this case NRV is substantially less than the carrying value (NRV £120,000, carrying value £290,000). The FRS then requires management to compare NRV with the value in use. The value in use is £248,600 (£100,000 for three years discounted at 10% per annum). As value in use is not lower than NRV, the recoverable amount will be based on value in use.

It would appear therefore that in this case the management of AB would write down the asset to its net present value of £248,600 and recognise the loss in the profit and loss account.

(ii) AB will recognise the impairment losses relating to the taxi business in the following way. (Impairment losses should be recognised if the recoverable amount of the income generating unit is less than the carrying value of the items of that unit.)

At 1 February 20X8

	1.1.X8	*Impairment loss*	*1.2.X8*
	£000	£000	£000
Goodwill	40	(15)	25
Intangible assets	30		30
Vehicles	120	(30)	90
Sundry net assets	40		40
	230	(45)	185

An impairment loss of £30,000 is recognised first for the stolen vehicles and the balance (£15,000) is attributed to goodwill.

At 1 March 20X8

	1.2.X8	*Impairment loss*	*1.3.X8*
	£'000	£'000	£'000
Goodwill	25	(25)	
Intangible assets	30	(5)	25
Vehicles	90		90
Sundry net assets	40		40
	185	(30)	155

AB recognises a further impairment loss of £30,000 although the value in use of the business is lower (£150,000), the carrying amounts of the individual assets are not reduced below their net realisable value.

Any impairment loss should usually be allocated in priority to those assets which have the most subjective valuations. Thus impairment identified in this way should usually be allocated firstly to goodwill, thereafter to intangible assets for which there is no active market and finally to any tangible assets in the unit. However, in doing this no asset should be written down to below its net realisable value.

(***Tutorial Note:*** Since this question was originally set, SSAP 12 has been superseded by FRS 15 *Tangible fixed assets*. As a result, one sentence has been deleted from the answer to part (b)(i); the rest of the answer is still valid.)

29 Aztech

Key answer tips

Part (b) effectively requires you to value the assets on an annual basis and depreciate them, applying the requirements of FRS 15.

(a) Accounting for tangible fixed assets has been a source of concern and contention in the UK particularly when inflation was high. However the principles used in determining the cost of tangible fixed assets when initially measured and recognised in financial statements were generally accepted by preparers and auditors of financial statements. However there was no accounting standard prior to FRS 15 'Tangible Fixed Assets' which dealt with these principles and thus differences arose in practice. Companies revalued fixed assets at their own discretion and whenever they wished to do so. There was no requirement to update these revaluations in subsequent accounting periods, thus reducing the value of the information.

Prior to FRS 15, a company could revalue part of their tangible fixed assets without having to treat similar assets consistently and thus achieving a particular effect in an accounting period. Thus the amounts attributable to a company's tangible fixed assets had 'mixed' values thus making inter temporal and inter company comparisons extremely difficult. Companies could capitalise or expense interest on a selective basis to massage earnings.

The requirement of SSAP 12 'Accounting for Depreciation' as regards depreciation required clarification. Several companies had charged depreciation in an exaggeratedly prudent way and had ceased depreciating certain assets, particularly property, on the grounds that they were increasing in value or that they were being maintained or refurbished on a regular basis. This policy had been a source of continual argument since SSAP 12 was published. This practice had been adopted particularly by hotels, retail organisations and the banks. FRS 15 addresses the above issues by specifying accounting rules on initial recognition, valuation and depreciation of tangible fixed assets (other than investment properties).

(b) (i) Where properties are not improved, then FRS 15 states that non-specialised properties should be valued on the basis of their existing use and where the open market value is materially different this fact should be disclosed. Specialised properties should be valued on the basis of depreciated replacement cost and properties surplus to a company's requirements should be valued on the basis of open market value less selling costs where material.

Thus on 31 March 20X0, the hotels will be deemed to be non specialised properties and will be valued as follows:

	£m	£m
Existing use value	20	
Less property to be sold	(3)	
		17
Property surplus to requirements		
(open market value)	2.5	
Less: selling costs	(0.2)	
		2.3
Balance sheet value		19.3

Expenditure on fixed assets to maintain the asset at its current level does not negate the need to charge depreciation. The only grounds for not charging depreciation under FRS 15 are that the depreciation charge and accumulated depreciation are immaterial. The depreciation charge would be almost £1 million per annum. If this charge were deemed immaterial, then the hotels should be reviewed for impairment every year in accordance with FRS 11 'Impairment of Fixed Assets and Goodwill'.

(ii)

At 31 March 20X0	£'000
Cost of manufacture	28,000
Interest capitalised	
(£20m × 10% + (£20m × 110% × 10% × ¾)	3,650
	31,650

Capitalisation of finance costs should cease when the fixed assets are physically complete (FRS 15 para 29). Hence only 1¾ years finance costs are capitalised. If the amount recognised when a fixed asset is constructed exceeds its recoverable amount then it should be written down to its recoverable amount. The recoverable amount is the higher of net realisable value and value in use. Thus the fleet of aircraft will be recognised in the balance sheet at £30 million (FRS 15 para 32).

31 March 20X1

	Carrying value 1/4/20X0	*Depreciation*	*Carrying value 31/3/20X1*
	£'000	£'000	£'000
Engines	9,000	3,000	6,000
Body	21,000	2,625	18,375
	30,000	5,625	24,375
Revaluation to STRGL			2,625
Closing carrying value - revalued amount			27,000

31 March 20X2

	Carrying value 1/4/20X1	*Depreciation*	*Carrying value 31/3/20X2*
	£'000	£'000	£'000
Engines	6,646	(3,323)	3,323
Body	20,354	(2,908)	17,446
	27,000	(6,231)	20,769
To STRGL			(2,019)
			18,750
To profit and loss account			(250)
			18,500
To STRGL			(500)
Closing carrying value			18,000

FRS 15 (para 65) states that where there is a revaluation loss which has been caused by a clear consumption of economic benefits, then the loss should be recognised in the Profit and Loss account. Other revaluation losses should be recognised in the STRGL until the carrying amount reaches depreciated historical cost and thereafter in the profit and loss account. Depreciated historical cost is

Engines	9,000 × $\frac{1}{3}$	3,000
Body	21,000 × $\frac{6}{8}$	15,750
		18,750

However if it can be demonstrated that the recoverable amount (£18.5 million) is greater than its revalued amount (18 million), then this portion of the loss should be recognised in the STRGL.

31 March 20X3

	Carrying value 1/4/20X0	*Depreciation*	*Carrying value 31/3/20X3*
	£'000	£'000	£'000
Engines	2,880	(2,880)	
Body	15,120	(2,520)	12,600
	18,000	(5,400)	12,600
Add cost of new engines			15,000
Closing book amount before revaluation			27,600

30 Strained plc

Key answer tips

Not required: calculation of the annual profit and loss account charge in part (a); calculation of the carrying amount of the loan for the year ended 31 March 20X7 in part (b); discussion as to whether the lease is a finance lease in part (c) (you are told that it is an operating lease).

Remember to explain your calculations and to relate them to the scenarios in the question.

(a)

(i) FRS 4 para 40 requires shareholders' funds to be analysed between the amount attributable to equity interests and the amount attributable to non-equity interests. The amount of shareholders' funds attributable to equity interests is the difference between total shareholders' funds and the total amount attributable to non-equity interests. Para 41 states that immediately after the issue of a non-equity instrument the amount of non-equity shareholders' funds attributable to it should be the net proceeds of the issue.

This is achieved by a two column analysis for equity and non-equity and inclusion of the premium as follows:

	Equity shareholders' interest	*Non-equity shareholders' interest*	*Total*
	£m	£m	£m
Share capital	4.95	2.0	6.95
Share premium	5.50	0.3 [0.4 – 0.1]	5.80
Profit and loss account	4.40		4.40
	14.85	2.3	17.15

(ii) The finance cost of the non-equity shares is calculated as follows:

	£
Redeemable amount	2,500,000
Dividends (7% of £2,000,000) for 10 years	1,400,000
	3,900,000
Less: Net proceeds	2,300,000
Total finance cost	1,600,000

This amount will be shown as an appropriation of the company's profit and loss account at a constant rate based on the carrying amount of the preference shares.

(b) The carrying amounts are

	£'000
31.3.X5	5,100
31.3.X6	5,059

They are calculated as follows:

Loan	*Overall effective rate interest 9%*	*Cash paid*	*Carrying amount*
£'000	£'000	£'000	£'000
5,000	450	350	5,100
5,100	459	500	5,059
5,059	455	5,514	–

The reasoning for the treatment is that the stated rate of interest does not reflect the true economic cost of borrowing in any period during the time the loan is outstanding, since low rates of interest in one period are compensated for by higher rates in another.

The payments required by the debt should be apportioned between a finance charge for any accounting period at a constant rate on the outstanding obligation and a reduction of the carrying amount. The effect of this accounting on a stepped interest loan is that an overall effective interest cost will be charged in each accounting period; an accrual will be made in addition to the cash payments in earlier periods and will reverse, partially offsetting the higher cash payments, in later periods.

(c) The transaction falls within the provisions of para 47(c) of SSAP 21 *Accounting for leases and hire-purchase contracts*. However, the provisions of FRS 5 also require to be taken into account and the substance of the transaction considered.

Profit and loss entries

The company will recognise a profit on the sale of £500,000 which is equal to the fair value of £8.5m less the carrying value of £8m at the date of sale.

Prior to the issue of FRS 5, the excess of the sale price over the fair value was not regarded as a realised profit and arose because the operating lease rentals in future years were deemed also to be above fair value. The excess was therefore deferred and amortised over the period of the lease term with the net annual operating rental charged in the profit and loss account being reduced to £625,000 [£1m – (£1.5m/4)].

However, the substance would appear to be that the company has received a loan of £1,500,000 for four years on which interest will be paid. The annual payment of £1,000,000 would consequently need to be divided into three elements, namely, the capital repayment of the loan, the interest element and the operating lease payment. The profit and loss account entries will be:

		£
Interest		150,000
Operating lease payment	£1,000,000 – (£1,500,000/3.170)]	526,814

Note: 3.170 is the four year annuity factor at 10%.

Balance sheet entries

The vehicles will no longer appear in the balance sheet as an asset. Prior to FRS 5 there would have been a deferred gain of £1.5m as at 1 April 20X4 which would have been reduced by £375,000 per annum as it was amortised.

Under FRS 5, there will be a loan account showing the balance of the £1,500,000 as at 31 March 20X5 as follows:

	£
Loan account [£1,500,000 + 150,000 – 473,186]	1,176,814

(d) The question that needs to be addressed is whether the transaction is really a sale in substance or whether it is simply a borrowing transaction with the trade debtors being used as collateral and the £4m retained by Blue Factors plc being in substance an interest charge. The overall terms of the agreement would need to be examined in aggregate. The focus is on the risks of ownership.

The two main risks associated with trade debtors are the risk of slow payment which gives rise to a finance cost and the risk of non-payment.

Risk of non-payment

The risk of non-payment is regarded as remaining with the seller if one of the terms of the agreement is that unpaid debts are sold back to the seller. In such a case the transaction is regarded as a financing transaction; the amount received from Blue Factors plc will be shown as a loan; any amounts expected under a recourse agreement will be disclosed within provisions.

Risk of slow payment

This will depend on whether the factor has assumed any substantial risk of slow payment of the debts. For example, the discount charged by the factor will normally be estimated at a rate of interest related to the time between payment to Strained plc and collection by Blue Factors plc from the debtors. If the actual time for the debtors to be collected can substantially exceed the expected time without cost to Strained plc then it may be assumed that the risk lies with the factor and there has been a sale. Otherwise it will be treated as a finance arrangement.

31 Timber Products plc

Key answer tips

In part (a) do not waste time by giving a general description of all the requirements of FRS 5. There are only 5 marks available.

Approach each of the transactions in part (b) in the same way: determine the substance of the transaction by asking yourself who bears the benefits and risks; draw up the accounting entries required and explain them.

There is no single right answer to part (c) and so the Examiner is primarily interested in your reasoning.

(a) (i) The objective (FRS 5 para 1) of the FRS *Reporting the substance of transactions* is to ensure that the substance of an entity's transactions is reported in its financial statements. The commercial effect of the entity's transactions, and any resulting assets, liabilities, gains or losses, should be faithfully represented in its financial statements. This will affect the accounting for any arrangement the effect of which is to inappropriately omit assets and liabilities from the balance sheet. It achieves this by requiring financial statements to be prepared reporting the substance rather than the legal form of transactions.

(ii) The FRS recognises two types of transaction where an asset might cease to be recognised.

The first is where all significant benefits and risks relating to an asset are transferred. An example is where a car manufacturer supplies parts at listed trade price to a service station customer.

The second is where not all significant benefits and risks relating to an asset are transferred, but it is necessary to change the description or monetary amount of the original asset or to record a new liability for any obligation assumed. An example is where a car dealer supplies a car subject to a guaranteed residual repurchase price.

(b) (i) **Disclosure using linked presentation**

The transaction appears to satisfy the criteria set out in FRS 5 for linked presentation in that the finance will be repaid only from the proceeds generated by the specific item it finances and there is no possibility of any claim on the entity being established other than against funds generated by that item and there is no provision whereby the entity may either keep the item on repayment of the finance or reacquire it at any time.

The accounting treatment for linked presentation is as follows:

		£m	£m
Current assets			
Receivables subject to financing arrangements			
Gross receivables			14.40
(After providing £600,000 for bad debts)			
Less:	Non-returnable proceeds		
	90% of net debtors £14.4m	12.96	
	Less potential recourse	0.20	
			(12.76)
			1.64
Current asset: Cash			12.96
Creditors: Recourse under factored debts			0.20

(ii) How to determine the substance/whether to include in balance sheet/recognition

Under FRS 5 the transaction would be regarded as a financing transaction in that Timber Products plc has not transferred the risks and rewards of ownership of the timber. It has in fact borrowed money on the security of the timber. The timber will therefore appear as stock in the balance sheet and the loan will appear as a creditor. Each year there will be an interest element charged to the profit and loss account and added to the liability.

The balance sheet as at 31 October 20X5 will show:

	£m
Stock	40.0
Loan payable after more than one year	42.8

Note: The loan is secured by stock of £40m at cost.

The profit and loss account will show:

Interest payable [7% of £40m]	£2.8m

(iii) **How to determine the substance/whether to include in balance sheet/derecognition**

The problem in this transaction is to determine the substance of the transaction i.e. whether or not the 'outstanding' stock of £4m at selling price (£3m cost price), has been sold. If it has this would mean that the stock appears in the balance sheet of the retailers at £4m.

Possibly the principal point that would support recognition of a sale and derecognition of the stock in the balance sheet of Timber Products plc is the fact that the retailers are able to purchase at the trade price as at the date of delivery. If they were required to pay the trade price as at the end of the six month display period then the substance would be that the rewards remained with Timber Products plc and the stock would continue to be recognised by their balance sheet at cost of £3m, or net realisable value if lower.

Thus, the more prudent view, treats the transaction as a genuine sale or return with the manufacturer holding the price for six months.

There is a further point, which is that the retailers could take the opportunity immediately prior to the end of the six months to return all unsold consignment stock. This would support the view that the risk and rewards remained with Timber Products plc.

The decision in this case has to be taken on balance i.e. giving weight to those matters that are likely to have a commercial effect in practice. There is no absolute answer. The persuasive factor is probably the date of fixing the price which would support treating the item as sold and therefore derecognised from the Timber Products plc balance sheet.

The accounting entries on that basis would be:

Profit and loss account for the year ended 31 October 20X5

Sales	£10m
Cost of sales	£7.5m
Other income	£50,000
Insurance costs	£15,000
Carriage costs	£10,000

Balance sheet as at 31 October 20X5

Debtors	£4m

A provision for returns should be made based on past experience.

However, a case could also be made under the prudence concept for the stock to appear on both the manufacturer's and the retailer's balance sheets.

(iv) **Quasi-subsidiary**

The arrangement with Inter plc has been structured so that it does not meet the legal definition of a subsidiary within the provisions of FRS 2 para 14. However, the commercial effect is no different from that which would result were Inter plc to be a subsidiary of Timber Products plc and under FRS 5 it falls to be treated as a quasi-subsidiary.

Under FRS 5, the factory will appear as an asset in the Timber Products consolidated accounts and it will be reduced to £8.5m being cost to the group and the profit on disposal will be cancelled out; the fee will be cancelled as an intra group transaction; the loan interest will appear at £1.5m in the consolidated profit and loss account; the loan of £10m will appear as a creditor in the consolidated balance sheet.

(c) There would appear to be two possible approaches. One would be to approach the transaction as a secured loan; the other as a leasing arrangement.

Secured loan considerations

The question to be answered is what risks has Timber Products plc borne in this transaction.

It clearly bears the operating risk in the form of maintenance and insurance costs. It needs to be determined whether it has also borne the charge for covering the finance cost of the equipment during construction. Further information is required in considering this transaction to assess whether Extractor-Plus plc is in effect receiving a lender's return. If that were the case, the equipment would appear as an asset in the balance sheet and an amount equal to the cost of the asset as a loan secured on the asset.

Leasing considerations

More information is necessary to establish whether there has been an attempt to word the agreement so that it falls outside the SSAP 21 definition of a finance lease. The additional information would include matters such as the cost of the equipment, the length of the contract, any minimum lease payments particularly in the event of low hourly usage. However, FRS 5 with its substance approach, might influence the accounting treatment.

32 Mortgage Lend Ltd

Key answer tips

Your answer to parts (a) and (b) must do more than state the relevant requirements of FRS 5; it must explain them.

Answer part (c) by analysing the transaction from the viewpoint of Borrow Ltd, Mortgage Lend Ltd and Lendco Group plc in turn. Discuss the extent to which each experiences the risks and benefits associated with the mortgages. This will indicate which accounting treatments may be appropriate. The requirement for this part of the question is to *discuss*, so you should look at alternative possibilities.

(a) Once a transaction's commercial purpose has been determined, it is necessary to ascertain whether a new asset or liability has arisen or whether the entity's existing assets or liabilities have changed. Assets are defined in FRS 5 'Reporting the substance of transactions' as 'Rights or other access to future economic benefits controlled by an entity as a result of past transactions or events'.

The control over the rights to economic benefits should entail the right to obtain the future economic benefits relating to the asset and the ability to restrict the ability of others to access those benefits. Management of the assets is not the same as control. Management of the assets is the ability to direct the use of the asset as a fund manager may do. However, the fund manager will not gain the economic benefits from those assets. Evidence of whether an entity is exposed to the risks associated with the asset is taken as evidence that the entity has access to the asset's future economic benefits. Therefore if the entity controls the rights to the economic benefits an asset may arise.

Liabilities are defined as 'an entity's obligations to transfer economic benefits as a result of past transactions or events'. If an outflow of resources arises as a result of an obligation then a liability will arise. If the entity is unable to avoid the outflow of funds either legally or commercially, then such an obligation will exist. Where this obligation is contingent upon the outcome of a future uncertain event, a liability will not necessarily be recognised. Such an obligation will be accounted for under FRS 12 and a liability will arise where the future event confirms a loss already estimated with reasonable accuracy at the time of the financial statements.

(b) (i) Once an asset or liability has been identified, it should be recognised in the entity's balance sheet if there is sufficient evidence of the item's existence and the item can be measured with sufficient reliability at a monetary amount. The problem with those principles is that conventional accounting recognises most transactions when they are performed. For example when goods are physically sold under a contract. However one interpretation of the recognition criteria might be that an asset is created when a contract (for example) for the sale of goods has been entered into. The assets created are the sale proceeds and the liability is the right to the goods by a third party. However, this interpretation of the recognition criteria would create a radical change in practice.

(ii) Where a transaction transfers all the significant benefits and risks relating to an asset, the asset should cease to be recognised. 'Significant' should not be judged in relation to all possible benefits and risks that could occur but only those which are likely to occur in practice. The importance of the risk retained by the transferor of the asset must be assessed in the context of the total risk which relates to that asset.

If a high quality asset is sold, for example debtors, and the seller agrees to compensate the buyer for any subsequent loss of up to 5% of the assets value, then if the risk of bad debts is very low, then effectively all the risk may be being retained by the seller, in which case the transaction may not be a sale.

FRS 5 addresses the issue of derecognition only in relation to assets and not liabilities.

(c) Securitisation of assets is often used by originators of mortgage loans to package assets together to sell to a sparsely capitalised vehicle or company. As securitisation makes use of the Special Purpose Vehicles (SPV), it is necessary to consider the accounting treatment in three sets of financial statements, the originator's, the SPV's and the originator group's financial statements.

(i) Borrow Ltd

The financial statements of Borrow Ltd (the SPV) are perhaps the easiest to deal with. Borrow Ltd will treat the transaction as a separate presentation assuming the company has access to all of the future benefits and risks related to the securitised assets and the loan noteholders have recourse to all the assets of Borrow Ltd including assets other than the mortgages. For example the cash balance of Borrow Ltd.

Borrow Ltd is exposed to the inherent risks of collecting the cash from the mortgagors. Hence derecognition would not be appropriate. Because Borrow Ltd's exposure to loss does not appear to be limited, the use of the linked presentation will also not be appropriate.

(ii) Mortgage Lend Ltd

In the financial statements of Mortgage Lend Ltd there are again three possible accounting treatments:

- derecognition
- linked presentation
- separate presentation.

If the transaction is to be derecognised then the price of the sale of the mortgages should have been determined at an arm's length, for a single, non-returnable fixed sum and there should be no recourse to Mortgage Lend Ltd for losses. If these conditions are met then the mortgages will be taken off the balance sheet of Mortgage Lend Ltd and the value of the mortgage will be offset against the proceeds with the difference taken to the profit and loss account. If significant benefits or risks are retained by Mortgage Lend Ltd then derecognition cannot be utilised. However in such a situation a linked presentation might apply.

It is common in securitisation schemes for the originator of the scheme (Mortgage Lend Ltd) to retain some benefits relating to the securitised assets. This benefit may be in the form of earning income from the management of the mortgages. However the linked presentation is only appropriate where the risk exposure is limited to a fixed monetary amount and the conditions under FRS 5 for a linked presentation are met. Indicators which may point to a linked presentation are that the transaction price is not at arm's length and the right of the originator to further sums other than the non-returnable proceeds. Where a linked presentation is applied the mortgages will remain on the assets side of the balance sheet. Extensive disclosure requirements apply in this situation.

If the conditions for derecognition or linked presentation do not apply then a separate presentation is required. This means that the mortgages will remain on the balance sheet of Mortgage Lend Ltd and the proceeds will be shown as a loan in creditors.

(iii) Lendco Group plc

In the context of the Lendco Group plc, the important consideration is the nature of the relationship between Borrow Ltd and the group. If Borrow Ltd is owned by an independent third party which has made a large investment and has the benefits and risks of Borrow Ltd's net assets, derecognition may be appropriate. If Borrow Ltd is essentially a quasi-subsidiary of Mortgage Lend Ltd and the conditions for a linked presentation are met from a group perspective, then the latter presentation will be effected even if separate presentation has been used in Borrow Ltd's financial statements.

If Borrow Ltd is a subsidiary of Mortgage Lend Ltd, then separate presentations may be appropriate in the group accounts and Borrow Ltd should be consolidated in the normal way unless the linked presentation is possible in the subsidiary. It is normal in securitisation schemes for the SPV to fall within the definition of a quasi-subsidiary.

33 Tall plc

(a)

MEMORANDUM

To: Assistant Accountant

From: Chief Accountant

Subject: Accounting treatment of capital instruments **Date:** 30 November 20W9

Under FRS 4 *Capital instruments* the bonds must be treated as debt and will be shown as long term creditors in the balance sheet. This is because they fall within the definition of liabilities, as there is an obligation to transfer economic benefits when they are redeemed. In addition, the bonds are not legally shares. Although it is probable that the bonds will eventually be converted to shares, FRS 4 states that conversion of debt must not be anticipated.

In contrast, the preference shares should be reported as part of shareholders' funds, despite the fact that they also contain an obligation to transfer economic benefit on redemption. This is because they have the legal status of shares. However, they are classified as non-equity shares, because they are redeemable and must be disclosed separately from equity shares. The disclosure may be given on the face of the balance sheet or in a note to the financial statements.

Although no interest or dividends are payable there *is* a finance cost associated with both the debt and the preference shares: the difference between the issue proceeds and the amount payable on redemption. FRS 4 requires that finance costs of capital instruments are allocated to accounting periods over their terms at a constant rate on the balance sheet amounts.

(b) Balances at 1 October 20W9 (immediately after the issues)

	£m
Equity share capital	100.0
Non-equity share capital	10.0
Share premium (W1)	37.7
Profit and loss account	89.7
	237.4
Net assets (W2)	237.4

Workings

(W1) Share premium

	£m
Balance at 30 September 20W9	35.8
Premium on preference shares (10 × 20p)	2.0
Issue costs	(0.1)
	37.7

(W2) Net assets

	£m
Balance at 30 September 20W9	225.5
Net proceeds of issue of bonds	15.0
Net proceeds of issue of preference shares (12 – 0.1)	11.9
Less: long term creditor (bonds)	(15.0)
	237.4

(c) Finance costs for the year ended 30 September 20X0

Bonds

Interest is reported under 'Interest payable and similar amounts':

Charge for the period (15 × 10%) £1.5 million

Working:

$$\frac{\text{Existing carrying value of bond}}{\text{Terminal value of bond}} = \frac{15.00}{24.15} = 0.621$$

Using present value tables, the implicit rate of interest is 10% (the term of debt is five years).

Preference shares

Finance costs are shown as an appropriation of profit.

Charge for the period (11.9 × 12%) £1.428 million

Working:

$$\frac{\text{Existing carrying value of preference shares}}{\text{Terminal value of preference shares}} = \frac{11.9}{23.5} = 0.506$$

Using present value tables, the implicit rate of interest is 12% (the term of debt is six years).

34 Financial instruments

Key answer tips

The fair value of the debenture is the total interest and capital payable discounted to present value using the market rate of interest at the balance sheet date.

(a) (i) In recent years the growth and complexity of financial instruments has been quite significant. Companies use a range of instruments to transform and manage their financial risk. However, accounting standards have not developed at the same rate as the growth in the instruments. The main concern of standard setters is that many derivatives are not recognised on the balance sheet. The main reason for this is the use of the historical cost concept in financial statements together with the fact that many derivatives have a nil cost. However, derivatives may be substantial assets and liabilities and may expose the entity to significant risk. Additionally many companies measure financial assets at amortised cost even though there are reliable quoted market prices that differ from amortised cost and the assets are readily saleable.

At present unrealised gains and losses arising from changes in the value of many financial instruments are often ignored. Unrealised losses are recognised if the instrument is valued on the basis of the lower of cost or market value but ignored if the instrument is classed as a hedge. The danger is that such unrealised losses are overlooked. Additionally companies can choose when they recognise profits on instruments in order that they can smooth profits. This applies both to derivatives and non-derivatives.

The use of hedge accounting currently causes significant problems. The practical problem with hedge accounting is translating business decisions into an accounting transaction that satisfies the hedging criteria. Hedge accounting relies on management intent and the result of this is that identical instruments can be accounted for differently depending upon the intentions of management in relation to them. Hedge accounting is often used for hedges of uncontracted future transactions and in these circumstances can be used to justify deferring almost any gain or loss on the derivative.

Circumstances can change quickly in the financial markets and the resultant effect on a company's derivatives can quickly transform the risk profile of a company. The present accounting framework does not adequately make this movement in the position and risk apparent to users of financial statements.

(ii) Disclosure of the risk of an entity in relation to financial instruments is an important element of accounting for financial instruments and the ASB has developed FRS 13 'Derivatives and Other Financial Instruments: Disclosures' to deal with this issue. However disclosure requirements alone are not sufficient to deal with the problem. Recognition and measurement issues need to be dealt with. Many derivatives are kept off the balance sheet with unrealised gains and losses being ignored. Hedge accounting problems cannot be dealt with purely by requiring narrative disclosures of the hedging instrument or of any deferred or unrecognised gain or loss. It is important that some consensus is achieved over the possible measurement bases which can be used. The use of current values for financial instruments requires agreement as it is a critical measurement issue. For example, could current values be used for derivatives but not for non-derivatives. There are issues of impairment of financial instruments and the recognition of such instruments which need to be dealt with in a standard. Most issues in accounting are dealt with by standards focusing on measurement, recognition and disclosure issues. A financial instrument is no exception in this regard and it is such an important issue that disclosure alone could never effectively deal with the issues satisfactorily.

(b) (i) There are four alternative ways in which gains and losses on financial instruments can be reported:

(i) all gains and losses in the profit and loss account

(ii) certain gains and losses in the profit and loss account and others in the statement of total recognised gains and losses (STRGL)

(iii) some gains and losses could be recorded within assets and liabilities or as a separate component of shareholders funds and transferred to the profit and loss account in a future period once they are realised

(iv) some gains and losses could be held temporarily in equity via the STRGL, and recycled to the profit and loss account once they are realised.

Method (i)

The main arguments for reporting all changes in value in the profit and loss account are that all gains and losses represent the performance of management who are responsible for the decision to buy or hold certain instruments. Additionally if all changes in value are recorded in the profit and loss account it restricts abuses and the manipulation of profits although decisions will have to be made about how the gains and losses are reported. For example should the interest expense be shown separately from other changes in value. However if unrealised gains and losses on fixed rate debt were recorded in the profit and loss account it might imply that such debt carried risk and companies might fear that the reporting of gains and losses on this debt in this manner might be misunderstood. Additionally such gains and losses are of a different character to trading profits and losses but would be amalgamated with the latter in the profit and loss account.

Method (ii)

The advantage of this approach is that the different types of gains and losses would be reported separately. Gains and losses on long-term instruments could be reported in the STRGL and those on short term investment in the profit and loss account. The profit and loss account could be protected from volatile movements if this method were adopted. The main problem however is drawing a distinction between those gains and losses to be reported in the profit and loss account and those to be reported in the STRGL. There are principles and a code of practice to be developed. The question is simply about which performance statement they should be shown in and the rationale for such a distinction.

Method (iii)

Under this method, gains and losses are deferred until a future period when the gain or loss is transferred to the profit and loss account. This 'recycling' could occur on realisation or at a constant rate over the remaining life of the instrument. This approach would avoid the volatility which would result from recording all changes in value in the profit and loss account. If the gains and losses were transferred on realisation then present practice would not be significantly altered. However, gains and losses would not be reported in the year in which they occurred but are deferred and this gives opportunities for abuse. Also the balance sheet will record amounts which are meaningless. The deferred debits and credits are not assets and liabilities and the alternative of showing the items as a component of shareholders funds amounts to reserve accounting and is difficult to justify in principle.

Method (iv)

This is a similar method to (iii) above. Certain gains and losses are recorded in STRGL and are transferred to the profit and loss account at a later date perhaps when realised or at a constant rate over the life of the instrument. All gains and losses would be recorded in the year they occur. However, under this method the reported figures can be meaningless as a loss can be reported in two performance statements at different times. The STRGL becomes an account which temporarily holds gains and losses that have not been reported in the profit and loss account and this conflicts with the rationale for the current usage of the statement. Also the approach conflicts with FRS 3 'Reporting Financial Performance'. It might appear that the best solution is method (ii) as it enables separate reporting of different gains and losses.

(Candidates need only discuss three of the above four methods.)

(ii)

AX plc

	20W9	*20X0*	*20X1*
	£'000	£'000	£'000
Historical cost interest 5%	1,500	1,500	1,500
Adjustment to fair value for market rate of interest	-	267	(288)
Effective interest cost	1,500	1,767	1,212
(Gain)/Loss due to change in fair value	(550)	571	-
Net charge to 'profit'	950	2,338	1,212

Fair value of debenture at 30 November 20W9

	£m	Disct at 6%
Interest payable 30.11.20X0	1·5	1,415,094
Interest and capital payable 30.11.20X1	31·5	28,034,887
		29,449,981
Gain on fair valuation is £30m–£29·45m =		£550,000

Fair value of debenture at 30 November 20X0

			Disct at 4%
Interest and capital payable 30.11.20X1		31·5	£30,288,461
Loss/(Gain) due to change in fair value	£30,288,461 – (266,999 + 29,449,981)		i.e. £571,481

Interest adjustment
20W9 – No adjustment
20X0 – 6% of £29,449,981 = £1,766,999
20X1 – 4% of £30,288,461 = £1,211,538

(***Tutorial Note****:* This question was set before the issue of the Joint Working Group's Consultation Paper: *Financial Instruments and Similar Items* (see Section 5 *Updates*), but this does not affect the answer.)

35 Flow Ltd

(a) Finance lease and operating lease

SSAP 21 *Accounting for leases and hire purchase contracts* defines two types of lease. A finance lease is a lease that transfers substantially all the risks and rewards of ownership of an asset to the lessee. An operating lease is a lease other than a finance lease.

The distinction between the two types of lease is designed to ensure that the financial statements reflect the commercial substance of lease agreements entered into by entities. Although legal title never passes to the lessee, the commercial substance of a finance lease is that the lessee has an asset which is financed by a loan from the lessor. Therefore the asset is capitalised and depreciated like any other fixed asset, while the capital portion of the outstanding lease payments is included in liabilities.

In contrast, an operating lease has the substance of a rental agreement and the lessee does not enjoy the benefits of owning the asset throughout its useful economic life. (Most operating lease agreements are for a shorter period than the total useful economic life of the asset.) In order to reflect this, lease rentals for the period are charged to the profit and loss account on a straight line basis over the lease term, unless another systematic and rational basis is more appropriate. In most cases, this means that the lease rentals for the period are charged on an accruals basis.

SSAP 21 also requires lessees to disclose details of future operating lease commitments in a note to the accounts. The amount disclosed is the annual rental for the following year, rather than the total future payments and this must be analysed between amounts relating to leases which expire within one year, in the second to fifth years inclusive and after five years. The annual rental must also be analysed between amounts relating to land and buildings and other operating leases.

(b) **Journal entries**

Sale of the property to River plc on 1 April 20X8

	£'000	£'000
Dr Bank	850,000	
Cr Loan		300,000
Cr Property disposal		550,000
Dr Property disposal	500,000	
Cr Property: Cost		500,000
Dr Property: Accumulated depreciation	60,000	
Cr Property disposal		60,000
Dr Property disposal	110,000	
Cr Profit and loss account		110,000

Being the sale and leaseback of property

Comments:

Flow Ltd has entered into a sale and leaseback agreement with River plc which must be accounted for in accordance with the requirements of FRS 5 *Reporting the substance of transactions*. Because the leaseback is an operating lease, rather than a finance lease, the substance of the agreement is that Flow Ltd has sold the property to River plc and no longer has the risks and rewards of ownership. Therefore the property is removed from the balance sheet.

SSAP 21 requires that the profit on disposal of the property should be calculated as the difference between the fair value of the property and its net book value at the date of sale (550,000 – 440,000).

The property was sold for an amount in excess of its fair value and so the difference between the sale proceeds and the fair value of the property (850,000 – 550,000) is treated in accordance with the commercial substance of the transaction – it is an interest bearing loan from River plc.

Payment of the first rental to River plc on 31 March 20X9

	£'000	£'000
Dr Operating lease rental	50,000	
Dr Interest charge (300,000 × 10.56%)	31,680	
Dr Loan (50,000 – 31,680)	18,320	
Cr Bank		100,000

Being the first rental payment to River plc

Comments:

FRS 5 requires that the lease is treated in accordance with its commercial substance, which is that of an operating lease for the continued use of the property, plus an interest bearing loan. The loan is effectively treated as a capital instrument, with the normal commercial rate of interest being applied to periods over the term of the debt at a constant rate on the carrying amount. Therefore the repayment is divided into three parts:

- Normal annual operating lease rental of £50,000. This is accounted for on a straight line basis over the term of the lease, as required by SSAP 21.
- Interest on the loan of £300,000, charged at the rate which River plc normally applies to similar fixed rate loans.
- Repayment of the capital portion of the loan.

(Tutorial Note: The interest bearing loan is accounted for over its full term as follows:

Year ended 31 March	Balance b/f	Interest @ 10.56%	Repayments (loan only)	Balance c/f
	£	£	£	£
20X9	300,000	31,680	(50,000)	281,680
20Y0	281,680	29,745	(50,000)	261,425
20Y1	261,425	27,607	(50,000)	239,032
20Y2	239,032	25,242	(50,000)	214,274
20Y3	214,274	22,627	(50,000)	186,901
20Y4	186,901	19,737	(50,000)	156,638
20Y5	156,638	16,541	(50,000)	123,179
20Y6	123,179	13,008	(50,000)	86,187
20Y7	86,187	9,101	(50,000)	45,288
20Y8	45,288	4,782	(50,000)	–
rounding		(70)		
		200,000	500,000)	

36 AB plc

Key answer tips

Your answer to part (a) should explain the treatment of leases without going into lengthy detail, as there are only 7 marks available.

In part (b) you should make a variety of points (the key requirement word is *discuss*) and include examples, as requested.

Your answer to part (c) should not only describe the accounting treatment in each case, but must explain the reasoning behind it.

(a) (i) SSAP 21 'Accounting for leases and hire purchase contracts' requires a distinction to be made between finance leases and operating leases. A finance lease is defined as one that 'transfers substantially all of the risks and rewards of ownership of an asset to the lessee', whilst an operating lease 'is a lease other than a finance lease'. A finance lease should be capitalised in the financial statements at the present value of the minimum lease payments utilising the lease term and the interest rate implicit in the lease contract. Any residual payments guaranteed by the lessee should also be taken into account. The capitalised asset is then depreciated on a basis similar to owned assets. For finance leases the depreciation should be calculated over the lease term if this is shorter than its useful life.

The interest and principal components of the periodic lease payments must be identified, allocated to accounting periods and the lease liability reduced accordingly. The finance charge is calculated as the difference between the undiscounted total of the minimum lease payments and the value given to the fixed asset in the financial statements. The discount element will be the finance charge. The lease obligation will be the present value of the minimum lease payments and the double entry will be completed by capitalising the fixed asset. Finance charges must produce a constant periodic rate of charge.

Operating lease rentals are charged to the profit and loss account on a straight-line basis over the lease term irrespective of when payments are due. This reflects the pattern of benefits derived from the leased asset.

The classification of leases can therefore have significant financial reporting consequences.

(ii) Current accounting standards do not deal adequately with leases. They do not require the rights and obligations arising under operating leases to be recognised in the lessee's financial statements. However addressing the situation presents a problem for standard setters. When the current standard on leasing (SSAP21) was developed, the principles as regards recognition of assets were left largely intact with those transactions which were essentially purchase agreements appearing on the balance sheet. The principle which was generated from the standard was one of the transfer of the risks and rewards of ownership. Those leases which transferred the benefits and risks of ownership were classified as finance leases and accounted for as assets and liabilities. All other leasing transactions were classified as operating leases. SSAP21 contains specific guidance regarding lease accounting and one would look to the standard as the primary source of authoritative guidance although the general principles of FRS5 are also relevant in ensuring that leases are classified as finance or operating in accordance with their substance.

Where a lease contract secures SUBSTANTIALLY all of the risks and rewards of ownership to a lessee, a recognisable asset and liability exists. 'Substantially', however has been judged against quantitative rather than qualitative criteria. If the lease is non-cancellable and the present value of the minimum lease payments is equal to or greater than 90 per cent of the fair value of the leased asset then the lease is normally classified as a finance lease.

The quantitative criteria have been perceived as the effective rules rather than the qualitative criteria set out in SSAP21 and FRS5. The standards have been thwarted by the fact that many lease arrangements have been designed to fail the specific quantitative tests for classification as a finance lease by the smallest of margins. Even where the substance of a lease contract can be objectively assessed, different weightings can be given to different factors by different accountants thus causing failure in the classification of a finance lease. For example the relative responsibilities of the lessor and lessee for maintenance, insurance, and bearing of losses can be blurred.

Long-term financing leases can be packaged as operating leases to secure the benefits of off balance sheet finance. The problem which arises is that substantially the same leasing arrangement will be accounted for in a substantially different way depending upon the satisfaction of the quantitative criteria and the perception of the relevant risks and rewards criteria. The following examples set out the ways in which contracts which in substance are finance leases may be classified as operating leases:

(i) The criterion that the present value of the minimum lease payments must be less than 90 per cent of the fair value of the asset for a lease to be classified as an operating lease may be satisfied by the use of contingent rentals which are not included in the present value calculation. Alternatively the present value of minimum lease payments may be reduced by lessening the guaranteed residual value or capping the lessee's liability at an amount less than the residual value.

(ii) The interest rate implicit in the lease may be impossible to calculate. Normally the lessee would then estimate the rate which would be paid on a similar lease. This estimated rate might then bring the present value below the 90% threshold.

(iii) Leases of land and buildings are classified as operating or finance leases in the same way as other assets. As land has normally an indefinable useful life, and if the title is not expected to pass to the lessee, then the lessee does not receive substantially all of the risks and rewards of ownership. Thus such a lease will normally be an operating lease. Some leases however may have the characteristics of a finance lease (for example a lease of a building with a short useful life). However, even in these cases companies will allocate as large a value as possible to the land so that it will automatically be classified as an operating lease.

It is worth noting that although some lease contracts do not satisfy the quantitative criteria for classification as a finance lease, they often do not change the substance of the lease agreement which may include certain criteria regarding the rights and obligations of the lessee which in themselves will determine the fact that it is a finance lease.

The various methods employed to avoid the standards can be seen as a shortcoming of the current rules. The arbitrary criteria used to determine 'de facto' ownership are easily circumvented and the difficulty of establishing the substance of leases raises serious questions about the adequacy of the arbitrary separation of leases into finance and operating leases. A major deficiency of the current accounting standards is the non-recognition in lessee's balance sheets of material assets and liabilities arising from operating leases.

(b) (i) Electrical distribution system

Where a lessee enters into a sale and leaseback transaction which results in an operating lease then the original asset should be treated as being sold and the operating lease should be accounted for under SSAP21. If the transaction is at fair value then immediate recognition of the profit or loss on the sale of the asset should occur. However where the transaction is above fair value, the following should happen:

(i) the profit based on fair value should be recognised immediately (£98m – £33m, i.e. £65m)

(ii) the balance of the sales value over the fair value should be deferred and amortised over the shorter of the lease term and the period to the next lease rental review (£198m – £98m, i.e. £100m divided by 10 years = £10m per annum)

If the sales value is not the fair value, then the operating lease rentals (£24m) are likely to have been adjusted for the excess price paid for the assets. In the case of AB plc the sales value is more than double the fair value of the asset and FRS5 may dictate that the substance of the transaction is essentially that of the sale of an asset and also a loan which equates to the deferred income element. Thus part of the commitments under the distribution agreement may in fact be more in the way of a financing cost (£12m). The company may therefore show the excess over the fair value as a loan (£100m) and part of the costs of the operating lease will essentially be a repayment of capital and interest on this amount.

(ii) Sale and leaseback of plant

The sale and leaseback of the plant appears to result in the creation of a finance lease as the present value of the minimum lease payments is greater than 90% of the fair value of the plant and AB plc has to pay all of the costs of maintaining and insuring the plant. Additionally the lease runs for the remaining useful life of the plant after which it can be purchased by AB plc for a nominal amount, i.e. the lease contains a bargain purchase option. (£43.5m + £43.5m × 2.49 = £151.82m: fair value £152m).

FRS5 states that the asset remains in the lessee's balance sheet at the carrying value and the sale proceeds (£152m) are shown as a creditor (Application Note B4 and B20). The creditor balance represents the finance lease liability and as the payments are made, they are treated partly as repayment of that creditor and partly as a finance charge against income. The revaluation reserve (£30m) will continue to be treated as before and if it is being transferred to the profit and loss reserve, this will now be over the lease term/assets life of four years.

37 Leese

Key answer tips

You must do more than calculate ratios in your answer to part (b) (ii). You must also discuss the impact of capitalising operating leases on the key performance ratios *and* on the business generally.

(a) Operating lease finance is used by a large number of companies. It is used for short-term financing of cars and long-term financing of land and buildings. Companies seek to preserve scarce capital and 'rent' resources rather than own them. They will not own the leased assets but will incur significant obligations under lease arrangements. A major deficiency of current accounting standards is that they do not require recognition in the lessee's balance sheets of material assets and liabilities arising from operating leases.

Because operating leases do not appear on the balance sheet companies have drawn up leasing agreements which are essentially finance leases as off balance sheet operating leases. If balance sheets are to represent faithfully an entity's assets and liabilities, then operating leases ought to be shown on the balance sheet. Current standards have promoted the structuring of financial arrangements so as to meet the classification of an operating lease so that the effects of capitalisation are avoided in financial statement ratios. The ability to achieve this off balance sheet treatment detracts from the comparability and usefulness of financial statements. The off balance sheet effect is so material that it cannot be ignored if there is to be meaningful analysis of financial statements. (Beatti.e. Edwards and Goodacre calculated that in their sample of companies the average operating lease liability was £51 million as opposed to the average reported liability for finance leases of £4 million.)

Current lease standards make it clear that quantitative criteria are to be used as guidance only and that the determination of whether a lease is to be classified as a finance lease or operating lease is a matter of professional judgement. However, in practice, quantitative criteria have been perceived as precise rules and in some cases have been applied as absolute thresholds. Thus leasing arrangements being packaged to fail by a small margin any specific quantitative tests for classification as a finance lease has thwarted the intent of standards.

Opposing conclusions can be reached when trying to assess the substance of the agreement such as the relative responsibilities of lessors and lessees for maintenance, insurance and the bearing of losses. This can lead to similar leases being classified differently. Thus the arbitrary and judgemental nature of standards and the ease with which such standards can be circumvented, have led to calls from standard setters to bring operating leases onto the balance sheet.

There is disclosure of future operating lease commitments so that it is possible to make an 'inspired' assessment of operating lease assets and liabilities. Thus the market can 'price in' the effect of capitalising operating leases which leads one to ask why companies are afraid of showing such commitments on the balance sheet.

(b) (i) Profit and Loss account after adjustment for capitalisation of operating leases

	£m
Profit on ordinary activities before taxation	88
Add back operating lease rentals	40
Less depreciation	(28)
Profit before taxation	100
Taxation on profit on ordinary activities (30 + (30% of 40 – 28))	(33.6)
	66.4

Balance Sheet after adjustment for capitalisation of operating leases

	£m
Fixed Assets (200 + 404 + 32 – 28)	608
Net Current Assets	131.4
Creditors: amounts falling due more than one year	(411)
	328.4
Share Capital	200
Profit and Loss account	128.4
	328.4

Workings

Net Present Value of operating lease commitments

	Land and Buildings £m	*Motor Vehicles* £m	*Total* £m
30 November 20X1	26.67	8.57	35.24
30 November 20X2	22.68	7.26	29.94
30 November 20X3	17.27	6.05	23.32
Thereafter	306.96		306.96
	373.58	21.88	395.46
plus rentals 30 November 20X0	30	10	40
	403.58	31.88	435.46
Capitalise at	404	32	436
Depreciation 5%/25%	20.2	8	28.2

Creditors: amounts falling due more than one year

	£m
Balance in balance sheet	50
add NPV of operating lease rentals	436
less rental paid 30 November 20X0	(40)
less operating lease NPV to NCA	(35)
	411

Net Current Assets

Balance per balance sheet	170
less operating lease current liability	(35)
taxation increase	(3.6)
	131.4

Profit and Loss Account

Balance per balance sheet	120
add increase in profit/loss account (66.4 – 58)	8.4
	128.4

(ii) Ratios

	Before Capitalisation	*After Capitalisation*
Net profit margin $\frac{\text{Profit before tax}}{\text{Sales}}$	$\frac{88}{580} \times 100$ i.e. 15.2%	$\frac{100}{580} \times 100$ i.e. 17.2%
Return on capital employed $\frac{\text{Profit before tax}}{\text{Share capital + Res. + Lt liabilities}}$	$\frac{88}{370} \times$ i.e. 23.8%	$\frac{100}{739.4} \times 100$ i.e. 13.5%
Gearing $\frac{\text{(Lt Liabilities}}{\text{Share capital \& Reserves)}}$	$\frac{50}{320} \times 100$ i.e. 16%	$\frac{411}{328.4} \times 100$ i.e. 125%

Discussion

The capitalisation of operating leases has a major impact on the critical performance measures. The net profit margin has increased from 15.2% to 17.2% which is almost certainly a significant increase. This increase represents the increase in the profit arising from the replacement of the operating lease charges with depreciation on the capitalised leased assets.

The impact on Return on Capital Employed (ROCE) is quite dramatic. The ROCE falls from 23.8% to 13.5% due to the capitalisation of the operating leases. However, the most striking impact is on the gearing ratio, which increases from 16% to 125%. The company would be concerned at the absolute changes in the ratios but most performance assessments are based on comparisons with other 'similar' companies or industry averages. It is likely that the relative performance and financial risk within the sector is going to be substantially affected by the capitalisation of operating leases as it is unlikely that all companies will use this form of finance to the same extent and over the same lease terms.

American corporations monitor ROCE particularly closely and the dramatic decline may be of concern to the holding company particularly if they are considering selling the company. Operating lease rentals are allowable for taxation and if capitalised as finance leases these agreements will attract a depreciation allowance and a finance cost deduction in the profit and loss account (Inland Revenue SP3/91). The finance cost for the year will be zero. This results in an increase in the tax payable for the period.

Leese may consider some other form of financing the usage of land and buildings, and motor vehicles. Sale and leaseback agreements will be affected by the capitalisation rules. However, motor vehicles can remain off the balance sheet by using 'Personal Contract Plans' whereby finance houses purchase the vehicles and sell the vehicles on to an employee. If operating leases are to be capitalised, the finance industry will probably create an instrument, which will still enable certain assets to remain off the balance sheet.

Whether the capitalisation of operating leases will affect the company's value or share price is debatable. There is already disclosure of future operating lease rentals so that analysts can already estimate the net present value of the liability. So it can be argued that this information is already priced in the market.

The problem arises with those users of financial statements who are not so well informed of the complexities of financial statements.

38 AZ plc

Key answer tips

In part (a)(i), concentrate on the information that segmental disclosures give to users and why it is useful, rather than restating the disclosure requirements of SSAP 25.

In part (b), you must consider the requirements of both FRS 3 *and* SSAP 25.

(a) (i) Many companies and groups of companies conduct their business in several industrial sectors and in a number of different countries. Such companies also may manufacture in one country and supply goods to customers in another country. These different parts of the business will be subject to different risks determined by the business environment in which they are operating. Additionally each segment may have a different growth potential because of the region of the world in which it is trading and may have different regional problems to deal with. For example, there may be high inflation in that part of the world, or currency problems. There is greater awareness of cultural and environmental differences between countries by investors and therefore geographical knowledge of business operations is increasingly important.

The provision of segmental information will enable users to better understand the company's past performance and to make more informed judgements about the company as a whole. If users are to be able to assess the performance of a company and attempt to predict likely future results, then disaggregation of the data in the financial statements is necessary. It is important that users are aware of the impact that changes in significant components of the business may have on the business as a whole. Several companies are currently demerging their activities and as a result of this, the provision of segmental information becomes increasingly important. The computation of key accounting ratios for the different segments is important information for potential investors in the demerged activities.

(ii) If a company analyses its segmental information using the 'risk and returns' approach then this will reflect the approach taken in the financial statements for external reporting. If information is analysed segmentally on any other basis than that required for external reporting, then there will be difficulty in reconciling the segmental information to the financial statements. Segmental reporting on the risks and returns basis will produce information which is more consistent over time and comparable between companies, although the use of directors judgement in segmental analysis affects comparability. The greater consistency of this method occurs because the managerial method is subject to fluctuations due to the changing allocation of managers to the task of producing segmental information. This method assists in the assessment of profitability, and returns and the risks of the component parts of the enterprise. The determination of business segments under this method had been somewhat subjective and it is thought segments based on an existing internal structure should be somewhat less subjective. In any event knowledge of the internal structure of a company is valuable information in itself and may enhance a user's ability to predict the actions of the management.

Utilising the managerial approach will be more cost effective as the incremental cost of providing segmental information will be low. If segmental information is reported on the same basis as for internal decision making, then this will reflect the classifications used by managers to discuss the progress of the business. However, the information produced by this form of classification is more likely to be sensitive because of the strategic way in which business is organised. Also segments with different risks and returns will be combined thus affecting the quality of the financial information produced. If the managerial approach is adopted, the definition of a segment will be determined solely by management which means that the nature of the information disclosed will be highly variable.

(b) (i) SSAP 25 states that the definition of a segment should be made by the management of the company and gives guidance but only in general terms. SSAP25 states that the directors should have regard to the main purpose of presenting segmental information and the need of information to users. There is no single set of factors which are universally applicable although the standard sets out the factors to be taken into account (for example these factors may be the nature of and markets for the products). Once the features of a segment have been distinguished it has to be significant to warrant separate disclosure and a 10 per cent threshold as regards third party turnover, results and net assets is set out in SSAP25. Thus the directors of AZ will take into account the above and perhaps may look to how the company is organised into divisions or subsidiaries, and may look to the management accounts for guidance.

In the case of an airline, the segments may be determined by the destination of the aircraft, or the location in which the sale was made. The geographical analysis of the net assets may be difficult as the aircraft will be deployed across the world-wide route network. Companies which operate in global markets will have difficulty in analysing their operations geographically.

(ii) Turnover for each segment should be split under SSAP25 between sales to external customers and sales to other segments. Thus the sales of aircraft to its domestic airline should be disclosed. However, the basis of inter segment sales is not required to be disclosed by SSAP25 and therefore the fact that the companies can negotiate a price for the aircraft with the possibility of resultant creativity in the intersegmental analysis need not be disclosed.

(iii) SSAP25 requires the results of the segments to be analysed before accounting for 'taxation, minority interests and extraordinary items'. The standard was issued before FRS 3 'Reporting Financial Performance' and the resultant impact on the categorisation of exceptional and extraordinary items. Exceptional items are not specifically dealt with in SSAP25 but by implication should be included in the analysed results. However, because specific guidance is not given some companies do not disclose the segments to which the exceptional items belong. In this case the nature of the exceptional item will be disclosed in the financial statements so that whatever the policy chosen by the directors, users should be able to allocate the loss to a particular segment.

(iv) FRS 3 requires the disclosure of the impact of a discontinuance on a major business segment where this is material. Many companies in the UK do not give comprehensive segmental analysis of discontinuance but show discontinued operations as a residual category, analysing only results from continuing operations into segments which was not the purpose of FRS 3. It is however, normally self evident in the financial statements as to what the discontinued operations relate to. It is likely that the holiday company would have been disclosed separately in the segmental analysis and also in the financial statements as it would be classified as a discontinued activity under FRS 3.

(v) The standard requires groups to give segmental disclosure of the profit/loss before tax, minority interests and extraordinary items of associates and the groups share of the net assets. The results of the associate need only be disclosed if the associate forms a material part of the groups results or assets. (Materiality has a 20% threshold in the context). If publication of the information is thought to be prejudicial to the business of the associate then segmental information need not be disclosed. Additionally where the holding company is unable to obtain the information concerning the associate it need not be disclosed. Thus Eurocat Ltd. may feel that the publication of information about its business (specialist aircraft engines) is prejudicial and may either request non publication or refuse to supply information on the above grounds then the standard has not been contravened.

39 C Ltd

(a) **MEMORANDUM**

To: Board of Directors

From: Financial Controller

Subject: Accounting for retirement benefits **Date:** XX.XX.XX

The difference between a defined contribution scheme and a defined benefit scheme

There are two main types of pension scheme. These are defined contribution schemes and defined benefit schemes.

Under a defined contribution scheme the employer pays a pre-determined rate of contribution on behalf of the employees. The rate of contribution is often specified in the rules of the scheme. The benefits available to the members of the scheme are directly determined by the value of the contributions paid. Therefore the cost of the scheme to the employer is reasonably certain.

Under a defined benefit scheme the rules of the scheme specify the benefits which are to be paid to each member. These normally depend upon factors such as the final or average salary of the employee and his or her period of service. This means that it is impossible to be certain in advance that the contributions to the scheme will generate sufficient returns to pay the benefits. The employer may have to increase the level of contributions in order to make good a shortfall. Alternatively, a surplus may arise and the employer may then be entitled to a refund of contributions or to a reduction in contributions.

The requirements of FRS 17

FRS 17 states that the cost of a defined contribution scheme is the contributions payable to the scheme for the accounting period. This is recognised within operating profit in the profit and loss account.

The cost of providing pensions under a defined benefit scheme is calculated on the basis of an actuarial valuation of the scheme assets and liabilities. The scheme assets should be measured at fair value and the liabilities should be measured actuarially using the projected unit method. Because the scheme liabilities will normally be payable in several years' time, they should be discounted to their present value.

The actuarial valuation normally results in a surplus or a deficit and the level of contributions to the scheme is then adjusted. If there is a deficit, contributions are increased, because the employer has an obligation to make good the deficit. A deficit is recognised as a liability of the employer. If there is a surplus, contributions may be reduced or there may be a period during which no contributions are paid (a contribution holiday). A surplus is recognised as an asset of the employer to the extent that the employer can recover it through reduced contributions and refunds.

The change in the asset or liability in the period, other than that arising from contributions to the scheme, is analysed into its components. Each of the components is reported in the performance statements (the profit and loss account and the statement of total recognised gains and losses) in a way that reflects its characteristics.

The current service cost is reported as an operating expense in the profit and loss account. The interest cost and the expected return on assets are netted against each other and reported as a financing item adjacent to interest. Actuarial gains and losses are recognised immediately in the statement of total recognised gains and losses and are not recognised in the profit and loss account in subsequent periods. Because actuarial gains and losses largely consist of market fluctuations, the ASB believes that these are similar in nature to unrealised gains and losses on revaluation of tangible fixed assets. Therefore they are treated in the same way.

Why the accounting objective is difficult to satisfy

Accounting for the cost of a defined benefit scheme is difficult because there are so many uncertainties involved. In contrast, the cost of a defined contribution scheme is predictable.

The amounts involved are frequently material. Typically, many years elapse between making contributions and actually meeting the liabilities. Valuing a pension fund is a complicated exercise requiring specialist knowledge. The actuary must make many assumptions. Returns from investments may fluctuate and may be affected by many factors which cannot be easily predicted. It is difficult to estimate the amount needed to provide pensions as this depends on salary increases and the estimated future service lives and life expectancy of employees. The choice of assumptions and the choice of valuation method can have a major effect on the contribution rate.

(b) **Profit and loss account charge for the year ended 30 June 20X5**

	£
Current service cost (W)	2,500,000
Net finance cost	600,000
Total charge	3,100,000

Balance sheet at 30 June 20X5

Creditors: amounts falling due within one year (15,000 × 18% × 1/12)	225,000

FRS 17 states that the defined benefit pension liability should be presented separately on the face of the balance sheet below other net assets:

Net assets excluding pension liability	XXXXXXX
Defined benefit pension liability	2,400,000
Net assets including pension liability	XXXXXXX

(Tutorial Note: The current service cost of £2.5 million is charged against operating profit and the net finance cost of £600,000 is reported as a financing item adjacent to interest. The actuarial loss of £2 million is recognised immediately in the statement of total recognised gains and losses.***)***

Working

	£
Current service cost (balancing figure)	2,500,000
Contributions (15,000 × 18%)	(2,700,000)
Other finance cost	600,000
Actuarial loss	2,000,000
Deficit in scheme at end of year	2,400,000

40 Diverse plc

(a) The principles outlined in FRS 17

There are two types of pension scheme: defined contribution schemes and defined benefit schemes.

Under a defined contribution scheme the pension received by the member is determined by the size of the fund arising from the contributions paid. Under a defined benefit scheme the rules of the scheme specify the pension which is to be paid to each member. This is normally based on the final or average salary of the employee and his or her period of service.

The cost of a defined contribution scheme is reasonably certain. FRS 17 states that the charge to the profit and loss account should be the amount of contributions payable to the scheme during the period.

In contrast, the ultimate cost of a defined benefit scheme depends on a number of factors, such as increases in salaries, returns on investments, changes in interest rates and the service lives of the members. None of these can be predicted in advance. The amounts involved are frequently material and many years may elapse between making contributions and actually meeting the related liabilities.

Therefore FRS 17 requires the assets and liabilities of defined benefit pension schemes to be valued at regular intervals by a professional actuary. Scheme assets are valued at fair value (in practice often equivalent to market value). Because there is no market value for scheme liabilities these are valued actuarially using the projected unit method. The actuarial valuation reveals whether there is a surplus or a deficit.

A defined benefit pension scheme is normally a separate entity from the employing company and the scheme assets and liabilities are not owned by the employer. Therefore the scheme assets and liabilities are not recognised in the employer's financial statements. However, a surplus is an asset of the employing company because it gives access to future economic benefits. The employer may be able to reduce the level of contributions or contributions may be refunded. A deficit is a liability of the employer because the employer has a legal or constructive obligation to transfer economic benefits (in the form of increased contributions) to make good the deficit.

Under FRS 17 a surplus should be recognised as an asset in the balance sheet of the employer to the extent that the employer is able to recover it and a deficit should be recognised as a liability. The movement in the surplus or deficit during the period, (less the contributions paid into the scheme) is analysed into its component gains and losses. The current service cost and the net finance cost (or income) are recognised in the profit and loss account. Because actuarial gains and losses are largely caused by variations in market value they are treated in the same way as unrealised gains and losses on revaluation and recognised in the statement of total gains and losses for the period.

The approach taken by FRS 17 is consistent with the ASB's Statement of Principles. Gains and losses arise as a result of changes in assets and liabilities.

(b)

Amounts to be recognised in the profit and loss account for the year to 31 December 20X8

	£m
Current service cost	6.5
Curtailment	(3.0)
Total operating charge	3.5
Other finance income	0.7

Amount to be recognised in the statement of total recognised gains and losses for the year to 31 December 20X8

	£m
Actuarial loss (W)	3.2

Note: The part of the surplus that arose as a result of the significant reduction in scheme members is a curtailment. FRS 17 requires this to be recognised as a gain in the profit and loss account for the period in which the redundancies took place (which is assumed to be the year to 31 December 20X8).

(c) Pension asset in the balance sheet at 31 December 20X8

The defined benefit asset or liability should be presented separately on the face of the balance sheet below other net assets:

	£m
Net assets excluding pension asset	XXX
Pension asset (4 – 3)	1.0
Net assets including pension asset	XXX

Working

	£m
Deficit in scheme at the beginning of the year	(6.0)
Current service cost	(6.5)
Contributions (5 + 6)	11.0
Curtailment	3.0
Other finance income	0.7
Actuarial loss	(3.2)
Surplus in scheme at the end of the year	1.0

41 Harmonise plc

Key answer tips

In part (c), concentrate on the *group situation* (including the requirements of FRS 7), rather than on the general application of deferred tax.

(a)

Profit and loss account and balance sheet extracts

(i) **Flow-through method**

	20X6	20X7	20X8	20X9
	£	£	£	£
Taxable profit	850,000	1,120,000	1,020,000	440,000
Tax at 33%	280,500	369,600	336,600	145,200
Deferred tax	nil	nil	nil	nil
Balance sheet extract				
Provision for liabilities and charges	nil	nil	nil	nil

(ii) **Full provision method**

	20X6	20X7	20X8	20X9
	£	£	£	£
Taxable profit	850,000	1,120,000	1,020,000	440,000
Tax at 33%	280,500	369,600	336,600	145,200
Deferred tax W1	105,600	(26,400)	(52,800)	132,000
Balance sheet extract				
Provision for liabilities and charges	105,600	79,200	26,400	158,400

W1 Deferred tax calculations				
Capital allowances	400,000	80,000	80,000	560,000
Depreciation	80,000	160,000	240,000	160,000
	320,000	(80,000)	(160,000)	400,000
Tax at 33%	105,600	(26,400)	(52,800)	132,000

(iii) **Partial provision method**

£79,200 of the timing difference will reverse in 20X7 and 20X8.

	20X6	20X7	20X8	20X9
	£	£	£	£
Taxable profit	850,000	1,120,000	1,020,000	440,000
Tax at 33%	280,500	369,600	336,600	145,200
Deferred tax W1	79,200	(26,400)	(52,800)	
Balance sheet extract				
Provision for liabilities and charges	79,200	52,800	nil	nil

(b) The following discussion considers the arguments for and against each of the methods.

The flow-through method

This method is based on the principle that only the tax payable in respect of a period should be charged in the profit and loss account of that period. The effect on the balance sheet would be that it would only show the current liability relating to that tax payable.

On grounds of commercial reality, flow-through avoids the need to make assumptions about the future which are uncertain as to outcome; on revenue grounds, recognising income tax when assessed is consistent with the government's policy of assessing tax for the time period in accordance with the fiscal policy of the time. On accounting principle grounds, the flow-through method complies with the matching principle whereby the amount charged in the profit and loss account is based on tax payable in relation to the taxable profit of the accounting period.

The arguments against the method are that the commercial reality is that tax has been deferred and not eliminated and the uncertainties surrounding deferred tax provisioning are similar to many other areas where management exercise judgement. On the question of accounting principle and the matching concept, it is argued that the tax should be matched against the operating results of the accounting period and not the taxable profit. A particular problem is that the EPS is affected by any deferred tax charge. EPS can therefore be distorted by fiscal policy rather than give a fair reflection of operating performance which it is supposed to measure.

Full provision

This method has strong support based on the accounting principles of matching and prudence. The tax charge is matched with the operating results and is prudent because the amount is the full potential tax liability based on the timing differences known at the date of the accounts.

The arguments against the method are largely based on commercial reality in that the result of full provisioning may be to accumulate provisions over time to the extent that they become a material item in the balance sheet without representing a genuine liability of the business. There has been discussion about the advisability of discounting the provision which would reduce its significance in the profit and loss account and balance sheet. However, it could be argued that discounting an accounting allocation is invalid and even if cash flows were identified they would be a subjective estimate of both the amounts and the years of reversals and a subjective choice of the most appropriate discount rate to use.

Even where there has been agreement that full provisioning should be the preferred method, there has been disagreement as to the use of the liability or deferral method. The deferral method places the primary emphasis on the matching concept i.e. matching the tax charge in each period with the accounting profit; the liability method places the primary emphasis on maintaining the provision at the best estimate of future tax payable considering the initial charge to be a tentative estimate requiring reassessment over time.

The ASB has now issued FRS 19 *Deferred tax*, which requires full provision.

Partial provision

Until the issue of FRS 19, the approach in the UK was to apply the partial provision method calculating the charge using the liability method.

The arguments in favour of this method are largely based on realism. The tax charge reflects the amount of tax that will become payable based on current knowledge and intention; the provision in the balance sheet is a realistic estimate of the tax liability that will need to be discharged.

The arguments against the method are mainly based on the need to consider the foreseeable future with a prediction of future events. This is subjective and can result in differing treatments of identical situations depending on the business's forecasts of future activity and profitability.

In conclusion, it is unclear whether a decision should be based on commercial reality or accounting principles. There is a conflict between the two which SSAP 15 attempted to resolve. Similar debates to that in the UK have occurred in other countries and within the IASC. One of the main reasons why the ASB has abandoned partial provision is that the UK was out of step with international practice which overwhelmingly uses full provisioning.

(c) Assuming that all of the shares in Harmonise plc were acquired for cash by Grab plc on 1 May 1995, explain the factors that would be taken into account in determining the fair value of deferred tax as at the date of acquisition.

Determine on a group basis

FRS 7 provides that deferred tax assets and liabilities recognised in the fair value exercise should be determined on a group basis by considering the enlarged group as a whole. At the end of the accounting period in which the acquisition occurred, the enlarged group's deferred tax provision will be calculated as a single amount, on assumptions applicable to the group and to determine the deferred tax of the acquired company as at the date of acquisition using different assumptions from those applying to the group as a whole would result in the post-acquisition profit and loss account reflecting the change from one set of assumptions to another, rather than any real change in the circumstances of the group.

Existing timing differences

The recognition of deferred tax in the context of a fair value exercise falls into two areas. First there will be the existing timing differences within the acquired company which will have been quantified in determining the potential tax liability to deferred tax.

Quasi-timing differences arising from fair value exercise

In addition, the adjustments made as a result of the fair value exercise may lead to quasi-timing differences which in theory would also require provision for deferred tax, as differences between accounting profits and taxable profits will arise in subsequent periods as items pass through the profit and loss account. However, FRS 7 has been amended so that deferred tax recognised in a fair value exercise is measured in accordance with the requirements of FRS 19. This means that deferred tax is not recognised on fair value adjustments in an acquisition.

(***Tutorial note*** Part (a) (ii) of this question has not been reproduced. This asked candidates to calculate the deferred taxation arising from accrued interest on debentures. Following changes in a recent Finance Act, interest is now generally taxed on an accruals basis rather than a cash basis. This means that timing differences no longer arise on accrued interest. Changes have also been made to the Examiner's answer to reflect the abolition of ACT and the issue of FRS 19.)

42 XL plc

Key answer tips

In part (a), give as many reasons as possible why SSAP 15 was criticised. Write a short paragraph explaining each reason. This approach will attract more marks than exploring one or two criticisms in depth.

In part (b), examine several arguments for and against providing deferred tax in each situation. This will meet the requirement to *discuss*.

Approach part (c) by calculating the deferred tax expense under full provision (part (i)). Then calculate the timing differences for the group at 30.11.X7 and work out the maximum reversal to give the profit and loss account under partial provision. Adjust this for the revaluation of land and buildings to give the final answer.

(a) The main reasons for the criticism of SSAP 15 'Accounting for Deferred Tax' are as follows:

(i) The recognition rule of SSAP 15 is different from that of other standards. Deferred tax assets and liabilities are only recognised when they will not be replaced by equivalent assets and liabilities. If this rule were applied to current assets such as stock or debtors then a significant part of such assets may not be recognised in the financial statements as in many companies these values remain static with a hard core of the asset remaining. This problem led to the issue of an amendment to SSAP 15 in 1992 in respect of post retirement benefits.

(ii) SSAP 15 was dependent upon future events and the intentions of management. It is thought this may be contrary to the Statement of Principles which defines assets and liabilities in relation to past events and states that management's intentions alone do not give rise to assets and liabilities.

(iii) There have been variations in practice in the application of SSAP 15. There are variations in practice over fair value adjustments made in acquisition accounting as some companies provide for deferred tax on such adjustments and others do not. Similarly there was no specific guidance given in SSAP 15 as regards the effects of revaluation on the calculation of deferred tax relating to timing differences between the depreciation charged in the financial statements and tax allowances.

(iv) The partial provision method is not internationally acceptable. It is required only in a small number of countries and the global trend is towards full provision particularly where there is a conceptual framework similar to the Statement of Principles.

(b) (i) Fair value adjustments

The issue is whether fair value adjustments in acquisition accounting give rise to deferred tax if the full provision method is used. Fair value adjustments were not timing differences in SSAP 15 but permanent differences. It is felt that deferred tax should not be provided on fair value adjustments because these adjustments are made as a consolidation entry only. They are not taxable or tax deductible and do not affect the tax burden of the company.

It is argued that providing for deferred tax on fair value adjustments is not an allocation of an expense but a smoothing device. Finally the difference between the carrying value of the net assets acquired and their fair value is goodwill and therefore no deferred tax is required. The arguments in favour of deferred tax are conceptual by nature. If the net assets of the acquired company are shown in the group accounts at fair value, then this will affect the post acquisition earnings of the group. For example, an increase in the stock value by £10,000 will result in profit being reduced by £10,000 in the post acquisition period. Therefore it seems consistent to exclude the tax on these profits from the post acquisition period also.

Additionally since an acquisition gives rise to no tax effect, the effective tax rate in the profit and loss account should not be distorted as a result of the acquisition. Providing for deferred tax ensures that distortion does not occur.

Some commentators feel that deferred tax should be provided on assets purchased in an acquisition as a 'valuation' adjustment. If the asset had been purchased in an arm's-length transaction for example stocks, then this cost would have been totally tax deductible. As this is not the case then the asset is worth less to the company because it is not tax deductible. Therefore deferred tax should be provided as an adjustment to reflect the reduction in the true value of the asset.

(ii) Revaluations of fixed assets

The revaluation of a fixed asset can be seen as creating a further timing difference because it reflects an adjustment of depreciation which is itself a timing difference. An alternative view is that it is a permanent difference as it has no equivalent within the tax computation. The revaluation is not seen as a reversal of previous depreciation, simply that the remaining life of the asset will be measured at a different amount. The additional depreciation charge has no tax equivalent and it would be incorrect to make any tax adjustments in respect of this amount. If however the revaluation takes the asset value above its original cost, then a chargeable gain may arise and a provision for tax should be considered if disposal is likely.

As with fair value adjustments, it can be argued that deferred tax is a valuation adjustment and whilst a revaluation does not directly give rise to a tax liability, the tax status of the asset is inferior to an equivalent asset at historical cost and therefore provision for deferred tax should be made in order to reflect the true after tax cost of the asset. The revalued asset would not attract the same tax allowances as an asset purchased for the same amount and therefore if deferred tax was not provided it would distort the post revaluation effective tax rate. (This would only be the case if the asset is the type which is deductible for tax purposes. Rollover relief postpones rather than extinguishes any tax liability and therefore should not affect the recognition of deferred tax.)

(c) (i) **Full provision**

	Valuation	*Tax value*	*Temporary difference*
	£'000	£'000	£'000
XL plc			
Buildings	50,000	7,500	42,500
Plant and equipment	60,000	13,000	47,000
Health care benefits	(300)	-	(300)
	109,700	20,500	89,200
BZ Ltd			
Buildings	500	100	400
Plant and equipment	40	15	25
Stock	124	114	10
Retirement benefit	(60)	-	(60)

	604	229	375
Total	110,304	20,729	89,575
Deferred tax liability	89,935 at 30%	26,980	
Deferred tax asset	(360) at 30%		(108)
	89,575 at 30%		26,872
less opening deferred tax liability			(9,010)
Adjustment due to change in tax rate	$9{,}010 \times \frac{100}{35} \times 5\%$		1,287
Deferred tax expense for year			19,149

The deferred tax expense relating to the revaluation of assets would not be shown in the group profit and loss account as it relates to items credited to equity.

(ii) *Partial provision*

Group Position Based on Carrying Values Before Any Fair Value Adjustments or Revaluation

	£'000
Balance at 30.11.X7	
Buildings XL plc	33,500
BZ Ltd	300
Plant and equipment	
XL plc	52,000
BZ Ltd	30
	85,830
Tax values at 30.11.X7	
Buildings XL plc	7,500
BZ Ltd	100
Plant and equipment	
XL plc	13,000
BZ Ltd	15
	20,615
Timing differences	65,215

Timing differences	30.11.X7 £'000	30.11.X8 £'000	30.11.X9 £'000	30.11.20Y0 £'000
Depreciation		(7,040)	(8,432)	(7,594)
Tax allowances		8,040	4,536	3,030
	65,215	1,000	(3,896)	(4,564)
Cumulative	65,215	66,215	62,319	57,755

Maximum reversal 65,215 - 57,755 = 7,460
Provision required 7,460 at 30% = 2,238

Therefore there will be a release of the existing provision if deferred tax were calculated using the partial provision method. However because the land and buildings had originally cost £45 million and the revaluation takes the value above this amount an additional provision of £50 - 45 million at 30% i.e. £1.5 million needs to be provided.

Thus the deferred tax provision will be reduced to:

£'000	
2,238	Timing differences
1,500	Tax on revaluation—chargeable gain
3,738	

The deferred tax released to the profit and loss account will be (9,010 – 3,738) i.e. **£5,272,000**

There will be no deferred tax consequences of the retirement benefit liability or healthcare costs under the partial provision method as it is anticipated that there will be no movement in the balance sheet amount.

(***Tutorial note:*** This question and answer were set before the issue of FRS 19 *Deferred Tax.* FRS 19 has been developed from the proposals in the ASB's Discussion paper 'Accounting for Tax' which was mentioned in the original question**).**

Part (c) (i) calculates the expense under full provision using the 'temporary differences' approach of IAS 12. FRS 19 takes a different approach, based on 'timing differences'. Under FRS 19, deferred tax would not be provided on either the effects of the revaluation or the fair value adjustments and the answer would be as follows:

(c) (i) Full provision

Valuation £'000	Temporary Tax value £'000	difference £'000	
XL plc			
Buildings	33,500	7,500	26,000
Plant and equipment	52,000	13,000	39,000
Health care benefits	(300)	-	(300)
	85,200	20,500	64,700
BZ Ltd			
Buildings	300	100	200
Plant and equipment	30	15	15
Retirement benefit	(60)	-	(60)
	270	115	155
Total	85,470	20,615	64,855
Deferred tax liability	65,215 at 30%		19,564
Deferred tax asset	(360) at 30%		(108)
	64,855 at 30%		19,456
less opening deferred tax liability			(9,010)
Adjustment due to change in tax rate $9{,}010 \times \frac{100}{35} \times 5\%$			1,287
Deferred tax expense for year			11,733

)

43 DT

Key answer tips

Notice that the requirement to part (c) has two parts: calculate the provision *and* comment on the effect.

(a) (i) Timing differences arise because the accounting effect of a transaction is recognised in a different period to the tax effect. They are differences between an entity's taxable profits and its results as stated in the financial statements that arise from the inclusion of gains and losses in tax assessments in periods different from those in which they are recognised in financial statements. Timing differences originate in one period and may reverse in one or more subsequent periods. This approach to calculating deferred tax is essentially a profit and loss account approach. The objective of the temporary difference approach is to recognise the future tax consequences inherent in the carrying. amounts of assets and liabilities in the balance sheet. The approach looks at the tax payable if the assets and liabilities were realised for the pre tax amounts recorded in the balance sheet. The presumption is that there will be recovery of balance sheet items out of future revenues and tax needs to be provided in relation to such a recovery. This involves looking at temporary differences between the carrying values of the assets and liabilities and the tax base of the elements. Most temporary differences are created by timing differences but temporary differences can also be created by permanent differences, which is where the two approaches differ.

Timing differences are readily identifiable from tax computations but it can be more difficult to identify and measure temporary differences, particularly when assets and liabilities denominated in foreign currency are deductible for tax purposes in some instances but not in others.

Thus timing differences differ from temporary differences in approach (profit and loss account v balance sheet) and in categorisation as temporary differences include permanent differences.

(ii) By definition, deferred tax involves the postponement of the tax liability and it is possible, therefore to regard the deferred liability as equivalent to an interest free loan from the tax authorities. Thus it could be argued that it is appropriate to reflect this benefit of postponement by discounting the liability and recording a lower tax charge. This discount is then amortised over the period of deferment. The purpose of discounting is to measure future cash flows at their present value and, therefore, deferred tax balances can only be discounted if they can be viewed as future cash flows that are not already measured at their present value.

Some timing differences clearly represent future tax cash flows. For example, where there is an accrual for an expense that is to be paid in the future and tax relief will only be given when the expense is paid. Some expenses are already measured on a discounted basis (e.g. retirement benefits), and it is not appropriate to discount the resulting deferred tax.

However, there is controversy over whether it is valid to discount deferred tax when tax cash flows have already occurred as in the case of accelerated capital allowances. It is argued that this timing difference does not give rise to a future cash flow and there is no basis for discounting. An alternative view is that an accelerated capital allowance is a liability that will be repaid in the form of higher tax assessments in the future. It can be argued that there are two cash flows, with the second cash flow occurring on the reversal of the timing difference, as the tax payment will be higher.

Discounting, however, makes the deferred tax computation more difficult to calculate and more subjective. Also there will be an additional cost in scheduling and calculating deferred taxation, as well as the problem of the determination of the discount rate. However, the ASB appears to support the idea of discounting in FRS 19 even though IAS 12 and US accounting standard FAS 109 specifically prohibit it.

(b)

Calculation of deferred tax liability

	30.11.20X1	*30.11.20X2*	*30.11.20X3*
	£m	£m	£m
Capital allowances in excess of depreciation reversal	50	60	70
Other timing differences	90		
Tax losses (42 ÷ 0.3 = 140)	(70)	(70)	
Corporation tax on capital gain (165 ÷ 0.3)			550
Inter company profit in stock	(6)		
	64	(10)	620
Tax rate	30%	30%	30%
Deferred tax liability (30% of £64m plus div. £2m)	21.2	(3)	186
Discounted (4%)	20.4	(2.8)	165.4

	£m
Total discounted liability (20.4 – 2.8 + 165.4)	183
Plus pension provision undiscounted	90
Total deferred tax provision	273

Notes

1 Taxation should not be provided on the unremitted earnings of subsidiaries unless there are dividends accrued as payable or there is a binding agreement to distribute past earnings. Thus a provision of £2m is required in this case. A provision needs to be set up for the inter company profit in stock at the rate of tax used by the supplying company (DT).

2 Deferred tax should not be provided on revaluation gains or losses unless the company has a binding sale agreement and has recognised the expected gain or loss. If rollover relief is likely to be utilised, then tax on the sale of assets should not be provided for. However, if taxation has merely been postponed then tax should be provided.

3 The pension provision will already have been discounted by reason of the actuarial valuation and therefore does not require further discounting.

Comment

The deferred tax provision of DT will rise by £196 million, thus reducing net assets, distributable profits, and post tax earnings. The borrowing position of the company may be affected and the directors may decide to cut dividend payments. However, the amount of any unprovided deferred tax, analysed into its major components, was required to be disclosed under SSAP 15. FRS 19 brings the majority of this liability onto the balance sheet but because the liability has already been disclosed the impact on the share price should be minimal.

44 Brachol plc

(a) (i) The statement of movements on reserves can be produced in different formats. The following is a common layout:

Reserves	*Share premium account* £'000	*Revaluation reserve* £'000	*Profit and loss account* £'000	*Total* £'000
At beginning of year as previously stated	2,025	4,050	2,700	8,775
Prior period adjustment			(1,350)	(1,350)
Restated at 1.12.X1	2,025	4,050	1,350	7,425
Premium on issue	2,755			2,755
Transfer from profit and loss account			135	135
Transfer of realised profits		(810)	810	
Decrease in value of investments		(405)		(405)
Currency translation difference			(270)	(270)
Surplus on property revaluation		540		540
	4,780	3,375	2,025	10,180

(ii) Statement of total recognised gains and losses

The format follows that used in FRS 3 and would be as follows:

	19X2 £'000
Profit attributable to members of the company	810
Unrealised surplus on revaluation of warehouse	540
Unrealised loss on investments	(405)
Total gains and losses for year before currency adjustment	945
Currency translation difference	(270)
Total recognised gains and losses for the year	675
Dividends	675
Total recognised gains and losses for year after dividends	0
Prior year adjustment	(1,350)
Net (deduction from) addition to net assets	(1,350)

(b) (i) The purpose of the statement of total recognised gains and losses

The statement is designed to highlight changes that have been recognised in the financial statements other than those resulting from capital payments or repayments.

If the company were to follow the historic cost convention and operate in its own currency, the balance on the profit and loss account for the year would represent the movement in net assets. However, the use of historic cost convention modified by the revaluation of fixed assets or the use of alternative accounting rules will give rise to unrealised movements that do not currently go through the profit and loss account. The statement will contain these unrealised adjustments to the net assets.

Clearly, it will not contain contra movements between different reserves nor will it contain the realisation of gains that have been recognised in previous periods as these will also be contra movements between reserves.

(ii) The extent to which a user of the accounts will be better able to make decisions by referring to a statement of total recognised gains and losses rather than the statement of movements on reserves that is produced to comply with the Companies Act 1985.

The statement of movement on reserves produced in (a) above shows that there was a change in net assets of £1,405,000 (£10,180,000 - £8,775,000). This change arose from:

	£'000
Premium on issue of new shares	2,755
Retained profit for 20X2 applying realisation concept	135
Revaluation movements (£540,000 - £405,000)	135
Currency translation movements	(270)
Prior period adjustment	(1,350)
	1,405

This is substantially the same information that appears in the statement of total gains and losses with the exception of the dividend distribution.

Why should there be a need for another statement described by FRS 3 as a primary statement when it is a re-arranged statement of movement on reserves?

One explanation might be that the statement of movement on reserves has not a regulatory or mandatory format so that it is clear that the movements contained in the statement are not presented in a uniform format and are not well understood by the user. The statement of total recognised gains and losses is intended to highlight all the gains and losses recognised in the period, including items that might otherwise be 'lost' in reserves.

Users of the financial statements need information which helps them to assess the performance of an entity as a whole. The ASB's concept of performance is wider than reported results. Gains and losses on revaluation of assets, gains and losses on retranslation of foreign subsidiaries and prior period adjustments are not included in reported results for the period, but can have a significant effect on the overall performance of an entity. The statement of total recognised gains and losses is designed to encourage users to analyse and interpret the financial statements as a whole.

(c) (i) The nature of the adjustments that would be required to reconcile the profit on ordinary activities before tax to the historical cost profit.

The differences will arise from the modification of the historical cost concept in the preparation of financial statements. This can occur

- when fixed assets that have been revalued are depreciated under FRS 15 and the carrying value is depreciated;
- when there is a realisation of fixed asset revaluation gains of previous years.

(ii) There have been criticisms that because there is no mandatory requirement for companies to follow a uniform procedure in the treatment of revaluations either with regard to timing or method of revaluing it is impossible to carry out effective inter-company comparisons or inter-period comparisons. The inter-company comparisons are impeded because the depreciation charges and realised gains on disposal are influenced by management decision in the individual companies and we have seen examples where the company has refrained from revaluation because of the impact on its future profits which could, in the directors' view, put it at an apparent disadvantage when compared to other companies that had not revalued. The inter-period comparisons are impeded because the depreciation charges and realised gains on disposal of fixed assets can vary from period to period depending on management decision.

45 Shiny Bright plc

Key answer tips

In part (a) (i) you should not simply explain the meaning of the terms, but also the difficulties in applying them.

In part (a) (ii)you should explain both columnar layering and row layering.

In part (b) (i) you are required to propose treatments which would be as advantageous as possible, yet which would still comply with FRS 3. For each item give a suggested treatment, with appropriate figures and an explanation.

An illustrative example (real or invented) is helpful in part (b) (iii), even though it is not explicitly required.

(a) (i) *Size*

Size refers to the value of a transaction in monetary terms. It is relevant when assessing effect or significance to the performance of the enterprise

There are two major problems in assessing whether size is significant, namely, the setting of a benchmark and the determination of a base figure.

There are differences of opinion amongst accountants and auditors as to what benchmark to use. Some, for example, assume that if the value exceeds say 10% of a base figure then it is significant. This is not however a universally accepted percentage for determining significance.

There are also differences of opinion over an acceptable base. Some use profit from all activities but there are other acceptable bases e.g. profit from continuing activities, profit after tax, related functional expense items or even turnover.

Incidence

This relates to the frequency of occurrence of a transaction with a transaction being exceptional if it is infrequent. This is in practice a most difficult area requiring a review of past experience, an assessment of possible future frequency and a knowledge of management intentions. Incidence changes over time and an item can change from exceptional to ordinary over time.

(ii) Explain how companies might be able to make use of FRS 3's layered approach to the profit and loss account to direct attention from the overall total result for which management was accountable.

The summary of FRS 3 states that a layered format is to be used for the profit and loss account to highlight a number of important components of financial performance:

- results of continuing operations (including the results of acquisitions)
- results of discontinued operations
- profits or losses on the sale or termination of an operation, cost of a fundamental re-organisation or restructuring and profits or losses on the disposal of fixed assets
- extraordinary items.

It also states that in presenting the profit and loss account the following requirements should be observed.

- The analysis between continuing operations, acquisitions (as a component of continuing operations) and discontinued operations should be disclosed to the level of operating profit. The analysis of turnover and operating profit is the minimum disclosure required in this respect on the face of the profit and loss account.
- All exceptional items, other than those in the item below should be included under the statutory format headings to which they relate. They should be separately disclosed by way of note or, where it is necessary in order that the financial statements give a true and fair view, on the face of the profit and loss account.
- The following items, including provisions in respect of such items, should be shown separately on the face of the profit and loss account after operating profit and before interest:
  - profits or losses on the sale or termination of an operation;
  - costs of a fundamental reorganisation or restructuring; and
  - profits or losses on the disposal of fixed assets.

There is therefore columnar layering with the classification between continuing and discontinued operations and row layering between pre and post operating profit items.

Columnar layering

The classification is important because it provides an indication of future sustainable operating profits. It could therefore be beneficial for loss making operations to be classified as discontinued. Such a treatment would need to satisfy the FRS 3 criteria for discontinued operations. There are opportunities for the exercise of judgement which could influence the classification. These include:

- downsizing

  This falls to be considered within the criteria of material effect on the nature and focus of the reporting entity's operations and represents a material reduction in its operating facilities resulting from either its withdrawal from a particular market (whether class of business or geographical) or from a material reduction in turnover in the reporting entity's continuing markets.

Judgement is required concerning the definition of material.

- partial disposal of non-core business resulting in loss of control

  There are differences of opinion as to whether a partial disposal should be classified as a discontinuance. If approached in the same way as downsizing, a decision to treat as a discontinuance may be supportable.

Row layering

This offers an opportunity to influence the operating profit figure by attempting to structure transactions to satisfy the criteria for disclosure as exceptional items after operating profit. In addition these exceptional costs are themselves required to be separated under continuing and discontinued headings.

The decision as to what constitutes a fundamental reorganisation or restructuring is a highly subjective and judgmental exercise.

(b) (i) 1 **Profit on disposal of a fixed asset**

Profit on disposal of fixed assets is required under FRS 3 to be disclosed on the face of the profit and loss account after operating profit. The profit is required to be based on the carrying value of the asset i.e. £1.5m resulting in a profit of £1m to be disclosed in the profit and loss account. The £500,000 that had been credited to the Revaluation Reserve will be transferred to the profit and loss reserve as a transfer on realisation.

In order to bring the profit on sale into the operating profit the company could consider reclassifying the fixed asset as a current asset in anticipation of sale. In making this decision attention should be given to FRS 5 para k which states that where the nature of any recognised asset or liability differs from that usually found under the relevant balance sheet heading, the difference should be explained. The effect of this is that there should be a time delay between the asset being used and being sold. It should also be remembered that such an accounting treatment could be considered by the Financial Reporting Review Panel.

2 **Loss on the sale of an operation**

The hotels acquired from Retort Hotels Ltd which were located in Ireland were sold on 31 August 20X6 for £12.5m. They had been valued at £16m at the date they were purchased from the receiver. No depreciation has been provided by the company.

The loss satisfies FRS 3 para 20 for the treatment as an exceptional loss to be disclosed after operating profit either as a loss on disposal of an asset or as a loss on sale of an operation.

If the company is able to support the judgement that the sale has a material effect on the nature and focus of the reporting entity's operations and represents a material reduction in its operating facilities resulting from its withdrawal from a particular geographical market then it can classify the loss under the discontinued heading.

It could support such a judgement in Shiny Bright plc based on the fact that the company has changed the positioning of its services by withdrawal from a geographical area, namely, withdrawal from Ireland and the amounts appear material.

The other criteria relating to discontinuance appear to have been satisfied.

3 **Cost of fundamental re-organisation**

Shiny Bright plc has incurred costs of £1.1m arising from the reorganisation of the hotel administration. This comprised £0.5m for the centralisation of the accounting and booking function, £0.4m for retraining staff and £0.2m for redundancy payments. The refurbishment costs have been treated as fixed assets.

If the company is able to support a judgement that the re-organisation is fundamental then the costs will be treated as exceptional and reported after the operating profit.

It might be able to argue that the centralisation of the booking system had a material effect on the nature and focus of the reporting entity's operations which justified treating it as a fundamental re-organisation.

Failing this, the costs will be shown as an increase in the administrative expenses under continuing operations.

4 **Permanent diminution in asset values**

The fixed assets used for cleaning were estimated to have fallen by £0.75m following the discovery that cleaning equipment had suffered damage due to staff failing to follow the manufacturers instructions.

This cost is an exceptional operating expense which is required to be analysed under the statutory format heading to which it relates i.e. the whole amount would be allocated to cost of sales.

5 **Decision to close the loss making hotel**

Although there is a proposal on the agenda, it has not yet been accepted by the Board.

If the proposal is accepted at the October 20X6 Board meeting it will be necessary to consider whether it can be classified as discontinued. The fact that the completion of the sale is not expected until May 20X7 means that the sale cannot be treated under the discontinued heading in the 20X6 accounts. It would however be necessary to consider the creation of a provision for loss on operations to be discontinued in the 20X6 accounts. This would be disclosed after the operating profit but it would reduce the EPS figure for 20X6.

It would be preferable therefore to delay the decision to close until after the accounts for 20X6 have been signed. This would also avoid it being treated as a post balance sheet event in the 20X6 accounts. If this route is followed it would be advisable to delete it from the agenda and not to minute the decision at this point.

(ii) Revised operating profit

	Continuing operations £m	*Discontinued operations* £m	*Total* £m
As stated in question	4.0	0.1	4.1
1. Restaurant sale treated as operating profit	1.0		1.0
4. Cost of sales increased	(0.75)		(0.75)
Revised figure	4.25	0.1	4.35
Exceptional items			
3. Cost of fundamental reorganisation	(1.1)		(1.1)
2. Loss on sale		(3.5)	(3.5)
	3.15	(3.4)	(0.25)

(iii) Describe the presentation of profit and loss account that would concentrate attention on the profit figure most favourable to the company.

The company is required to disclose the EPS as calculated under FRS 14. However, it is also permitted to disclose additional EPS figures and the format used by Imperial Chemical Industries plc (1992) attempts to focus the reader's attention on the profit before exceptional items using the layout:

	Continuing operations Before exceptional items £m	*Discontinued operations* £m	*Exceptional items* £m	*Total* £m
As stated in question	4.0	0.1		4.1
4. Cost of sales increased			(0.75)	(0.75)
Exceptional items				
1. Restaurant sale treated as operating profit			1.0	1.0
3. Cost of fundamental reorganisation			(1.1)	(1.1)
2. Loss on sale			(3.5)	(3.5)
	4.0	0.1	(4.35)	(0.25)

There is therefore a certain amount of flexibility in the layout of the profit and loss account which could assist the company to direct the readers' attention.

The company could produce an EPS figure based on the profit from continuing operations. However, where it does this, FRS 3 insists that the reason is given and a reconciliation to the FRS 14 EPS figure is given on an item by item basis.

There are alternative presentations that could be used, such as that proposed by the Institute of Investment and Management Research but provided companies give an explanation and a reconciliation to the FRS 14 defined EPS figure, they are able to tell their own story.

46 Reporting Financial Performance

Key answer tips

You are not required to describe the detailed requirements of FRED 22 in part (a).

(a) (i) FRS 3 'Reporting Financial Performance' was innovative in its time and still represents a more sophisticated approach to reporting financial performance than that found in many countries. However, various accounting practices have occurred in the UK, which have indicated the need to review the standard. FRS 3 did not attempt to change practice in the cases where law or previous accounting standards permitted items to be taken to reserves but it did ensure that such gains and losses were reported in a primary statement of financial performance (STRGL). However, preparers of financial statements have used the manner in which the different components are displayed so as to give undue prominence to the favourable aspects of the management's performance. It seems that users are often misled by innovative use of the profit and loss account so that attention is diverted from the total results for which management is accountable. A single performance statement would make such practices less effective.

A key objective of financial reporting is to provide information that may be of use in making and confirming predictions of the amount, probability and timing of future cash flows. Therefore, in principle, all gains and losses are relevant to an understanding of financial performance although the significance of each gain or loss will depend upon its individual characteristics. Thus full disclosure in a single statement of all transactions will enable users to make their own judgement as to the importance of the elements of financial statements and produce appropriate measurement of current and future income to meet their own specific needs. Only by assessing all relevant elements can users gain insight into past performance and be capable of estimating likely future trends.

Historically accounting has recognised changes in net assets but excluded them from the profit and loss account. (Foreign currency translation adjustments, gains on revaluation of fixed assets.) Thus the content of the profit and loss account has remained intact. The change in the net assets has been shown clearly but often because the gain/loss has not been included in the profit and loss account, such elements have been obscured in equity movements. FRS 3 introduced the STRGL to mitigate the problem. However it is now felt that all components of recognised performance should be reported in a single statement rather than changes in net assets being reported alongside changes in equity such as dividends and contributions from owners.

Items appear in the profit and loss account when they are realised. This traditional view is now being questioned as being an adequate basis for determining where and how elements of financial performance should be reported. Basing the reporting of financial performance on the realisation of assets permits the management of reported profits, whereas if all gains and losses were reported the manipulation of reported profits would be less of an issue.

The issue of reporting financial performance in one statement or more is a pragmatic issue rather than a conceptual one. However a disadvantage of the two or more statements approach is that disproportionate significance can be attached to one statement at the expense of the others. Additionally if a single statement is produced it leads to easier comparison of financial statements of different entities.

(ii) There are conflicting rules internationally as to whether recycling is an appropriate method of reporting certain aspects of financial performance. FRS 3 takes the view that gains and losses are reported only once in the period when they arise. (IAS 21 'The Effects of Changes in Foreign Exchange Rates' however, allows the recycling of gains/losses on overseas net investments on disposal.)

There are three main arguments for the recycling of gains and losses. Firstly realised profits have traditionally been recognised in the income statement with unrealised items reported in a second performance statement. When the unrealised items are realised, then 'recycling' would need to take place to record the realisation of the items in the income statement. This approach has been refuted by FRS 3 (but is used in the USA). However, realisation is now being discredited as being the basis for reporting financial performance. Realisation may provide information that is of limited value, merely confirming the nature of the gain already recorded. For example, a gain on the revaluation or disposal of a fixed asset is always a holding gain and its realisation does not warrant further inclusion in the performance statements. The cash flow statement is the best source of information about the effect of realisation on the entity.

Recycling is often used because of the uncertainty over the changes in value of elements of financial statements. The initial recognition of the gain/loss in a second performance statement is then subsequently confirmed or changed by realisation and the subsequent recycling into operating activities when the uncertainty of the measurement has been removed. However, if measurement is sufficiently certain to allow a gain or loss to be recognised, then it is the nature of the item itself which determines its classification in financial statements and recycling is, therefore, not required.

It is often felt that all items should be shown in the profit and loss account under operating or financing activities and that there is a critical event, which triggers the introduction or recycling of again/loss. However it can be argued that there is no conceptual basis for delaying recognition of these items unless there is some concern over the volatility or size of those items rather than their nature. In any event if an item is volatile and material it should not be disguised in the financial statements.

(b) (i) Under FRS 15 'Tangible Fixed Assets', gains and losses on disposal are treated in accordance with FRS 3 and calculated as the difference between the carrying amount and the net sale proceeds. They are reported in the profit and loss account as part of profit (loss) on ordinary activities before taxation. Any element of the revaluation reserve will not pass through the profit and loss account but will be transferred to retained earnings by an inter-reserve transfer. This transfer would be disclosed in the reconciliation of the opening and closing carrying amounts of the reserve. Under FRED 22, they would be recorded in the 'other gains and losses' section of a single performance statement which is broadly equivalent to the STRGL. If the disposal gains represent adjustments to depreciation or reversals of impairments, or the disposal losses represent impairments or adjustment to depreciation, then to that extent they are reported in the 'operating' section.

(ii) Revaluation gains are recognised in STRGL except to the extent that they reverse revaluation losses on the same asset which were recognised in the profit and loss account, in which case they too are recognised in the profit and loss account (after adjustment for depreciation). Revaluation losses caused by consumption of economic benefits are shown in the profit and loss account. Other revaluation losses are recognised in the STRGL until the carrying value falls below depreciated historical cost when the losses are recognised in the profit and loss account. An exception to this is where it can be demonstrated that the recoverable amount is greater than the revalued amount, the loss can be recognised in the STRGL to the extent that the recoverable amount is greater than its revalued amount and taken to revaluation reserve.

Under FRED 22 all revaluation gains are shown in a single performance statement under 'Other gains and losses'. Revaluation losses are shown under the same heading except to the extent that there has been impairment, when the impairment will be reported in the 'operating' section.

(iii) Foreign currency translation adjustments arising on the net investment in foreign operations should be shown as a movement in equity rather than as part of income. Thus the adjustment would be shown in the STRGL, that is outside the profit and loss account. Under FRED 22, the adjustments should be reported in single performance statement under 'other gains and losses' not as part of operating activities.

(***Tutorial Note:*** Minor changes have been made to the original question and answer following the issue of FRED 22.)

47 X plc

(***Tutorial note***: This question was originally based on the proposals in a Discussion Paper 'Earnings per share', which has since been developed into FRS 14. Minor amendments have been made to both the question and the answer as a result.)

Part (c) of the original question required the calculation of diluted EPS according to both the Discussion Paper/FRS 14 and SSAP 3.

Part (d) of the original question required a discussion of the results of the two calculations and comments on the acceptability of the possible revisions to SSAP 3.

Key answer tips

Your answer to part (b) could include examples of situations in which disclosure provides useful information.

Approach to part (c): calculate the number of shares deemed to be issued for no consideration when the options are taken up (Working 1). Then calculate the earnings per incremental share arising on each of the three types of potentially dilutive share. This determines the order in which the securities are included in the calculation. (See Tutorial Note.)

(a) The Accounting Standards Board (ASB) recognised the importance of international developments in accounting standards to companies raising capital overseas. The International Organisation of Securities Commissions (IOSCO) has now recognised International Accounting Standards as a basis for listing by foreign companies on world-wide stock markets (subject to some conditions). The ASB therefore has included on its agenda most of the issues that are the subjects of standards being developed by the International Accounting Standards Committee. This approach means that the ASB can form views on a subject so that it can exert influence on the IAS being developed. It also ensures that future FRSs are as consistent as possible with international accounting requirements.

Earnings per share is a widely quoted statistic in financial analysis and the ASB supported the attempt to reach agreement on an internationally acceptable level of computation and disclosure. The publication of the Discussion Paper allowed the financial community to express views on international developments at an early stage.

(b) Diluted earnings per share is an attempt to show the effect of a future issue of dividend earning shares. The future dilution will affect shareholders who should be informed of the impact on EPS. This is particularly important where the financial instruments giving rise to the dilution carrying a low interest rate in compensation for the future rights they give. (Disclosure of these rights is required under FRS 4 'Capital Instruments'). Where a company finances an acquisition through the use of convertible loan stock or preference shares, the securities often carry a low interest or dividend coupon due to the conversion privilege. Therefore, it is possible to achieve illusory growth in basic EPS as consolidated earnings will be boosted without any increase in ordinary share capital (assuming that the post tax finance cost is covered and current profits are maintained). Diluted earnings per share will however show the 'real' growth in EPS for existing shareholders since the 'cost' i.e. conversion privilege of using convertible finance is reflected in the calculation of EPS.

(c)

Diluted earnings per share - FRS 14

	£'000 *Ordinary shares*	£'000 *Net profit*	*EPS*	*Status*
Net profit after tax & Minority Interests		18,160		
less preference dividend		(160)		
	40,000	18,000	45p	
Options (Working 1)	400			
	40,400	18,000	44.6p	dilutive
Convertible preference shares	3,200	160		
	43,600	18,160	41.7p	dilutive
Convertible loan stock				
Interest (6% × 20 million × .67)		804		
Discount		200		
Shares converted $\frac{20 \text{ million}}{200} \times 23$	2,300			
	45,900	19,164	41.8p	Anti-dilutive

Since the convertible loan stock increases diluted earnings per share, they are anti-dilutive and are ignored in the calculation of diluted earnings per share. Diluted EPS is therefore 41.7p per FRS 14.

Working

(W1) Fair value of one ordinary share	£1.50
Number of options	2,000,000
Exercise price	£1.20
Proceeds from exercise of options	£2,400,000
Number of shares assumed to be issued at fair value	1,600,000
Number of shares issued for no consideration (2 million - 1.6 million)	400,000

(***Tutorial note:*** The order in which dilutive securities are included in the EPS calculation is determined as follows:

	Increase in earnings	*Increase in no of ordinary shares*	*Earnings per incremental share*
	£'000	000	
Options	NIL	400	NIL
Convertible loan stock	1,004	2,300	44p
Convertible preference shares	160	3,200	5p

The options are the most dilutive and the convertible loan stock is the least dilutive. The most dilutive must be included in the calculation first, so the order is: options, convertible preference shares, convertible loan stock.)

48 Mayes plc

Key answer tips

When determining which potential ordinary shares are dilutive you must base your calculations on earnings from *continuing operations*.

(a) Basic EPS takes account only of those shares which are in issue (FRS 14) and does not take account of obligations that could dilute the EPS in future. The company could have convertible stock, options or warrants to subscribe for shares. Additionally, a company could have entered into deferred consideration agreements under which additional shares may be issued at a future date. Investors are not only interested in past performance but also with forecasting future earnings per share. Thus it is important to disclose the effect of any dilution in the future. Many companies use convertible stocks to achieve the illusion of growth in basic EPS. Where convertible loan stock or shares are used to finance expansion, the securities normally carry a low rate of interest due to the fact that they can be converted into shares. If current performance is sustained and the incremental finance cost is covered, then EPS can be increased. Diluted EPS, however, will reveal the true growth in earnings as an attempt is made to show the true cost of using convertible stock to finance growth in earnings.

The disclosure is intended to help users assess the potential variability of future EPS and the risk attaching to it. It can function as an indicator to users that the current level of basic EPS may not be sustainable in future. However, it is also felt that the objectives of the basic and diluted EPS should be the same and act as a performance measure. The diluted EPS is a theoretical measure of the effect of dilution on basic EPS and analysts do not use this measure as much as basic EPS because of its hypothetical nature. However, the diluted EPS can serve as a warning device to equity shareholders that future earnings will be affected by diluting factors.

(b) **Earnings per share – basic**

	£'000
Profit attributable to the members of the parent company.	12,860
less preference dividend	(210)
other appropriations	(80)
Earnings – basic	12,570

Weighted average number of shares. (000)

	Shares	Weight	No.
1 June 20X8	10,100 ×	1	10,100
1 January 20X9 – issued	3,600 ×	5/12	1,500
1 March 20X9 – options	1,200 ×	3/12	300
1 April 20X9 – purchased	(2,400) ×	2/12	(400)
31 May 20X9	12,500		11,500
Bonus issue 1 July 20X9 1 for 5			2,300
Number of shares			13,800

Basic Earnings Per Share $\frac{12{,}570}{13{,}800}$ = 91p

FRS 14 states that the shares used in the basic EPS calculation should be based on the weighted average number of equity shares in issue. FRS 14 also states that a bonus issue should be taken into account in calculating basic EPS if the issue was before the publication of the financial statements.

Diluted Earnings per Share.

Computation of whether potential ordinary shares are dilutive or antidilutive

	£'000 *Net profit from continuing operations*	*Ordinary Shares* (000)	*Per share pence*
Net profit from continuing operations	18,270	13,800	132
Options			
$1{,}200 \times \frac{5-2}{5} \times 9/12$		540	
$2{,}000 \times \frac{5-3}{5}$		800	
$1{,}000 \times \frac{5-4}{5}$		200	
	18,270	15,340	119 Dilutive
6% Bonds (6% × 6,000 × .65)	234	12,000	
	18,504	27,340	67.7 Dilutive
Convertible Redeemable Preference Shares	210 80	2,000	
	18,794	29,340	64.1 Dilutive

Therefore all adjustments are dilutive and should be taken into account. FRS 14 states that potential ordinary shares which increase earnings per share from continuing operations are deemed to be anti-dilutive and are ignored in calculating diluted EPS. However in this case all dilutive elements would be taken into account.

Diluted Earnings Per Share Calculation

	£'000
Profit/Earnings – basic	12,570
6% Bonds – interest	234
Convertible preference shares	290
Earnings – diluted EPS	13,094
Ordinary shares	29,340
Diluted Earnings per Share	44·6p

Working

Net Profit from continuing operations.

	£'000
Operating Profit – continuing operations	26,700
Profit on fixed assets	2,500
Interest payable	(2,100)
Taxation (7,500 – 100)	(7,400)
Minority Interest (540 + 600)	(1,140)
Dividends – preference	(210)
Other appropriations	(80)
Net profit from continuing operations	18,270

(***Tutorial note:*** The order in which dilutive securities are included in the EPS calculation is determined as follows:

	Increase in earnings £'000	Increase in no of ordinary shares 000	Earnings per incremental share
Options	NIL	1,540	NIL
Convertible preference shares	290	2,000	14.5p
6% convertible bonds	234	12,000	1.9p

Options are always more dilutive than other securities because there is no increase in earnings. The order in which the securities must be included in the calculation is: options, convertible bonds, convertible preference shares.)

49 Worldwide Nuclear Fuels

Key answer tips

This question only concerns provisions. You are not required to write about contingencies in part (a).

(a) (i) A provision for a liability or charge is defined in the Companies Act as 'any amount retained as reasonably necessary for the purposes of providing for any liability or loss which is likely to be incurred, or certain to be incurred but uncertain as to the amount or as to the date on which it will arise'. However, the ASB is anxious to ensure that only those amounts that meet its definition of liabilities are reported in the balance sheet. Thus the ASB proposes to edit the Act's definition to 'liabilities in respect of which the amount or timing of the expenditure that will be undertaken is uncertain', as the Companies Act definition is more discretionary than that in FRS 12. The Board is keen to prevent companies from providing for future operating losses as in the ASB's opinion they should be accounted for in the future.

It is often quite difficult to differentiate between provisions and liabilities and reclassification from one category to another is not uncommon. The importance of the distinction is that provisions are subject to disclosure requirements which do not apply to other creditors. For example the Companies Act requires disclosure of the movement on a provision in the year but not creditors. However even such disclosure does not solve the difficulty with provisioning as quite often the largest disclosed balance is 'other provisions' with no information being disclosed in the financial statements.

The transparency of disclosure is possibly the most important issue in accounting for provisions. Once a provision has been established it is possible to bypass the profit and loss account with expenditure that is charged to it. Some of the provisions that have been set up in this manner have been very large. Planned expenditures for several years may be aggregated into one large provision that is reported as an exceptional item. The user of financial statements may then add the provision back to income in the year and fail to take account of charges made to that provision in future years. (This is often referred to as 'big bath accounting'.)

There has been concern that the basis on which provisions have been recognised has not been clear. In some cases the recognition of provisions has been based on management's intentions rather than on the basis of a present obligation. Thus management have been able to exercise discretion over the timing of recognition of provisions with the following effects:

(i) inconsistency between the accounting for provisions between different companies
(ii) the smoothing of earnings by management
(iii) the impairment of the balance sheet as a useful statement.

It is important that provisions are recognised and measured on a consistent basis and that sufficient information is disclosed in the notes to the financial statements to enable users to understand their nature, timing and amount.

(ii) FRS 12 utilises the ASB's 'Statement of Principles for Financial Reporting' and concludes that provisions are an element of the liabilities and not a separate element of the financial statements. Provisions should be recognised when and only when:

(i) an enterprise has a present legal or constructive obligation as a result of past events

(ii) it is probable that a transfer of economic benefits will be required to settle the obligation

(iii) a reliable estimate of the amount required to settle the obligation can be made. A reliable estimate can always be made if there is a reasonable range of possible outcomes.

An obligation exists when the entity has no realistic alternative to making a transfer of economic benefits. This is the case only where the obligation can be enforced by law or in the case of constructive obligation (see below). No provision is recognised for costs that need to be incurred to operate in the future. The only liabilities recognised are those that exist at the balance sheet date. The obligations must have arisen from past events and must exist independently from the company's future actions. If the company can avoid the expenditure by its future actions then no provision is recognised. These rules are designed to allow a provision to escape recognition only in rare cases. In these rare cases there is an obligation if having taken into account all available evidence, it is more likely than not that a present obligation exists at the balance sheet date.

It is not necessary to know the identity of the party to whom the obligation is owed in order for an obligation to exist but in principle there must be another party. The mere intention or necessity to incur expenditure is not enough to create an obligation. Where there are a number of similar obligations, the whole class of obligations must be considered when determining whether economic benefits will be transferred.

There is a need to provide for legal obligations although there is the important issue of timing and the identification of the past event which triggers the recognition. However FRS 12 also deals with the concept of 'constructive obligation'. For example where a retail store gives refunds to dissatisfied customers even though there is no legal obligation to do so in order that it will preserve its reputation. Therefore, an entity may be committed to certain expenditure because any alternative would be too onerous to contemplate. The determination of a constructive obligation is extremely difficult and is a somewhat subjective concept.

An event may give rise to an obligation at a later date because of changes in the law or because of a constructive obligation. Provision will be made when the law is virtually certain to be enacted or the entity publicly accepts responsibility for the event in a way which creates a constructive obligation.

The rules for recognition are expanded to deal explicitly with certain specific cases:

(i) no provision should be recognised for future operating losses

(ii) a present obligation for restructuring only exists and thus a provision recognised when a constructive obligation to restructure exists at the balance sheet date and the criteria for recognition laid out in FRS 12 are satisfied.

(iii) If an entity has a contract that is onerous, the present obligation under the contract should be recognised and measured as a provision.

FRS 12 essentially looks at the problem of provisions from a balance sheet perspective choosing to concentrate on liability recognition rather than the recognition of an expense.

(b) (i) FRS 12 has a significant impact on decommissioning activities. It appears that the company is building up the required provision over the useful life of the radioactive facility often called the 'units of production' method. However FRS 12 requires the full liability to be established as soon as the obligation exists to the extent of the damage already done or goods and services received. The provision should be capitalised as an asset if the expenditure provides access to future economic benefits. If this is not the case, then the provision should be charged immediately to the profit and loss account. The asset so created will be written off over the life of the facility. Thus the decommissioning costs of £1,231m (undiscounted) not yet provided for will have to be brought onto the balance sheet at its discounted amount and a corresponding asset created.

The current practice adopted by the company as regards the discounting of the provision is inconsistent. The provision is based on future cash flows but the discount rate is based upon current market rates of interest. FRS 12 states that companies may use current prices discounted by a real interest rate or future prices discounted by a nominal rate. The company is currently utilising a mix of these practices. FRS 12 states that a risk free rate should be used where a prudent estimate of future cash flows already reflects risk. (The government bond rate is recommended.)

The company currently makes a reserve adjustment for changes in price levels. However this adjustment should have two elements and be charged to the profit and loss account. The first element would be the current adjustment on the total provision for changes in the discount rate and the second element would be an element representing the unwinding of the discount. Thus the profit and loss account would be charged with the amortisation of the asset created by the setting up of the provision, and also with an adjustment for the change in price levels and the unwinding of the discount. FRS 12 requires this latter amount to be shown as a financial item adjacent to but separate from 'interest'.

It appears that any subsequent amendment of the provision should be recognised in the profit and loss account if it does not give rise to future economic benefits (paragraph 66). However the company appears to be treating the adjustment of £27m as a movement on reserves. This would not be allowed under FRS 12.

(ii) One of the quite explicit rules of FRS 12 is that no provision should be made for future operating losses. However, if the company has entered into an onerous contract then a provision will be required. An onerous contract is one entered into with another party under which the unavoidable costs of fulfilling the contract exceed the revenues to be received and where the entity would have to pay compensation to the other party if the contract was not fulfilled. Thus it appears that the contract should be loss-making by nature. Thus in this case the provision of £135m would remain in the financial statements and would affect the fair value exercise and the computation of goodwill.

Provisions for environmental liabilities should be recognised when the entity becomes obliged (legally or constructively) to rectify environmental damage or perform restorative work on the environment. A provision should only be made where the company has no real option but to carry out remedial work. The mere existence of environmental contamination caused by the company's activities does not in itself give rise to an obligation. Thus in this case there is no current obligation. However it can be argued that there is a 'constructive obligation' to provide for the remedial work because the conduct of the company has created a valid expectation that the company will clean up the environment. Thus there is no easy solution to the problem as it will be determined by the subjective assessment of the directors and auditors as to whether there is a 'constructive obligation'. It is a difficult concept and one which will result in different interpretations. If one takes example 2B in FRS 12 as a guide then a provision should be made.

50 Maxpool plc

Key answertips

In part (a) do not simply state the requirements of the Companies Act and FRS 8. Instead, explain the ways in which FRS 8 differs from and goes further than previous requirements.

Answer part (b) by considering each of the three companies in turn. Determine whether each company was a related party of the other two during each of the two years. This will enable you to decide on the disclosures needed in each case. You should not simply state what disclosures would be required, but explain why.

(a) (i) There are extensive Companies Act and Stock Exchange requirements regarding the disclosure of transactions with related parties. However, these provisions, such as the disclosure of transactions with directors and the disclosure of group companies are designed to highlight the stewardship nature of the director's work and not necessarily the users' perspective. As a result the need for greater disclosure was recognised by the ASB.

There are many transactions carried out by companies that are not on commercial terms and DTI reports on failed companies have highlighted the need to disclose such transactions. One of the first major cases in the UK involving related party transactions investigated by the DTI was that of Pergamon Press Ltd in 1969 where the chairman was Robert Maxwell. Further, the publishing of an FRS on related party transactions places a greater onus on auditors to identify related party transactions and to prevent the deliberate concealment of such transactions by the directors. (The Auditing Practices Board has also responded by providing guidance to auditors in SAS 460 'Related Parties'). The ASB felt that a much wider perspective was required as regards related party transactions and FRS 8 concentrates on the relevance of information to users of financial statements.

The amount of the disclosure required extends existing requirements. The definition of a related party is different in FRS 8 to that in the Stock Exchange's listing rules. The specific disclosures relevant to related parties required by the Stock Exchange relate only to the directors and shareholders of the company.

FRS 8's definition is much more comprehensive dealing with the wider issues of control, common control, influence and common influence. Further, FRS 8 states that all material related party transactions ought to be disclosed and this brings the standard broadly in line with International Accounting Standard 24. The ASB felt that it was important to provide an appropriate standard which would ensure consistency with international practice in this area. In the absence of contrary information, users will assume that all transactions have been undertaken at arms length. Where related party relationships exist this assumption is not justified because free market dealings have not occurred. Such transactions between these parties are susceptible to alteration or may not have occurred if the relationship did not exist or may be on terms different from those with an unrelated party.

Thus the ASB felt that existing legislation and rules did not adequately safeguard users of financial statements in these areas and require disclosure of such related party transactions.

(ii) It is important to gain comment on any accounting issue as it gives the Accounting Standards Board an insight into the views of preparers and users of financial statements as well as occasionally the views of academics. The ASB is keen to hear views on possible alternative solutions to issues and the needs of users of financial statements. Further it is important to obtain information on how the proposed standard conflicts or is consistent with existing practice in a particular area.

Additionally, comments on the consistency of the proposed treatment with current requirements and practices that are applied around the world to these accounting issues and the reasons for these requirements and practices, are most helpful to the ASB. Also the consistency of the proposed treatment with existing UK pronouncements, statute and the Statement of Principles will have been considered by the ASB but occasionally anomalies will arise and constructive comment in this area will be of use.

(b) For the financial year ending 31 December 20X6, the following related party disclosures would be made. Bay plc is an investor owning more than 20% of Ching Ltd and therefore is a related party of this company. Thus details of the transaction will have to be included in both sets of financial statements. Disclosures will include any elements of the transactions necessary for an understanding of the financial statements. As the factory outlet site was sold to a major investor, it is important that the financial statements note that the price was determined by an independent surveyor.

Maxpool plc and Bay plc both have an investment in Ching Ltd but this fact does not by itself make these companies related parties. There would appear to be no related party relationship between them and therefore there will be no disclosure in Maxpool plc's financial statements. Maxpool Group plc may be a related party of Bay plc only if they fall within the definition of FRS 8 paragraph 2.5(a) which states that such a relationship exists where there is the necessary control or influence by one party. This influence may be for example where Bay plc persuaded Maxpool plc to sell the factory at below market value.

The question of one party having subordinated its interests is unlikely as the value of the factory outlet site was determined independently and therefore in this situation no disclosure would be made in the group financial statements under FRS 8. However, as Maxpool plc is a listed company, the transaction may require disclosure under the Stock Exchange rules. The disclosure will depend upon the size of the transaction in relation to specified criteria laid down by the Stock Exchange. For listed companies and their subsidiaries transactions with related parties include shareholders holding 10% or more of the voting rights.

During the financial year to 31 December 20X7, there were significant changes in the shareholdings within the group. As a result the following related party relationships exist under FRS 8:

(i) Maxpool plc is presumed to be a related party of Bay plc as Maxpool plc has a holding of more than 20% (FRS 8 paragraph 2.5c).

(ii) Maxpool plc is a related party of Ching Ltd but any transactions between the two companies are exempted from disclosure under FRS 8 as Maxpool plc holds a 90% stake in Ching Ltd (FRS 8 paragraph 3c).

(iii) Bay plc is not necessarily a related party of Ching Ltd as there is no presumption that 10% shareholders have the requisite level of influence. Additionally although Maxpool plc controls Ching Ltd and has influence over Bay plc, FRS 8 indicates that the relationship between Bay and Ching would not normally justify being treated as related parties of each other. However, one would have to see if one party has subordinated its interests to the other before being definite about this relationship. In this instance, as regards the disclosure of the purchase of the vehicles by Bay plc, it appears that under FRS 8 that Bay and Ching are not related parties and therefore no disclosure would be required in the financial statements of either company.

Although Bay plc is not a related party of Ching Ltd it is an associate of Maxpool plc and by definition is a related party of Maxpool plc. Thus, Maxpool plc will have to disclose details of the transaction between a group member and Bay plc in the group financial statements. Financial statements should disclosure material transactions undertaken by the reporting entity (Maxpool group) with a related party (FRS 8 paragraph 6).

As Bay plc is a listed company, the Stock Exchange rules include as related parties shareholders holding 10% or more of the voting rights. Thus the transaction between Bay and Ching may need disclosure under the listing rules.

51 RP Group plc

Key answer tips

The key requirement word in part (b) is *discuss*. Therefore your answer should look at all the potential issues and should be *specific* to the events described in the question. You are not required to make general comments about related party relationships.

(a) (i) Related party relationships are part of the normal business process. Entities operate the separate parts of their business through subsidiaries and associates and acquire interests in other enterprises for investment or commercial reasons. Thus control or significant influence can be exercised over the investee by the investing company. These relationships can have a significant effect on the financial position and operating results of the company and lead to transactions which would not normally be undertaken. For example, a company may sell a large proportion of its production to its parent company because it cannot and could not find a market elsewhere. Additionally the transactions may be effected at prices which would not be acceptable to unrelated parties.

Even if there are no transactions between the related parties it is still possible for the operating results and financial position of an enterprise to be affected by the relationship. A recently acquired subsidiary can be forced to finish a relationship with a company in order to benefit group companies. Transactions may be entered into on terms different from those applicable to an unrelated party. For example, a holding company may lease equipment to a subsidiary on terms unrelated to market rates for equivalent leases.

In the absence of contrary information, it is assumed that the financial statements of an entity reflect transactions carried out on an arm's length basis and that the entity has independent discretionary power over its actions and pursues its activities independently. If these assumptions are not justified because of related party transactions, then disclosure of this fact should be made. Even if transactions are at arm's length, the disclosure of related party transactions is useful because it is likely that future transactions may be affected by such relationships. The main issues in determining such disclosures are the identification of related parties, the types of transactions and arrangements and the information to be disclosed.

(ii) The disclosure of related party information is as important to the user of the accounts of small companies as it is to the user of larger entities. If the transaction involves individuals who have an interest in the small company then it may have greater significance because of the disproportionate influence that this individual may have. The directors may also be the shareholders and this degree of control may affect the nature of certain transactions with the company. It is argued that the confidential nature of such disclosures would affect a small company but these disclosures are likely to be excluded from abbreviated accounts made available to the public. In any event if these disclosures are so significant then it can be argued that they ought to be disclosed.

It is possible that the costs of providing the information to be disclosed could outweigh the benefits of reporting it. However, this point of view is difficult to evaluate but the value of appropriate related party disclosures is particularly important and relevant information in small company accounts since transactions with related parties are more likely to be material. The Financial Reporting Standard for Smaller Entities (FRSSE) requires disclosure of material transactions with related parties including personal guarantees given by directors in respect of borrowings by the reporting entity. There are exemptions from disclosure if the reporting entity applies the FRSSE and these include non disclosure of pension contributions paid to a pension fund and transactions with certain parties such as providers of finance, and government departments.

It is felt by some that the Companies Acts requirements in this area were sufficient to enable adequate disclosure. However the Companies Acts gave a certain amount of information as regards the disclosure of directors and other officers transactions but these requirements only give limited assurance and therefore FRS 8 and the FRSSE requirements were required in order to extend the disclosure and produce a comprehensive set of regulations in the area.

(b) (i) FRS 8 does not require disclosure of the relationship and transactions between the reporting entity and providers of finance in the normal course of their business even though they may influence decisions. Thus as RP is a merchant bank, there are no requirements to disclose transactions between RP and AB because of this relationship. However, RP has a twenty-five per cent equity interest in AB. FRS 8 states that in order to avoid any doubt there are certain relationships that are deemed to be related parties. One of these relationships is that of investor and associate. Thus under FRS 9 'Associates and Joint Ventures' the entity has to have a participating interest and be able to exercise significant influence over the operating and financial policies of the company in order for associate status to exist. In order to exercise significant influence the company must actively be involved and be influential. Thus the equity holding in AB may not necessarily mean that AB is an associate especially as the remaining seventy-five per cent of the shares are held by the management of AB who are likely to control decisions on strategic issues. Also merchant banks often do not regard companies in which they have invested as associates but as investments and such 'portfolio investors' are acknowledged in FRS 9. FRS 9 says that if the business of the investor is to provide capital to the entity accompanied by advice and guidance then the holding should be accounted for as an investment rather than an associate.

However, FRS 8 presumes that a person owning or able to exercise control over twenty per cent or more of the voting rights of the reporting entity is a related party. An investor with a twenty-five per cent equity holding and a director on the board would be expected to have influence over the financial and operating policies in such a way as to inhibit the pursuit of their separate interests. If it can be shown that such influence does not exist, then there is no related party relationship. The two entities are not related parties simply because they have a main board director on the board of AB (directors in common do not make the companies related parties FRS 8). Thus it is apparent that the establishment of a related party relationship in this case involves consideration of several issues.

If, however, it is deemed that they are related parties then all material transactions will require disclosure including the management fees, interest, dividends and the terms of the loan.

(ii) No disclosure is required in consolidated accounts of intragroup transactions and balances eliminated on consolidation. Thus transactions between related parties will be disclosed to the extent that they were undertaken when X was not part of the group. Disclosure has to be made of transactions between related parties if they were related at any time during the financial period. Thus any transactions between RP and X during the period 1 July 20X9 to 31 October 20X9 will be disclosed but transactions prior to 1 July 20X9 would have been eliminated on consolidation. There is no related party relationship between RP and Z, as it is simply a business transaction unless there has been a subordinating of interests when entering into the transaction due to influence or control.

(iii) Pension schemes for the benefit of employees of the reporting entity are related parties of the entity. This requirement of FRS 8 was inevitable after the problems associated with the Maxwell affair. Contributions paid to the pension scheme are exempt from the disclosure under FRS 8 but it is the other transactions with RP which must be disclosed. Thus the transfers of fixed assets (£10m) and the recharge of administrative costs (£3m) must be disclosed. The pension scheme's investment managers would not normally be considered a related party of the reporting sponsoring company and it does not follow that related parties of the pension scheme are also the company's related parties. There would however be a related party relationship if it can be demonstrated that the investment manager can 'influence the financial and operating policies' of RP through his position as non-executive director of that company. Directors under FRS 8 are deemed to be related parties. The fact that the investment manager is paid £25,000 as a fee and this is not material to the group does not mean that it should not be disclosed. Materiality is defined in the context of its significance to the other related party which in this instance is the investment manager. It is likely that the fee will be material in this respect.

52 Industrial Estates plc

(a) The information in the question is that the units under construction are not subject to a legal contract of sale as at the date of the balance sheet. It is therefore inappropriate to treat them as long-term contracts.

The correct accounting treatment is to classify them as work in progress and show them in the balance sheet at the lower of cost or net realisable value.

The balance sheet figure would be £2,500,000 made up as follows:

(i) **Two units at cost**

	£
Two units at cost 2 × 75% of £1,000,000	1,500,000

(ii) **One unit at NRV**

Third unit on which additional costs were incurred:

	£	£
Cost incurred to date		
Per budget		750,000
Additional		300,000
		1,050,000
Selling price	1,250,000	
Less: Cost to complete	250,000	
	1,000,000	
Carrying value lower of cost and NRV		1,000,000
Written off		50,000
Balance sheet entry:		
Work in progress at lower of cost and NRV		£2,500,000

In the absence of a contract of sale it is unacceptable to bring attributable profit into account. There is no legal contract and the partly completed units should be shown at the lower of cost and net realisable value. The deposits of £50,000 will be shown as current liabilities.

(b)

MEMORANDUM

From: Chief Accountant

To: Assistant Accountant

Re: Treatment of sales effected under our new scheme.

This year we will need to decide on the effect of the new scheme on our year end accounts.

I have set out my views and indicated a proposed treatment. We will clearly need to have discussions with the auditors but before that could you please review the following and let me have your comments.

I don't see any particular problem with the figures for the profit and loss account or balance sheet here.

(i) The sales turnover figure

The legal position is quite clear. The company has sold its entire interest and retained a charge to cover 40% of the sales proceeds. I think we can happily record the full selling price as sales turnover.

(ii) The treatment of the 40% unpaid

We will show this balance as a debtor in the accounts under amounts falling due after more than one year. There is no interest or rental income arising so there will be no profit and loss account entries.

There is the question of the effect of UITF 4 to which we will need to give some thought. We will need to comply with the provisions of UITF 4 (covered in a Technical Department Student Newsletter article) with regard to the way we disclose the debtor.

As I read it, UITF 4 requires that in applying the Companies Legislation requirement to distinguish between debtors due within one year and in more than one year, it will usually be sufficient to disclose the size of debtors due after more than one year in the notes to the accounts. However, we might fall foul of the provision that where the amount of a debtor due after more than one year is particularly material it should be disclosed on the face of the balance sheet as leaving such information as a note may mislead users.

My own view is that the debtor figure is not material in relation to the total assets and we need only make a reference in the notes to the accounts.

Again, could we discuss this before we meet the auditors.

(c) Journal entries to record the unit repurchased during the year would be as follows:

	Dr	Cr
	£	£
Sales	1,250,000	
Stock	1,100,000	
Debtors	850,000	
Debtors		1,350,000
Cost of sales		1,000,000
Cash		850,000

Note: the entries recording the original sale are reversed. The cash payment to the debtor of £1,350,000 – the outstanding amount of £500,000 is recorded with a resulting debit balance transferred to the stock carrying figure.

(d) The terms of repurchasing units are that the company undertakes to pay the original purchaser 60% of the market value as at the date of repurchase.

This means that the company is entitled to share in the increase in value of the property and is subject to the risks of a fall in its value. Because of this, the transactions fall within the scope of FRS 5 *Reporting the substance of transactions* and the company should report in accordance with the commercial substance of the transactions.
Accounting for the transactions in accordance with their legal form would not give a true and fair view because the commercial substance is so different from the legal form that no amount of notes could correct the potentially misleading impression given by accounts prepared in accordance with the legal form.

It would be necessary to apply the provisions of FRS 18 in these circumstances. This would mean providing a clear and unambiguous statement that there has been a departure from the requirements of the Companies Act and that the departure is necessary to give a true and fair view. The company should also provide a statement of the treatment that the Companies Act would normally require and a description of the treatment actually adopted: a statement as to why the treatment prescribed would not give a true and fair view and a description of how the position shown in the accounts is different as a result of the departure with a quantification if necessary.

The effect on the profit and loss account

The company should treat the initial transaction as the sale of a 60% interest.

This means that the sales would be recorded at £750,000 per unit sold rather than at the existing figure of £1,250,000 per unit.

The cost of sales will be recorded at £600,000 per unit being 60% of total cost per unit.

The 40% interest will not affect the profit and loss account until it is sold when there will be a profit or loss on disposal.

The effect on the balance sheet

The 40% interest will be treated as a fixed asset or work in progress depending on the circumstances and carried at £400,000 per unit. The buildings element will need to be depreciated in accordance with the provisions of FRS 15.

On a sale of the 40% interest the profit or loss calculated in relation to the depreciated cost amount will be taken to the profit and loss account.

The transfer value from current asset to fixed asset must comply with UITF 5 which provides that where an asset is transferred from current to fixed assets the current asset rules should apply up to the date of transfer and the transfer should be made at the lower of cost or net realisable value. In the present situation, the net realisable value exceeds cost, and the fixed asset will therefore be transferred at £400,000 per unit.

(***Tutorial note:*** Part (d) of the original question and answer have been substantially re-written, following the issue of FRS 18 *Accounting policies* and changes in the syllabus.)

53 Badger plc

MEMORANDUM

To:	Assistant Accountant	
From:	Chief Accountant	
Subject:	Accounting treatment of three transactions	**Date:** 25 November 20X8

Transaction One

The lease appears to be a finance lease, because the present value of the minimum lease payments of £16 million (5 × £3.2 million) is likely to be more than 90% of the fair value of the asset and also because the lease gives Cub Ltd (the lessee) the right to use the machine for the whole of its expected useful economic life of 5 years. This means that the risks and rewards of owning the machine have been transferred to Cub Ltd. Under SSAP 21 *Accounting for leases and hire purchase contracts* the financial statements must reflect the economic substance of the agreement, which is that the machine is held by Cub Ltd. The machine should be removed from the balance sheet. Outstanding lease rentals are treated as a loan to Cub Ltd (i.e. as a debtor of Badger plc). Rentals received are split between capital (which reduces the outstanding debt in the balance sheet) and interest (which is treated as income in the profit and loss account).

Your treatment of the tax free grant is correct. SSAP 4 *Accounting for government grants* requires that capital grants are credited to deferred income and released to the profit and loss account over the useful economic life of the related assets. However, a recent amendment to SSAP 21 has prohibited the grossing up of tax free grants, so the tax charge in the profit and loss account should be adjusted to remove the notional amount of tax on the grant income.

Transaction Two

Although the company does not own the individual assets and liabilities of the scheme, the company has an obligation to provide the specified level of pensions to the employees in the scheme. Therefore the company has a liability to pay increased contributions to make good the deficit. FRS 17 *Retirement benefits* requires the deficit of £25 million to be recognised as a liability in the balance sheet.

The cost to the company of providing a pension is not the actual contributions paid during the year. It is the £5 million increase in the deficit between 1 November 20X7 and 31 October 20X8, plus the contributions paid of £2.5 million.

The actuarial loss of £4 million should be reported in the statement of total recognised gains and losses. Therefore the total charge to the profit and loss account is £3.5 million (W). This amount should be analysed between the current service cost (which is charged against operating profit) and the interest cost and the expected return on assets (the net amount is reported in the profit and loss account as a financing item).

Working

	£
Deficit at beginning of year	20.0
Contributions paid	(2.5)
Actuarial loss	4.0
Charge to profit and loss account (balancing figure)	3.5
Deficit at end of year	25.0

Transaction Three

FRS 12 *Provisions, contingent liabilities and contingent assets* states that provisions should only be recognised in the financial statements if:

- there is a present obligation as a result of a past event; and
- it is probable that a transfer of economic benefits will be required to settle the obligation; and
- a reliable estimate can be made of the amount of the obligation.

In this case, there is no obligation to incur expenditure. There may be a constructive obligation to do so in future, if the Board creates a valid expectation that it will protect the environment, but a Board decision alone does not create an obligation. There is also some doubt as to whether the expenditure can be reliably quantified. The sum of £100,000 could be appropriated from profit and transferred to an environmental protection reserve, subject to formal approval by the Board. A note to the financial statements should explain the appropriation.

54 Portfolio plc

MEMORANDUM

To: Assistant

From: Management Accountant

Subject: Treatment of three transactions **Date:** 22 November 20X0

I set out below my comments on your proposed accounting treatment of three transactions.

Transaction One

FRS 5 *Reporting the substance of transactions* includes application notes on the treatment of debt factoring. The correct accounting treatment depends on whether Portfolio plc has sold the debtors to the factor, or whether the company still 'owns' the debtors with the factor making a loan to the company and using the debts as security. To decide the true nature (commercial substance) of the transaction it is necessary to determine who experiences the risks and benefits associated with holding the debtors. In this case, any debts which are not recovered within three months are transferred back to the company and the amounts advanced must be repaid. Although the factor has assumed legal title to the debts, Portfolio plc bears the risk of slow payment and bad debts. This suggests that the factoring arrangement is in fact a loan secured on the debts. Therefore your proposed accounting treatment, which treats the arrangement as a sale, is incorrect.

The debtors should appear as an asset, with 90% of the debtors (representing the loan from the factor) being treated as a liability. The factor makes charges for administration and interest costs and these should be accrued as administrative expenses and finance charges respectively. Finally, a note should disclose the amount of factored debts outstanding at the balance sheet date.

Transaction Two

Because the legislation requiring the subsidiary to make the chemical plant environmentally safe was passed on 15 July, at the balance sheet date the company had a legal obligation as the result of a past event. The company will have to incur expenditure to meet this obligation (transfer economic benefits). A reliable estimate of the amount has been made and evidence of the existence of the liability is provided by the continuing contamination of the plant. Therefore a liability (as defined by FRS 5 *Reporting the substance of transactions*) exists and FRS 12 *Provisions, contingent liabilities and contingent assets* requires that full provision is made immediately. It is incorrect to build up the amount over the next four years.

Because the effect of the time value of money is material, the provision should be discounted to its net present value at 12%. The amount to be recognised and reported under 'provisions for liabilities and charges' is £25.44 million (40 × 0.636). The discount should be unwound over the next four years and the unwinding of the discount will be charged to the profit and loss account as a financing charge. (This is similar to interest, but is reported separately.) The effect of this treatment is that the carrying value of the provision will have built up to £40 million by the time that the closure takes place in July 20X4. However, the amount of the provision must be reviewed at each balance sheet date and adjusted if necessary to reflect the current best estimate of the expenditure to be incurred.

By incurring the expenditure to make the plant safe, the group gains access to future economic benefits (the ability to continue to make profits from operating the plant). Therefore the company should recognise a tangible fixed asset of £25.44 million and this will be depreciated over the next four years in the same way as the plant.

Transaction Three

Your proposed treatment of the loan stock is incorrect. Although it carries no interest as such, there is a finance charge to the company because the loan stock is redeemable at a higher value than the issue proceeds. FRS 4 *Capital instruments* requires that this finance cost is recognised over the term of the instrument at a constant rate on the carrying amount. Each year, the carrying value of the loan stock increases by the amount of the finance charge, so that at the date of redemption the carrying value is equal to the amount payable of £128.8 million (80 × 1.61).

The total finance cost is £48.8 million (128.8 – 80). Interest of £8 million (80 × 10%) should be charged to the profit and loss account for the year ended 31 July 20X0. This amount is also added to the carrying value of the loan stock so that this is shown at £88 million in the balance sheet.

The quoted price of the loan stock is probably of little direct relevance to the company. However, it is likely to be relevant to the users of the financial statements, because they need information about the risks faced by the company as the result of its use of financial instruments. FRS 13 *Derivatives and other financial instruments: disclosures* requires the company to disclose the fair value of the loan stock, which is its quoted market value. Therefore a note to the financial statements should show that the fair value of the loan stock is £94.4 million (80 × 1.18) at 31 July 20X0.

55 Dragon plc

MEMORANDUM

To: Assistant Accountant

From: Chief Accountant

Subject: Accounting treatment of various items
Date: 24 November 20X9

I set out below my responses to your queries about the correct treatment of each of the three items.

Item 1

FRS 15 *Tangible fixed assets* requires that all tangible fixed assets with a finite useful economic life should be depreciated over that life. Land is normally treated as having an infinite life, unless it is used for mining, but virtually all other fixed assets have finite economic lives. Although buildings may have very long useful economic lives, they are not excepted from the requirement to charge depreciation. The market value of the building is irrelevant. Depreciation applies the accruals concept to the cost or revalued amount of a fixed asset by allocating this amount to the periods expected to benefit from the asset's use. It is not a measure of market value.

In the past some businesses have not charged depreciation on buildings on the grounds that they are maintained to such a high standard of repair that their economic lives are extended indefinitely. This treatment has been particularly popular in the hotel industry. FRS 15 does recognise that in exceptional circumstances the useful economic life of a building may be so long that the annual depreciation charge is immaterial. This would apply to some heritage properties. However, the company's policy would seem to be in conflict with the 'spirit' of FRS 15. FRS 15 requires that fixed assets should be subjected to an annual impairment review if:

- the entity has adopted a policy of non-depreciation on the grounds that the useful economic life of the asset is so long that the charge would be immaterial; or
- the estimated remaining useful economic life of the asset is more than fifty years at the end of the reporting period.

Item 2

FRS 12 *Provisions, contingent liabilities and contingent assets* defines a provision as a liability of uncertain timing or amount. For there to be a liability there must have been a present obligation (legal or constructive) as a result of a past event. A provision should not be recognised unless this is the case and unless it is also probable that the company will have to transfer economic benefits as a result of this obligation. A constructive obligation exists where the entity has indicated, by past practice or published policies, that the actions it has taken will give it no realistic alternative to discharging the obligation.

The public announcement of the rationalisation plans would normally create a constructive obligation. However, it did not take place until two weeks after the period end. At the balance sheet date the board of directors had merely the intention to rationalise and could have subsequently decided not to proceed with the plan. Therefore there was no obligation and no provision should be made.

Item 3

The interest rate futures give the company the right to receive a fixed amount of cash at a specified future date and are therefore financial instruments. The underlying value of the futures is derived from the level of interest rates and therefore they are derivative financial instruments. At present there is no financial reporting standard that deals with the accounting treatment of derivatives, although the Accounting Standards Board (ASB) is currently developing such a standard.

Accounting for derivatives creates problems because the costs incurred by an entity in buying or selling them normally bear no relation to their value. Therefore it is not appropriate to use historic cost to account for them. The ASB is expected to require that current values are used instead. In the meantime, FRS 13 *Derivatives and other financial instruments: Disclosures* requires the disclosure of information about an entity's financial instruments. An entity must make narrative and numerical disclosure. Narrative disclosures explain the role that financial instruments have had during the period in creating or changing the risks faced by the entity. Numerical disclosures include information about and analyses of interest rate risks, currency risks, liquidity and fair values.

56 Finaleyes plc

Key answer tips

For each of the four parts to this question there are two steps: determine the nature of the problem; and explain the appropriate accounting treatment and disclosures. Make sure that you explain the reasoning behind your choice of accounting treatment (e.g. how and why adjustments are made). Calculate the materiality of each item in relation to the financial statements as a whole. This will enable you to determine what level of disclosure is required.

Because items (1) and (3) are non-adjusting post balance sheet events, FRS 4 and SSAP 21 are irrelevant.

(1) (a) This is a non-adjusting post balance sheet item. Although the decision was made within the financial year ended 30 April 20X6 it was not put into effect until the following year i.e. the receipt or entitlement to the receipt of cash was not a condition that existed at the date of the balance sheet.

(b) Disclosure is required because it is an event of such materiality that its non-disclosure would affect the ability of the users of the financial statements to reach a proper understanding of the financial position i.e. that the share capital has been increased by 5%.

An appropriate note would read:

'On 31 January 20X6, it was announced that the company was raising £14m (before expenses) by an issue for cash of 2m new ordinary shares of 25p each (representing 5% of the company's issued capital). The proceeds of the cash placing will assist towards the financing of further identified acquisition opportunities.'

(2) (a) The main issue is whether a provision can be recognised in respect of the expected future replacement of the heating system at 30 April 20X6.

The provision has been recognised on the grounds that the expenditure to replace the heating system complies with the ASB's definition of a liability i.e. an obligation to transfer economic benefits as a result of past transactions or events. However, FRS 12 'Provisions, contingent liabilities and contingent assets' now sets out the conditions for recognising a provision in the financial statements. The entity must have a present obligation as a result of a past event; it must be probable that a transfer of economic benefits will be required to settle the obligation; and it must be possible to make a reliable estimate of the amount of the obligation.

It is probable that the expenditure will take place and the expected cost is known, but in practice, the entity will be able to choose whether or not to continue to use the building after fifteen years. Therefore there is no present obligation and the provision cannot be recognised.

Our advice is that replacing the heating system would increase Finaleyes assets, not its liabilities and Finaleyes should depreciate the cost of the new system over its expected life thereby achieving matching. However, the matching will be over the useful life of the heating system not over the useful life of the building.

(b) Finaleyes should not have depreciated the £4m over 40 years. It should have separated the cost into buildings and plant and machinery and depreciated these separately i.e. the heating system over 15 years at £30,000 per annum and the buildings (minus the heating system) over 40 years at £88,750 per annum [(£4m - £450,000)/40 years].

The depreciation charge for the year should be £118,750.

The difference of £11,250 [£100,000 - £88,750] on the buildings' depreciation should be credited to the profit and loss account and debited to the buildings; the provision of £30,000 should be debited and the profit and loss account credited; there should be a charge for depreciation of plant and machinery of £30,000.

(3) (a) This is a non-adjusting event. Disclosure is required because it is an event of such materiality that its non-disclosure would affect the ability of the users of the financial statements to reach a proper understanding of the financial position i.e. that the company has disposed of net tangible assets representing 12.5% of the net tangible assets.

If the sale had been agreed before the year end on 30 April 20X6 with the purchase price determined after the balance sheet date, it would have been treated as an adjusting event.

(b) An appropriate note would read:

'On 15 May 20X6, Finaleyes exchanged contracts with the Helpful Friendly Society Ltd for the sale and leaseback of the main offices of the company. The total consideration was £12m payable in cash and the associated lease is for an initial 20 year term with rentals at market rates. The carrying value of this property at 30 April 20X6 was £10m. Completion of the disposal is to take place on 14 June 20X6.'

(4) (a) The management treatment of the £238,000 as a prior period adjustment is incorrect.

FRS 3 defines a prior period adjustment as 'material adjustments applicable to prior periods arising from changes in accounting policies or from the correction of fundamental errors. They do not include normal recurring adjustments or corrections of estimates made in prior periods'.

In this case, although the reductions in stock value relate to previous years they are not sufficiently material to qualify as a fundamental error. Even if it were a prior period adjustment, it would not be the cumulative figure that needed adjusting as stock errors reverse in the following period.

The reductions have arisen because of a failure to apply an adopted accounting policy correctly and not from a change in an accounting policy.

(b) The adjustment of £238,000 to the stock and profit and loss account balance brought forward needs to be reversed.

The appropriate accounting treatment is to charge the £115,000 in the 20X6 accounts as part of the cost of sales and to disclose £105,000 of this as an exceptional item. £10,000 would have been charged without disclosure in the cost of sales in any event.

Balance sheet stock at 30 April 20X6 needs to be reduced by a credit of £115,000.

The £105,000 is classified as exceptional because it is a material item which derives from events that fall within the ordinary activities of the reporting entity and which need to be disclosed by virtue of their size and incidence in order to give a true and fair view.

(***Tutorial note***: Since this question was originally set, the ASB has issued FRS 12 Provisions, contingent liabilities and contingent assets and FRS 15 Tangible fixed assets.

The answer to (2) (a) has been amended to reflect this.)

57 Look Ahead & Co

(a) Discuss the relevance of dividends in the valuation of D Dodd's shareholding on the assumption that it is sold to his son W Dodd illustrating your answer from the data given in the question.

There is a problem for the valuer in that the dividend policy is outside the control of the shareholder wishing to sell his shares and, because the company is a private company, there is not the same pressure on the directors to maintain a consistent dividend policy or, indeed, to even pay a dividend.

This means that there is uncertainty. At one extreme the valuer could value the shares at nil because there is the possibility of no dividends being declared in future years; at the other extreme the valuer could value the shares on an earnings basis in the hope that the earnings will be fully distributed in future years.

In between these two extremes the valuer could make a valuation based on the probability of the level of dividends.

A prudent approach might be to assume that the current dividend will be maintained. If this were to be assumed the valuation of the shares would be £3,703.70. This is calculated as follows:

The valuation of each share would be based on the gross dividend of 6.67p per share to produce a valuation of 37.04p per share. (5p/75 × 100/.18 = 37.04p per 25p share).

The 10,000 shareholding would be valued at £3,703.70.

This method is referred to in 'Valuation of Unquoted Securities' by C G Glover as the initial yield method. It is simple to use and has a wide following in practice.

An inappropriate choice of comparator company would clearly be misleading but it should be recognised that the use of sector averages published in the FT Actuaries Share Index can be even more misleading because the prices arising from dealings by institutional investors often reflect short-term political and economic circumstances whereas the investor in a private company may be looking for long-term considerations.

This method does not take account of a possible range of dividends and required rates of return. It is a normal practice for a valuer to produce a table of values to indicate to a client for negotiation purposes the range of possible values. For example, the following table could be produced on the assumption that the future net dividend would be between 5p and 7p; that the investor's required gross rate of return would be between 16% and 22%; and that the rate of tax was 25%.

Dividend		*Investor's required rate of return*			
Net	*Gross*	*16%*	*18%*	*20%*	*22%*
5p	6.67p	41.7	37.1	33.4	30.1
6p	8.00p	50.0	44.4	40.0	36.4
7p	9.33p	58.1	51.8	46.7	42.4

This is simplistic but the table indicates that from the estimated dividends and required rate of return a share price can be derived that lies between 30.1p and 58.1p. It indicates the sensitivity of the share price to a variation in the assumption of dividend per share and required rate of return. In relation to the shares being considered, that indicates an offer of between £3,010 and £5,810.

The tabular method is attempting to allow for a growth in the dividend by setting out three levels of dividend. An alternative approach that features in the academic texts is to estimate the rate of growth. In the present example, it is clear that there has been a consistent dividend policy.

The directors have followed a policy of increasing the dividends at the rate of 5% per year. The dividend cover has varied between 4 and 10 indicating a policy of maintaining dividend growth rather than maintaining the dividend cover and relating the dividend directly to the earnings of the year in which the dividend is paid.

Applying the growth formula, the value of a share would be:

$$\frac{\text{Gross dividend} \times \text{growth rate}}{\text{Required rate of return - growth rate}} = \frac{(5\text{p}/75 \times 100) \times 1.05}{18-5}$$

$$= 53.85\text{p}$$

The 10,000 shares would have a value of £5,384.62.

On the data given in the question, there is a clear dividend policy and a valuation could be based on that. The earnings are not relevant unless there is some indication that they will fail to support the dividend or some indication that the dividend policy will change to reflect the earnings growth e.g. following a flotation on the AIM.

(b) (i) Explain briefly the factors that the firm would take into account when estimating the future net dividends.

In order to estimate the likely range of future dividends, the firm needs to evaluate the directors' dividend policy.

In Arbor Ltd there has been a consistent policy of increasing the dividend per share by 5% per annum. The future dividends can be related to that policy assuming that there are no contra-indications such as liquidity pressures or expansion plans that could affect the maintenance of the existing policy. There is less need to consider the future rate of increase in the profits.

However, if the directors appear to have adopted an identifiable dividend cover policy, then efforts should be made to determine the future profitability and to apply the historic dividend cover rate to the forecast profits.

If the directors have a restrictive attitude towards paying dividends, this might result in the payment of a constant amount regardless of earnings growth or even in the payment of no dividends with profits taken as directors' remuneration or ploughed back into the business.

Where there is no discernible pattern, this could have an impact on the investor's required rate of return.

(ii) Explain briefly the factors that the firm would take into account when making an initial estimate of the investor's required gross yield.

The rate of return on a security has to take account of:

(1) forgoing the pure or risk-free rate of interest;
(2) bearing the risk of equity investment;
(3) suffering any lack of marketability; and
(4) possible changes in the marketability.

The firm usually considers three main sources of information.

(1) in order to assess the risk-free rate of interest

The current market statistics of average gross interest yields to redemption of British government stocks together with the gross returns available from local authority loans and building societies, will give a fairly reliable guide to the interest rates prevailing at the date of the valuation.

These rates of return after deducting the investor's top rate of tax and after deducting the rate of inflation will indicate the real return obtainable by the investor.

(2) in order to assess the premium for equity investment

The second source of information is the current market statistics of gross dividend yields on minority holdings of equity shares that are quoted. The market will have taken business risk arising from the nature of the company's operations and financial structure into account in arriving at a price.

However, it is often difficult to identify a company whose business, trading record and financial structure are similar to the company whose shares are being valued and an adjustment might be needed to take account of any material differences.

Adjustment for differing operating conditions is subjective. It will involve a consideration of a number of factors. For example, it could involve comparing the workforce if the target has a new workforce and the comparator has a long established, experienced workforce; or comparing the products/services; or the pricing structures; or the tangible assets e.g. the target might have new fixed assets and the comparator heavily depreciated ones.

Adjustment for different capital structures is also subjective. It may involve a consideration of present gearing levels and also future changes e.g. arising from changes in the working capital requirements.

(3) in order to assess a premium for lack of marketability

An adjustment is required for the lack of marketability. This is a subjective adjustment. It will be influenced by the valuer's knowledge of the market in unquoted minority shares that prevails at the date of the valuation.

(4) Possible changes in the lack of marketability

If there is any indication that the minority interest will become more marketable then the premium for this risk will be reduced.

For example there may be some indication of an exit route other than by sale within the existing articles and memorandum of association e.g. flotation or take-over.

(c) Explain how the approach adopted by the firm when valuing a minority interest might be influenced by the size of the shareholding or its relative importance to the other shareholdings.

The firm will need to consider the ownership of other shares before and after the transaction and the effect that this has on the control and management of the company assuming that the shares passed into the ownership of one or more of the other shareholders. It is important to consider the powers attaching to the shares.

The powers attaching to degree of ownership

With a holding that exceeds 10% a shareholder has the power to prevent a complete take-over by another company (Companies Act 1985 Ss428-430) that might have sought to enforce a compulsory acquisition of the minority that has not accepted the offer.

With a holding that exceeds 25% the minority shareholder has the power to block a special resolution such as that required to change the objects of the company (Companies Act 1985 s.4) without recourse to the court as a dissenting minority.

With a holding that exceeds 25% the minority shareholder has the power to block extraordinary resolutions such as that required to wind up a company voluntarily when because of its liabilities it cannot continue to trade: IA 1986 s.84.

With a holding that exceeds 50% the shareholder is able to control the constitution of the board of directors and the dividend distribution policy of the company.

This effect of the above considerations is that there may be a special buyer to whom the shares have a value that is greater than that based on dividend yields. The special buyer might be acting to achieve a positive effect e.g. to control dividend distribution policy or to achieve a negative effect e.g. to frustrate control being achieved by a single person.

Powers attaching to existing shareholding

In the present situation the shares are held so that no single shareholder can pass ordinary resolutions but A Arny is able to prevent a special or extraordinary resolution being passed e.g.

Shareholder	*Shareholding*	*% holding*
A Arny	61,250	49%
B Brady	30,000	24%
D Brady	20,000	16%
E Brady	11,250	9%
D Dodd	2,500	2%

Existence of special buyer(s) in Arbor Ltd

In the present situation, where there are shareholdings on the margins of 10%, 25% and 50% there are clearly potential special buyers.

The sale to A Arny would allow A Arny to control the company and the dividend distribution policy. This could have an effect on the value of the other minority shareholdings if he were to change the dividend policy from its present pattern of 5% increase each year. If there were any likelihood of this then the other shareholders would consider a premium to protect the valuation based on the dividend growth model.

The sale to B Brady would allow him to prevent the passing of a special or extraordinary resolution.

The sale to any of the Bradys would allow them, acting in concert, to control the company.

The effect of a special buyer on the share valuation method

The point that needs to be considered is whether the existence of a special buyer has an implication for the share valuation method that is applied.

For example, should the shareholding being sold be valued on an earnings basis rather than on a dividend basis.

If an earnings basis is applicable, then a profit forecast and earnings yield approach would be followed.

This could be significant in the case of Arbor Ltd because the growth of earnings has been at a substantially greater rate of approximately 40% than the 5% growth in the dividends distributed.

58 Old Parcels Ltd

Key answer tips

Approach part (a) by using the introductory paragraph as a source of ideas. Your answer should cover several issues: criteria for determining 'small'; objectives of the FRSSE; usefulness of the FRSSE. You are not required to describe the detailed requirements of the FRSSE.

The solution to part (b) depends upon several assumptions and alternative solutions are possible. Therefore you must do more than produce a detailed calculation; you must discuss the nature of your calculations.

(a) The main aim of developing an accounting framework for small companies is to provide users with a reporting framework which generates reliable, relevant and useful information. It is important that the accounting standards which are used by small companies are of value to them and therefore it is necessary to determine which companies are to be within the definition of a small company. Very few accounting issues need to be addressed by a small company simply because of its size. The criteria for a small company need not be determined by reference to size but would be more meaningful if the definition were based on the relationship between the shareholders and management. Small companies could be defined by reference to the ownership and management of the company. It is inaccurate to assume that small companies are simply smaller versions of large public companies.

The basis for developing an accounting framework for small companies ought to be based around the issues of recognition, measurement and disclosure. The question to be answered is whether alternative standards should be developed in recognising, measuring and disclosing transactions of small companies.

The objectives of financial reporting differ between large companies and owner managed companies. The nature of accountability is different between large and small companies and thus there is a major distinction between the objectives of financial reporting for the two types of company. The needs of users of financial statements should determine the nature of those statements. It is intellectually and commercially sound to develop an accounting framework on the basis of the objectives of the financial statements.

The ASB has developed an accounting standard 'Financial Reporting Standard for Smaller Entities' (FRSSE) which uses size criteria to determine the nature of a small company.

It is often stated that the purpose of producing an accounting framework for smaller companies is to reduce the administrative burden on those companies. In reality the financial statements are produced by external accountants and thus the production of such a framework on the pretext of reducing the administrative costs is an unrealistic objective. Additionally many of these accounting standards will have a negligible impact on a small company and those standards which are selected for application to small companies may apply to some and not to others. It might appear that an approach which takes existing accounting standards and eliminates those which are thought not to be applicable to small companies is going to result in a framework which is simply a hybrid version of the large company's regulatory system.

The FRSSE in the UK has been received with mixed feelings as it aims to simplify and reduce the financial reporting requirements of small companies. It selects certain elements of certain accounting standards as a basis of reporting for small companies and exempts entities from compliance with the other extant accounting standards and UITF Abstracts. It applies the size criteria set out in the Companies Acts for a small company and utilises the same measurement bases as for large companies. Measurement requirements of a complex nature have been omitted but small companies do undertake complex transactions and in these cases they are referred to the full standard. It is not surprising that this accounting standard will in fact increase the amount of work involved in preparing financial statements in the short term whilst companies change the nature of the information disclosed and become expert in the application of the standard.

(b) When valuing the shares of an unlisted company, it is unlikely that one value will be used in isolation. The more common methods include a dividend yield basis, the present value of future dividends, the earnings basis, the accounting rate of return, the net assets basis, the use of the Capital Asset Pricing Model, the super-profits method and the present value of future maintainable earnings. The dividend bases are only really applicable to preference shares or the sale of a small number of shares. In general all of the methods set out above will provide a guide to a share price but the final price will be negotiated between the parties after taking into account intangible factors such as personal circumstances, business consideration and the market for the shares.

(i) **Net Assets Basis of Valuation**

The valuation of the ordinary shares can depend upon how the ownership of the ordinary shares is dispersed, the holding of the shares being sold and the use to which the assets are to be put after the sale. As the whole of the capital of the family is being sold and the companies are to merge, a dividend yield basis is not realistic.

Asset valuation (Going concern basis)

Valuation (£'000)	
Intangible asset - licence (note (i))	15
Tangible assets (278 × 1.05) (note (ii))	292
Current assets	835
Creditors due within one year	(365)
Creditors: falling due after more than one year (note (iv))	(121)
Preference shares (note (iv))	(34)
Deferred taxation (note (v))	-
Other items not in balance sheet	
Millennium costs (note (vi))	(30)

Inflow of cash for share issue (note (vii))	30
Total net asset value	622
Shares in issue	170,000
Options	30,000
	200,000
Price per ordinary share	£3.11

Notes on asset valuation

As the company is being sold as a going concern, this basis has been used to calculate the value of the net assets.

(i) The intangible asset has an estimated market value of £15,000. If the intangible asset is valued on an income basis then its valuation is £10,000 per annum discounted for two years at a rate of 8%, i.e. £17,832. As the income stream is perhaps more subjective than a current market valuation the latter value has been taken in the answer.

(ii) As the assets are being valued on a going concern basis, the net realisable value of the tangible fixed assets has not been used as a valuation method. An estimate of current value has been made utilising the information concerning the increase in the value of the assets. Taxation has been ignored as there is no intention to sell the assets.

(iii) The FRSSE does not deal with UITF13 'Accounting for employee share ownership plan trusts' and therefore the company is currently in compliance with the standard by not including the assets of the ESOP in the valuation of the assets of Old Parcels Ltd. As the assets of the trust cannot be transferred to the company they are not included in the asset valuation.

(iv) The company has complied with the FRSSE regarding FRS 4 'Capital Instruments'. However, the 'true' value of the debenture liability could be calculated as the net present value of the future interest payments and redemption cost.

	£
Loan interest payable 31 May 20X9	6,000
Loan and premium payable 31 May 20X9 on redemption	125,000
	131,000
Discounted at 8% per annum	121,296

Similarly, the preference shares might be valued at their net present value.

	Dividend amount	*Redemption factor*	*Discount value £*	*Present*
31 May 20X9	4,200	-	8%	3,889
31 May 20Y1	2,100	33,000	8%	30,093
				33,982

(v) Deferred taxation has been eliminated from the asset value as the timing differences represent a liability that is unlikely to crystallise in practice.

(vi) The cost of converting the computer to allow for the millennium could be taken into account or ignored depending upon the use to which New Parcels plc would put the existing system. The shareholders of Old Parcels Ltd would not be happy with a calculation which takes into account the renewal of the system.

(vii) It is assumed that the holders of the share options would exercise them as the option price will be well below the offer price.

(ii) **Earnings method of valuation**

The price earnings ratio is the market value of a share divided by the earnings per share. Therefore, the market value of a share can be assessed by multiplying the P/E ratio by the earnings per share.

The FRSSE does not require companies to disclose the results of discontinued operations but obviously they will be included in the Profit or Loss for the year. The results from discontinued operations ought to be excluded from any profit calculation.

	£'000
Profits (20X4-X8)	216
Less: Discontinued activities (20% of 216)	(43)
Preference dividends 3 years × 7% × £30,000	(6.3)
Preference share appropriation (510 + 554 + 603)	(1.7)
Net profits available to ordinary shareholders	165
Average profits (divided by 5)	33

The average profits for the last five years are £33,000 and the projected profits are £35,000 – £2,100 (preference dividend) – £654 (preference share appropriation) i.e. **£32,246**. Therefore the figure of £33,000 seems to be a reasonable one to use in the earnings based calculation of the price of the ordinary shares. New Parcels plc has a P/E ratio of 14 but because any growth in the profits is uncertain and because Old Parcels Ltd is an unquoted company, a lower P/E ratio may be more suitable for the valuation of Old Parcels Ltd's shares. However because additional capital will be provided by the holders of share options, future profits may result from this inflow, therefore, the discount applied to the P/E ratio need not be too severe.

$$\text{Market value per share} = \frac{\text{P/E ratio} \times \text{Earnings}}{\text{Number of shares}}$$

$$= \frac{10 \text{ (say)} \times 33{,}000}{200{,}000}$$

Market price per share is **£1.65**

If the P/E ratio of New Parcels is applied to the earnings of Old Parcels Ltd then the price per share is

$$\frac{14 \times 33{,}000}{200{,}000} \text{ i.e. } \mathbf{£2.31}$$

If one assumes that Old Parcels Ltd has future maintainable earnings of £33,000 at a discount rate of 8%, then a value can be placed on the shares of

$$\frac{£33{,}000}{8\%} \text{ i.e. £412,500 or } \mathbf{£2.06} \text{ per share}$$

Conclusion

It would appear that the owners of the ordinary shares of Old Parcels Ltd would require a price for their shares of around £3.11 but New Parcels may attempt to acquire the ordinary shares for between £1.65 and £2.31 per share. The above answers are a basis for valuing the shares of Old Parcels Ltd, candidates will be given due credit for alternative assumptions and solutions.

59 Prospect plc

REPORT

To: Mr Green

From: Accountant

Subject: Prospect plc **Date:** 24 November 20X9

As requested, I have examined the consolidated profit and loss accounts of Prospect plc for the two years ended 30 June 20X9 and the consolidated balance sheets at 30 June 20X8 and 30 June 20X9. I have also examined the notes to the financial statements. My calculations are set out in the attached Appendix.

I have analysed the figures as they stand, but it should be noted that the group is exposed to considerable foreign currency exchange risk. Exchange rates have been particularly favourable during the year ended 30 June 20X9, with gains of £140 million being taken to reserves compared with £90 million for the year ended 30 June 20X8. This means that any apparent increases in profit and loss account items, assets and liabilities that have taken place during the year to 30 June 20X9 are likely to have been exaggerated by the movement in exchange rates. Without more information it is difficult to assess the extent of the distortion.

Major reasons for the decline in profits and dividends

Turnover has increased by 30% during the year to 30 June 20X9, although some of this increase may be due to exchange effects. However, the gross profit percentage has fallen from 55% in the year ended 30 June 20X8 to 46% in the year ended 30 June 20X9. Operating profit percentage has fallen even more dramatically, from 28% to 19%. Lower profits in 20X8/X9 have resulted in lower dividends.

Return on capital employed (ROCE) has fallen from just over 19% to 13.5%. ROCE is normally regarded as the key measure of performance and this fall indicates that the group is generating less profit in relation to the resources available to it in the form of net assets. This decline in performance in 20X8/X9 appears to be almost entirely due to falling profit margins as asset turnover (the measure of turnover generated in relation to capital employed) is very slightly increased from 20X7/X8. This indicates that the group is not using its assets any less efficiently than before.

Cost of sales, operating expenses and interest payable have all increased. However, operating expenses have remained about the same in relation to turnover. Cost of sales has increased by 55% in 20X8/X9 and this appears to be the main cause of the fall in profits.

One possible reason for the increase in cost of sales is the group's policy of capitalising the cost of locating new mineral sources and amortising the costs over the periods during which the source provides economic benefits. As turnover has increased in the period it seems likely that amortisation charges have increased correspondingly. Another possible reason for the increase is that it may be becoming more difficult and costly to extract minerals in particular locations. This is borne out by the segmental information, which shows that the profitability of European operations has fallen significantly although turnover has risen slightly. As Europe is the largest segment in terms of turnover, this fall in profits has had a significant effect.

Other factors to be taken into account in making a hold or sell decision

Although profits and dividends have declined, there are a number of other significant factors which should influence your decision to hold or sell the investment.

The current ratio and the quick ratio have both increased in 20X8/X9, from 2.3:1 to 2.7:1 and from 1.4:1 to 1.5:1 respectively. An increase in turnover often results in liquidity problems at least in the short term, but Prospect plc appears to be in a healthy position. Although the group has increased its debt finance during the year, the gearing ratio has remained at 54%. This is high, but not excessively so, given the group's liquidity. Given the exchange rate movements during the year it is possible that gearing has actually fallen in real terms. All these factors suggest that the company will continue to trade for the foreseeable future and is therefore a relatively safe investment. In addition, the company has the liquid resources available to enable it to continue to expand.

There are some indications that the company will expand its operations. For example, there appears to have been some capital investment (fixed assets have increased from £950 million to £1,100 million) and intangible fixed assets have doubled. As intangible fixed assets represent the cost of locating new mineral sources, this suggests that the group is about to start extracting minerals from new sources.

The segmental information reveals that the company's European operations are becoming less profitable. However, the segmental information also reveals that the group's operations are changing:

	% of total turnover for the group		
	20X9	*20X8*	*Increase in segment turnover*
Europe	37	47	+3%
Africa	29	19	+100%
Far East	34	34	+27%

Turnover generated by the group's African operations has doubled in the year and it now forms a larger proportion of total turnover. In addition, the net asset information shows that there has been significant investment in Africa during the year. Segment net assets have increased by 80% as opposed to 9% for Europe and 17% for the Far East, which indicates that the growth in African operations is likely to continue. This is very encouraging, as Africa is the most profitable of the three segments and its profitability appears to be increasing.

If these trends are borne out in future periods, profits for the group are likely to increase, resulting in an increase in dividends.

Conclusion

The decline in the group's profits appears to be due to the poor performance of European operations. There is a case for continuing to hold your investment, as expansion in Africa may lead to increased profits in future periods.

APPENDIX: Ratio calculations

	20X9	*20X8*
Gross profit percentage		
$\frac{\text{Gross profit}}{\text{Turnover}}$	$\frac{600}{1{,}300} \times 100\% = 46\%$	$\frac{550}{1{,}000} \times 100\% = 55\%$
Operating profit percentage		
$\frac{\text{Operating profit}}{\text{Turnover}}$	$\frac{250}{1{,}300} \times 100\% = 19\%$	$\frac{280}{1{,}000} \times 100\% = 28\%$
Operating expenses/sales		
$\frac{\text{Operating expenses}}{\text{Turnover}}$	$\frac{350}{1{,}300} \times 100\% = 27\%$	$\frac{270}{1{,}000} \times 100\% = 27\%$
Return on capital employed		
$\frac{\text{Operating profit}}{\text{Capital employed}}$	$\frac{250}{1{,}850} \times 100\% = 13.5\%$	$\frac{280}{1{,}470} \times 100\% = 19.0\%$
Asset turnover		
$\frac{\text{Turnover}}{\text{Capital employed}}$	$\frac{1{,}300}{1{,}850} = 0.70$ times	$\frac{1{,}000}{1{,}470} = 0.68$ times
Current ratio		
$\frac{\text{Current assets}}{\text{Current liabilities}}$	$\frac{875}{325} = 2.7{:}1$	$\frac{735}{315} = 2.3{:}1$

Quick ratio

$\frac{\text{Current assets - stock}}{\text{Current liabilities}}$	$\frac{495}{325} = 1.5:1$	$\frac{435}{315} = 1.4:1$

Gearing

$\frac{\text{Long term loans}}{\text{Capital employed}}$	$\frac{1,000}{1,850} \times 100\% = 54\%$	$\frac{800}{1,470} \times 100\% = 54\%$

60 Heavy Goods plc

(a)

To: Managing Director **Dated:** 1 December 20X4

From: Chief Accountant

Re: Report on performance of Modern Tractors plc based on ratios for 20X2-X4 and Industry Averages for 20X4.

In this report I propose to comment on five aspects of the company's performance, namely, liquidity, asset utilisation, interest cover, capital gearing and profitability based on the inter-period ratios for 20X2-x4 and the inter-company ratios for 20X4.

Liquidity

The liquidity ratios i.e. current and quick ratios have increased in each of the past three years. However, compared to the industry average they are giving apparently conflicting signals with the current ratio being below and the quick ratio being above the industry average. This would appear to arise from the company's relatively lower stock holding and relatively higher debtors/cash holding confirmed by the stock turnover ratio and the stock/total assets figures.

Liquidity has progressively improved with less dependence on realising stock to meet short-term liabilities to the point where its quick ratio is higher than that for the industry.

The company is cash rich and not vulnerable in this area which is confirmed by the cash/total assets ratio.

Asset utilisation

To assist with the evaluation of the company's asset utilisation, 'Turnover' ratios have been calculated.

Starting with the sales to total assets ratio, this has fluctuated over the past three years and is currently lower at 1.6 than the industry average of 2.43.

This could indicate that the company is less efficient at generating sales with the economic resources available to it.

However, a more detailed analysis is required of the constituents of the total asset figure. For example they may include investments that are not generating sales but do provide investment income which might well fluctuate between years.

The turnover of each class of asset has been calculated to identify any that exceeds the industry average. This has been done for each class of asset, starting with the fixed asset and working capital turnover rates.

Fixed asset turnover

In 20X4, the company is only generating £2.74 per £ of net fixed asset whereas the industry is on average generating £16.85 per £ of fixed asset. There can be a number of explanations. For example, it could reflect adversely on the management of Modern Tractors or it could indicate a capital investment programme geared up to continuing sales growth. This will require further evaluation.

Working capital turnover

The company's turnover rate of 38.33 is much higher than the industry average of 10.81. A review of the constituent ratios will indicate which item(s) within the current assets/current liabilities is responsible for the difference.

The report considers each constituent in turn.

Stock turnover

The company is turning over its stock at more than twice the average industry rate. This might be due to higher sales or to lower stock holdings. This therefore needs to be investigated in the context of the balance sheet which shows that the company's stock represents only 14.63% of total assets as opposed to the 41.90% for the industry.

This requires further enquiry to identify any downside e.g. a low stock holding might be associated with stockouts and lost sales.

In many acquisitions there is an immediate advantage available to the acquirer by improving stock control – this would not appear to be available to us in this case.

Debtors turnover

The ratio for Modern Tractors is substantially higher than the industry average. We need to assess the significance of the amount and one indication is that debtors represent only 1.70% of the total assets as opposed to the industry average of 18.40%. The difference might be due to an efficient debtors ledger operation but the difference is so great that it is more likely to reflect a difference in policy e.g. Modern Tractors factors its debtors ledger with only four days sales appearing as debtors. The industry average is also low at 23 days and would indicate that factoring is an industry practice.

Cash

The cash to total assets at 25.08% is high and might support the view that the debtors are being factored.

Creditors turnover

The company is taking twice as long to pay its creditors than the industry average. However, the balance sheet ratio, current liabilities to total assets, indicates that even so the company is less reliant on short-term credit than the industry.

From the above, we can see that the company is significantly different from the industry average on all of the turnover ratios we have examined. Management should investigate this further to assess whether there is a problem e.g. consider if the mix of fixed assets is appropriate; consider if there is a likelihood of a stock-out; consider the make-up of the working capital. If there is no problem then it could be determined whether company policy is significantly different from competitors and whether the industry comparisons are not valid comparators.

Interest cover

The company's cover is almost three times that of the industry average. This indicates that the company is well able to service the existing debt and that it could expand this form of financing if it required additional capital.

Gearing

The company's long-term debt to total assets is 29.27% which is higher than the industry average of 19%. Modern Tractors has a higher dependence on long-term debt (gearing), but a lower level of short-term financing (current liabilities), overall debt is at a similar level to the industry average.

At the same time, although there is a higher level of long-term debt, the interest cover is substantially higher than the industry average as mentioned above. Information is also required on rates of interest as the company might have renegotiated its loans or obtained additional finance at a lower rate than the rest of the industry is paying. It is noted that the interest cover in 1993 was 26 times and further information would be required to assess the extent to which this is the result of differences in the interest charge rather than in the profit available to cover the interest.

The debt equity ratio can be calculated from the ratios given in the question, as follows:

(Long-term debt/Total assets) / (Equity/Total assets)

which produces debt equity percentages as follows:

20X2	*20X3*	*20X4*	*Industry average 20X4*
200%	50%	87%	58%

The 20X4 debt equity ratio for the company is higher than the industry average but this does not pose a problem for servicing the debt.

Profitability

The gross profit at 19.57% is a little lower than the industry. However, the initial thought is that its pricing is similar to that of the industry and its manufacturing costs are similar.

At an operating level, the company has an operating profit percentage that is more than twice the industry average. This may be due to one factor or a combination of factors e.g. lower operating expenses, lower interest costs, other income as mentioned above.

The company's profit after tax to total assets is 48% higher than the industry's average and its return on equity 37% higher. Assuming that there is scope to increase the financial leverage, the return on equity could be significantly improved.

Conclusion

The company appears to have increased its fixed asset base in 20X4 following two years of substantial sales growth in 20X2 and 20X3. It has not maintained the same level of growth and it would be helpful to obtain forecasts for the following three years.

The make-up of the fixed assets has not been given. Information is required about this with a view to considering an improvement in their utilisation.

The gross profit margin has remained at about the same level. However, there has been a fluctuation in the profit before tax figure. Further information is required to ascertain the reason for this. It is possible that there has been fluctuations in other income e.g. arising from the disposal of investments. This will need to be taken into account when assessing future maintainable profits.

The company appears to be financially sound with cash increasing to 25.08% of total assets by 20X4 compared to the industry average of 9.6%.

Considering the financial structure of the company, there appears to be scope for increasing the amounts borrowed without endangering the capacity to service the loans. This could lead to a significant improvement in the return on equity and share price if the funds could be used as effectively as at present within the business. However, this method of increasing the return on equity brings with it an increase in the financial risk.

The company appears to be poised for growth with new fixed assets and a high level of cash. This might be an opportune moment to initiate an approach – before this sound base is translated into sustained profit growth.

(b) **Memo to management Dated**

(i) **Re: Limitations of inter-period and inter-company comparisons**

The following is a brief comment to bring out the fact that there are limitations which may make the interpretation of inter-period and inter-firm comparative ratios difficult to accurately evaluate.

These include:

- The data might need to be adjusted for inflation if valid comparisons are to be made over time. Some companies achieve this by adjusting their five-and ten-year summaries to take inflation into account.

- The financial statements might have been prepared using different accounting policies e.g. choice of fixed asset depreciation and stock valuation policies.

- Accounts may be made up to a different date which can significantly affect ratios if the business is seasonal e.g. before or after the start of the new season's models.

- Traditional analysis tends to focus on profitability. Greater attention is needed to be paid to assessing liquidity and the capacity to adapt by reference to the cash flow statement.

- Informal typologies of ratios have been long established and certain ratios have come to be accepted as suitable indicators of each characteristic of firm performance to be investigated. This in itself can limit the investigation and care is required to explore beyond the conventional ratios. For example, productivity ratios could be extremely important in an industry such as tractor manufacture. Appropriate ratios could include average sales per employee, operating profit per employee, capital employed per employee and stock and work in progress per employee.

- The balance sheet is prepared at a single point in time. This means that it is possible to practise window dressing e.g. by selecting a year end date when stocks are low, dispatching stock which may not have been as carefully inspected as normal in order to improve the current year's sales and stock levels.

- The industry average does not indicate the distribution of results around the average. It would be helpful to also have quartile and decile figures.

(ii) **Specific comments**

Liquidity ratios

The liquidity ratios appearing in the inter-firm comparison scheme are not strictly measures of liquidity as there is no indication of the timing of their conversion into cash. The assumption behind the quick and current ratios is that the current assets will be converted into cash sufficiently readily to meet the liabilities on their due dates.

The liquidity ratios are at one particular point in time. Other companies might have taken steps to produce liquidity ratios that are not representative of their normal ratios that exist throughout the year. For example, levels of stock might be changed – this might be achieved by simply delaying purchases or by unacceptable techniques such as selling stock to associated companies and reversing the transaction after the year end; creditors might be paid early and overdrafts reviewed by negotiating term loans with the bank to remove them from the classification of being payable within one year. Some of these practices are perfectly acceptable commercially and by the auditors e.g. restricting purchases; others are window dressing and would be objected to by the auditors if they were to become aware that they had occurred e.g. sale to and buy back from an associated company by a subsidiary – in practice however they might not be readily detected.

Asset utilisation

Turnover ratios can be affected if the sales trend is different from previous years in either our own or other companies. For example, if the sales were skewed towards the end of the year, the debtor turnover would be lower than in previous years or in other companies not having the same pattern. Such a skewing could result from market conditions, e.g. the economy picking-up or from internal decisions e.g. commercial decisions to promote heavily or window dressing decisions to ship out uninspected goods to contractees although aware that there will be heavy returns due to warranty claims for defective work after the year end.

They can also be affected by the choice of accounting policies e.g. Modern Tractors plc might revalue its fixed assets and competitors leave their fixed assets at depreciated cost which could result in significant differences in fixed asset turnover ratios.

They can also be affected by commercial changes that are being put in place but not yet effective e.g. building factory space, acquiring machinery, introducing robotics which will come into operation in 20X5 or later.

Questions that need answering in relation to the fixed asset turnover ratios include the following:

- Are other companies using older written-down equipment?
- Are any of the companies leasing?
- When were the new fixed assets acquired by Modern Tractors?
- Were they acquired late in the year?
- Is Modern Tractors still commissioning its fixed assets?
- What is the make-up of fixed assets in Modern Tractors and in the industry?
- Is there a different mix e.g. properties that will produce a capital rather than revenue profit?

The stock level of Modern Tractors is lower than the industry average. This might indicate that the company has stock financing arranged and there might be recourse liabilities that need to be taken into account.

Gearing

This could be affected by a number of factors. For example, the choice of accounting policies such as a decision to revalue fixed assets would affect the debt/equity ratio by increasing the equity amount and so improving the ratio; a decision to re-negotiate an overdraft to a term loan would increase the debt/equity ratio and improve the quick ratio, a policy of borrowing rather than relying on short-term credit will increase gearing.

There might be different pressures on the management of different companies to influence the gearing percentages e.g. a company that is likely to breach loan covenants relating to acceptable debt/equity levels might resort to commercial or artificial measures to contain or reduce the debt/equity relationship that appears in the year end financial accounts. For example, there might be an increase in the use of leasing with lessor companies structuring the agreement to fall outside the finance lease classification. A detailed reading of the financial statements and the notes to the accounts will give indications of the existence of such arrangements and changes in company practice.

Profitability

Sales growth per cent is based on historic transaction data. They indicate that the company has achieved growth in each of the past three years. However, this should be adjusted for inflation if one is to be able to identify whether there has been a growth in the sales volume. It is possible that adjusted for inflation the company's sales have actually fallen in volume terms.

Gross profit per cent could be affected by changes in the choice of accounting policies e.g. the choice of depreciation method; or by technical manipulation e.g. structuring leasing agreements so that they become classified as operating leases with no depreciation charged in the cost of sales.

Net profit could be affected by company attitudes to provisioning and releasing deferred income into the profit and loss account e.g. debtor provisioning and decisions on releasing grants into the current year's profit.

Conclusion

The comparative ratios are a useful initial indicator. They identify symptoms not causes. Causes require further enquiry but they do provide useful signposts. For example, there is a clear need for us to consider the causes of the differences in the relative fixed asset levels (which are higher) and stock levels (which are lower) and the apparent debtor factoring.

I would be pleased to produce a follow up report on dealing with any questions that you raise on the basis of this initial report.

61 Lewes Holdings plc

Key answer tips

Part (a) can be answered almost directly from the Operating and Financial Review itself. Notice that you are not required to discuss the OFR in general, but specific aspects of it.

Your answer to part (b) must address the specific concern of the reader; the fall in profitability relative to the increase in turnover. Notice that very few ratios are presented in the answer below, but that they are all relevant to the central concern of the reader. Notice also that one of them is an alternative measure of EPS. This is particularly appropriate because the draft profit and loss account shows the information required under FRS 3 and because the reader is specifically concerned with EPS. Gearing should be covered because of its effect on profit, but your answer should not discuss gearing in terms of liquidity or solvency. The fact that a segmental report has been included in the question is a fairly clear indication that your answer must use that information.

In part (b) (ii) your answer should consider not only what has happened, but what may happen in the future. This is important because the hold or sell decision is concerned with future earnings.

(a) (i) The principal aim of the financial review section is to explain to the user of the annual report the capital structure of the business, its treasury policy and the dynamics of its financial position – its sources of liquidity and their application, including the implications of the financing arising from its capital expenditure plans.

The discussion should concentrate on matters of significance to the position of the business as a whole. It should be a narrative commentary supported by figures where these assist understanding of the policies and their effect in practice.

(ii) Specific matters that should be addressed when discussing capital structure and treasury policy include:

Discuss the capital structure in terms of maturity profile of debt, type of capital instruments used, currency, and interest rate structure including comments on relevant ratios such as interest cover and debt/equity ratios.

The *policies* and *objectives* covering the management of the maturity profile of borrowings, exchange rate and interest rate risk and the implementation of such policies in the period under review in terms of:

- the manner in which the treasury activities are controlled
- the use of financial instruments for hedging purposes
- the extent to which foreign currency net investments are hedged by currency borrowings and other hedging instruments
- the currencies in which borrowings are made and in which cash and cash equivalents are held

- the extent to which borrowings are at fixed interest rates
- the purpose and effect of major financing transactions undertaken up to the date of approval of the financial statements
- the effect of interest costs on profits and the potential impact of interest rate changes.

(b) (i) **Report to an existing shareholder**

To:

From:

Re: Performance of the Lewes Group Date: 15 June 20X5

In accordance with your instructions we have reviewed the consolidated profit and loss account and balance sheet of the Lewes Group as at 31 December 20X4 and certain supporting notes in relation to your concern that a substantial increase in turnover was not reflected in the earnings per share for 20X4.

Profitability

Although the profit on ordinary activities has increased by 45% from £121,600,000 to £176,300,000 in 20X4, the percentage of profit on ordinary activities to turnover has actually fallen from 6.2% in 20X3 (121.6/1,966.3 × 100) to 5.2% in 20X4 (176.3/3,381.8 × 100).

A key question is whether it is because the operations of the group have become less profitable that the above ratio fell. The fall therefore needs to be evaluated taking account of the changes that have occurred during 20X4 i.e. the acquisitions, the restructuring costs and increased gearing.

The operating profit to turnover percentage has improved slightly from 6.2% in 20X3 (122.6/1,966.3 × 100) to 6.3% in 20X4 (213.1/3,381.8 × 100) indicating that, at the group level, operating does not appear to have become less efficient or to have suffered from cost increases that it could not pass on to customers.

We then considered the impact of new acquisitions, restructuring costs and increased gearing on the profit before tax percentage.

New acquisition

The turnover and operating costs of the new acquisitions have been given so that we can calculate the impact on the operating profit percentage. From these we see that the new business is producing an operating profit slightly higher than the consolidated business i.e. 6.6% (29.9/453.2 × 100), however this has had no significant effect on the group's overall results.

Restructuring costs

Exceptional costs of £18.9m have been incurred in 20X4. Prior to FRS 3 these might well have been disclosed as extraordinary and not had an impact on the earnings per share figure. However, they are now classified as exceptional and an EPS figure is required to be disclosed after deducting such costs. However, in recognition of the fact that they are non-recurring, a number of companies disclose two EPS figures – one in accordance with FRS 3 and a further company defined figure that would exclude such exceptional items.

The EPS figure adjusted for restructuring costs is 18.3p [16 × ((133.9 – 4.2) + 18.9)/129.7]. This shows an increase of 31% over the 20X3 figure.

Capital gearing

The amounts falling due after more than one year have increased from £97.3m in 20X3 to £212.4m in 20X4. There is a consequent increase in the interest charged from £5.6m in 20X3 to £23.9m in 20X4. The percentage increase in the interest far exceeds the change in the level of debt at the respective year ends which may indicate that the debt has increased from a low level at the beginning of 20X3 and/or the interest rates have increased. Also some of the interest may relate to a seasonal overdraft that does not appear in the year end balance sheet.

When preference share capital is included in the debt figure, the debt to equity ratio was 52% in 20X3 [(97.3 + 47.0)/(325.2 – 47.0) × 100] falling to 40% in 20X4 [(212.4 + 47.0)/(693.4 – 47.0) × 100].

The effect of the increased borrowings has been to increase the interest charge but, because the ROCE is greater than the rate of interest, the earnings available for distribution in 20X4 have increased and the change has been to the advantage of the equity shareholders.

The above comments are based on the consolidated profit and loss account and balance sheet. Any decision on realising your investment should also take into account future prospects. In assessing these, the segmental information can be helpful.

The significance of the segmental information

The geographical analysis shows that the group is diversifying into overseas markets. In 20X4 56% of the turnover arose in the UK and 30% in the USA which is a material change from the position in 20X3 when 60% of the turnover was from the UK and 20% from the USA.

The profit percentage on UK sales has fallen from 11.5% in 20X3 (137.5/1,191.5 × 100) to 7% in 20X4 (133.3/1,892.3 × 100). There could be a number of possible reasons for this change of 4.5% e.g. the exceptional restructuring cost of £18.9m related to UK subsidiaries.

Also, the increase in the UK turnover by 59% [(1,892.3 – 1,191.5)/1,191.5] might be related to the fall in profitability e.g. a conscious decision to reduce margins stimulated demand.

The profit percentage on US sales has improved from a loss in 20X3 of 4% to a profit of 4% in 20X4. The majority of the US turnover was derived from automated manufacturing systems and the profit per cent on these appears to be lower in the US at 4% than in UK and Europe where it is 5%.

The segmental analysis indicates that the group has diversified geographically and in classes of business with entry into the US market and that it has successfully addressed the losses that were occurring in the US in 20X3.

However, it is important to note that despite the decline in UK profitability and the improvement in the US profitability, the UK operations are still more profitable than the US operations.

(ii) **Additional information**

The following additional information would be helpful in considering whether to hold or sell the investment in Lewes plc.

(1) *New acquisitions*

The net assets acquired (other than goodwill) indicate that the group has acquired net assets that represent 40% of the pre-acquisition net assets (133.6/325.2 × 100). For certain individual classes of asset it represents a significant addition in relation to its pre-acquisition size e.g. the acquired stock of £117.8m was 90% of the 20X3 group stock figure at 31 December 20X3.

An important consideration is the relative size of the goodwill as this alone represents 77% of the pre-acquisition net assets (251.8/325.2 × 100) which raises the question as to the extent to which this represents a payment to gain control rather than a valuable asset that would result in the generation of future profits. In this context, it would be useful to review the financial statements of the acquired business for prior years to identify trends in turnover, product mix and profits and to ascertain from the management of Lewes plc the reason for the acquisition.

Restructuring costs were incurred in 20X4 which reduced the EPS for that year. The likelihood and extent of restructuring costs arising from the new acquisition might have a similar depressing effect on future years. Conversely restructuring may be complete and future earnings may be increased by the absence of such costs.

Goodwill of £251.8m has been capitalised and is now included in intangible fixed assets. This means that profit on ordinary activities will be reduced in future years as a result of amortisation charges. The useful economic life of the goodwill is not known and therefore it is difficult to quantify the effect on profit, but the amortisation charge might be approximately £25m per annum (10% of the goodwill). The effect on profit in future years will depend on any increase in future profits arising from the acquisition. The return from the acquisition (29.9/133.6 or 385.4) is much lower than the overall ROCE, and is thus depressing profitability, however, this may be partly due to the fact that under acquisition accounting the 20X4 results may not include a full year's profit from the acquired company(ies) i.e. they would only include post-acquisition profits.

(2) *Liquidity*

At the working capital level, the current ratio has remained at 1.2:1 in 20X3 and 20X4 and the acid-test ratio has remained at approximately 1:1.

However, at the financing level, the long-term liability has more than doubled and there are issued preference shares.

Further information is required as to the maturity dates of the loans, the redemption terms for the preference shares (if any) and any capital commitments for fixed assets.

The significance for the investor is that Lewes plc might be looking to making a rights issue in the near future if operating cash flows are not sufficient to meet any investment or financing outflows.

Conclusion

On the information provided, the Lewes Group is expanding and diversifying internationally and by class of business. The group is expanding its automated manufacturing systems business with an increase of 60% in turnover [((889.2 + 962.2) – (666.7 + 497.7))/(666.7 + 497.7)]. This produced a slightly lower rate of profit but there appears to be an increasing market. Previous losses in North America have been eliminated and the group has made significant acquisitions in 20X4. In deciding whether to hold or sell, much will depend upon the investor's assessment of the management skills of the Lewes management in integrating the new acquisitions and improving profit levels.

In addition, the investor would take into account the possibility that there might be an early need for a rights issue.

(Tutorial notes: This question and answer have been amended slightly to reflect the changes to the accounting treatment of goodwill introduced by FRS 10 'Goodwill and intangible assets'.*)*

The Examiner's Answer discusses the return from the acquisition compared to overall ROCE. In practice, there are several possible calculations:

	Acquisition	**Group 20X4**	**Group 20X3**
$\frac{\text{Operating profit}}{\text{Capital employed}}$	$\frac{29.9}{150.1} = 19.9\%$	$\frac{213.1}{942.3} = 22.6\%$	$\frac{122.6}{429.3} = 28.6\%$
$\frac{\text{Operating profit}}{\text{Net assets employed}}$	$\frac{29.9}{133.6} = 22.4\%$	$\frac{213.1}{693.4} = 30.7\%$	$\frac{122.6}{325.2} = 37.7\%$
$\frac{\text{Operating profit}}{\text{Net assets employed}}$ (taking into account the effect of the goodwill)	$\frac{29.9}{385.4} = 7.7\%$	$\frac{213.1}{693.4} = 30.7\%$	$\frac{122.6}{325.2} = 37.7\%$

The Examiner's Answer uses the second and third calculations, which are not based on conventional ROCE, but provided that like is compared with like, all these calculations illustrate the point being made and all are acceptable in the context of this question.*)*

62 Bewise plc

Key answer tips

Remember to:

- use observation as well as ratio analysis
- arrive at a logical conclusion.

Avoid errors of principle in calculating ratios, (e.g, not matching the numerator and the denominator in ratios such as ROCE).

To: Bewise Bank Manager

From:

Date: 30 June 20X5

Re: Request for increase in short-term loans by Bewise plc

The following report is submitted in accordance with your instructions following a request by Bewise plc to increase its short-term loans having forecast that its overdraft will exceed its agreed overdraft level of £240m as at 31 December 20X5.

The report considers the company's performance in four key areas, namely, turnover rates, profitability, liquidity and solvency and concludes with our recommendation concerning the short-term loan request.

Turnover

Sales turnover has increased by 9%, and 20% over the past two years and is forecast to increase by 12% in the current year.

The rates of total asset and debtor turnover have remained reasonably steady over the four year period with the asset turnover remaining at around 1.6 and the debtor turnover at around 3.4 as shown in Appendix A.

The rate of stock turnover based on selling prices, however, has fallen from 4.9 to 4.1 as stock levels have increased. This fall might possibly have partly arisen from the fluctuations in the rate of percentage growth in sales. If the company achieved the same rate of turnover as in 20X2, it would reduce its stock by approximately £92m [609 – (2,512 × 351/1,706)].

If based on cost of sales, it would reduce stock by approximately £75m [609 – (1,731 × 351/1,138)].

If the return were calculated as net assets deducting creditors but not the overdraft because of its permanence, the ROCE for 20X2 would be 16% (93 + 28)/(85 + 277 + 62 + 135 + 197) and the trend would be similar to that based on gross assets.

Profitability

The return on gross assets has been falling over the four years from 12.2% in 20X2 to 8.0% in 20X5, although it has remained fairly static in 20X4 and 20X5.

The return on equity remained fairly constant from 20X2 to 20X4. However, in 20X5 there is forecast to be a dramatic fall in the ratio to 4.2%. We have seen that the rate of asset turnover had remained reasonably steady and that the reason for the declining returns resulted from the fact that the profit after tax had not increased at the same rate as the sales turnover.

Gross profit

The gross profit percentage has fallen steadily from 33.3% in 20X2 to 31.1% in 20X5.

Finance cost

The finance cost has risen significantly to 11.5% in 20X5 from 7.1% in 20X2 based on year end figures in the balance sheets. The ratios are set out in Appendix B.

Liquidity

The current and acid-test ratios have remained reasonably steady over the four year period. As set out in Appendix C, the current ratio has remained at 1.5 to 1.7 and the acid-test ratio at 0.8 to 1.0. Both of these ratios are within normally acceptable ranges. However, with HP debtors it is likely that some of the current assets (debtors) are receivable after more than one year and this would affect the current ratio.

Solvency

The gearing has increased significantly in every year since 20X2.

The debts were 1.1 times the equity in 20X2; by 20X5 they are forecast to be 2.4 times the equity as set out in Appendix D. This indicates that the increase in working capital to support the increase in the sales turnover of 47% that the company has achieved since 20X2, and the increases in fixed assets have been financed almost entirely by external borrowing. This is an important feature when considering the company's request for additional short-term support and it is towards this aspect of the company's operating that we have directed our attention.

With regard to the stocks, it is noted that although they have increased by 74% from the 20X2 figure, this has not been matched by a similar increase in the creditors figure which has only increased by 16%.

Other matters that should be noted are that the company has maintained its dividends although the EPS has been declining since 20X2 and there appear to be high cash balances and increasing investments at a time when the company has been experiencing solvency problems.

Financing Bewise plc's increased activity

To assess more clearly the impact of the increased level of activity on the cash position of the company we have prepared cash flow data. This shows that the company has had a negative cash flow from operations in each year since 20X2 as shown in Appendix E.

Conclusion

The company has not financed its expansion from equity or from operating cash flows. Until therefore the company reaches a position where it is generating a positive cash flow from operations, it will continue to need loan capital to support its operations.

In our view the failure to generate positive operating cash flows is a long standing problem. The fact that it has been allowed to continue reflects adversely on the effectiveness of the senior management of the company. There is an indication of lack of effective planning to provide adequate finance to support the growth in the company's activity and also a failure to adequately control the working capital of the company as evidenced by the falling rate of stock turnover.

Our recommendation is therefore that

(i) the bank should not increase the facility offered to Bewise plc; and

(ii) the bank should take immediate action to ensure that the company puts into place positive measures to improve its operating performance and control its working capital.

We realise that the latter suggestion might well be dependent upon changes of management at a senior level and for this reason it is our view that representation of the bank's interest on the board of directors is essential. We would be pleased to advise further if you decide to pursue such a policy.

Please advise us if you wish to arrange a meeting to discuss the report or any matters relating to this assignment.

Reporting accountants

Dated:

Appendix A – Turnover rates

Asset turnover		20X2	[1,706/995]	=	1.7
		20X3	[1,867/1,169]	=	1.6
		20X4	[2,233/1,386]	=	1.6
	Forecast	20X5	[2,512/1,597]	=	1.6
Stock turnover based on sales		20X2	[1,706/351]	=	4.9
		20X3	[1,867/404]	=	4.6
		20X4	[2,233/540]	=	4.1
	Forecast	20X5	[2,512/609]	=	4.1
Debtor turnover		20X2	[1,706/483]	=	3.5
		20X3	[1,867/551]	=	3.4
		20X4	[2,233/633]	=	3.5
	Forecast	20X5	[2,512/730]	=	3.4

Appendix B – Profitability ratios

Return on gross assets		20X2	[(93 + 28)/995]	× 100	=	12.2%
		20X3	[(78 + 24)/1,169]	× 100	=	8.7%
		20X4	[(82 +30)/1,386]	× 100	=	8.1%
	Forecast	20X5	[(20 + 107)/1,597]	× 100	=	8.0%

In defining this ratio, the bad debts have been treated as an operating expense, the finance income has been assumed to be related to the debtors and, as the debtors have been included in the denominator, it has been included in the profit figure to be consistent. Note that the return on net assets would be 16%, 11.4%, 10% and 9.6% for 20X2 to 20X5 respectively:

Return on equity		20X2	[50/362]	× 100	=	13.8%
		20X3	[43/377]	× 100	=	11.4%
		20X4	[48/397]	× 100	=	12.1 %
	Forecast	20X5	[16/385]	× 100	=	4.2%
Gross profit %		20X2	[568/1,706]	× 100	=	33.3%
		20X3	[610/1,867]	× 100	=	32.7%
		20X4	[714/2,233]	× 100	=	32.0%
	Forecast	20X5	[781/2,512]	× 100	=	31.1%
Finance cost %		20X2	[28/394]	× 100	=	7.1%
		20X3	[24/515]	× 100	=	4.7%
		20X4	[30/720]	× 100	=	4.2%
	Forecast	20X5	[107/934]	× 100	=	11.5%

Appendix C – Liquidity

Acid-test ratio		20X2	[530/571]	=	0.9
		20X3	[618/598]	=	1.0
		20X4	[674/795]	=	0.8
	Forecast	20X5	[793/889]	=	0.9
Current ratio		20X2	[881/571]	=	1.5
		20X3	[1,022/598]	=	1.7
		20X4	[1,214/795]	=	1.5
	Forecast	20X5	[1,402/889]	=	1.6

Appendix D – Solvency

Debt/Equity		20X2	[394/362]	=	1.1
		20X3	[515/377]	=	1.4
		20X4	[720/397]	=	1.8
	Forecast	20X5	[934/385]	=	2.4

Appendix E – Operating cash flows

	20X3	*20X4*	*20X5*
Profit after tax	43	48	16
Depreciation	14	16	18
Creditor increase	38		9
	95	64	43
Less: Stock increase	(53)	(136)	(69)
Debtor increase	(68)	(82)	(97)
Creditor decrease		(8)	
Negative cash flow from operations	(26)	(162)	(123)

63 Thermo Ltd

Key answer tips

Your answer must interpret and make connections between the ratios rather than merely observing changes (e.g. profitability has improved).

In part (a) you are required to report to the bank on the client's behalf. Notice the way in which the answer below attempts to mitigate the effect of potentially damaging information (leverage has worsened) by drawing attention to the improvement in interest cover. As well as ratio analysis, the report must cover cash flows as these will be the prime concern of the bank.

The focus of the report in part (b) is quite different from that of part (a). Whereas the tone of the report in part (a) has to be positive, the report in part (b) must be realistic and must analyse the projections from a critical perspective. Start part (b) by calculating a selection of ratios based on the projections. These will enable you to decide whether: (a) the projections appear realistic; (b) the bank will agree to restructure the loan. Notice that the answer below does not simply comment on the figures, but focuses firmly on the questions that the bank will ask. Your answer should state the important fact that the restructuring is unachievable and then make firm recommendations.

(a) **Draft of report on the company's performance in the two periods from incorporation to 31 March 20X6**

Date: 14 June 20X6
To: Bank
From: Mike Ried and Jane Thurby

Re: Thermo Ltd

This is a report on the performance of Thermo Ltd based on the audited accounts of the company for the nine months period to 31 March 20X5 and for the year ended 31 March 20X6.

The first period of nine months was a start-up period and the second year will be more indicative of the ratios that can be used for establishing norms for the business and estimating future trends.

Profitability

Profitability has improved considerably in 20X6. The gross profit % is up by two percentage points. The operating profit has increased from the low opening figure of 0.04% to 8.90% due to the improvement in the gross profit percentage and because the fixed cost elements of the administrative and selling expenses have been spread over a greater volume of sales which have increased by 35% in 20X6.

The increase in interest charges has meant however that the profit before tax has shown a lower increase of 6.8 percentage points thereby partially diluting the gain from the improved operating.

The company incurred a tax charge in 20X6 and achieved a profit after tax rate of 4.3%.

Liquidity

The current ratio has improved from 0.94 to 0.98. However, the liquid ratio has moved in the opposite direction weakening from 0.71 to 0.58 due to the large increase in the inventory period from 52 to 114 days and a more than doubling of the overdraft from £74,567 to £188,235.

This increase in the overdraft means that it has exceeded the limit of £175,000 that was agreed on commencing the business.

The collection period has improved from 136 to 127 days but it is higher than the payment period in both trading periods. The payment periods remained stable at 85 and 86 days and is indicative of reasonable credit taking terms.

If the collection period were reduced to the same level as the payment period the overdraft would be reduced by £61,068 which would have brought the overdraft within agreed limits.

[£190,539 – (£549,500/365 × 86) = £190,539 – £129,471 = £61,068]

Leverage

The bank debt/tangible net assets ratio has worsened from 0.43 to 0.96 which reflects the significant rise in the bank overdraft. However, although the bank has almost as much money in the business as the owners, the profit cover for interest has improved significantly from 0.03 to 2.65.

Cash generation

The 20X6 accounts show that with a profit of £30,457 and depreciation of £20,150 the company generated a positive gross cash flow from trading operations of £50,607. Increased capital was required for working capital following the 35% increase in sales and there was an increase in the stock holding period. The working capital increase was £125,525 as follows:

	£
Stock increase	(90,600)
Debtors increase	(39,339)
Prepayments increase	(8,750)
Cash increase	(1,253)
Creditors increase	32,230
Accruals decrease	(17,813)
	(125,525)

This meant that there was a net cash outflow from operations of £74,918 [125,525 – 50,607] which together with the capital investment of £36,750 in machinery and office furniture was financed by an increase in the bank overdraft.

Deferred income

The company received a grant of £20,000 in 20X4. This has been credited to income at the rate of £2,000 each financial year and is not a material consideration.

Conclusion

The company has established itself in the market achieving a sales growth of 35%. It has improved the asset turnover rate and is achieving 15.6% return on tangible net assets. Its trading profitability has improved to show 4.3% profit after tax.

The increase in activity and the lengthening of the stockholding period has put pressure on the liquidity and increased the banks' exposure to risk when considered from a capital leverage viewpoint. However, the company is able to service the loan and shows a healthy interest cover of 2.65.

For information

Appendix to part (a)	*20X5*	*20X6*
Profitability		
Sales growth [(549,500 – (304,500/9*12))(304,500/9*12)*100]	-	35.34%
Gross profit % [51,713/304,500*100][106,330/549,500*100]	16.98%	19.35%
Operating profit %	.04%	8.90%

[123/304,500*100][48,912/549,500*100]		
Profit before tax %	(1.25%)	5.54%
[(3,799)/304,500*100][30,457/549,500*100]		
Profit after tax %	(1.25%)	4.33%
[(3,799)/304,500*100][23,820/549,500*100]		
Return on capital employed	(2.22%)	15.60%
[(3,799)/171,201*100][30,457/195,201*100]		
Net asset turnover	1.78	2.82
[304,500/171,201][549,500/195,201]		
Liquidity		
Current ratio	0.94	0.98
[198,975/211,787][338,917/345,723]		
Liquid ratio	0.71	0.58
[151,200/211,787][200,542/345,723]		
Collection period (days)	136	127
[151,200/(304,500/273)][190,539/(549,500/365)]		
Stock period (days)	52	114
[47,775/(252,787/273)][138,375/(443,170/365)]		
Payment period (days) using purchases		
[93,445/(252,787 + 47,775)*365*9/12]	85	
[125,675/(443,170 – 47,775 + 138,375)*365]		86
Leverage		
Total liabilities/tangible net worth	1.24	1.77
[211,787/(171,201)][345,723/(195,021 + 786)]		
Bank debt/tangible net worth	0.43	0.96
[74,567/171,201][188,235/(195,021 + 786)]		
Long-term debt/tangible net worth		
Profit cover for interest	0.03	2.65
[123/3,922][48,912/18,455]		

(b) Report on projections

To: Mike and Jane
From:
Date:

Report on projections and restructuring of bank facilities

In accordance with your instructions, we have reviewed the projected accounts for 20X7, 20X8 and 20X9 and your proposals for restructuring the bank facility.

The bank will be viewing the projections to establish whether they are realistic in the light of your 20X6 achievement. In particular they will be considering sales growth, operating profit, interest cover, assumptions for working capital changes and the bank's exposure to risk as a result of leverage.

Sales growth

The company is forecasting 21.8%, 11.9% and 28% in 20X7, 20X8 and 20X9. There will need to be a clear explanation of the reason for the change in 20X9 e.g. change in company policy as regards type and quality of product or geographical area; change in market share. The essential aspect will be to demonstrate that the assumptions are realistic.

Operating profitability

The operating profit is 10.4%, 12.0% and 14.3%. This increase does not arise from improved margins with the gross profit per cent remaining reasonably constant at 19 – 21%. Given that this is a new start-up and a growth business then it could be expected that the benefits of spreading fixed administration and selling costs would continue. However, the assumption that a 75% increase in sales from 20X6 to 20X9 will only lead to an increase of 17% in the administration costs will need to be explained.

Interest cover

The interest cover improves from 2.6 to 27.4 as the bank liability is repaid over the three years. This is of course dependent on the company being able to reduce its borrowing.

Working capital

Debtors

The projections show the collection period reducing significantly from 127 days in 20X6 to 79 days in 20X7, 61 days in 20X8 and 76 days in 20X9.

We recognise that it is the management's intention to strenuously address this area and this should of course be reflected in the projections. However, the reasonableness of the projected improvement and a reduction of such an amount will be questioned.

Strong evidence would need to be produced that trading conditions can reasonably be assumed to change to this extent or the projections will need to be restated to reflect an approach that is more in line with 20X6 performance.

On an initial assumption that the company brings the collection period from 127 days in 20X6 down in line with the agreed credit period of 90 days at say 10 days per year the debtors figure would be as follows

	20X7	*20X8*	*20X9*
Sales	£670,000	£750,000	£960,000
Collection period (days)	117	107	97
	£	£	£
Debtors	215,000	220,000	255,000
Debtors in projection	145,000	126,000	200,000
Increased working capital	70,000	94,000	55,000

These revisions will have a material effect on both the amount and the timing of projected borrowing.

Stock

The stock period achieved in 20X6 was 114 days. The period projected for 20X7 is 81 days. Again, accepting that the company will improve the stock period the speed of the change is questionable and will be regarded as too optimistic without strong evidence that it is achievable.

If it were assumed that an improvement of 10 days per year could be achieved the stock levels would be as follows:

	20X7	*20X8*	*20X9*
Cost of sales	£545,000	£600,000	£760,000
Stock period (days)	104	94	90
	£	£	£
Stock	155,000	155,000	187,000
Stock in projections	120,000	170,000	190,000
Increase/(decrease) in working capital	35,000	(15,000)	(3,000)

Payment period

The payment period is projected to remain reasonably constant at 84 days by 20X9 [£180,000/(£760,000 – 170,000 + 190,000)*365] which appears reasonable.

Fixed assets

We note that in your projections the fixed assets have not been depreciated. Unless the additions each year equal the depreciation, a depreciation charge needs to be built into the projections.

Revision of projections

The increase in working capital would be reflected in an overdraft figure in the balance sheet. If the revised stock and debtor figures are incorporated, the effect of the difference between the original and revised figures on the projected overdraft would be as follows:

	20X7	*20X8*	*20X9*
	£'000	*£'000*	*£'000*
Projected overdraft	(5)	(5)	(50)
Stock (increase)/decrease	(35)	15	3
Debtors increase	(70)	(94)	(55)
Revised overdraft	(110)	(84)	(57)

This indicates that the proposed restructuring in the form of a term loan with a repayment of £100,000 in 20X7 will be unachievable and that there would be an overdraft requirement at the end of 20X9.

If the revisions are realistic, the company will need to retain an overdraft facility. The revised projections show that there will be £210,000 owing to the bank at 31 May 20X7 reducing to £57,000 by the end of 20X9.

In our opinion, the projections will need revision before submission to the bank and/or additional supporting information e.g. assumptions on administrative expenses and sales growth.

We have approached the review in the same manner as we feel the bank will approach it and raised questions such as they will no doubt raise when you meet.

Please let us know if we can be of further assistance either in revising the projections or at your meeting with the bank.

64 Language-ease Ltd

Key answer tips

You will need to calculate some ratios, but you should also compare the narrative part of the scenario with the figures in the profit and loss accounts and balance sheets. This should show you the key areas on which to comment in part (a). You must make connections between the ratio analysis and the information in the scenario and identify possible reasons for the changes.

Your answer must address the needs of the recipient (the potential acquirer). Cold Pack Ltd are concerned with future profitability, and so your answer should analyse the profit figures in detail.

The explicit requirement is to comment on the action that might be needed to improve profitability, but the answer below also comments on liquidity. This is because the lack of finance indirectly affects profitability, but also because the liquidity problems are so severe that any acquirer would need to deal with them urgently.

In part (b), you must explain the reasoning and assumptions behind the calculation.

(a) (i) Prepare comments on the financial position of Student-Food Ltd as at 31 October 20X6 and on the changes that have occurred during the three years to that date for inclusion in a report in Cold Pack Ltd.

The following comments have been drafted:

Financing capital asset expenditure

Student-Food Ltd has achieved sales of £1,240,000 in 20X6 which is an increase of 37.8% [(1,240,000 - 900,000)/900,000] over the 20X4 figure. However, it has increased its gross cost of fixed assets by £660,000 in 1995 and £500,000 in 20X6. This is a 178% [1,160,000/650,000] increase over the 20X4 gross cost figure partly due to health and safety considerations and partly due to refurbishment to improve the company's competitiveness with local restaurants. In considering the financial position, it is necessary to identify how the fixed assets were financed. From an inspection of the balance sheets it is clear that the fixed assets acquisitions were largely financed by additional loan capital.

For the purpose of the report a more detailed analysis would be appropriate identifying the extent to which the fixed assets have been financed by internally generated funds, new share capital, long term loans and from changes in working capital.

A statement such as the following could be helpful:

		20X5 £'000		*20X6* £'000
Cost of additional fixed assets		660		500
Financed by:				
Internally generated funds				
- Profit	33		(16)	
Depreciation	60		100	
	93		84	
Less dividends	36		-	
		(57)		(84)
		603		416
New equity capital		-		-
		603		416
Loan capital		(240)		(520)
Reduction/(Increase in working capital)		363		(104)
Stock increase	120		40	
Debtor increase	200		120	
Creditor increase	(300)		(76)	
Bank (increase)/decrease	(383)		20	
		(363)		104

This indicates that 66% of the increase in fixed assets was financed by loan capital [760,000/1,160,000]; 22% by a reduction in working capital [(363,000 - 104,000)/1,160,000]; 12% by internally generated funds [(57,000 + 84,000)/1,160,000]; and nil % by new share capital.

Depreciation
The depreciation policy and amounts needs further enquiry. There has been £800,000 expenditure on fittings during 20X5 and 20X6 and rental agreements having only a further four years to run. *Prima facie* this would indicate that a significantly higher rate of amortisation might be appropriate.

Working capital
The internally generated funds have been insufficient to finance either the fixed assets or the increase in working capital in 20X6. The company has become heavily dependent on loans and increases in its creditors.

The stock turnover was:

2.7 in 20X4 [(900,000 - 252,000)/240,000];
2.6 times in 1995 [(1,200,000 - 272,000)/360,000]; and
2.3 times in 20X6 [(1,240,000 - 320,000)/400,000].

The decrease in the stock turnover could be related to the company failing to meet the increased sales for which it had planned. Although the food packs are stated to be long life, enquiry should be made as to the shelf life of stock and the possibility of stock being out of date and unsaleable. The company sells both direct to students and also to colleges with the debtor figure arising from sales to the colleges. There has been a material change in the percentage of debtors to sales rising from 17.8% in 20X4 to 38.7% in 20X6. This could simply be a shift to credit sales from cash sales. However, enquiries are necessary to establish how this increase arose. Given the related party relationships it is possible that the company is accommodating the colleges by granting them increasing credit periods or, alternatively, that the colleges are accommodating the company by allowing the company to invoice in order to conceal the increase in stocks and improve the liquidity ratio.

The liquidity ratio [acid test] was:

1.5:1 in 20X4 [(160,000 + 80,000)/(112,000 + 48,000)];
0.47:1 [360,000/763,000] in 1995; and
0.59:1 in 20X6 [480,000/819,000].

However, if the debtors remained at 17.8% in 20X6 as in 20X4 the liquidity ratio would have worsened to 0.26:1 [(1,240,000 × 17.8%)/819,000]

The creditors turnover based on cost of sales was:

5.8 in 20X4 [(900,000 - 252,000)/112,000];
2.2 times in 1995 [(1,200,000 - 272,000)/431,000]; and
1.8 times in 20X6 [(1,240,000 - 320,000)/518,000]

Turnover

The directors planned to sell four £5 packs per week to at least 15% of the students. For 1995, this would have resulted in the sale of 288,000 packs [40 colleges × 400 students × 15% × 4 packs × 30 weeks] and a turnover of £1,440,000. This would have produced an increase in turnover of £540,000 [1,440,000 - 900,000]

Although therefore the actual sales were 33.3% higher than 20X4 they were 16.7% under budget [240,000/1,440,000 × 100]. The plan therefore to increase the sales to 30% of the student population in 20X6 appeared unrealistic as evidenced by the modest 3% increase actually achieved [40,000/1,200,000 × 100].

Profitability

The gross profit % has fallen from 28% in 20X4 [252,000/900,000 × 100] to 25.8% in 20X6 [320,000/1,240,000 × 100].

Enquiry should be made to obtain the reason for this fall. It was noted that the company experiences competition from local city centre restaurants.

The profit before tax has fallen from a profit of 13.3% in 20X4 [120,000/900,000 × 100] to a loss of 1.3% in 20X6. Expenses have increased from 7.2% in 20X4 [66,000/900,000 × 100] to 11.8% in 20X6 [146,000/1,240,000 × 100]. Enquiry should be made to obtain a detailed analysis of the expenses to identify which of the expenses have increased and reasons for the increase.

The rental currently charged is lower than that which would apply in the market. If the market rates were applied the rental charge would be £39,000 per annum - an increase of £33,000 and the profit before tax would have been £87,000 in 20X4, £7,000 in 1995 and a loss of £49,000 in 20X6.

The bank overdraft carried interest of 20% and on the basis that it arose evenly over the year, the interest charge in 1995 was £24,000 [((303,000/2) × 289/365) × 20%] assuming that the overdraft existed for 289 days in 1995 i.e. $\frac{303}{(80+303)} \times 365 = 289$.

The loan would therefore appear to carry interest of 3.3% [(28,000 - 24,000)/(240,000/2) × 100].

The bank overdraft carried interest of 20% and on the basis that it arose evenly over the year, the interest charge in 20X6 was £59,000 [((303,000 + 283,000)/2) × 20%]. The loans appear to carry interest of 5% [(84,000 - 59,000)/((240,000 + 760,000)/2) × 100].

There is a significant difference in this 5% and the market rate of 12% and enquiry should be made to establish the terms and conditions attaching to loans raised by the company. It could possibly be that loans have been raised at below market rates from related parties.

The worsening operating profit figures are reduced further by interest charges incurred in 1995 and 20X6. If the market rate of 12% was applied to the loans, the interest charged would be increased by £10,400 in 1995 [(12% of 120,000) - (4,000)] and £35,000 in 20X6 [(12% of 500,000) - (5% of 500,000)].

The effect on the profit before tax figure of commercial rents and interest rates would have been to turn 1995 into a loss of £3,400 and increase the 20X6 loss to £84,000.

There is also the question of the adequacy of the depreciation charge made in 20X6, in particular, that relating to the fittings but this will clearly be influenced by the length of rental agreements negotiated with the colleges.

Summary
Although Student-Food Ltd increased its sales by 38.8% from 20X4, it failed to achieve its planned sales in 1995 by 16.7% and failed by 13.9% even in 20X6 to achieve the sales level planned for 1995. The actual increase achieved in 1995 appears to have misled the directors into assuming that such significant growth would continue. Their planned increase for 20X6 was consequently totally over-optimistic.

The company has been unable to finance its sales growth by internally generated funds and is overtrading. It has financed its growth with loans and an increase in current liabilities, thereby incurring interest charges in the profit and loss account which it is unable to fully cover in 20X6.

Its gearing in the balance sheet has increased so that loans exceeded shareholders' funds by 20X6. The rate of interest charged on the loans is significantly lower than the market rate which might be due to related party relationships.

The company has a liquidity problem and it is in a potentially dangerous financial position.

The company is suffering from falling gross profit margins and falling net profit percentages which means that it will be unable to pay a dividend.

(ii) Comment on the action that Cold Pack Ltd might need to take to improve the company's profitability.

Profitability improvement
An analysis is required of the sales and cost of sales to identify whether the fall in gross profit is due to a fall in selling prices and/or an increase in costs.

If there is a fall in selling prices, ascertain whether there has been a general fall in selling prices or whether it relates to any particular sales area e.g. any particular college. Consider pricing and market strategies.

If there is an increase in costs, review purchasing policy and procedures to ascertain the extent to which the company could benefit from centralised buying.

The terms of licensing agreements should be examined and reviewed.

An analysis is required of the expenses by function and an investigation made of significant changes with a view to their reduction.

Where possible, it would be helpful to calculate a return on capital employed for each business segment to establish whether there are any particular segments that are underperforming.

If any segment is underperforming, ascertain whether it is feasible to improve performance to an acceptable level. For example, it might be necessary to improve the location of the outlets or there might be strong local competition which will require combating by advertising or other measures such as staff incentives.

If any segment or location is not able to produce an adequate return on capital employed, it might be necessary to consider closure.

Liquidity - investment in assets
In addition to increasing the operating profit, consideration must be given to substantially increasing the sales or reducing the overall investment in assets.

Monetary asset management needs to be improved.

The stock turnover has fallen since 20X4. The rate needs to be increased by reducing stock or increasing sales and enquiries are needed to establish the shelf life of stock. A possible approach would be to decide on the number of days stock to hold at each college taking into account the demand and the shelf life of the stock. Assuming that four weeks supply is to be held in stock - the stock should be reduced to approximately £123,000 [(1,240,000 - 320,000)/30 × 4]. There is also the point to consider that, because sales are not occurring in 22 weeks due to the college year, the timing of the balance sheet date could give unrepresentative figures for current assets and current liabilities.

The debtor position is unclear. There is a significant increase in the period of credit allowed which should be reviewed to secure significant reduction. This is an area that requires further enquiry. Assuming that 50% of the sales are to colleges direct and that 30 days credit is allowed, debtors should be reduced to approximately £83,000 [(1,240,000/2)/30 weeks × 4]. The point made above about the timing of the balance sheet date also applies to debtors.

Credit periods and terms with suppliers should be re-negotiated.

The major expenditure on fixed assets appears to have been on fixtures and fittings. Consequently, it is possible that these may not be capable of being easily reduced or disposed of. However, asset disposals should be considered.

The reduction in current assets would reduce them from £880,000 to £206,000 a saving of £674,000 which would be used to reduce the creditors and overdraft from £819,000 to £145,000.

Finally, budgets and forecasts should be recomputed.

(b) Assuming that you are Joseph Tan, prepare an initial valuation of the shares in Student-Food Ltd based on the information available at 25 November 20X6.

Share valuation method
As Cold Pack Ltd is acquiring the whole of the issued share capital of Student-Food Ltd the initial valuation is calculated using the earnings method.

Level of gross profit
The draft accounts for 20X6 show loss before tax of £16,000 and it will be necessary to ascertain from Cold Pack Ltd how they propose to bring the company into profit.

Our enquiries appear to indicate that this loss is increased to £84,000 if a market rate is used for the loan interest and rental charges. Enquiries are needed to establish whether the rental and/or loan will continue at the same preferential rate. The question of a possible change in the depreciation charge is to be considered further.

There is information that Cold Pack Ltd will be able to improve gross profit margins by centralising purchasing and obtaining better terms from suppliers. Assuming that the 20X6 level of sales will be maintained and that a gross profit of 42.5% is achievable, this would have produced a gross profit in 20X6 of £527,000.

Level of trading profit
The trading expenses have been around 12% for the past two years.

Assuming that there is little scope for cost reduction of the expenses of £146,000 and that the depreciation charge should be higher, say, £225,000 i.e. 15% of the fixed assets at the end of the year (15% of £1,500,000) the profit after interest will be £55,000.

[527,000 – expenses 146,000 – rental 6,000 – depreciation 225,000 – loan interest 38,000 – bank interest 57,000].

Applying a PE multiple of 10, the shares are valued at £550,000 i.e. £1.375 per share.

However, the position would change significantly if the preferential rent and loan interest were not available resulting in a loss of £31,000.

[527,000 – expenses 146,000 – rental 39,000 – depreciation 225,000 – loan interest 91,000 – bank interest 57,000].

Asset backing
The earnings based share valuation should be compared with the asset valuation per share.

Based on the book value of the assets, each share has asset backing of £1.75. Current values e.g. insurance values should be obtained immediately from Student-Food Ltd.

65 Accounting ratios

Key answer tips

The requirement is to *evaluate the usefulness* of ratio analysis, not simply to state its limitations. Because of the requirement to *evaluate*, some description is needed. A list of 'bullet points' would not fully address the requirement.

Your answer to part (b) should make a number of points in a descriptive way, meeting the requirement to *discuss the value*. You need only describe the Altman and Argenti models in so far as is necessary to explain their advantages and limitations; avoid lengthy description and explanation for its own sake.

(a) Ratio analysis can be a useful way of interpreting financial information but its predictive powers should not be overestimated. Ratios calculated from historical cost accounts do not reflect the current values of assets or the current costs of operations and as a consequence if users wish to predict a company's future performance, they are restricted in their analysis by the provision of historical cost information in corporate financial statements. Comparison of ratios between companies is very difficult. Companies are inherently different in structure and use different accounting policies and although these may be disclosed in financial statements, it is difficult sometimes to adjust the accounts for these differing policies as the information required to carry out the adjustment may not be disclosed.

The environment within which the company operates may change. If the rate of inflation changes or the business environment changes, then performance over time using ratio analysis may be distorted.

The potential usefulness of many ratios both as an indicator of current performance and as a guide to future performance would appear to require that the constituent elements of the profit and loss account and balance sheet should be expressed in comparable prices. The use of profitability ratios is limited if the numerator is expressed in current prices (for example turnover) and the denominator is based upon historical values (for example capital employed). An organisation showing a satisfactory gross profit percentage may not be generating sufficient funds to replace stock at current prices or to meet its operating costs, and ratio analysis based on published data would not pick up this weakness.

Return on capital employed is a key investment ratio but the figure for capital employed is based upon the historical value of capital provided. The real cost of the shareholders' investment in the company is the opportunity cost of their investment which is the amount sacrificed by not selling their shares (i.e. market price). Similarly the return to ordinary shareholders is dependent upon dividends received and expected to be received. Neither of these components are used in the calculation of return on capital employed traditionally used by users of financial statements.

Traditional ratio analysis is dependent upon items included in the financial statements. Companies, despite the introduction of FRS5 'Reporting the substance of transactions', still leave assets and liabilities 'off the balance sheet'. The accounting for pension costs and leases are still areas where traditional accounting rules allow companies to leave assets and liabilities off the balance sheet. In many cases, the balance sheet is a repository for elements not charged in the profit and loss account under accrual accounting. Thus certain items in the balance sheet are 'sunk costs'. For example research and development expenditure. Companies still use creativity in formulation of financial statements and directors still believe that capital markets are 'fooled' by 'creative' accounting practices. If the remuneration of managers (including share options) is linked to profit and if their value in the labour market is enhanced by running a 'profitable' company, then management may attempt to influence the accounting treatments adopted by the company. Although analysts are aware of the above facts, it is not always easy to adjust financial statements for them. Thus the effectiveness of ratio analysis is reduced.

These limitations do not necessarily mean that ratio analysis should be discarded as an interpretative mechanism. If the cost of providing such information was greater than its usefulness then understandably ratio analysis would not be used. Financial statements are part of conventional accrual accounting and are subject to the preferences, judgements and objectives of management. Analysts need to be aware of these limitations. Ratio analysis is part of the process of information gathering for decision making and is not an absolute performance measure in itself.

(b) Empirical studies have been undertaken to determine the extent to which financial ratios can be used to predict corporate failure. The ability to predict corporate failure is important from the investors viewpoint and from a social perspective, and an early warning system would allow investors and management to take preventative action. Both univariate and multivariate (Altman) approaches have been used to predict corporate failure and essentially these analyses are capable of saying whether a company exhibits characteristics similar to companies which have failed in the past without being able to determine whether a particular company is going to fail.

Altman (1968/1983) determined multiple predictors of business failure using multiple discriminant analysis for the development of a linear function which purported to predict corporate failure. The 'Z' score selected five (out of 22 utilised in the research) financial ratios for his final discriminant function. The ratios and weighting were derived from an empirical study of US companies. The effectiveness of the 'Z' score in predicting corporate failure declined when used on data other than that used in the empirical study.

Argenti developed a failure model only partly based on financial information and developed the failure model to include such variates as the nature of management, response to change, the accounting systems and financial problems and mistakes.

All models which predict corporate failure from financial statements suffer from the underlying weakness of a lack of comparability of financial statements. Also managers may start creative accounting practices when they realise that their company is having problems. It is unlikely that corporate failure can be predicted on the basis of a univariate or multivariate model alone. There are several other factors such as those outlined by Argenti that one has to take into account.

The accounting ratios used by researchers are based on historic information but ideally prospective information is likely to be more useful in predicting corporate failure. Historic information is often published too late to be of use in determining the going concern status of companies and contains information which has 'mixed values' inasmuch that some items will be at net replacement cost, others will be at historic cost and some items at current value.

The underlying theory behind the models is suspect and little attempt has been made to explain the logic of the models. As a result confidence in the models varies and their ability to predict corporate failure has been undermined. The ability of the models to predict the time-scale of the failure has been criticised. The models were developed in the 1960s, 70s and 80s when business transactions and the sophistication of accounting techniques were different to those of the current generation of companies. Therefore, the application of 'Z' scores to the current business environment may be unrealistic. Additionally these models do not take account of inflation in their calculations.

Despite the criticisms of multivariate analyses they are used by banks to analyse credit risk, by companies to monitor credit worthiness and audit firms in their analytical review procedures. However, they are not used in isolation but are utilised alongside other information about a company.

(c) Financial analysts may undertake several adjustments to financial statements. The reasons for this may vary from the fact that the basis of several balance sheet items is the subjective assessment of the directors to the fact that balance sheet write-offs reduce the carrying value of net assets to 'unrealistic' levels.

Analysts often review the depreciation rates of capital intensive businesses as the profitability of such businesses is affected by accelerated depreciation rates. Such depreciation rates cause a concave decline in net asset values whereas often the asset values decline in convex terms. Analysts therefore often add back depreciation, thus charging it at a slower rate. Differences in depreciation methods and revaluations of assets also cause distortions in the ratios. Many analysts are looking to adjust accounts in order that they might arrive at 'economic' value and profit.

(***Tutorial note:*** Part (c) of the original question asked candidates to describe, with reasons, an accounting adjustment which analysts might wish to make to financial statements before evaluating corporate performance in the case of each of the following elements: goodwill; deferred taxation; and depreciation.

When this question was originally set, SSAP 22 and SSAP 15 were still in force. Under SSAP 22, purchased goodwill could be written off against reserves and analysts often made adjustments to the financial statements to bring it back onto the balance sheet. FRS 10 has now prohibited this treatment. Similarly, SSAP 15 required that deferred tax should be accounted for using the partial provision method. Analysts often adjusted the financial statements because of the subjectivity of partial provision. FRS 19 now requires full provision.)

66 Changeling plc

(a)

Extract from profit and loss account for the year ended 31 March 20X3

	£'000		CPP units '000
Net operating profit	750	given	247
Tax	(338)	-	(338)
Profit/(loss) after tax	412		(91)
Gain/(loss) on net monetary assets		working	(98)
Gain/(loss) on long-term loans		working	213
Net profit/(loss) for year	412		24
Dividends	(187)	-	(187)
Retained profit/(loss) for the year	225		(163)
Brought forward	750	given	1,305
Carried forward	975		1,142

(***Tutorial note:*** The transaction date for tax and dividends is the last day of the accounting period and therefore there is no index adjustment.)

Workings

Gain/(loss) on net monetary assets

	£'000	*Index*	*CPP units* 000
Opening net monetary assets:			
Debtors	1,050		
Creditors	(875)		
	175	$\frac{2,000}{1,750}$	200
Increase in net monetary assets:			
Sales	6,500	$\frac{2,000}{1,875}$	6,933

Decrease in net monetary assets:

Purchases	(4,250)	$\frac{2,000}{1,875}$	(4,533)
Expenses	(1,150)	$\frac{2,000}{1,875}$	(1,227)
Tax	(338)	-	(338)
Dividends	(187)	-	(187)
(Debtors 1,150, Creditors 400)	750		848

Loss in purchasing power = £750 – £C848 = £C98.

Gain/(loss) on long-term loans

Opening balance	1,125	$\frac{2,000}{1,750}$	1,286
Increase in loan	500	$\frac{2,000}{1,813}$ (As per equipment purchased with loan)	552
Closing balance	1,625		1,838

Gain in purchasing power = £1,625 – £C1,838 = £C213.

(b) The indexing used in the current purchasing power method of accounting for price level changes is attempting to measure the profit or loss for a period in terms of the increase or decrease in the current purchasing power of shareholders' funds. The use of indexing results in profits or losses being stated after allowing for the declining purchasing power of money due to price inflation. When applied to Historic Cost Accounting the indexing results in CPP accounts that reflect adjustments to income and capital values to allow for the general rate of price inflation.

CPP attempts to maintain the shareholders' capital in terms of its general or consumer purchasing power. However, this proprietorship concept will only be of relevance to the company's owners (proprietors) if the general index used reflects their own consumption pattern which in most cases it will not. The CPP accounts will not therefore automatically be of relevance to the proprietors.

Indexing may be of use to the entity because it does result in the recognition of gains and losses on monetary items in periods of changing prices and does provide financial statements in which all the items are expressed in constant units. However, the indexing will not result in values of individual assets which will be of relevance. A replacement cost or mixed value system needs to be applied to achieve a real terms asset value which may be of relevance.

(c)

To: Principal shareholder — Date: X-X-XX
From: An accountant
Subject: Financial statement analysis

Attached is a set of financial statements for Changeling plc for the year to 31 March 20X3. This set includes accounts expressed in purely historic cost terms and accounts that have been adjusted to allow for the effect of general price inflation on the historic cost figures. At present no details of other companies are available for an inter-company analysis. This analysis is therefore based on the concepts - Historic Cost and Current Purchasing Power, and emphasises the level of profitability, liquidity and financial structure reflected in these two sets of accounts.

Profitability

The return (operating profit before tax) achieved on the capital employed (share capital plus retained profit) for the year is 21.7% according to the historic cost figures. However, this return is reduced to a mere 3.9% when adjustments are made to the measure of profit and capital for the effects of inflation.

The level of gross profit achieved on the sales for the period is 37.7% based on historic cost figures, with price inflation adjustments resulting in only a minor decrease to 36.1%. However, there is a dramatic decrease in the level of the profit available for distribution (as dividends) from the £412,000 shown in the historic cost accounts to only £24,000 in the inflation adjusted CPP accounts. The dividend of £187,000 is therefore not covered by profits measured in current purchasing power terms. It may be useful to find out if this is normal for companies similar to Changeling plc.

Liquidity

The company does not appear to have any short-term liquidity problems. The debtors are nearly 3 times the creditors at the end of the year but the company must remember that holding monetary assets in periods of changing prices results in a loss in purchasing power as reflected in the profit and loss account using CPP units i.e. £98,000 loss on net monetary assets.

Financial structure

The historic cost accounts show that loans constituted nearly 26% $\left(\frac{1,125,000}{3,250,000+1,125,000}\right)$ of the long-term funds at the end of 20X2 and this had increased to nearly 32% $\left(\frac{1,625,000}{3,475,000+1,625,000}\right)$ by the end of 20X3. This may indicate an unfavourable trend but it is necessary to investigate the financial structure of other similar companies before such a conclusion can be reached.

The CPP figures also show a similar trend moving from over 16% $\left(\frac{1,286,000}{6,568,000+1,286,000}\right)$ at the end of 20X2 to over 20% $\left(\frac{1,625,000}{6,405,000+1,625,000}\right)$ by the end of 20X3. The CPP profit and loss account does reflect the benefit of holding fixed repayment loans in periods of increasing general price levels i.e. the £213,000 gain on the long-term loan.

67 Air Fare plc

(a) (i)

Profit and loss account for the year ended 31 December 20X3

		£'000	£'000
Sales			11,441
Cost of sales		10,292	
Cost of sales adjustment		412	
Depreciation adjustment			
Freehold property	£6.0m/40 years	150	
Equipment	£0.60m/15 years	40	
			10,894
Current cost operating profit			547
Less: Interest			625
Current cost profit (loss) before tax			(78)
Tax		(124)	
Current cost profit (loss) after tax			(202)

Add:	Realised holding gains			
	Cost of sales adjustment		412	
	Depreciation adjustment		190	
			602	
Unrealised holding gains				
		1.1.X3 *31.12.X3*		
	Stock	£45,000 – £10,000	35	
	Freehold premises	(£14m – 13.8) × 32/40	160	
	Equipment	(£12.6m – 12.5m) × 13/15	87	
			282	
Less:	Depreciation adjustment previously recognised as unrealised		(190)	
Total holding gains				694
Total gains				492
Less:	Inflation adjustment to shareholder's funds 3% of £25m			(750)
Total real loss				(258)
Dividend				(100)
				(358)

Note the depreciation adjustment could have been based on average current values for the year, the result would not have been materially different from the depreciation adjustment based on the year end current value.

(ii) The company achieved a current cost operating profit of £547,000 after deducting the realised holding gains on the stock and fixed assets i.e. £547,000 after maintaining the operating capacity of the company and ignoring the MWCA. The historic cost gross profit of £1,149,000 has been reduced by the realised holding gains of £602,000.

The holding gains which are stated in money terms and calculated by reference to the specific price changes of the assets are reduced by the general inflation adjustment to the opening shareholders' funds stated at current cost representing a charge for general inflation. The result is a total real loss before dividends of £258,000. This implies that the declaration of the proposed dividend of £100,000 is imprudent.

(b)

Report to Directors of Air Fare plc **Dated:**

Re: Non-depreciation of freehold property

I have reviewed the circumstances in which other companies have not made a property depreciation charge in the profit and loss account. It would appear that they have rarely been able to make a case for exemption from the provisions of FRS 15 *Tangible fixed assets* with the exception of property companies who are subject to the provisions of SSAP 19.

In my view we need to present a case that the amount is immaterial and that the original decision to depreciate was a passive decision rather than an active assessment of the life and residual value of the freehold properties. My draft of the points to raise are set out below.

There have been references made to the Financial Reporting Review Panel in respect of non-compliance and they have made decisions both for and against such a practice.

In my view it will be important for the company to be able to show that it has substance for such a decision.

Draft points to be raised in support of non-depreciation

The following points are raised for your consideration with the auditors.

(1) *Materiality of current charge*

The profit before tax for the year ended 31 December 20X3 was £524,000. This figure was arrived at after making a depreciation charge for the year of £200,000 on the freehold property. The amount is therefore material. Even if the charge were immaterial in relation to the profit and loss account, the accumulated figure would probably not be immaterial and the user of the accounts would have lost the benefit of this piece of information.

Users of the accounts tend to refer to the relationship between the balance outstanding and the cost to assess the extent to which the life of the asset has been exhausted and at what point they are likely to need to be replaced.

(2) *Basis of current rate of depreciation*

The company has been depreciating its freehold properties using a rate of 2.5% straight line.

I would like to emphasise that this was not a thought through decision on the part of the company in as much as it reflected the group policy of the American parent company.

We certainly did not base it on an estimate of the life of the building and the residual value at the date of purchase.

In our view the assumptions underlying the choice of rate of depreciation need to be defined. I won't say redefined because, as I have mentioned, they were never actually defined by our company's management.

(3) *Determining a true and fair charge*

To arrive at a true and fair charge, I think we should recognise that the buildings are subject to Health and Safety and Public Health inspections because we are preparing food. This means that the company is required to maintain the premises in a continual state of sound repair.

In the directors' view this means that the life of the premises is so long and residual value, based on prices prevailing at the time of acquisition, so large that depreciation is insignificant.

We should, however, note that FRS 15 states that subsequent expenditure that maintains or enhances an asset does not negate the need to charge depreciation.

(4) *Impairment*

The directors undertake to charge any impairment in the value of the premises to the profit and loss account as appropriate. Indeed, FRS 15 requires that the premises are reviewed for impairment when no depreciation charge is made on the grounds that the charge is immaterial.

(5) *Costs incurred on maintenance*

The maintenance and repair costs have been separately recorded each year and I will prepare a schedule of these on an annual basis if you consider that to be relevant.

Could you please consider the points raised and let me know how you would like to take this forward.

(Tutorial Note: At the time that this question was originally set, FRS 15 had not yet been issued and the answer has been amended slightly to reflect this development.

One of the arguments against depreciating the premises (i.e. that they are maintained to such a high standard that their useful economic life is very long) has become much less valid since the issue of FRS 15. However, although the ASB has attempted to discourage non-depreciation, it has not actually prohibited it.*)*

68 Measurement systems

Key answer tips

The requirement in part (a) is to *describe*. This means that simply listing the disadvantages as 'bullet points' will not be sufficient. You are not required to give detailed explanations of CPP and CCA accounting.

In part (c) you are required to illustrate your answer using AB, in other words, with figures. A description of the 'real terms' system on its own would not earn maximum marks.

(a) Replacement cost accounting is often thought to be more relevant to investors than historical cost accounting. However there are disadvantages with this form of accounting:

1 Replacement cost accounting (RCA) is often criticised on the grounds that the measurements can be subjective. Indices are often used in the measurement of assets and these values may be unreliable.

2 This system is based on the assumption that the firm is a going concern and that reliable entry price data is available and can be readily obtained. This may be a problem during a period of technological change as the replacement cost may relate to a new generation of asset rather than the existing asset.

3 RCA does not take account of changes in the general price level and gains and losses on holding monetary assets and liabilities.

4 There is a problem in correctly specifying what 'replacement cost' price actually means. The question arises as to the purpose of holding the assets as this will determine its value. There are alternative interpretations of 'replacement cost'. For example it can mean the used value or the reproduction cost or the cost of an equivalent asset.

Similarly there are significant disadvantages with a net realisable value method of valuation:

1 This system is only relevant for assets that are expected to be sold and for which a second-hand market exists. It will be more difficult to determine an exit value for specialised equipment with little or no alternative use.

2 The exit price has little relevance for assets that the firm expects to use. The disclosure of the cash value is not likely to be relevant to a user interested in the profitability of the company.

3 It is difficult to value certain assets/liabilities at their exit value. There is a problem of valuing intangibles and goodwill, and also of the valuation of liabilities. The problem arises as to whether liabilities should be valued at their contractual amounts or at amounts required to fund the liabilities.

4 There is a contradiction between the realisation principle and the established assumption that the company is a going concern.

5 As with RCA an exit based system does not take into account changes in the general price level.

(b)

Profit and loss accounts

	(i) CPP	*(ii) CCA*
	£m	£m
Turnover	4,950	4,500
Cost of sales	(3,300)	(3,000)
Gross profit	1,650	1,500
Distribution and administrative expenses	(550)	(500)
Current cost operating adjustment (W1)		(1,150)
Loss on net monetary items (W2)	(280)	
Operating profit (loss)	820	(150)
Gearing adjustment		423

Profit before taxation	820	273
Taxation	(300)	(300)
Profit/(loss) after taxation	520	(27)

Balance sheets

Fixed assets (net of depreciation)	2,200	2,400
Current assets and liabilities		
Stock	1,320	1,600
Debtors	2,400	2,400
Cash	300	300
Creditors: amounts falling due in one year	(1,200)	(1,200)
Net current assets	2,820	3,100
Creditors: amounts falling due after one year	(1,500)	(1,500)
	3,520	4,000
Capital and reserves		
Share capital	3,000	2,500
Reserves – Profit/(loss)	520	(27)
Capital maintenance		1,527
	3,520	4,000

Note that there are alternative presentations of the above information.

Workings

1 **Current cost operating adjustments**

	£m
Monetary working capital adjustment	400
Depreciation adjustment	120
Cost of sales adjustment (3,750 – 3,000 – 120)	630
	1,150

2 **Capital maintenance**

	£m	£m
CPP – Loss on short-term monetary items		
Bank movements		
Capital	(500)	
Fixed assets (2,860 – 2,600)		260
Turnover (4,950 – 4,500)		(450)
Distribution costs (550 – 500)		50
Purchases		360
Loan raised		(20)
		(300)

Purchases = COS (3,300 – 3,000) + stock (1,320 – 1,200) – depreciation (660 – 600) i.e. 360

Loss on short-term monetary items		(300)
Gain on long-term monetary items		20
		(280)
CCA		
Current cost adjustment		
MWCA	400	
COSA 630		
Gearing	(423)	
		607

Fixed assets		520
Stock	400	
		1,527

(c) If general inflation is a significant factor in an economy, it may be suitable to adjust a current value system for the effects of inflation in order to produce a 'real terms' system. This system can be presented in several ways. Normally the total real gains are determined by utilising CPP accounting. This essentially takes account of the increase in asset values and deducts a charge for general inflation.

Working 4 shows this calculation which results in a real holding gain of £560m. The profit for the year would be adjusted for this amount. Additionally current cost adjustments would be dealt with in the financial statements as well as a computation of the amount required to maintain the capital of the company. The profit for the period could be calculated as follows:

	£m
Operating loss – CCA	(150)
Real holding gains	560
Taxation	(300)
Profit	110

The balance sheet could be shown as follows:

Net assets – CCA	4,000
Share capital	3,000
Profit	110
Capital maintenance (working 3)	890
	4,000

Workings

3 **Real terms CCA**

	£m	£m
Current cost reserve (above without gearing adj.) (1,527 + 423)		1,950
Real holding gains		(560)
Capital maintenance		(500)
		890

4 **Real holding gains adjustment**

Stock – current value	1,600	
– CPP	1,320	
		280
Fixed assets – current value	3,120	
– CPP	2,860	
		260
Gain on monetary items		20
		560

69 CIC plc

(a)

To: The Directors   Date: X-X-XX
From: A.N. Accountant
Subject: **Analysing foreign financial statements**

In order that we can assess the financial performance and position of our group on an international scale, it is necessary to attempt to analyse financial statements produced by comparable multinational groups in other countries. Such statements will usually have been produced for 'home market' users and follow national accounting regulations. Such users and regulations will often be different from the user orientation that is reflected in UK financial statements produced within the UK regulatory framework. Such differences will present problems and the most important are set out below.

Data accessibility

Some countries do not require companies to publish their accounts, and in others that do, the level of accessibility is not as high as it is in the US and the UK.

Timeliness of information

Countries vary in the delay between the end of the accounting period and the date the financial statements are made available publicly e.g. UK usually around six months, US usually around ninety days. (Note that for some countries there is a considerable delay in producing accounts in the English language.)

Language and terminology barriers

Language is often the major barrier which must initially be overcome and, even when it has been, there are terminology problems. If the foreign enterprises do produce English versions, they may still use terms not easily understood in the UK and some of the important information content of the financial statements may be lost in the translation.

Currency translation

This will probably involve using arbitrary exchange rates. The use of such rates may result in a loss of the relative values of items in the accounts.

Statement formats

These tend not to be too vital after the initial 'shock' of seeing statements in 'foreign' formats. This problem will be most apparent outside the EU where the Fourth Directive standard formats do not apply.

Disclosure requirements

These will be dependent on the main user target. In some countries disclosure will be less than in the UK, making interpretation and analysis very difficult.

Accounting principles

Comparison of companies on an international scale suffers from the same problem as comparisons on a national scale - unless the accounts are prepared on the same accounting principles, direct comparisons are inappropriate. Reconciliations and/or adjustments to allow for the use of different accounting principles must be made.

Environment

The environment in which financial statements are prepared will differ from country to country. Allowances must be made for cultural differences towards risk, creditor protection, secrecy and finance methods. Such differences will often present barriers which cannot be overcome.

(b) Should domestic accounting standards be abandoned?

There would be advantages in adopting International Accounting Standards (IASs) in preference to domestic standards in some cases. The financial statements of multinationals are used by investors in many different countries and a 'common language' of accounting standards would be helpful to these users. The requirement to prepare financial statements based on domestic standards leads to additional costs for multinationals.

However, many countries would not wish to abandon domestic standards, which have often been developed in response to particular cultural and political conditions. For example, in the UK and the US, the regulatory system reflects the fact that most capital is provided by external shareholders, while in other countries the regulatory system has been designed to protect the interest of banks and the government. There are many different legal systems in operation around the world (e.g. the common law system and the codified system).

IASs that reflected such diversity would need to be so flexible that their usefulness would be reduced.

However, many experts now believe that the advantages of international harmonisation outweigh the disadvantages and that eventually domestic accounting standards will be replaced by IASs. The European Commission has recently recommended that all EU listed companies should prepare financial statements in accordance with IASs by 2005. This has brought the abandonment of domestic accounting standards significantly closer.

70 AHS SA

REPORT

To: Managing Director

From: Chief Accountant

Date: 24 May 20XX

Ref: AHS SA

(a) **The performance of AHS SA**

The income statement

A comparison of 20X5 with 20X4 is useful in highlighting trends in income and expenditure.

	20X4 *FFr million*	*20X5* *FFr million*	*% increase*
Material purchased	400	740	
De-stocking of materials	40	90	
Material cost	440	830	89%
Labour cost	285	500	75%
Depreciation	150	200	33%
Current assets written off	20	30	50%
Other operating expenses	40	50	25%
Finished goods stock increase	(80)	(120)	50%
Cost of sales	855	1,490	
Sales	1,270	1,890	49%
Operating profit before other operating income	415	400	
Profit rate on turnover	32%	21%	

- Turnover has increased significantly over the year, showing a 49% rise. However, profitability has fallen from 32% to 21%, apparently due to a disproportionate rise in material and labour costs which have increased by 89% and 75% respectively.

- Depreciation has risen by 33%, and there is a corresponding 39% increase in fixed assets.

- Other operating income has increased by 50%. As there are no investments shown in the balance sheet this income may be attributable to rent of property, leasing or other sundry activities.

- Interest costs have doubled whilst the debt to equity ratio has remained at 22% (20X5: $\frac{425}{1,925}$; 20X4: $\frac{350}{1,540}$) and trade and other creditors have only increased by 22.5%.

Balance sheet

- Overall, stocks have increased by 25%. This increase comprises a FFr 120 million increase in finished goods stocks and a FFr 90 million decrease in raw materials stocks. Both figures are significant and this trend is apparent in both 20X4 and 20X5. It suggests that the company is moving away from manufacturing, preferring to buy-in the goods ready made.

- Trade debtors have increased by 80%, outstripping the increase in sales. This could be due to the increased sales occurring towards the end of the financial year, or a longer credit period taken by customers. The debtors collection period has increased from 28 days ($\frac{100}{1,270} \times 365$) to 35 ($\frac{180}{1,890} \times 365$) days in 20X5, assuming that all sales are on credit.

- Creditors have increased by 13% whilst materials costs have increased by 89%. Again, this could be explained by increased purchases in the earlier part of the year or a decreased period of credit taken. Calculation of a creditors payment period is relatively meaningless without an analysis between current and long term creditors.

- Shares have been issued at a premium of 100%.

Cash flow

- The cash position has worsened considerably over the year, from a balance of FFr 200 million to FFr 20 million. This decrease is analysed below:

FF million	
Flows giving rise to an increase in cash:	
Retained profit with depreciation added back (185 + 200)	385
Increased creditors	75
Decreased prepayments	20
Share capital issues	200
	680
Flows giving rise to decreased cash:	
Purchases of plant (550 + 200)	750
Increased stock	30
Increased debtors	80
	860
Overall decrease in cash (680 – 860)	180

Conclusion

The company's liquidity situation gives cause for concern; the cash level needs to be increased by reducing stock levels, collecting debts more quickly and delaying payments to creditors. If this does not happen the company would need to increase its borrowings in order to pay taxes and other creditors.

(b) **Comparison of XYZ plc and AHS SA**

Direct comparison of the companies is meaningless without further explanation of their accounting policies; different policies may have been adopted in respect of, for example:

- depreciation;
- stock valuation;
- fixed asset valuation; and
- bad and doubtful debts.

Such inconsistency would prevent direct comparison of profit and the balance sheet items involved. There are a number of figures in the income statement of AHS SA which are not fully explained. Further information is required to ascertain:

- how 'sale of goods' is computed;
- the sources of 'other operating income';
- the basis of the tax computation;
- the basis for current assets written off;
- the whereabouts of dividends, if any; and
- the contents of 'other operating expenses'.

Without this information the profit figure cannot be understood.

The balance sheet also presents problems for comparison:

- 'legal reserves' may arise for different reasons under French law compared with the Companies Act;
- local customs regarding trade credit may affect a comparison of debtors and creditors; and
- lack of analysis between current and long term creditors prevents the calculation of meaningful gearing, current and acid test ratios.

71 Badgo plc

REPORT

To: Non-Executive Director

From: Chief Accountant

Subject: Draft consolidated financial statements for the year ended 31 December 20X9

Date: 24 May 20Y1

As requested, I am responding to your questions about the draft consolidated financial statements for the year ended 31 December 20X9. Supporting calculations are shown in the Appendix.

(a) **Fall in profits and dividend for the year**

There has been a modest increase of 5% in turnover, which you have correctly noted, while the gross profit margin has remained at 30%. One of the reasons for the fall in profits is that operating expenses have increased by one third during 20X9. In addition, interest charges have increased by 30% during the year, as a result of increases in borrowings. It was necessary for us to raise additional finance in order to acquire our 35% investment in Stateside Inc and this was partly in the form of long term loans and a 110% increase in the overdraft.

The total dividend proposed for 20X9 has fallen by one quarter compared with that of 20X8. In addition, we have issued a further 100 million shares and this means that the dividend per share has halved. Dividend cover remains at just under 2 times. There are good reasons for this, despite the reduction in the dividend per share. If we distributed all our earnings for the year, we would not retain sufficient profits in the business to finance future operations. In addition, because of the current level of the bank overdraft we would have difficulty in financing a large cash payment. Paying the existing proposed dividend of £60 million will strain our cash resources considerably.

(b) **Increase in retained profits**

As you have noted, retained profit for the year ended 31 December 20X9 is £57m while the profit and loss account reserve in the balance sheet has increased by £62m (£321m – £259m).

The balance on the profit and loss account reserve has been increased by the retained profit for the year of £57m and also by a currency translation gain of £5m. This additional gain results from our investment in Stateside Inc, which was translated from US$ into sterling at the date of acquisition. On 31 December it was subsequently revalued (retranslated) at the rate of exchange ruling at that date. We have recognised an exchange gain of £5m because the movement in currency between those two dates was favourable. This contrasts with the year ended 31 December 20X8, when we recognised an exchange loss of £4m on our short term foreign currency investments.

Currency translation gains and losses are reported in the Statement of total recognised gains and losses (STRGL). This shows any gains and losses that are not recognised in the profit and loss account. The currency translation gain cannot be included in the profit and loss account because it is not realised and therefore is not yet distributable as a dividend.

(c) **Carrying value and financing of investment in Stateside Inc at 31 December 20X9**

You have noted that during the year the group paid £380m for its investment in Stateside Inc. However, this cannot simply be included in the balance sheet at its cost, because the group owns a significant proportion (35%) of Stateside Inc's equity share capital. This means that the group can exercise significant influence over Stateside Inc. Therefore FRS 9 *Associates and joint ventures* requires it to be included in the consolidated financial statements under the equity method.

Under the equity method, the carrying value of the investment is shown as the group's share of the net assets of Stateside Inc at 31 December 20X9. Since the date of acquisition Stateside Inc has earned profits and therefore the carrying value of the investment includes the group's share of these, as well as the exchange gain discussed above.

You have also noted that the acquisition was partly financed from the funds raised from shareholders during the year. The company issued 100 million shares at £2 each, raising £200 million. It raised a further £100 million by selling short term investments (assuming that these were sold at net book value) and borrowed an additional £24 million in the form of long term loans. An increase in the bank overdraft provided the remaining finance. Capital gearing (including the bank overdraft) has remained at around 33%, which is not yet alarmingly high. However, it is not appropriate to use the bank overdraft to finance long term investments as, in theory, they are repayable on demand.

*(**Tutorial Note:** There is insufficient information to reconcile the cost of the investment of £380 million with the carrying value of £400 million at 31 December 20X9.)*

(d) **Financial statements of Stateside Inc**

It is quite possible that the financial statements of Stateside Inc in US dollars report a loss while the sterling accounts report a profit. The difference is not caused by the translation from US dollars to sterling. The company's results would have been translated either at the closing rate (the exchange rate ruling at 31 December 20X9) or at the average rate for the period since the acquisition.

Stateside Inc's individual financial statements would have been prepared in accordance with accounting standards and generally accepted accounting principles in the United States (US GAAP). Although US GAAP is broadly similar to the accounting principles and standards generally accepted in the UK (UK GAAP), there are still some significant differences. US GAAP is generally more conservative and prescriptive than UK GAAP. Users of the consolidated financial statements need useful information about the group's financial performance and position and therefore the same accounting policies must be applied consistently throughout the group. Therefore it was necessary to adjust Stateside Inc's financial statements so that they complied with UK GAAP before they were included in the consolidated financial statements. The difference could be explained by preparing a reconciliation of the effect of all differences between US GAAP and UK GAAP.

I hope that this report has explained the various issues that you have raised. Please do not hesitate to contact me if you have any other queries about the draft consolidated financial statements.

Appendix: ratios

		20X9	***20X8***
Gross profit margin	$\frac{\text{Gross profit}}{\text{Turnover}}$	$\frac{600}{2,000}$ **= 30%**	$\frac{570}{1,900}$ **= 30%**
Operating expenses/sales	$\frac{\text{Operating expenses}}{\text{Turnover}}$	$\frac{400}{2,000}$ **= 20%**	$\frac{300}{1,900}$ **= 15.8%**
Dividend cover	$\frac{\text{Profit after tax}}{\text{Dividends}}$	$\frac{117}{60}$ **= 1.95 times**	$\frac{155}{80}$ **= 1.94 times**
Dividend per share	$\frac{\text{Dividends}}{\text{No of shares}}$	$\frac{60}{300}$ **= 20 pence**	$\frac{80}{200}$ **= 40 pence**
Capital gearing	$\frac{\text{Long term liabilities + overdraft}}{\text{Capital employed (inc overdraft)}}$	$\frac{351}{1,072}$ **= 33%**	$\frac{237}{696}$ **= 34%**

72 Stateside plc

Key answer tips

In part (a) the requirement is to discuss, so you must cover a range of points.

Approach part (b) by describing the standard UK accounting treatment for each item. This will give you the reason for each adjustment.

(a) There is no definitive answer and credit will be given for valid points raised.

Potential benefits of greater harmonisation include:

(i) **A user's perspective**

Cross border investment is increasing and it is important that potential investors are not misled by the financial statements. For example, there could be an assumption that the liquidity position of a company that makes a full provision for deferred tax liabilities is worse than that of a company that is only required to provide an amount that is likely to crystallise as a liability.

(ii) **A preparer's perspective**

There is an increase in the cost of preparing financial statements that need to be adjusted to comply with different national accounting standards.

Obstacles hindering greater harmonisation include:

(i) **Different legal systems**

Countries vary in the amount of detailed legislation on accounting that has been enacted. In Europe for example this meant that prior to the issue of EC Directives accounting requirements in the UK differed substantially from those in France.

(ii) **Different capital financing systems**

Types of business organisation and their financing differ internationally and it therefore follows that if financiers and owners differ then the primary users of accounting information will differ. The rule makers in the US and UK regard the existing and potential investors as the primary users. However, there are other ways of financing business and capital provided by banks may be very significant. In Germany and Japan the banks are important owners of companies as well as providers of debt finance. This enables them to appoint directors and they will therefore be able to obtain information other than that which is included in the published annual report.

Where there are fewer outsider shareholders external reporting has been largely for the purposes of government, as tax collectors or controllers of the economy.

(iii) **Degree to which taxation regulations determine accounting measurements**

In some countries the tax rules are the accounting rules. For example, although depreciation in the UK differs from the capital allowance for tax purposes, in other countries the accounting depreciation is the same as the equivalent of the capital allowance for tax purposes.

(iv) **Differences in the size and competence of the accounting/auditing profession**

The lack of a substantial body of private investors and public companies in some countries means that the need for and status of the auditors is much smaller than in the US or UK. Also there is an impact on the type of accounting that is or could be practised. Without a strong profession there is a limit to the extent to which national accounting standards can be developed.

(v) **Environmental/cultural factors**

These include educational standards which can be an important factor in developing countries; political factors where there is central control over the accounting and reporting system and cultural factors where for example cultures that tend towards secrecy are unlikely to adopt full disclosure-based financial reporting practices.

(b) (i) *Capitalised interest*
Under FRS 15 *Tangible fixed assets* companies have a choice of writing off or capitalising and amortising. Stateside plc appears to have written off interest costs. In the US the interest relating to this fixed asset would be capitalised and amortised with an amortisation charge of £5m.

Merger accounting adjusted to acquisition accounting
There has been a merger during the year which has satisfied UK criteria for treatment as a merger. The adjustment indicates that this has not however satisfied the US criteria. Consequently pre-acquisition profits of £150m are eliminated on reconciliation, together with additional depreciation and amortisation of goodwill of £200m.

(ii) *Capitalised interest*
The equity will be increased by any unamortised balance outstanding.

Merger accounting adjusted to acquisition accounting
The equity will be increased by any increase in net assets (most likely) and decreased by any decrease in net assets (unlikely) arising from fair value adjustments. The equity would also be increased by the unamortised amount of any consolidated goodwill that would arise under acquisition accounting.

(iii) *Proposed dividend*
The shareholders' equity will be increased by the amount of the proposed dividend because in the UK dividends are accounted for in the fiscal year to which they relate.

(c) (i) Year to 31.5.X4: Statement of total recognised gains and losses

This will disclose the £10m gain

Year to 31.5.X4: Profit and loss account

There will be a depreciation charge of £3m based on revalued amount

Year to 31.5.X4: Note of historical cost profits and losses

Difference between a historical cost depreciation charge and the actual depreciation charge of the year calculated on the revalued amount £1m

Year to 31.5.X4: Revaluation reserve

A revaluation reserve of £10m will be created via the Statement of total recognised gains and losses and £1m will be transferred to realised profit

Year to 31.5.X5: Note of historical cost profits and losses

Realisation of property gains	£8m
Profit and loss account profit [£40m – (£27m – £3m)]	£16m
Working note: Total = £40m – (£20m – £2m – £2m)	£24m
Difference between a historical cost depreciation charge and the actual depreciation charge of the year calculated on the revalued amount	£1m

Year to 31.5.X5: Revaluation reserve

There will be a transfer from the revaluation reserve of £9m to realised profits comprising £1m excess depreciation and the £8m shown above.

(ii) The reasons lie in the ASB's balance sheet approach to the recognition of assets, liabilities, gains and losses.

According to the Statement of Principles, recognition of a gain is triggered where a past event indicates that there has been a measurable change in assets which has not been offset by an equal change in liabilities unless the change relates to a transaction with the entity's owners, in which case a contribution from owners or distribution to owners will be recognised.
Gains which are earned but not realised are recognised in the statement of total recognised gains and loses. Gains which are realised are recognised in the profit and loss account. However, it follows from this approach that gains should not be recognised twice i.e. at the point of revaluation and at the point of realisation. Once an asset has been revalued in an entity's balance sheet any subsequent transactions must be based on the balance sheet carrying amount of that asset.

The ASB has taken account of the fact that it is common practice for companies to produce modified historical cost basis and that there is currently no mandatory requirement for regular revaluations by requiring a note of historical cost profits and losses. This note will reconcile the modified profit to the pure historical cost profit where material differences exist.

The ASB stance might be seen to be at odds with the statutory approach of using historical cost accounts to determine capital maintenance and distributable profits. However, the ASB is basing its approach on the view that the income statement should be primarily concerned with the measurement of performance which can be distorted when reported figures are not related to current values. In such cases, there can be over- or under-statement of performance as measured by profits and return on assets.

(***Tutorial note:*** This question and answer have been slightly amended to reflect the changes to accounting for goodwill, tangible fixed assets and deferred tax introduced by FRS 10 'Goodwill and intangible assets', FRS 15 'Tangible fixed assets' and FRS 19 'Deferred tax'.*)*

73 Morgan plc

Key answer tips

Start by setting up a columnar working to adjust the financial statements (see answer). Take each of the points in the scenario in turn. Do any calculations required and determine the adjustment(s). Enter the adjustments on the main working schedule. Your answer should not only show the calculations, but explain the reasons for them. (See the requirement.) If time allows, set out the results of your calculations using the UK Group plc ratios from the question as comparative figures. This will make it easier for you to compare the two sets of ratios in part (b). You are *not* required to prepare revised accounts for publication.

In part (b) your answer should not simply compare the two sets of ratios, but should concentrate on the implications of the revisions to the Overseas Group ratios.

You are not required to discuss accounting policy differences in part (c). Instead, your answer should describe and explain economic and cultural considerations, with examples.

(a) **Revised Financial Ratios of Overseas Group Inc**

			UK group plc from question
Current ratio	$\frac{92,800}{79,400}$	1.17 to 1	1.75 to 1
Stock turnover	$\frac{(110,100-6,000)}{39,520}$	2.62 times	6.5 times
Average collection period unchanged		85.5 days	41.7 days
Interest cover	$\frac{7,052}{1,036}$	6.81 times	6 times
Profit margin	$\frac{6,016\times100}{132,495}=$	4.5%	5.4%
Return on total assets	$\frac{7,052\times100}{243,682}=$	2.9%	7.4%
Return on net worth	$\frac{6,016\times100}{64,401}=$	9.3%	12.2%
Gearing ratio	$\frac{99,881}{243,682}=$	41.0%	27.7%
Price earnings ratio	$\frac{147}{19.1}=$	7.7	15

Earnings per share calculation

		Weighted	Total
Shares issued 1.6.96 - purchase of subsidiary	8,000	1	8,000
Shares issued - options	100	6/12	50
Balance	21,900		21,900
	30,000		29,950

Earnings per share $\frac{5,710}{29,950}$ ie 19.1c

Workings (all in $000)

Overseas Group Inc
Summarised Financial Statements
Period ending 31 May 20X7

Balance sheet

		Purchase of subsidiary	*Software*	*Share option*	*ESOT*	*Stock and extraordinary item*	*Total*
Fixed assets	135,200	9,432	(750)		7,000		150,882
Current assets							
Stock	42,020					(2,500)	39,520
Debtors	31,050						31,050
Cash	22,230						22,230
	95,300						92,800
Current liabilities	(79,400)						(79,400)
Long term debt	(99,700)	(165)					(99,881)
		(16)					
Shareholders funds	51,400						64,401
Share capital	30,000						30,000
Other reserves inc		(40)					
minority interest	20,806	10,000		(75)	7,000	(9,000)	28,691
Profit for year	594	(60)	(750)	75		6,500	5,710
		(16)					
	51,400	(633)					64,401

Profit and loss account

Profit before interest and tax	1,840	(100)	(750)	75		120	7,052
		(633)				6,500	
Interest	(1,020)	(16)					(1,036)
Profit before tax	820						6,016
Tax	(200)					(30)	(230)
Profit/loss for year before minority interests	620						5,786
Minority interests	(80)	40				(36)	(76)

Earnings available for ordinary shareholders	540		5,710
Extraordinary item	54	(54)	
Net profit	594		5,710
EPS	1.8c		19.1c

Computer software

In the UK the development costs of computer software products are expensed in the year in which they are incurred hence fixed assets will be reduced by the costs not yet written off and profit will be reduced also.

Share options and ESOT

Under FRS 4 the share options should be recorded at their discounted price i.e. the net proceeds received. Hence the discount on the market price has to be adjusted to allow for UK GAAP.

DR Other reserves (Share premium a/c)	75
CR Profit/loss account	75
Market price	250
Proceeds	(175)
Directors remuneration to be eliminated	75

In the UK UITF 13 states that ESOT's should be recorded as fixed asset investments and not deducted from shareholders funds.

Purchase of subsidiary

Purchase consideration

8 million ordinary shares of $1 - value $2	16,000
Cash	2,000
Deferred consideration (200 discounted for two years)	165
	18,165
less fair value of assets acquired 60% of 25,000	15,000
Goodwill	3,165
Less: Amortisation (3,165 ÷ 5)	(633)
	2,532

So therefore the negative goodwill of 2,000 should be added back to fixed assets. The adjustments required in the financial statements of Overseas Group Inc are therefore:

Fixed assets-	negative goodwill added back	2,000
	-revaluation	5,000
	increase depreciation	(100)
	goodwill	2,532
		9,432

Profit and loss account

There will be a charge for depreciation on the increased value of the fixed asset ($100) and this will affect the minority interest (40% of 100 i.e. 40). Also there will be a notional charge of (10% of 165 for the interest on the long term loan i.e. 16) and the amortisation charge for the year of 633.

Other reserves

Share premium	8,000
Minority interest 40% of 5,000	2,000
	10,000

Extraordinary item

The extraordinary profit of $54 would be treated as normal profit under FRS 3 'Reporting Financial Performance'. Therefore it should be included in the pre tax and pre minority interest calculation of profit. Therefore as the holding company's share of this item is $54, the minority's share must be $36 ($\frac{40}{60}$ × 54), thus the pre tax and pre minority interest value of this item will be:

	HC	*MI*	*Total*
Extraordinary profit	72	48	120
Tax	18	12	30
	54	36	90

Stock

Closing stock adjustment	(2,500)
Opening stock adjustment	9,000
Net profit increase	6,500

The policy of 'marking to market' value has developed in the UK where commodities are being dealt with on a recognised market and dealing in such commodities is the company's principal activity. In this case however in order to ensure consistency, the stock should be valued at the lower of cost and net realisable value. The latter value can be equated in this case to market value.

The result of this adjustment will be as follows:

DR	Opening reserves	9,000
CR	Cost of sales	6,500
	Closing stock	2,500

(b) The revision of the financial ratios for the differing accounting policies has enhanced those ratios determined by the pre tax profitability of the company. There has been little change in the liquidity ratios which seem to indicate that the UK Group plc is more liquid and solvent than the Overseas Group Inc. The interest cover ratio has been significantly improved. The profit margin, return on total assets and return on net worth ratios were quite poor compared to UK group plc prior to the revision and therefore the improvement in these ratios may have a major impact on the decision to purchase one of the companies.

Overseas Group Inc is significantly higher geared than UK Group plc although the adjustment for differing accounting practices has in fact slightly reduced the level of gearing of Overseas Group Inc. The PE ratios of the two companies are significantly different. The adjustments have affected the PE ratio of Overseas Group Inc to the extent that it has been significantly reduced.

Overall it would appear that the UK group is more liquid, more profitable and has a lower gearing ratio. However, although one might automatically advise Morgan plc to acquire UK Group plc there are other factors which ought to be taken into account when analysing such ratios. These factors are set out in part (c) of the answers.

(c) Financial ratios may be appropriate measures of risk efficiency and profitability in a UK context but they may be misinterpreted when applied to an international situation because an investor may not understand the foreign environment and business conditions. Restatement of foreign companies financial statements for UK GAAP does have some effect on observed ratio differences as is evidenced by part (a) and (b) of this answer.

However, in many cases these accounting effects only explain a minor portion of the reasons for difference in ratios. Highly geared companies may be the norm in the country concerned. The relationship between the banks/loan creditors may be quite close even to the extent of the bank holding shares in the company. In this situation a bank would be loathe to impose financial penalties for slow payment of a debt. A key bank official may be on the board of directors to provide assistance in financial matters. The nature of business finance may therefore be quite different with long-term debt being more like an equity shareholding.

If this is the case then interest is essentially a dividend and lower interest coverage ratios will not therefore be viewed with as much concern. Institutional and cultural factors can cause liquidity ratios to differ without necessarily changing the basic financial risk being measured. The low current ratio of Overseas Group plc may indicate a weak short-term debt paying ability. However, if short-term interest rates are more attractive than long-term interest rates and short-term debts are rolled over by banks into long-term loans, then such a low current ratio does not indicate corporate illiquidity. In the UK, the use of short-term debt to finance long-term assets is frowned upon but this may be the norm in the overseas country.

Debtors collection periods may also reflect differences in business customs. Repayment terms may be longer for several reasons. For example economic downturns may result, not in tighter credit controls being exercised but exactly the opposite may occur in order to ensure more business stability. Lower stock turnover statistics may be indicative of employment policy rather than obsolete stock or slow sales. During slack periods, companies may prefer to continue production rather than make workers redundant. Short-term profitability may not be the main concern of corporate shareholders. If banks, customers and suppliers own shares in the company they will be more interested in strengthening the business rather than short-term stock market profits. If management are more secure in their employment, then short-term profits will not be as important to them. Companies such as Overseas Inc may wish to increase their market share on the basis that profits will come in the long-term. In order to do this, profit margins may suffer due to intense price competition. Hence this may be the reason for Overseas Inc's profitability ratios. Thus it is important that financial analysts not only understand major differences in accounting principles between the UK and other countries but also national business and financial customs. Additionally appropriate country and industry ratio aggregates may give analysts useful standards against which to compare and interpret ratios on a global basis.

74 Pailing

Key answertips

Set out your reconciliation statement in the format shown below and take each adjustment in turn, calculating the effect on net profit and on capital and reserves.

(a) (i) The main reasons why multinational companies might wish to adopt IAS are as follows

(a) In order to raise foreign finance by obtaining several stock market listings.

(b) To reduce the analytical cost associated with global investment and increase interest in non-US. based shares. At present there are costs involved in adjusting financial statements for differences in accounting practice.

(c) To improve the corporate image by publishing better quality financial information in some cases.

(d) To enhance financial transparency and reduce the practice of 'financial principle shopping'.

(e) To enhance the internal management of the company by the use of a common accounting language in the management of their operations. Irrational decision-making may be reduced.

(f) To improve comparability of financial information across borders. The rigid application and enforcement of IAS may be a problem.

(g) To increase the international visibility of a company with competitors. Customers and financial markets. Relatively few companies prepare their accounts using IAS and those that do use the standards receive wide publicity.

(h) To maintain the competitiveness of a company in comparison to others who use IAS, providing a reliable basis for corporate analysis.

(ii) The problems associated with IAS which may act as a barrier to their widespread adoption can be described as follows:

(a) Any delay in the acceptance of IAS by the United States may be seen as a dilution of their credibility. IAS have been accused of lacking 'appropriate rigour and detail' by US regulators.

(b) Some companies may not wish to lose the flexibility of their current accounting practices and apply IAS in full.

(c) Certain IAS allow alternative treatments through the 'benchmark' and 'allowed alternative' accounting practices. This can result in a loss of comparability and consistency of financial information.

(d) Some companies may lose a competitive advantage if they comply with IAS as there may be enhanced disclosure or items being brought onto the balance sheet.

(e) There will be a significant cost in converting information systems and training corporate personnel in the use of IAS.

(f) Many countries have a poor record in enforcing standards and this will lead to uncertainty in the quality of financial information produced. An audit by a 'Big 5' firm would enhance the credibility of such accounts.

(g) IAS do not deal with specialised industries and thus local rules may apply which might dilute the standards. Similarly national tax authorities may not accept IAS for taxation purposes.

(h) IAS do not lay down comprehensive guidelines for corporate governance, or any legal framework. This may result in local conflict with certain IAS and result in the modification of the standard.

(b) (i)

		£m	£m
Net profit for the year to 31 March 20X0		89	
Capital and reserves as at 31 March 20X0			225
(i)	**Change in Accounting Policy** Under UK GAAP the change in accounting policy would be adjusted against opening reserves. Thus current years profits (30–3) would be restated but the capital and reserves would remain the same	27	
(ii)	**Minority Interest** The profit for the period would remain the same as would the capital and reserves.		
	Increase in net assets		1
	Increase in minority interest (25% of 28 – 24)		(1)

(iii)	**Negative Goodwill** Negative goodwill arises on the acquisition of Odd. Purchase consideration (£1 6m) - net assets acquired (75% of £28m) i.e. £5m. Under UK GAAP the negative goodwill should be written off over the life of the non-monetary assets (five years) not against current profits unless the negative goodwill is in excess of the fair values of the non-monetary assets. Negative goodwill is presented as a negative asset immediately after positive goodwill.		
	Negative goodwill reinstated	(5)	(5)
	Negative goodwill written off over five years.	1	1
(iv)	**Gain on sale** The gain on sale shown in the group profit and loss account should be £(40 – 36)m i.e. £4 million not £8 million.	(4)	
	The exchange gain held in the exchange reserve cannot go to the profit and loss account as it has already passed through the STRGL Therefore it should be transferred to profit and loss reserve.	(3)	
		105	221

Candidates will not be penalised for commencing the write off of goodwill in the year to 31 March 20X1.

(ii) In theory, changes in accounting polices should not have any impact on the business decisions to buy a company as the underlying economic events have not changed but in reality this is not often the case. For example, the financial statements of the Rover group were turned from a profit of £147 million in the period 20X4 - 1997 to a loss of £363 million when German GAAP was applied to the UK financial statements and yet the underlying economic events were unchanged. As a result the image of Rover was tarnished by the change in policies and there was a threat of closure.

However, a knowledge of the differences in accounting practices of countries is essential in order to ensure that any business decision, which is at least partially made on the basis of financial information, is an informed decision. If Klese is considering the purchase of a UK or a non UK company then their financial statements should be, if possible, drawn up using common accounting principles. There are recent examples of differences in international accounting practices having economic consequences.

Thus on restatement the current year's profit is increased to £105 million with the subsequent impact on key ratios such as Return on Capital Employed (ROCE) and Earnings per share. The ROCE increases from 39.5% to 47.5%. If the purchase of the business is to be based on financial statistics then this change in the ROCE (and other ratios) could affect the decision significantly.

75 Daxon plc

Key answer tips

Your answer to part (a) should clearly state the directors' responsibilities. This is the issue that most concerns the readers of the memo. You are not required to discuss the Directors' Report.

In part (b), include a range of points both for and against a separate regime for small companies. You are not required to describe the requirements for small company financial statements or the contents of the FRSSE.

(a) **Memo to Board of directors**

From: Accountant

Dated: December 20X5

Following the enquiry concerning the directors' responsibilities statement that I included in the draft of the 20X5 annual accounts, I have set out the following information to explain how the need for the statement has arisen in order for the company to be following best practice.

(i) *The background to the inclusion in the annual report of a directors' responsibilities statement*

Major changes in corporate governance disclosures were recommended in the report of the Committee on the financial aspects of Corporate Governance (published by the Cadbury Committee in December 1992). In the report, the committee recommended that listed companies should state in their annual report whether they comply with a Code of Best Practice drafted by the committee, giving reasons for non-compliance.

The recommendations included a statement by the directors of their responsibility for preparing the accounts; a report on the effectiveness of their system of internal control; a report explicitly on whether the business is a going concern.

The Auditing Practices Board has included reference to directors' responsibilities in SAS 600 *Auditors' reports on financial statements* with a requirement that where there was not an adequate description of directors' relevant responsibilities, the auditors' report should include such a description (SAS 600.3). The sample wording in Appendix 3 of SAS 600 effectively covers the items in the draft presented to the directors of Daxon plc. The effect of this is that, if the board omit to do so, the statement will be included by the auditors in their report.

However, the essential point is that the primary responsibility for the preparation of financial statements lies with the directors; the auditors' responsibility is to express an opinion on the statements. The responsibilities statement is intended to emphasise this fact.

The requirement to include a statement is to give emphasis to the fact that the financial statements are the responsibility of the directors and, in this way, to reduce the expectation gap.

There is a view that users of the annual report have not distinguished between the directors' responsibilities and the auditors' responsibilities and have assumed that the audit responsibility was far greater than was actually the case.
There is also a view that the inclusion of the statement in the audit report is merely an attempt by the audit profession to transfer responsibility to another party. However, it is important to note that the acknowledgement of directors' responsibilities stemmed from the Cadbury Committee and not merely from the Auditing Practices Board.

Inclusion of a directors responsibilities statement is not mandatory for the company but it was my view that there was merit in bringing to the board's attention the changes that have been occurring in corporate governance and to make Daxon plc's annual report follow best financial reporting practices.

(ii) *How the board can determine whether the financial statements give a true and fair view*

There has always been a duty on the board to ensure that the financial statements are true and fair. However, it has in the past been the practice to regard this as a matter for the auditor. Inclusion in the directors' responsibility is merely recognition of a long standing duty.

Perhaps it would be helpful to first review the criteria for determining whether financial statements provide a true and fair view which is a step that we have not previously taken. The criteria are:

(i) They are prepared in accordance with accepted accounting principles.

(ii) The accounting principles applied are appropriate to the business i.e. it is not sufficient to be able to demonstrate that such principles have been applied by other companies and other accounting firms – they also need to be appropriate to the particular company.

The Foreword to Accounting Standards para 16/17 emphasise this approach in stating that compliance with accounting standards will normally be necessary for financial statements to give a true and fair view but that in applying accounting standards it is important to be guided by the spirit and reasoning behind them – the spirit and reasoning being set out in the individual FRSs and are based on the ASB's Statement of Principles for Financial Reporting.

(iii) They exhibit the qualitative characteristics of financial information set out in Chapter 3 of the Statement of Principles e.g. the two primary characteristics relating to content of relevance and reliability, the primary characteristics relating to presentation, such as comparability and understandability.

(iv) They provide sufficient information for the intended users to be able to comprehend and interpret i.e. there is an implication that the financial statements are a reflection of the economic position, regardless of particular accepted accounting policies and rules, which convey the nature of the business to a prospective or current shareholder with no inside knowledge of the company.

This latter criterion is generally referred to as reflecting the substance of transactions.

It is in order to reflect the substance of transactions that there is a requirement that, where the application of existing standards or statutes is not considered by the directors to result in a true and fair view, they are not to be applied. In such a case, there is a requirement to explain the departure. The nature of the disclosure is set out in RS F18 which effectively requires an explanation as to why the prescribed treatment would not result in a true and fair view.

The board's responsibility is therefore to ensure that the accountant in preparing the accounts has had regard to statutory, mandatory and voluntary pronouncements. The board's responsibility would be discharged by ensuring that the company employs appropriate professional staff and ensuring that their technical knowledge and competence is kept current.

Conclusion

Whilst the company is under no mandatory requirement to include such a statement in its annual report, it could be beneficial for the board to consider the proposals and consider their possible impact on current practices within the company.

(b) There has long been an argument that small companies should not be required to apply standards because they are unduly burdensome. However, the view expressed in UK GAAP has much merit in that it approaches the debate from a different aspect. It puts forward the view that it is necessary first to establish a sensible definition for a small company for financial reporting purposes, in contrast to the ASC's definition based on arbitrary size criteria. The definition would not assume that small companies are merely smaller versions of big companies but would relate to the difference in fundamental criteria i.e. the composition of its membership and management.

Existing standards cover recognition, measurement and disclosure. The appropriate approach to the question of standards for small companies is not to assess the extent to which the requirements attaching to listed companies should be relaxed but to assess what would be appropriate recognition, measurement and disclosure. This would recognise that the general purpose statements prepared for listed companies are intended for the range of users listed in the statement of principles whereas small companies might be preparing accounts for owner/managers, the bank and the Revenue. In the latter case, none of the users might be interested in information prepared to satisfy the information needs of such a broad spectrum of users.

***(Tutorial note**:* Since this question was originally set, the ASB has issued the Financial Reporting Standard for Smaller Entities (FRSSE). However, Daxon plc would *not* be able to adopt the FRSSE as it is a public company (and therefore not a 'small' company as defined by the Companies Acts.)

Section 9

NEW SYLLABUS EXAMINATIONS

Pilot Paper 2001 Questions

Section A – This question is compulsory and MUST be attempted

1 Portal Group

Portal Group, a public limited company, has prepared the following group cash flow statement for the year ended 31 December 2000:

Portal Group
Group Statement of cash flows for the year ended 31 December 2000 (draft)

	£m	£m
Net cash inflow from operating activities		875
Returns on investments and servicing of finance		
Interest received	26	
Interest paid	(9)	
Minority interest	(40)	(23)
Taxation		31
Capital expenditure		
Purchase of tangible fixed assets	(380)	
Disposal and transfer of fixed assets at carrying value	1,585	1,205
Acquisitions and disposals		
Disposal of subsidiary	(25)	
Purchase of interest in joint venture	(225)	(250)
Net cash inflow before use of management of liquid resources and financing		1,838
Management of liquid resources		
Decrease in short term deposits		(143)
Increase in cash in the period		1,695

The accountant has asked your advice on certain technical matters relating to the preparation of the group cash flow statement. Additionally the accountant has asked you to prepare a presentation for the directors on the usefulness and meaning of cash flow statements generally and specifically on the group cash flow statement of Portal.

The accountant has informed you that the actual change in the cash balance for the period is £165 million, which does not reconcile with the figures in the draft group cash flow statement above of £1,695 million.

The accountant feels that the reasons for the difference are the incorrect treatment of several elements of the cash flow statement of which he has little technical knowledge. The following information relates to these elements:

(a) Portal has disposed of a subsidiary company, Web plc, during the year. At the date of disposal (1 June 2000) the following balance sheet was prepared for Web plc:

		£m	£m
Tangible fixed assets	– valuation		340
	– depreciation		(30)
			310
Stocks		60	
Debtors		50	
Cash at bank and in hand		130	
		240	
Creditors: amounts falling due within one year (including taxation £25 million)		(130)	110
			420

	£m
Called up share capital	100
Profit and loss account	320
	420

The loss on the sale of the subsidiary in the group accounts comprised:

		£m
Sale proceeds	– ordinary shares	300
	– cash	75
		375
Net assets sold (80% of 420)		(336)
Goodwill		(64)
Loss on sale		(25)

The accountant was unsure as to how to deal with the above disposal and has simply included the above loss in the cash flow statement without any further adjustments.

(b) During the year, Portal has transferred several of its tangible assets to a newly created company, Site plc, which is owned jointly with another company.

The following information relates to the accounting for the investment in Site plc:

		£m
Purchase cost	– tangible non-current assets transferred	200
	– cash	25
		225
Dividend received		(10)
Profit for year on joint venture after tax		55
Revaluation of tangible non current assets		30
Closing balance per balance sheet – Site plc		300

The cash flow statement showed the cost of purchasing a stake in Site plc of £225 million.

(c) The taxation amount in the cash flow statement is the difference between the opening and closing balances on the taxation account. The charge for taxation in the income statement is £191 million of which £20 million related to the taxation on the joint venture.

(d) Included in the cash flow figure for the disposal of tangible non-current assets is the sale and leaseback of certain land and buildings. The sale proceeds of the land and buildings were £1,000 million in the form of an 8% loan note repayable in 2002 at a premium of 5%. The total profit on the sale of fixed assets, including the land and buildings, was £120 million.

(e) The minority interest figure in the statement comprised the difference between the opening and closing balance sheet totals. The profit attributable to the minority interest for the year was £75 million.

(f) The cash generated from operations is the profit before taxation adjusted for the balance sheet movement in stocks, debtors and ccreditors and the depreciation charge for the year. The interest receivable credited to the profit and loss account was £27 million and the interest payable was £19 million.

Required:

(a) Prepare a revised Group cash flow statement for Portal plc, taking into account notes (a) to (f) above. **(18 marks)**

(b) Prepare a brief presentation on the usefulness and information content of group cash flow statements generally and specifically on the group cash flow statement of Portal plc. **(7 marks)**

(Total: 25 marks)

Section B – THREE questions ONLY to be attempted

2 Axe

The financial director of Axe, a public limited company, has heard of the recent discussions over accounting for leases but is unsure as to the current position. Additionally the company has undergone certain transactions in the year and the director requires assistance as to how these transactions should be dealt with in the financial statements. The financial year end of the company is 31 December 2000.
On 1 January 2000, Axe sold its computer software and hardware to Lake, a public limited company, for £310 million. The assets were leased back for four years under an operating lease whereby Lake agreed to maintain and upgrade the computer facilities. The fair value of the assets sold was £190 million and the carrying value based on depreciated historic cost was £90 million. The lease rental payments were £45 million per annum, payable on 1 January in advance, which represented a premium of fifty per cent of the normal cost of such a lease.

Additionally, on 1 January 2000 Axe sold plant with a carrying value of £200 million. The fair value and selling price of the plant was £330 million. The plant was immediately leased back over four years which is the remaining useful life of the asset. Axe has guaranteed a residual value of £30 million and the plant is to be sold for scrap at the end of the lease. Axe will be liable for any shortfall in the residual value. The lease cannot be cancelled and requires equal rental payments of £87 million at the commencement of each financial year. The 'normal' cost of such a lease without the residual value guarantee would have been £95 million per annum. Axe pays the costs of all maintenance and insurance of the plant.

The company has also leased motor vehicles on 1 January 2000 for the first time. Fifty vehicles were leased at an annual rental of £5,000 each, payable on 1 January in advance. In addition an extra 20p per mile is payable if the mileage exceeds 60,000 miles over the three year rental period. The excess mileage charge reflects fair compensation for the additional wear and tear of the vehicle. Axe returns the vehicle to the lessor at the end of the lease. The lessee maintains and insures the vehicles. (A discount rate of 10% should be used in all calculations. The present value of an ordinary annuity of £1 per period for three years at 10% is £2·49.)

Required:

(a) Discuss the new approach to accounting for leases which is being developed by the Accounting Standards Board in its Discussion Paper 'Leases: Implementation of a New Approach'. **(8 marks)**

(b) Advise the financial director on the way in which the above transactions would be dealt with under current accounting standards and how this would change if the recommendations in the Discussion Paper were implemented. **(17 marks)**

(Total: 25 marks)

3 X, Y and Z

X, a public limited company, owns 100 per cent of companies Y and Z which are both public limited companies. The X group operates in the telecommunications industry and the directors are considering three different plans to restructure the group. The directors feel that the current group structure is not serving the best interests of the shareholders and wish to explore possible alternative group structures.

The balance sheets of X and its subsidiaries Y and Z at 31 May 2001 are as follows:

	X	*Y*	*Z*
	£m	*£m*	*£m*
Tangible fixed assets	600	200	45
Cost of investment in Y	60		
Cost of investment in Z	70		
Net Current Assets	160	100	20
	890	300	65
Share Capital Œ ordinary shares of £1	120	60	40
Accumulated reserves	770	240	25
	890	300	65

X acquired the investment in Z on 1 June 1995 when the profit and loss account balance was £20 million. The fair value of the net assets of Z on 1 June 1995 was £60 million. Company Y was incorporated by X and has always been a 100 per cent owned subsidiary. Goodwill is written off over four years. The fair value of the assets of Y at 31 May 2001 is £310 million and of Z is £80 million.

The directors are unsure as to the impact or implications that the following plans are likely to have on the individual accounts of the companies and the group accounts.

The three different plans to restructure the group are as follows:

Plan 1
Y is to purchase the whole of X™s investment in Z. The directors are undecided as to whether the purchase consideration should be 50 million £1 ordinary shares of Y or a cash amount of £75 million.
(10 marks)

Plan 2
A new company, W, is to be formed which will issue shares to the shareholders of X in exchange for X™s investment in Y and Z. W is to issue 130 million ordinary shares of £1 to the shareholders of X in exchange for their shares held in Y and Z. The group is being split up into two separate companies W and X which will be quoted on the Stock Exchange. **(8 marks)**

Plan 3
The assets and trade of Z are to be transferred to Y. Company Z would initially become a non trading company. The assets and trade are to be transferred at their book value. The consideration for the transfer will be £60 million which will be left outstanding on the inter company account between Y and Z. **(7 marks)**

Required:

Discuss the key considerations and the accounting implications of the above plans for the X group. Your answer should show the potential impact on the individual accounts of X, Y and Z and the group accounts after each plan has been implemented.
(The mark allocation is shown in brackets next to each 'plan'.) **(25 marks)**

4 Engina

Engina, a foreign company, has approached a partner in your firm to assist in obtaining a Stock Exchange listing for the company. Engina is registered in a country where transactions between related parties are considered to be normal but where such transactions are not disclosed. The directors of Engina are reluctant to disclose the nature of their related party transactions as they feel that although they are a normal feature of business in their part of the world, it could cause significant problems politically and culturally to disclose such transactions.

The partner in your firm has requested a list of all transactions with parties connected with the company and the directors of Engina have produced the following summary:

(a) Every month, Engina sells £50,000 of goods per month to Mr Satay, the financial director. The financial director has set up a small retailing business for his son and the goods are purchased at cost price for him. The annual turnover of Engina is £300 million. Additionally Mr Satay has purchased his company car from the company for £45,000 (market value £80,000). The director, Mr Satay, owns directley 10% of the shares in the company and earns a salary of £500,000 a year, and has a personal fortune of many millions of pounds.

(b) A hotel property had been sold to a brother of Mr Soy, the Managing Director of Engina, for £4 million (net of selling cost of £0·2 million). The market value of the property was £4·3 million but in the overseas country, property prices were falling rapidly. The carrying value of the hotel was £5 million and its value in use was £3·6 million. There was an over supply of hotel accommodation due to government subsidies in an attempt to encourage hotel development and the tourist industry.

(c) Mr Satay owns several companies and the structure of the group is as follows:

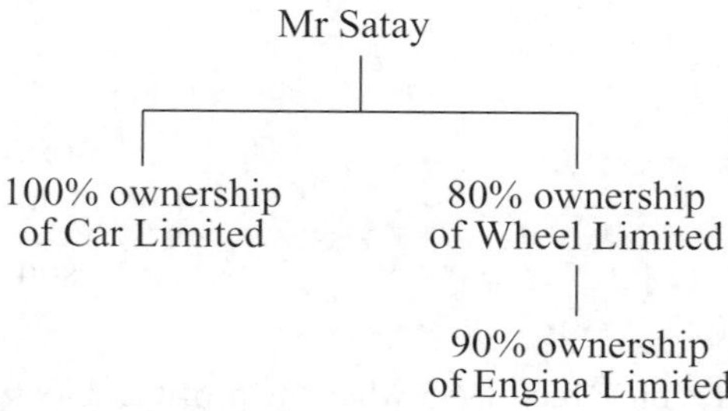

Engina earns 60% of its profit from transactions with Car and 40% of its profit from transactions with Wheel.

Required:

Write a report to the directors of Engina setting out the reasons why it is important to disclose related party transactions and the nature of any disclosure required for the above transactions under the UK regulatory system before a Stock Exchange quotation can be obtained. **(25 marks)**

The mark allocation will be as follows:

		Marks
Style/layout of report		4
Reasons		8
Transaction	(a)	4
	(b)	5
	(c)	4
		25

5 Glowball

The directors of Glowball, a public limited company, had discussed the study by the Institute of Environmental Management which indicated that over 35% of the world's 250 largest corporations are voluntarily releasing green reports to the public to promote corporate environmental performance and to attract customers and investors. They have heard that their main competitors are applying the 'Global Reporting Initiative'(GRI) in an effort to develop a worldwide format for corporate environmental reporting. However, the directors are unsure as to what this initiative actually means. Additionally they require advice as to the nature of any legislation or standards relating to environmental reporting as they are worried that any environmental report produced by the company may not be of sufficient quality and may detract and not enhance their image if the report does not comply with recognised standards. Glowball has a reputation for ensuring the preservation of the environment in its business activities.

Further the directors have collected information in respect of a series of events which they consider to be important and worthy of note in the environmental report but are not sure as to how they would be incorporated in the environmental report or whether they should be included in the financial statements.

The events are as follows:

(i) Glowball is a company that pipes gas from offshore gas installations to major consumers. The company purchased its main competitor during the year and found that there were environmental liabilities arising out of the restoration of many miles of farmland that had been affected by the laying of a pipeline. There was no legal obligation to carry out the work but the company felt that there would be a cost of around £150 million if the farmland was to be restored.

(ii) Most of the offshore gas installations are governed by operating licenses which specify limits to the substances which can be discharged to the air and water. These limits vary according to local legislation and tests are carried out by the regulatory authorities. During the year the company was prosecuted for infringements of an environmental law in the USA when toxic gas escaped into the atmosphere. In 1999 the company was prosecuted five times and in 1998 eleven times for infringement of the law. The final amount of the fine/costs to be imposed by the courts has not been determined but is expected to be around £5 million. The escape occurred over the sea and it was considered that there was little threat to human life.

(iii) The company produced statistics that measure their improvement in the handling of emissions of gases which may have an impact on the environment. The statistics deal with:

  (a) Measurement of the release of gases with the potential to form acid rain. The emissions have been reduced by 84% over five years due to the closure of old plants.

  (b) Measurement of emissions of substances potentially hazardous to human health. The emissions are down by 51% on 1995 levels.

  (c) Measurement of emissions to water that removes dissolved oxygen and substances that may have an adverse effect on aquatic life. Accurate measurement of these emissions is not possible but the company is planning to spend £70 million on research in this area.

(iv) The company tries to reduce the environmental impacts associated with the siting and construction of its gas installations. This is done in the way that minimises the impact on wild life and human beings. Additionally when the installations are at the end of their life, they are dismantled and are not sunk into the sea. The current provision for the decommissioning of these installations is £215 million and there are still decommissioning costs of £407 million to be provided as the company's policy is to build up the required provision over the life of the installation.

Required:

Prepare a report suitable for presentation to the directors of Glowball in which you discuss the following elements:

(a) current reporting requirements and guidelines relating to environmental reporting; **(10 marks)**

(b) the nature of any disclosure which would be required in an environmental report and/or the financial statements for the events (i-iv) above. **(15 marks)**

(The mark allocation includes four marks for the style and layout of the report) **(Total: 25 marks)**

Pilot Paper 2001 Answers

In the Part Three papers it is not always possible to publish a suggested answer which is fully comprehensive and therefore credit will be given to candidates for points not included in the suggested answers but which, nevertheless, are relevant to the questions.

The suggested answers presented below give more detail than would be expected from a candidate under examination conditions. The answers are intended to provide guidance on the approach required from candidates, and on the range and depth of knowledge which would be expected from an excellent candidate.

Answer to question 1

(a) **Group statement of cash flows for the year ended 31 December 2000**

	£m	£m
Net cash inflow from operating activities		692
Returns on investment and servicing of finance		
Interest received	26	
Interest paid	(9)	
Minority interest dividend	(31)	
Joint venture dividend	10	(4)
Taxation		(115)
Capital Expenditure		
Purchase of tangible fixed assets	(380)	
Sale of tangible fixed assets	195	(185)
Acquisitions and disposals		
Disposal of subsidiary	75	
Cash disposed of with subsidiary	(130)	
Purchase of interest in joint venture	(25)	(80)
Net cash inflow before use of liquid resources and financing		308
Decrease in short term deposits		(143)
Increase in cash in the period		65

Workings

1

		£m	£m
Net cash inflow from operating activities per cash flow			875
Sale of subsidiary	– stock	(60)	
	– debtors	(50)	(110)
	– creditors		105
Profit on joint venture (55 + 20)			(75)
Interest receivable			(27)
Interest payable			19
Profit on sale of fixed assets			(120)
Loss on disposal of subsidiary			25
			692

2

	£m
Disposals and transfers of tangible fixed assets per cash flow	1,585
Less: subsidiary disposed of	(310)
transfer to joint venture	(200)
sale and leaseback	(1,000)
Add: profit on sale of fixed assets	120
Cash proceeds	195

			£m
3	Taxation per cash flow		31
	Tax on joint venture		20
	Tax on subsidiary disposed of		25
	Tax on profit		(191)
	Taxation cash flow		(115)
4	Minority interest	– per cash flow	40
		– sale of Web (20% of 420)	(84)
		– profit for year	75
	Minority interest equity dividend		31

(b) **Presentation to the directors of Portal plc**

The analysis of cash flows under the headings specified in FRS1 'Cash Flow Statements' ensures that Portal's cash flow statement incorporates otherwise unpublished information. For example the cash payments made to settle taxation liabilities and the cash returns on investment and servicing of finance all incorporate information which is not published elsewhere. Some of this information can be computed from the published financial statements (for example the purchase of tangible fixed assets), but the published financial statements are complex sand the information therein is not always complete enough to calculate the cash flows (for example interest received and paid).

It is often argued that the disclosure of historical cash flows can be used in business valuation models. This may be true and, although the statement can provide additional information, it is unlikely to provide the necessary information for any particular need of a user of financial statements.

In order to arrive at the 'Net cash inflow from operating activities' reconciliation of operating profit to this figure is required to be disclosed in the financial statements. Some companies have presented this information on the face of the cash flow statements even though FRS1 requires that this should be shown as a note. The problem with the reconciliation is that naïve investors could misinterpret the adding back of depreciation and amortisation as sources of funds. This may cause the cash flow statement to be viewed as derivative, that is, the view may be that the cash flow statement is still derived from the accrual accounting utilised in the profit and loss account.

The group cash flow statement can hide the different cash flow profiles of group companies. For example, in cash based operations such as retail stores, cash from operations may predominate whereas in capital intensive firms, investing and financing cash flows may be important. The group cash flow statement may not show these profiles when the different group companies are consolidated. Additionally, restrictions on the remittability of cash (for example in the case of exchange controls) from one group company to another may not be apparent. (Although the Operating and Financial Review requires a commentary on such restrictions.)

Research into the incremental information content of cash flow statements over earnings information is inconclusive and contradictory. Similarly the usefulness of cash flow information as a predictor of financial failure has been studied with the results again being inconclusive.

Conventional accounting ratios can be enhanced by ratios based on the cash flow statement. For example interest cover based on the cash flow information of Portal plc is:

$$\left\{\frac{\text{Net cash flow from operating activities}}{\text{Interest paid}} = \frac{692}{9}\right\} \text{ 76·9 times}$$

This represents the number of times that the cash generated from operations covers the actual payment and may give additional information to the user.

Similarly the amount of the cash generated from operations which has been spent on purchasing non-current assets can be ascertained.

$$\frac{\text{Purchase of tangible fixed assets}}{\text{Net cash inflow from operating activities}} = \frac{380}{692} \quad \text{i.e. 54·9\%}$$

It is not possible to assess how much of the cash outflow on fixed assets relates to maintaining operations by replacing fixed assets that were worn out and how much related to increasing capacity with the potential for an increase in earnings.

A comparison of the net cash inflow before use of liquid resources and financing with the cash increase in the period shows how the cash flow after investment etc has been utilised. In the case of Portal 46·4% (143 /308) of this net cash inflow has been used to pay off short term deposits.

The arrangement of cash flows into the various categories provides users with additional information about the company. Whether it allows users to draw conclusions about future cash flows is debatable but it offers different information to the traditional accrual based data. There is an increase in the objectivity of the financial information being presented rather than the somewhat subjective information often found in accrual based accounts.

Answer to question 2

(a) Accounting standards currently draw a distinction between finance leases and operating leases. Leases that transfer to the lessee substantially all the risks and rewards of ownership of a leased item are accounted for in substance in the same way as a purchase by the lessee of the leased item, with the price being paid in instalments and the finance being provided by the lessor (a finance lease). Leases that do not transfer all the risks and rewards of ownership to the lessee are classified as operating leases with no asset or liability recognised by the lessee. The two types of leasing transactions are, therefore, accounted for very differently even though the two leases may be economically very similar.

The approach adopted in the Discussion Paper 'Leases: Implementation of a New Approach' would be to replace the finance/ operating lease classification with an approach which recognises the nature of the economic resource controlled by lessees and lessors and the obligation incurred by lessees. One objective of financial statements is to provide information of use to investors and those users who utilise financial statements for economic decisions. The financial performance of an entity comprises the return on the resources it controls and it is the latter control element which forms the basis of the new proposals for lease accounting.

Assets and liabilities are defined in terms of future economic benefits to be obtained or transferred. If these definitions are applied to leases, then all leases provide lessees with assets (the right to use the property for the lease term) and liabilities (the obligation to make payments). The Discussion Paper wants financial statements to reflect the economic resources the lessee controls and the related financing obligation.

The approach recognises that leases are a different form of asset financing than many other forms. Leases can be very flexible. The paper focuses on the assets and liabilities that arise under a contract without the need for artificial thresholdsand classifications. It, therefore, reduces the subjective judgement in lease accounting and different lease contracts would result in different amounts of assets and liabilities being recognised by lessees according to the different rights acquired and obligations incurred. Lessor accounting would be significantly affected as lessors would report financial assets receivable and residual interests as separate assets.

Marginal differences in the construction of lease contracts under this approach would no longer result in major differences in the financial reporting of leases. Transparency and comparability would be improved.

Capitalisation of operating leases has been supported for some time. The difference in the accounting treatment of operating and finance leases is unhelpful and obscures economic reality. Analysts and other users effectively utilise 'constructive' capitalisation of operating leases that would appear to indicate that present accounting practice is perhaps not relevant.

Users can only estimate with limited accuracy the value to be placed on operating leases in the financial statements and thus capitalisation of finance leases by preparers of financial statements is the preferred option, as it would reduce costs as the calculations need only be made once.

(b) The following advice would be given to the financial director on the treatment of the transactions under current accounting standards and the Discussion Paper:

(i) The assets which have been sold and leased back (the computer software and hardware) should be treated as a sale and the operating lease treated under SSAP21 'Accounting for leases and hire purchase contracts' which would keep the lease off the balance sheet and only charge the rentals against profit.

If the transaction is at fair value then immediate recognition of the profit or loss on the sale of the asset should occur. However, where the transaction is above fair value, the profit based on fair value should be recognised immediately (£190 million – £90 million, i.e. £100 million). The balance of the sales value over the fair value should be deferred and amortised over the shorter of the lease term and the period to the next lease rental review (£310 million – £190 million ÷ 4 years, i.e. £30 million per annum).

However, as the sales value is not the fair value, it is evident that the rental payments have been adjusted for the excess price paid for the assets and it appears that the substance of the transaction is the sale of an asset and a loan which equates to the deferred income element. Thus the premium of £15 million may be more a financing cost with the excess over the fair value being shown as a loan (£120 million) with part of the costs of the operating lease being treated as repayment of capital and interest.

Under the Discussion Paper, the accounting for this transaction would fundamentally change. The ASB has recommended the 'one transaction' approach which views the transaction as a single transaction with a double purpose. The double purpose is the raising of finance and the partial disposal of an interest in the property. Where the sale is for more than its fair value, and this is compensated for by an onerous lease then the following entries should result:

		£m	
DR	Cash	310	
CR	Lease liability	157	(£45m + £45m × 2·49)
	Carrying Value of assets	72·5	$\left(\frac{310 - 157}{190}\right.$ X £72.5m$\left.\right)$
	Profit	80·5	

The asset should be reviewed for impairment. The impact on the income statement and balance sheet of applying the Discussion Paper would be profound as it would reduce profit and increase gearing.

(ii) The sale and leaseback of the plant appears to create a finance lease as the present value of the minimum lease payments is substantially all (90%) of the fair value of the plant and Axe pays all the costs of maintenance and insurance of the plant. The lease runs for the useful life of the plant and Axe has guaranteed a residual amount of £30 million.
Thus the minimum lease payments are:

	£m
£87 million + £87 million × 2·49	303·6
£30 million residual value discounted at 10%	20·5
	324·1

FRS5 'Reporting the Substance of Transactions' states that the asset remains in the lessees balance sheet at the carrying value and the sale proceeds are shown as a creditor. The creditor balance represents the finance lease liability and as the payments are made they are treated partly as repayment of the creditor and partly as a finance charge against income. The rental payments have been reduced because the company has been prepared to guarantee a residual value of £30 million which is probably in excess of its scrap value which will potentially be low.

Under the Discussion Paper, the nature of this transaction would not be affected as the sale and leaseback conveys no significant residual interest to the lessor. The minimum lease payments are less than the fair value and selling price of the plant but not by a significant amount.

(iii) Under existing accounting standards, the lease would be treated as an operating lease with any rental being charged to the profit and loss account on a straight line basis over the lease term irrespective of the due dates of payment. However under the Discussion Paper, an asset and liability would be recognised representing the present value of three payments.

Annual payment 50 × £5,000	£250,000
Present value of three payments	£684,000

Axe also has the right to purchase additional usage of the vehicles at 20p per mile. As this rate is fair compensation for additional wear and tear, the option has little value and would be ignored. Such rentals based on contingent usage would be recognised as incurred.

Thus under the Discussion Paper, Axe would find that in the case of the operating leases, that assets and liabilities would be recognised on the balance sheet for such leases and would adversely affect the gearing ratio of the company.

Answer to question 3

Plan 1

The directors appear unsure as to the nature of the purchase consideration. The choice of purchase consideration has implications for the group. If the consideration is in the form of ordinary shares, then a share premium account ought to be set up in the books of Y.

In the case of a share for share exchange in a group reconstruction the ihminimum premium valuelm is the excess of the book value of the investment over the nominal value of the shares issued. Shares cannot be issued at a discount, therefore, it is important that Z is worth more than the nominal amount of shares issued. If the purchase consideration is in the form of cash, a gain or loss on the sale of Z will arise in the books of X. As the cash price (£75 million) is not in excess of the fair value of the net assets of Z (£80 million), there will be no question of there having been a distribution. This can only arise where the cash price is in excess of the fair value of the net assets.

Share for Share Exchange

	X	*Y*	*Z*	*Group*
	£m	*£m*	*£m*	*£m*
Tangible Fixed Assets	600	200	45	845
Cost of investment in Y	130			
Cost in investment in Z		70		
Net Current Assets	160	100	20	280
	890	370	65	1,125
Share Capital	120	110	40	120
Share Premium account		20		
Profit and Loss account	770	240	25	1,005
	890	370	65	1,125

The cost of the investment in Y is increased by the value placed on the shares issued (£70 million). The effect of this procedure is to preserve the book value of the investment. The changes should have no impact on the group accounts because they are internal and should not affect the group when it is portrayed as a single entity. Therefore goodwill arising on the purchase of Z of (£70 million – (Share Capital £40 million + Profit and loss account £20 million) £10 million will have been written off to group reserves. The Group profit and loss account balance is:

	£m
X	770
Y	240
Z (post acquisition)	5
Goodwill	(10)
	1,005

Cash Purchase

In the case of a cash transaction, the financial statements would be as follows:

	X	Y	Z	Group
	£m	£m	£m	£m
Tangible Fixed Assets	600	200	45	845
Cost of investment in Y	60			
Cost of investment in Z	75			
Net Current Assets	235	25	20	280
	895	300	65	1,125
Share Capital	120	60	40	120
Profit and Loss account				
(770 plus profit on sale (75-70))	775	240	25	1,005
	895	300	65	1,125

The profit on the sale of the investment in Z must be eliminated on consolidation as it is an inter group transaction. The group accounts will be the same using either a cash consideration or a share for share exchange.

Plan 2

This plan effectively involves the demerger of Y and Z from the group to form a separate group. The shareholders of X will hold shares in X and in W. Essentially the transaction involves a distribution by X to its shareholders in the form of the shares of W.

From the new holding company's viewpoint, there is a question as to whether the shares being issued should be treated as being issued at a premium. It would appear that this is a point of view that the directors of X should take into account, although on production of the financial statements of W, there is no requirement for a share premium account, in fact there is a debit balance arising. Additionally if all the conditions are met, merger accounting will probably be used for this transaction (group reconstruction under FRS6 "Acquisitions and Mergers") as long as no other inter group transactions involving share/cash transfer had preceded the demerger.

	X	W
	£m	£m
Tangible Fixed Assets	600	245
Net Current Assets	160	120
	760	365
Share Capital	120	130
Accumulated reserves (770 – distribution 130)	640	235
	760	365

The balance on W's income statement is made up as follows:

	£m	
Profit and loss account Y	240	
Profit and loss account Z	25	
Share capital – balance arising on merger account		
W shares issued	130	
Share capital Y	(60)	
Share capital Z	(40)	(30)
Profit and loss account		235

Plan 3

This plan is a method of rationalising and simplifying the group and can result in cost savings. The non trading company will have no current requirement for the cash consideration and therefore it will be left outstanding.

One complication that will arise in this transaction is the possible write down in the investment in Z in X's books as there may be an impairment in value. Z was originally purchased at a price which reflected goodwill of £10 million but the assets have been transferred at book value for a consideration of £60 million. Thus the cost of the investment of Z in X's books will be £70 million but the shell company Z will have a net asset value of £60 million being the value of the inter company current account. The cost of the investment in Z should, therefore, be reduced to £60 million.

	X	*Y*	*Z*	*Group*
	£m	*£m*	*£m*	*£m*
Tangible fixed assets	600	245	–	845
Cost of investment in Y	60			
Cost of investment in Z (70 – impairment 10)	60			
Net Current Assets	160	60	60	280
880	305	60	1,125	
Share Capital	120	60	40	120
Revaluation Reserve		5		
Profit and Loss account (770-10)	760	240	20	1,005
880	305	60	1,125	

Y's revaluation reserve is the gain on the purchase of the assets from Z of £5 million (£65 million – £60 million).
Y's net current assets are £60 million (£100 million + £20 million – intercompany creditor £60 million).
Z's income statement is £20 million (£25 million less loss on transfer of assets £5 million).

On consolidation it can be argued that the impairment loss of £10 million in X's books, the revaluation reserve gain of £5 million in Y's books, and the loss on the transfer of assets to Y in Z's books can be ignored as they are intercompany items. If this is the case then the Group reserves will be charged with goodwill arising on the purchase of X's holding in Z.

		£m
Group Reserves	X	770
	Y	240
	Z	5
Goodwill		(10)
		1,005

Conclusion

Plan 1 results in no change to the group financial statements. However such a change has advantages where closer linkage is required between Y and Z. For example there may be tax advantages to having a sub grouping of Y and Z or such a linkage may be useful for geographical reasons.

Plan 2 changes the group financial statements dramatically and results in a reduced figure for distributable profits (X group £1,005 million as compared with X £640 million; W group £235 million, i.e. £875 million). The demerger however might tighten the focus of management and thus enhance growth. The market value of the demerged companies may be greater than the market value of the former X group.

Plan 3 involves 'divisionalisation' in the context of transferring the assets and trade of Z into Y. It could result in cost savings and there is no effect on the group financial statements. This reconstruction of the group is a method being used currently to create a non trading company into which an internet company can be 'dropped'. Each method has its advantages and disadvantages and the determining factor is the purpose of the reconstruction of the group.

Answer to question 4

Brice and Partners
Brice Lane
Bridlington
31 December 2000

The Directors
Engina and Co.
Orange Lane
Edmond

Dear Sirs

Related Party Transactions

We are writing to explain the reasons why it is important to disclose 'Related Party Transactions' whilst at the same time explaining the nature of the disclosure required under current UK regulations. We appreciate the cultural and political sensitivity of the disclosure of such transactions in your country and the fact that such opinions will not change in the short term. However, a key factor in your thoughts about the disclosure of 'Related Party Transactions' is the fact that in addition to the requirements of the accounting standard (FRS8 'Related Party Disclosures') and the Companies Act, the Stock Exchange imposes additional disclosures on companies which require a listing. We hope that the following general discussion and specific comments on the transactions undertaken in your company will assist your understanding of quite a complex and sensitive area.

Related party relationships are part of the normal business process. Entities operate the separate parts of their business through subsidiaries and associates, and acquire interests in other enterprises for investment or commercial reasons. Thus control or significant influence can be exercised over the investee by the investing company. These relationships can have a significant effect on the financial position and operating results of the company and lead to transactions which would not normally be undertaken. For example, a company may sell a large proportion of its production to its parent company because it cannot and could not find a market elsewhere. Additionally the transactions may be effected at prices which would not be acceptable to unrelated parties.

Even if there are no transactions between the related parties, it is still possible for the operating results and financial position of an enterprise to be affected by the relationship. A recently acquired subsidiary can be forced to finish a relationship with a company in order to benefit group companies. Transactions may be entered into on terms different from those applicable to an unrelated party. For example, a holding company may lease equipment to a subsidiary on terms unrelated to market rates for equivalent leases.

In the absence of contrary information, it is assumed that the financial statements of an entity reflect transactions carried out on an arm's length basis and that the entity has independent discretionary power over its actions and pursues its activities independently.

If these assumptions are not justified because of related party transactions, then disclosure of this fact should be made. Even if transactions are at arm's length, the disclosure of related party transactions is useful because it is likely that future transactions may be affected by such relationships. The main issues in determining such disclosures are the identification of related parties, the types of transactions and arrangements and the information to be disclosed.

It can be seen that information about related parties can be an important element of any investment decision and the regulatory authorities in the UK consider disclosure of such information to be of paramount importance.

The following specific comments relate to the list of transactions with connected persons which you supplied to us.

Sale of goods to directors

Related party transactions need only be disclosed where they are material. These transactions are material where the users of financial statements might reasonably be influenced by such a transaction. Thus it is not possible to avoid disclosing such items on the grounds that they are non-numerically large enough. Additionally, where the related party is a director then the transaction should be viewed in relation to its materiality to that director. Contracts of significance with directors also require disclosure by the Stock Exchange.

In this case your director (Mr Satay) has purchased £600,000 (12 months × £50,000) of goods from the company and a car for £45,000 with a market value of £80,000. Although neither of these transactions is material or significant to the company or the directors, the spirit of good corporate governance would dictate that any transactions with directors are extremely sensitive and we would recommend disclosure of such transactions.

Hotel Property

Accounting standards (FRS8 'Related party disclosures') require 'any other elements of the transactions necessary for an understanding of the financial statements' to be disclosed. The hotel property sold to the brother of the Managing Director is a related party transaction which appears to have been undertaken at below market price. The disclosure of simply this fact would not reflect the reality of your company's position. The carrying value of the hotel needs to be adjusted as it has become impaired. The hotel should have been shown in your records under UK accounting standards at the lower of carrying value (£5 million) and the recoverable amount (higher of net realisable value (£4·3 million – £0·2 million, i.e. £4·1 million) and value in use £3·6 million). Thus the hotel should have been recorded at £4·1 million.

Thus the property has been sold at £100,000 below the impaired value and this is the nature of the disclosure which should be made, thus reflecting more closely the nature of the property market in your country and the nature of the transaction.

Group structure

The Companies Acts and Stock Exchange rules contain requirements to disclose directors interests in the share capital of a company. Mr Satay owns 10% of the share capital of Engina directly and 90% of the share capital through his ownership of Wheel Ltd.

Current rules in the UK (FRS8) give exemptions to disclosures of transactions with group investees (Wheel Ltd) in the accounts of 90% (or more) owned subsidiaries. Thus Engina need not disclose transactions with Wheel Ltd (assuming that Wheel Ltd prepares group accounts). However, the transactions with Car Ltd will have to be disclosed as both Car and Engina are under the common control of Mr. Satay and Car is not an investee of the Wheel group. We realise that the above disclosure requirements seem a little inconsistent but this is due to the current requirements of the accounting standards.

We hope that the above explanations are of use to you and realise that culturally and politically they may seem unacceptable. However, if you wish a quotation on the Stock Exchange in the UK, then the disclosure requirements set out above will have to be adhered to.

Yours faithfully,

Brice and Partners

Answer to question 5

Report to the Directors of Glowball plc
Environmental Reporting

Introduction

The following report details the current reporting requirements and guidelines relating to Environmental Reporting and specific comments on 'environmental events' occurring in the period.

(a) **Current Reporting Requirements and Guidelines**

The initial goal of environmental reporting was simply to demonstrate a company's commitment to the environment. However, the debate has moved on and the central objective of any environmental report is now to communicate environmental performance.

Wider ranging objectives may also be attributed to the report, such as acknowledging shared responsibility for the environment, differentiating the company from its competitors, obtaining social approval for operating practices and demonstrating regulatory compliance. Reports in practice vary from a simple public relations statement to a detailed examination of the company's environmental performance.

Environmental accounting disclosure is an assortment of mandatory and voluntary requirements. Not all companies report on environmental performance and those that do report often focus on only selected aspects of performance. It is typically only the leaders in environmental reporting that report in a comprehensive manner. In the UK, environmental reporting is voluntary although disclosure of environmental protection costs and potential environmental liabilities is required in the 'Operating Review' of companies and FRS12 'Provisions, contingent liabilities and contingent assets' requires the reporting of certain environmental liabilities. Other accounting standards on fixed assets and research and development costs mention environmental effects.

This voluntary position contrasts with the situation in Denmark and the Netherlands, which passed legislation in 1996 making environmental disclosure mandatory for the larger companies. In the USA, the SEC/FASB environmental accounting standards are obligatory, although recent press reports seem to indicate that the standards are not policed as closely as other accounting standards. The International Accounting Standards Committee has not as yet issued a standard in this area, although the IASC are considering the subject.

In the place of legislation on the subjects, there is a range of codes of practice and environmental reporting guidelines that have been published. Examples of these documents are as follows:

(i) In February 1999, the Global Reporting Initiative (initiated by CERES), published an exposure draft on sustainability reporting guidelines and 21 international companies are now participating in a pilot test of a programme for reporting corporate environmental sustainability.

(ii) The Confederation of British Industries published a guideline entitled 'Introducing environmental reporting'.

(iii) The Coalition of Environmentally Responsible Economies (CERES) has published formats for environmental reports and made a set of principles for investors and others to assess environmental performance.

(iv) The UNCTAD Report on 'Environmental Financial Accounting and Reporting at the Corporate level'(1998).

(v) The ACCA Guide to environment and energy reporting (1997).

There is a whole range of governmental, academic, professional body and international agencies that have published reports and guidelines that can be accessed and downloaded from the Web. Under the Eco Management and Audit Scheme (EMAS), companies can sign up to agree to a specific code of practice, but the report must be validated by an accredited environmental verifier.

In summary, environmental reports can enhance a company's reputation and standing, and the use of environmental reporting will expand. Currently, except in a few specific countries, this form of activity reporting is voluntary and, therefore, the extent of disclosure varies significantly. However, until regulation and standards are developed, the completeness and consistency of environmental reports will not be achieved. Similarly best practice in the attestation of the reports also needs establishing. However, environmental reporting is important to large companies as it is no passing phase. The main question is as to the form and content of the environmental report.

(b) **Comments on specific events**

All of the specific events outlined to us could be included in an environmental report but certain events will require disclosure or a provision in the financial statements.

Glowball has a reputation for ensuring the preservation of the environment and this fact, together with specific examples of the restoration of land, could be included in the environmental report. Additionally, however, provisions for environmental liabilities should be recognised when the company becomes obliged legally or constructively to rectify environmental damage or perform restorative work (FRS12). The mere existence of the restorative work does not of itself give rise to a specific obligation. There is no legal obligation to carry out the work but there is a 'constructive obligation' because of the company's conduct in the past and there is a valid expectation that the company will restore the farmland. It is a difficult concept but given the information currently provided by yourselves, it would seem that a provision of £150 million would be required in the financial statements.

In evaluating the environmental performance of the company, it would be useful to set out how many tests have been carried out by the regulatory authorities and how many times the company has passed the tests. Additionally, it appears that the number of times the company is prosecuted for infringements of environmental laws is reducing year by year. Thus this fact, together with the number of prosecutions in 1998, 1999 and 2000, could be presented in a small table.

An estimate of the fine to be imposed should be made and a provision set up for £5 million in the financial statements. The amount of the fine would also be disclosed in the environmental report together with the circumstances surrounding it.

The company should produce a report showing the environmental impact of the processes thus creating a measure of the overall environmental impact. The emissions should be categorised into:

(i) acidity to air and water;

(ii) hazardous air emissions;

(iii) aquatic oxygen demand and ecotoxity.

In each category, the reduction of emissions over the years should be set out and compared with target reductions. In the case of (c) above accurate measurements of emissions is not possible and this should be stated. The environmental report should not misstate the facts as this will affect the credibility of the report. The planned expenditure of £70 million on research should be mentioned in the environmental report but will not be accrued in the financial statements as the expenditure is avoidable and an obligation does not exist.

The fact that the company sites and constructs its gas installations in an environmentally friendly way can be disclosed in the section of the report dealing with direct environment impacts. Details of such policies can be explained in detail in this section of the report, setting out the criteria used for the sitings. Similarly the policy of dismantling the installations rather than sinking them can be set out together with the costs involved.

However, FRS12 has a significant impact on decommissioning activities. The company is building up the required provision over the useful life of the installation but FRS12 requires the full provision to be established as soon as the obligation exists.

Thus the decommissioning costs of £407 million (undiscounted) will have to be provided for and brought onto the balance sheet at the discounted amount and a corresponding asset created.

We hope that the above explanations are helpful and that we can assist you in the formal preparation of the environmental report.

Full provision as soon as obligation exsists.

Pilot Paper 2001 Marking scheme

This marking scheme is given as a guide to markers in the context of the suggested answer. Scope is given to markers to award marks for alternative approaches to a question, including relevant comment, and where well reasoned conclusions are provided. This isparticularly the case for essay based questions where there will often be more than one definitive solution.

					Marks
1	(a)	Net cash inflow			8
		Taxation			3
		Sale of tangible fixed assets			4
		Minority Interest			2
		Joint venture			2
		Disposal of subsidiary and cash disposed of			2
				Available	21
				Maximum	**18**
	(b)	Subjective			7
				Available	28
				Maximum	**25**
2	(a)	Subjective			8
	(b)	(i)	Current standards		4
			Discussion Paper		5
		(ii)	Current standards		4
			Discussion Paper		1
		(iii)	Current standards		1
			Discussion Paper		4
				Available	19
				Maximum	**17**
				Available	27
				Maximum	**25**
3	Plan 1		Share premium		2
			Shares at discount		1
			Gain or loss		1
			Distribution		1
			Calculations: share		5
			cash		3
					13
	Plan 2		Share premium		2
			Merger accounting discussion		2
			X financial statements		2
			W group		3
					9

			Marks
	Plan 3	Cash consideration	1
		Impairment	2
		Calculations	3
		Intercompany items	2
			8
		Available	30
		Maximum	**25**

			Marks
4	Style of letter/report		4
		Reasons	8
		Goods to directors	4
		Property	5
		Group 4	
		Available/Maximum	**25**

5	(a)	Current reporting requirements		10
	(b)	restoration		5
		infringement of law		4
		emissions		4
		decommissioning activities		4
			Available	27
		Report 4		
			Available	31
			Maximum	**25**